BLACK PEOPLE AND THE
SOUTH AFRICAN WAR 1899–1902

AFRICAN STUDIES SERIES   40

Editorial Board

John Dunn, Reader in Politics and Fellow of King's College, Cambridge

J. M. Lonsdale, Lecturer in History and Fellow of Trinity College, Cambridge

David M. G. Newbery, Lecturer in Economics and Fellow of Churchill College, Cambridge

A. F. Robertson, Assistant Director of Development Studies and Fellow of Darwin College, Cambridge

The African Studies Series is a collection of monographs and general studies that reflect the interdisciplinary interests of the African Studies Centre at Cambridge. Volumes to date have combined historical, anthropological, economic, political and other perspectives. Each contribution has assumed that such broad approaches can contribute much to our understanding of Africa, and that this may in turn be of advantage to specific disciplines.

AFRICAN STUDIES SERIES

BLACK PEOPLE AND THE SOUTH AFRICAN WAR 1899–1902

PETER WARWICK

CAMBRIDGE UNIVERSITY PRESS

CAMBRIDGE
LONDON   NEW YORK   NEW ROCHELLE
MELBOURNE   SYDNEY

PUBLISHED BY THE PRESS SYNDICATE OF THE UNIVERSITY OF CAMBRIDGE
The Pitt Building, Trumpington Street, Cambridge, United Kingdom

CAMBRIDGE UNIVERSITY PRESS
The Edinburgh Building, Cambridge CB2 2RU, UK
40 West 20th Street, New York NY 10011–4211, USA
477 Williamstown Road, Port Melbourne, VIC 3207, Australia
Ruiz de Alarcón 13, 28014 Madrid, Spain
Dock House, The Waterfront, Cape Town 8001, South Africa

http://www.cambridge.org

First published 1983
First paperback edition 2004

A catalogue record for this book is available from the British Library

Library of Congress catalogue card number: 82–17902

ISBN 0 521 23216 4 hardback
ISBN 0 521 27224 6 paperback

TO ALISON

'You must not think that you can frighten me, and my people, with your war talk. You know that I am a Son of the White Queen.'

Khama, the Ngwato ruler, to General F. A. Grobler,
23 October 1899

'I truly believe that if there is war again the people of the Transvaal will assist the Boers . . . The Natives of the Transvaal say "we expected deliverance whereas we have gone deeper into bonds".'

Segale, a Kgatla chief, writing in *Koranta ea Becoana*,
6 August 1903

Contents

Contents

Maps

Tables

Preface

'The first day of the first week of the first month in 1900. Not at all a lovely morning. The distant pop of the Mauser distinctly shows that there is no holiday for poor beleaguered us.' With these words Sol Plaatje began his diary entry for the first day of a new century, besieged by the Boers in Mafeking. John Comaroff's recovery of Plaatje's siege diary, and its subsequent publication in 1973, really marked the starting-point of the present study. Plaatje was one of more than 7000 blacks who shared the experiences of the siege with Baden-Powell's frontier force and the European townspeople of Mafeking. He was also one of more than four million black people in whose midst the familiar dramas of the South African War were played out. Yet at the time of the diary's publication almost nothing was known of the wartime experiences of South Africa's majority black population. How did black people interpret the issues over which the war was fought? What part did they play in military operations? How were their lives and livelihoods affected by the circumstances of military upheaval?

It was with questions such as these uppermost in mind that I embarked upon the research that has ultimately led to this book. It soon became evident that there was a wealth of material in archives in Britain and southern Africa on the experiences of black people during the war; that black people were far more than either spectators to, or passive victims of, a white man's quarrel; and that a thorough revision of accepted views on the war was called for, one that interpreted the struggle not from the vantage point of either London or Pretoria but rather in the context of a complex and rapidly changing colonial society increasingly shaped, but not yet transformed, by mining capital.

The book is the product of work that began when I was attached to the Centre for Southern African Studies at the University of York. I am grateful to the Social Science Research Council for supporting me for three years at the Centre, and to those who gave me assistance and encouragement while much of the archival research was being undertaken, in particular the Centre's Director, Christopher R. Hill, Anne Akeroyd, Tom Lodge, Robert Baldock and my supervisor, Harry Wilson. Professor Ronald Robinson made a number of perceptive criticisms when examining the thesis out of which the

Preface

book has emerged. Since leaving York a number of people have given valuable advice on drafts of the whole or parts of the book, and I would especially like to thank Brian Willan, Burridge Spies, Bill Nasson, Albert Grundlingh, Bob Edgar and John Lonsdale. Any inaccuracies of fact or interpretation that remain are of course my own responsibility. Ann O'Connor helped me enormously by typing the final manuscript in her usual efficient way. Writing a book demands considerable patience and understanding on the part of those around you, and I am deeply grateful to Alison, my wife, for showing these qualities in such abundance.

Cambridge
May 1982

A note on orthography

Throughout the book I have tried to discover and use the most modern and appropriate spelling of African proper nouns, so that Sekukuni becomes Sekhukhune, Linchwe becomes Lentshwe, Lerothodi becomes Lerotholi, and so on. In general I have omitted Bantu prefixes, though in one or two major cases these have been retained since in modern usage it is more common to do so, e.g. Barolong rather than Rolong. In quotations I have retained the original spelling in most cases unless this seemed likely to lead to misunderstanding.

Map 1   South Africa, 1899

Introduction

The South African War was a costly and bloody struggle. From the beginning of military operations in October 1899 to the signing of peace in Pretoria on the last day of May 1902 it claimed the lives of 22,000 imperial soldiers and over 7000 republican fighters. Almost 28,000 Boer civilians, most of them children under the age of sixteen, perished in British concentration camps during the war's protracted guerrilla phase. The conflict cost the British taxpayer more than £200 million and laid waste to large areas of the conquered Boer states.

The war owed its origin to the discovery in 1886 of gold deposits on the Witwatersrand in the South African Republic, the independent Boer state beyond the Vaal river. The region of the new mining capital, Johannesburg, thereafter began rapidly to industrialise, attracting international capital and a cosmopolitan immigrant (*uitlander*) population of mining engineers, artisans and fortune-seekers from Europe, America and the rest of South Africa. Thousands of migrant black workers from the subcontinent were also drawn to the Rand. By the end of 1895 the heavily mechanised and expensive extraction of gold from deep levels had begun, and by 1898 the Transvaal accounted for more than a quarter of the world's total gold output, the largest single source of supply.

The development of gold mining and its related industries, the geological and financial difficulties of extracting the Rand's gold deposits profitably, the regulation of the mining industry by the Boer oligarchy that controlled the Transvaal state, and the weakness of the state itself, all had profound political and economic consequences. The shift northward of the centre of economic activity in South Africa, from the Cape Colony to the Transvaal, was perceived as a threat to Britain's pre-eminent imperial influence in the subcontinent. The transformation of the South African Republic from near bankruptcy to prosperity gave new authority to the Pretoria regime; German commercial and political penetration of the Transvaal was a matter of no small concern to the British government; and in the corridors of Whitehall and Westminster there were many who believed the security of Britain's strategically important naval base on the Cape peninsula to be placed at risk. Britain's

1

erstwhile colonial ambition in the region, to amalgamate the settler states into a stable, self-governing federation in which British interests would be safeguarded, seemed further away from realisation than ever before.

Although the gold discoveries at once posed a threat to Britain's geo-political interests in the subcontinent, the successful long-term development of a profitable gold-mining industry in the Transvaal was nonetheless intrinsic to British interests. Between 60 and 80 per cent of foreign capital in the industry was British. During the latter part of the nineteenth century gold came to underpin and facilitate much of the world's expanding volume of international commerce, and by 1890 London had become the financial capital of world trade. A continuing increase in the world's stock of gold was essential to the stable growth of international transactions, and the Bank of England was especially keen to continue to strengthen its gold reserves, which doubled in value between 1890 and 1896.

Gold mining and industrialisation on the Rand were viewed from a different perspective by the regime in Pretoria. The government of President S. J. P. Kruger conceived of industrialisation as primarily serving the interests of a society rooted in the land, not the interests of the international financial community. Industry was therefore controlled and directed by the state on that basis. Concessions governing the railway system and the supply of dynamite raised mining costs, and little substantial progress was possible in reducing industrial labour costs. While a number of members of the Pretoria government supported the need for reforms to assist mining development in the 1890s, it nonetheless became apparent that the Boer regime was incapable of providing the large-scale state assistance that was needed to overcome the technical, economic and labour problems that confronted the gold-mining industry. It was increasingly recognised that Britain's interests, and those of her investors in the industry, could only be protected by the removal of the Boer oligarchy from control of the Transvaal state.

In these circumstances the interests of Britain and the Transvaal mining industry became closely entwined at the highest levels. In December 1895 the Jameson Raid took place, an abortive attempt to precipitate an *uitlander* insurrection that would provide a pretext for Britain intervening directly in the republic's affairs. It was organised by Cecil Rhodes, Kimberley diamond magnate and Cape prime minister whose Consolidated Gold Fields had substantial interests in the Transvaal, and was supported by Alfred Beit of Wernher-Beit & Eckstein, the largest mining group on the Rand responsible for about half the total production of gold. The conspiracy occurred with the connivance of various British colonial officials and, almost certainly, with the prior knowledge and general approval of the Colonial Secretary, Joseph Chamberlain. Afterwards diplomatic and political pressure was brought to bear on Kruger's government by sections of the *uitlander* population, by many of the leaders of industry in the Transvaal (especially those committed to long-range mining programmes), by the British government, and by its High Commissioner in South Africa, Sir Alfred Milner, with a view to bringing about the almost immediate enfranchisement of the *uitlander* community, and thereby ending the Boer oligarchy's domination of the Transvaal state. The Pretoria government, supported by the government of the sister Boer republic of the Orange Free State, was left with little alternative but to go to war to defend its control over the mineral revolution in the Transvaal.

Although both sides believed the conflict would probably be over by Christmas 1899, the Peace of Vereeniging, which brought the war to a conclusion, was not signed until almost thirty-two months later. During this period Britain mobilised in all 448,000 men and the Boers about 88,000 (including overseas volunteers and colonial rebels). The war passed through three distinct phases. At the start of the war the Boers launched three major offensives: commandos occupied northern Natal and besieged Ladysmith, invaded the Cape, and struck westwards to sever British communications with Rhodesia and lay siege to the British garrisons in Kimberley and Mafeking. On all three fronts – at Colenso, the Stormberg and Magersfontein – the Boers inflicted serious defeats on the British forces during 'black week' in December 1899.

Following the arrival in South Africa of heavy imperial reinforcements, and of Lord Roberts of Kandahar as Commander-in-Chief and Lord Kitchener of Khartoum as his Chief-of-Staff, a second phase of the war began during which the besieged towns of Ladysmith, Kimberley and Mafeking were relieved, the Boer advances beyond their frontiers reversed, and an offensive begun to conquer and occupy the Boer states. On 13 March 1900 Roberts's columns occupied Bloemfontein, and on 24 May the Orange Free State was annexed (to be known as the Orange River Colony). Johannesburg was entered by British troops on 31 May, and Pretoria captured on 5 June. President Kruger left the republic by the railway route to Lourenço Marques (Maputo), from where he sailed to Europe, dying four years later in Switzerland. On 1 September 1900 the Transvaal was annexed to the British crown. The war seemed to many all but won, and Roberts returned to London in triumph before the end of the year.

The period of conventional warfare was indeed over: but the third, more ruthless and prolonged phase of the war in which the Boers resorted to guerrilla tactics was only just beginning. Under the leadership of Louis Botha, Christiaan de Węt, J. C. Smuts and J. H. de la Rey, among many other astute and determined commando leaders, the Boers formed small, mobile military units which were able to evade capture by the British forces, and to continue to harass the imperial army by capturing supplies, disorganising the military's communications system and sometimes inflicting quite startling casualties on the army of occupation. At the end of 1900 and during the rest of the war a number of small-scale invasions into the Cape Colony were launched by the Boers to link up with rebel republican sympathisers. The success of the Boers' tactics enforced draconian methods of reprisal on the British, methods which began during the final period of Roberts's command and were intensified by Kitchener, his successor. To attempt to prevent the commandos from drawing shelter and sustenance from sympathetic civilians in the countryside, harsh penalties were introduced for aiding the guerrilla fighters, farms were burned and crops and livestock destroyed, and Boer women and children removed from the land and brought into concentration camps. To complement these tactics of 'scorched earth', 3700 miles of barbed-wire barricades and 8000 blockhouses were constructed to restrict the mobility of the guerrilla units. Finally, following the earlier failure of peace negotiations at Middelburg in March 1901, the war came to an end in Pretoria fourteen months later. The representatives of the Boer governments agreed to accept the British annexations of their states and to recognise the authority of the British monarch, Edward VII.

The impression has been perpetuated in numerous history books that the war was simply an Anglo-Boer struggle. In fact it was very much more than that. In a real sense it was a 'South African war', a conflict that directly touched the lives of hundreds of thousands of black people in whose midst the familiar dramas of the war unfolded. The war was fought in a region where white people made up only a fifth of the total population. In 1899 there were approximately one million whites in South Africa compared to four million Africans (including those living in Basutoland, the Bechuanaland Protectorate and Swaziland). Whites in the Cape Colony were outnumbered by Africans 3:1, in Natal the ratio was almost 10:1, in the Transvaal 4:1 and in the Orange Free State 2:1. South Africa also had a Coloured population of almost 500,000, most of whom lived in the Cape, and an Asian community of 100,000, most of whom lived in Natal. South Africa's majority population could not remain unaffected either by the two-and-a-half turbulent years of warfare or by the issues over which the war was fought and its subsequent implications.

Even before the formal beginning of military operations thousands of men were thrown out of work by the suspension of gold production on many of the Witwatersrand's gold mines, and by the dislocation of the migrant labour system in the subcontinent. Many rural communities whose economic prosperity and self-sufficiency had been undermined during the latter years of the nineteenth century found themselves having suddenly to support large numbers of men normally absent as migrant workers, on whose wages they had come to depend to stave off impoverishment. Black people became embroiled, often involuntarily, in some of the most celebrated episodes of the war, such as the three great sieges of Mafeking, Kimberley and Ladysmith. As the war dragged on into its ruthless guerrilla phase, the scorched earth tactics of the British army destroyed the livelihoods of many black peasants in the former Boer states; by the end of the war almost 116,000 Africans had been removed to concentration camps, in which over 14,000 refugees lost their lives.

But black people were not merely the victims of war. Over 100,000 became directly involved in the struggle as scouts, spies, guards, servants and messengers, and in a wide range of other occupations with the white armies.

4

At least 10,000, and possibly as many as 30,000, blacks were fighting with the British army as armed combatants by the end of the war. On a less formal basis, black people took action to resist the Boer invasions of the Cape and Natal and to stem the tide of rebellion, they supplied the British army with invaluable intelligence, and during the guerrilla war they effectively closed hundreds of square miles of the annexed states to commando penetration. Indeed the war often took the form of fierce localised struggles in which landlords were driven from their farms, and their lands systematically occupied and cultivated by their black tenants. Peasants in many regions accumulated capital and extended and modernised their holdings by taking advantage of short-term labour contracts and high wages in military employment, by leasing oxen and waggons to the British army at very favourable rates, and by selling livestock, cereals and other produce at inflated prices.

The economic leverage afforded some sections of the black population during the war did not completely disappear in its immediate aftermath, but Britain's military victory nonetheless represented a significant milestone in the development of social relations in South Africa. The conflict had been fought principally in the interests of mining capital, and it was a world made safe for the profitable long-term development of gold mining that was the overriding objective of British reconstruction after the war, not the engineering of social changes in the interests of South Africa's black population, which many members of the black elite had looked forward to with optimism as the two sides moved towards war during 1899. The extension of the franchise to black people in the former Boer states was effectively precluded by the terms of the peace agreement, the military assisted landlords to reoccupy their farms, and in the industrial heartland the wages of black mineworkers were reduced and labour more closely regulated and controlled. Rural unrest, worker resistance and profound criticism of British policy by black political leaders were the result. The foundations of modern South Africa were successfully laid between 1902 and 1910, the year in which the Union came into being, and in which Britain's attempt to create a stable and modernised state compatible with the needs of mining capital – a campaign that had begun a little over a decade before in October 1899 – finally drew to its close.

The following study seeks to look afresh at the tumultuous events of 1899–1902, not from the point of view of the British army or the Boer commandos, or from the standpoint of either the imperial or republican governments, but rather from a hitherto largely unexplored perspective: namely, by situating the war in the context of a complex and rapidly changing colonial society, and focusing on the involvement in the struggle and the reactions to the war of South Africa's majority black population.

1

Myth of a white man's war

At the beginning of the South African War the British and the Boers seemed in agreement on one issue at least: that the ensuing struggle would be a 'white man's war' in which the involvement of black people in the fighting would be confined to non-combatant roles. Until recently it had been generally assumed by historians that the shape this tacit agreement imposed on military operations was maintained throughout the course of the war. Rayne Kruger, in his book *Good-Bye Dolly Gray* (1959), described 'a phenomenon, so singular and astonishing, of a war fought across the breadth of a vast region, the majority of whose inhabitants were mere spectators'.[1] Writing of the war in the *Oxford History of South Africa* (1971), Leonard Thompson concluded that 'By tacit agreement both sides . . . refrained from involving the African peoples in their fighting, except as unarmed servants and scouts and, on the British side, as guards. Bitterly though the war was fought, it was a "white man's war".'[2]

Yet throughout the campaign allegations were persistently made that the opposing army was employing substantial numbers of black people as active participants in the war. In February 1900 General Sir Redvers Buller was informed by one of his officers in Natal that 'most men at the front are aware that there are armed natives fighting with the Boers'.[3] Later in the war a Boer commander, General J. C. G. Kemp, protested to Kitchener that in many instances the struggle was being fought 'contrary to civilised warfare on account of it being carried on in a great measure with Kaffirs'.[4]

In this chapter an examination will be made of white attitudes towards the involvement of black people in the struggle, and a study made of the extent to which the roles performed by blacks in the war differed in practice from those that had been conceived by both sides at the onset of hostilities. But first some consideration needs to be given to the nature of colonial society in South Africa, and an assessment made, related to this, of the roles undertaken by black people in the military systems of the white communities before the outbreak of war in 1899.

COLONIAL SOCIETY BEFORE THE WAR

South African society at the turn of the twentieth century was undergoing rapid and profound change. Thirty years before, in 1870, the majority of

Africans still lived in independent chiefdoms. Those who did not, and who had become incorporated into the white settler states of the Cape Colony, Natal and the Boer republics beyond the Orange and Vaal rivers, still generally had access to land and control over their own labour.

Society in the Cape Colony had been largely structured by the needs of British mercantile capital following Britain's occupation of the Cape for the second time in 1806. She took over a colonial outpost committed to slavery and serfdom which during the declining years of the Dutch East India Company had been unable to exercise effective control over frontier settlers and African communities along its borders. Britain sought to create a self-supporting agricultural-based colony producing wool and other goods for the British market, and in turn providing a market for British manufacturers, that was based on an ideology of free trade and a relatively unfettered labour supply. African societies along the colony's frontiers were gradually penetrated by missionaries and merchants and begun to be incorporated into the Cape's economic system. During the second half of the century a prosperous class of African peasant farmers grew up in the Ciskei and Transkei, responding to the food needs of the new colonial towns in the region and to the demands of Cape merchants for wool and other animal products for export. Members of this class were able to gain access to the colony's property-based 'colour-blind' franchise. By creating a stronger colonial state with a more efficient military system, Britain sought to secure and then extend in an orderly way the Cape's eastern frontier, especially against the Xhosa. Yet for much of the nineteenth century the achievement of enduring frontier stability proved elusive and the colony remained a drain on the British exchequer. Although the Xhosa were progressively deprived of important agricultural land in a series of frontier wars, and lost much of their wealth in a disastrous millennial cattle-killing in 1856–7, their capacity to resist white encroachment and pressure was not finally undermined until the last quarter of the century.

From the 1830s settler society in the interior remained weak and fragmented for more than a generation. In Natal the Voortrekkers remained in small groups and subsisted mainly by hunting and bartering African produce for cattle. Early British settlement took much the same form, and for most of the nineteenth century the colonial state in Natal was not powerful enough to restructure African society to create a stable and assured farm labour force. Instead Natal's economy was based mainly on plantation agriculture employing indentured Indian workers and on absentee landlordism whereby large landowners and land companies drew rents from African tenants. When Natal was annexed by Britain in 1843 the Zulu king, Mpande, was able to reassert his kingdom's independence from the Voortrekkers north of the Tugela river. The Zulu state remained intact and independent within its new frontiers until 1879.

In the region bounded to the north and south by the Limpopo and Orange rivers, Tswana lands to the west and the Zulu and Swazi states to the east, dispersed Boer communities were forced to compete with African societies for control of land, livestock and trading commodities such as ivory and hides. With limited human and capital resources at their disposal, and in constant need of funds for military expenditure yet unable to extract taxes systematically, the Boer states lacked the capacity to extend and stabilise their frontiers. Indeed, the Boers were confronted by new pressures once the African societies recovered from the worst ravages of the *difaqane* wars, which had followed the rise of the Zulu kingdom in the 1820s and had paved the way for colonial penetration south of the Tugela and on the highveld, and once these societies also began to acquire firearms in significant quantities. The Boer republic in the Zoutpansberg, essentially a raiding and hunting community founded in the 1840s, could not sustain itself in the mid-1860s against determined resistance from the Venda and other African groups of the region. On two occasions, in 1852 and 1876, the Boers tried vainly to conquer the Pedi. The overthrow of the Zulu state was beyond the Boers' resources.

The economic and political landscape of southern Africa was transformed dramatically by the mineral revolution during the final three decades of the nineteenth century. Diamond mining in Griqualand West, which had begun in 1867, developed rapidly during the 1870s. By the end of the decade there were 22,000 black workers on the diamond fields; by 1888 diamond production at Kimberley was controlled by a single company, Cecil Rhodes's De Beers Consolidated; and by the outbreak of the South African War De Beers was responsible for half of the Cape Colony's exports. The impact of the Witwatersrand gold discoveries in 1886 was even more profound. The economy of the Transvaal, and of southern Africa as a whole, was revolutionised, and by 1899 Johannesburg and its neighbourhood had attracted a mining workforce of almost 100,000 blacks and 12,000 whites. The mineral discoveries engendered rapid growth in all other sectors of the economy, creating a strong demand for labour in road, rail, harbour and building construction and in a variety of service industries. Industrial manufacturing, at first closely related to mining, began to develop, land values rose (in some districts spectacularly) and the creation of new markets led to an increased demand for foodstuffs and therefore for locally-grown agricultural produce and farm labour.

The political configuration of the subcontinent was transformed during these years by the colonial incorporation of the remaining independent African chiefdoms and states. Basutoland was annexed by Britain in 1868; it was governed by the Cape Colony until the Basotho successfully resisted disarmament in the Gun War of 1880–1, and was subsequently administered directly as a British possession. Griqualand West was annexed as a crown colony in 1871 and in 1880 incorporated into the Cape Colony. The independence of the Zulu state was destroyed first by British arms in 1879 and later by the civil wars that followed in the wake of military defeat. Zululand was annexed in 1887 and incorporated into Natal a decade later. The Pedi were conquered in 1879 during the period of British administration in the Transvaal, which had been inaugurated peacefully two years before and which was ended two years later by Boer force of arms. Sekhukhune, the Pedi paramount, was imprisoned, and following his release assassinated in 1882. In 1884 Britain annexed the lands of the Tswana people as the Bechuanaland Protectorate and the Crown Colony of Bechuanaland, the latter being incorporated into the Cape Colony eleven years later. In 1878 the forces of the Gcaleka- and Ngqika-Xhosa had been crushed and in 1894 the last remaining portion of the Transkei, Pondoland, was annexed to the Cape. In the same year Swaziland became, with British approval, a 'political dependency' of the South African Republic.

New colonial relationships were forged in the annexed territories. European officials were appointed, in some cases reserves demarcated, and taxes introduced to pay for the new administration and to provide a stimulus to further African participation in the regional economy, in particular in the labour market. In those regions administered directly by Britain colonial power and authority was largely developed in collaboration with African rulers who consolidated their wealth and influence within the framework of the new colonial order, such as the Koena chiefs in Basutoland and the Ngwato ruler in Bechuanaland, Khama. Other rulers in time came to accept collaboration with the colonial authorities, such as the Kgatla chief, Lentshwe. In those cases where the political independence of African societies had been brought to an end by military force, and when the exercise of colonial power or the major influence upon it rested with a settler state, different patterns of relationships developed. For example, the structure of the Zulu state was undermined by encouraging fragmentation as a means of hastening political and economic dependence; support was given by the colonial authorities to the opponents of the Zulu royal lineage and between 1889 and 1898 the head of the Zulu royal house, Dinuzulu, was exiled to St Helena. In the eastern Transvaal the power of the Pedi state was further weakened after military defeat by land alienation and the demarcation of locations, and by the undermining of the role of the paramountcy in Pedi affairs. Sekhukhune's heir was a small child, and a succession of regents were appointed whose exercise of authority largely depended upon the support of Boer officials.

The social changes throughout southern Africa set in motion by expanding commodity and labour markets on the one hand and colonial incorporation on the other were inescapable and profound. Labour mobilisation for farms, and above all industry, became of paramount importance. Though labour migration had been a feature of a number of African societies before the mineral revolution, its scale, and the means employed by the colonial states to procure labour, increased in scope and intensity thereafter. More and more it was a question of necessity rather than choice that drew men into labour migration. The imposition of colonial taxation followed hard on the heels of colonial incorporation. While those sections of the black population with continued access to land and markets prospered from the increasing local demand for agricultural produce, land dispossession, population growth, soil deterioration and changing patterns of agricultural production were already taking their toll on the economic self-sufficiency of increasing numbers of African homesteads in many areas. The rinderpest epidemic in 1896–7, a virulent cattle disease that accounted for the loss of as much as 90 per cent of African cattle in the subcontinent, pushed many homesteads into indebtedness and drove men on to the labour market in unprecedented numbers.

In the late-nineteenth century, therefore, powerful agents of social change were at work in South Africa. Within thirty years of the Rand gold discoveries a single capitalist state dominated by whites was to be created south of the Limpopo from the two British settler colonies and the two Boer republics of the Transvaal and Orange Free State. Yet on the eve of war, while the processes of social change created by the mineral revolution were clearly discernible, the structures of a society based on industrialisation were less rigid and secure than they were to become later. The acute shortage of labour in southern Africa during the 1890s bears testimony to the fact that mining capital was only in the early stages of transforming the colonial states of the region. The colonial incorporation of the major African chiefdoms of the region was a relatively recent occurrence. Twenty years before, the Zulu, Pedi, Swazi and the Tswana chiefdoms remained independent. In 1880–1 the Basotho successfully resisted the military forces of the Cape Colony. It was not until 1898 that Venda power in the northern Transvaal was at last defeated by the Boers. Indeed, in the late 1890s it was in the South African Republic, the scene of the gold revolution on the Rand, that the power of the settler state was weakest and relationships in the countryside between landlord and tenant most unstable.[5]

Social changes in South Africa in the late-nineteenth century had important implications for the way black people were regarded by the settler states as military collaborators. Before examining these implications, however, an analysis needs to be made of the ways in which Coloureds and Africans participated in the military systems of the white communities during the eighteenth and first half of the nineteenth centuries.

MILITARY COLLABORATION BEFORE 1899

The most distinctive form of white military organisation that evolved in South Africa during the eighteenth and nineteenth centuries was the commando – a body of men raised locally from among the civilian population that was summoned to deal with a particular emergency and disbanded when its task was completed. During the earliest period of white settlement at the Cape the commando originally consisted exclusively of soldiers provided by the Dutch East India Company, but settlers soon became involved directly in defence matters, and as early as 1715 the first entirely civilian commando, led by burgher officers nominated by the Company, was sent out against San groups on the northern frontier. As time passed by the defence of the frontier communities that grew up many miles away from Cape Town increasingly became the responsibility of the settlers themselves.

Those men raised on the frontier for commando duties, however, were not exclusively whites. So badly did many burghers respond to calls for military service, so proficient did many Khoikhoi and Coloureds become in the use of firearms, and so useful were Khoikhoi in tracking down cattle raiders, that whites often comprised only a minority of the men enlisted for the defence of the frontier communities. One of the three commandos assembled in 1774 under the overall leadership of Commandant G. R. Opperman, for operations against the San, consisted of 150 Khoikhoi and Coloureds and only 100 whites. The military duties imposed on Khoikhoi and Coloureds became sufficiently onerous for a complaint to be made in 1778 that on the northern frontier 'all the Hottentots and Bastards fit for commandos are going away to the Namaqua country to evade serving'.[6]

A similar pattern of military collaboration between white frontiersmen and Khoikhoi and Coloureds emerged on the eastern Cape frontier. J. S. Marais wrote of the importance of this cooperation in the arrangements for the defence of the Cape Colony during the eighteenth and first half of the nineteenth centuries.

> When an enemy attack threatened or had taken place, all the Colony's free inhabitants were liable to be called upon to join in its defence without distinction of colour. Hottentots and Coloured people fought side by side with Europeans . . . in all the Xosa wars on the eastern frontier from the 1780s to 1853. Indeed it is no exaggeration to say that in the Xosa wars of 1846–7 and 1850–3 the Coloured people played a greater part in the defence of their country than the European burghers, who responded badly to calls for service.[7]

It was in the Boer states of the interior that the commando system became most highly developed in the nineteenth century. During the Great Trek many of the Coloureds who accompanied the Voortrekkers participated in the struggles between the emigrant communities and the Zulu and other African peoples of the region. All behind-the-line services on commando were carried out by black people, who constructed fortifications, herded horses and cattle, drove waggons, and performed labour duties in the military camps. Many burghers were accompanied by one (or more) of their servants who acted as an *agterryer* (after-rider), performing such tasks as supervising his employer's horse, loading his rifles while in combat, and in exigent circumstances fighting alongside him.[8]

As well as participating in the commandos, Khoikhoi and Coloureds entered into professional military service at the Cape. Bodies of men were raised and garrisoned in Cape Town whenever peace was threatened in the colony or war in Europe seemed likely to spill over into a full-scale colonial struggle. Throughout the eighteenth century Coloured soldiers formed the backbone of colonial defences against both internal and external enemies.[9] There were Coloured soldiers in government pay continuously from 1793 until 1870. During the period of British administration at the Cape, Coloured troops were organised into the Cape Regiment or Cape Mounted Rifle Corps (after 1827 known as the Cape Mounted Riflemen) which took part in the frontier wars of the period, thereby making it unnecessary for Britain to keep a regular cavalry regiment in South Africa. After the war of 1812 the Cape Corps (*Kiepkor*), as the regiment was customarily known, regularly patrolled the eastern frontier to guard against Xhosa raids on the remote farming communities. The Corps also performed a general policing function for the colonial government, a role that was heartily disliked by Boer settlers in the frontier districts. Between 1806 and 1827 the strength of the Cape Corps was maintained at between 250 and 800 men, comprising after 1817 both cavalry and infantry units, though in 1827 only the cavalrymen were retained and the size of the regiment temporarily cut back.[10]

During the early years of the century British colonial officials and military commanders were extravagant in their praise of the qualities of Coloured soldiers; 'as good light troops as any in the world' was General Dundas's assessment in 1808.[11] But following the permanent transfer of the regiment to the harsh environment of the eastern frontier, relations between members of the Cape Corps and the government began to sour. Recruitment became a serious problem, the methods of enlistment increasingly severe and arbitrary, and desertions frequent and uncontrollable. Lack of morale among both Coloured soldiers and their white officers accounted for the Corps performing with little distinction during the frontier war of 1835. 'I never saw anything in the shape of regular soldiers so totally devoid of zeal, subordination, military discipline or feeling as the CMR', wrote Colonel Harry Smith to Sir Benjamin D'Urban in August of that year.

> Half-officered, bad non-commissioned officers, and intermixed with the dregs of the Hottentot rabble we picked up in the streets, or stole out of waggons, never having had previously a real system in the Corps, six months exertion of someone of ability, with every means, is required to make soldiers of those useful though most insubordinate drunken fellows.[12]

In 1838 sixteen Coloured soldiers mutinied and fired on their white officers, and in 1851 a section of the regiment defected to the rebel Coloureds of the Kat River Settlement. Not only were members of the Cape Corps found to be playing a leading role in the rebellion, but among those who deserted were some of the men most trusted by the military. Cory tells that the defectors 'were the oldest, the most steady and the most worthy of the regiment. Up to this time no soldiers could have done better service . . . they had been the admiration of all.'[13] After the rebellion the decision was taken to phase out Coloured members of the regiment.

When the frontier Coloureds allied themselves with the Xhosa, it was the Mfengu, a refugee people who had migrated south from Natal in the 1820s, who thereafter became the settlers' most important military collaborators on the eastern frontier. During the frontier war of 1846–7 1200 Mfengu levies had been mobilised, and in the war of 1850–3 greater reliance was placed on their cooperation because of Coloured defections. Many of the tasks performed in the earlier frontier wars by the Cape Corps and Coloured members of the militia were taken over by the Mfengu, of whom Richard Moyer has written

> they [were] . . . assigned many of the most dangerous tasks and . . . without them the successful conclusion of the wars would have been more difficult. There was no question of the British not committing the resources required to win the wars, but Mfengu assistance shortened their length, minimised their cost and reduced the number of injuries and deaths among the white combatants.[14]

In 1853 Governor Cathcart created a permanent Mfengu force of 240 men to patrol the eastern frontier. The Mfengu were acceptable military collaborators because their interests were closely related to those of the white settlers; both groups were seeking to secure for themselves a stable and independent livelihood on land formerly controlled by the Xhosa.

During the nineteenth century the emigrant white communities in the interior were from the outset dependent on military alliances with African peoples. The Barolong and the Voortrekkers jointly fought Mzilikazi's Ndebele in 1837, a struggle which forms the subject of Sol Plaatje's historical novel, *Mhudi*. Large numbers of Swazi participated in the Boer operations against the Pedi in 1876, and later, during General Wolseley's expedition against Sekhukhune in 1879, 6000 Swazi were mobilised.[15] For much of the nineteenth century the settler republics of the South African interior were weak and politically divided societies, possessing only limited capital, manpower and military resources. It was the power of other African societies in the interior that most rulers saw as the paramount threat to their authority and the security and prosperity of their people, not the emigrant white communities. The subsequent train of events in South African history was by no means evident at the time.

Between the late-eighteenth century and the middle of the nineteenth century black people played a significant part in 'white wars', if indeed they can be accurately called that. The entry of Coloureds into professional military service at the Cape in 1793 was prompted by the need to prepare for a possible attack from overseas, and Coloureds took part in the resistance to the British occupation of the Cape in 1795, and again, following the brief period of Batavian administration, to the British reoccupation of the colony in 1806. On both occasions, too, Malay slaves were mobilised by the authorities in Cape Town. In 1815 a detachment of the Cape Corps brought the Slagtersnek rebellion to an end, and members of the regiment, together with irregular Griqua troops, later played an active part in the operations of the British and colonial forces against the Voortrekkers, assuming important roles in the battles of Touwfontein in 1845 and Boomplaats in 1848.[16] Whites also from time to time negotiated for African military assistance in their disputes. During the 1790s the rebel burgher, Coenraad de Buys, attempted to enlist the cooperation of the Xhosa against the regime in Cape Town, and in 1815 the supporters of the rebel Frederick Bezuidenhout on two occasions made overtures to Ngqika for his military assistance against the government.

Hendrik Potgieter is reputed to have solicited the help of the Pedi chief, Sekwati, in his struggles against the Andries Ohrigstad Volksraad in the 1840s, and in 1857 the Basotho paramount, Moshoeshoe, received emissaries from Marthinus Wessel Pretorius (one of them Paul Kruger) who urged him to create a diversion in the southern Free State while the forces of the Transvaal attacked the republic from the north in a bid to overthrow the government of Jacobus Boshof and install Pretorius as president.[17]

During the period of colonial expansion and settler consolidation in South Africa, Coloureds and Africans can be seen to have played an important role in the military strategies and defence systems of the white communities. During the latter years of the nineteenth century, however, as economic take-off followed the mineral discoveries, as the frontiers closed and as social relations in the settler states became more stratified and established in pattern, so the use of black soldiers in warfare was increasingly opposed by settlers. In 1870 the Cape Corps was disbanded, by which time only ten Coloured soldiers remained in the force; when the Cape Mounted Riflemen was reborn in 1894 it was as an exclusively white regiment. In 1878 the Burgher Forces and Levies Act for the first time made a clear distinction between blacks and whites in determining the eligibility of men to serve in the Cape's militia, blacks being assigned to a new special category of 'levies'.[18]

Though never completely absent before, arguments against the use of black troops in warfare became more widespread and trenchant. Racial stereotypes, influenced by Social Darwinist notions current at the time, intruded more pervasively in opinions on the fighting qualities of black people: their methods of warfare were deemed unacceptably brutal; black troops were believed to eschew taking prisoners and instead preferred to slaughter women, children and the elderly caught up in their campaigns; once aroused in warfare, it was argued, blacks were almost impossible to restrain unless severe discipline was enforced; and so on.[19] All such stereotypes were patently false, as any appraisal of the earlier performance of black people in military service in South Africa would have indicated, but the ill-founded views of the time quickly assumed the status of accepted wisdom.[20]

In late-nineteenth century South Africa the temper of the times became markedly opposed to the use of black people as soldiers in wars between white adversaries. The wisdom of instructing blacks in the use of firearms was challenged, and it was argued that to become dependent on blacks for armed defence would lead them to exaggerate their own military strength. It was feared by settlers that once one side in a dispute accepted black people as collaborators against a white enemy, the other side too would be encouraged to employ black troops. Such dependence on the military collaboration of blacks, it was argued, would give them leverage to bargain for unacceptable liberties and economic rewards in the settler states. Ultimately, black people might even assume the role of arbiters in disputes between the white communities. Furthermore, unless blacks were excluded from military operations, it was feared that peasants and workers would rise against their landlords and employers on the pretext of supporting a rival white group. In a region ever more dominated by the demands of mining capital, the patterns of social relations in late-nineteenth century South Africa determined that the participation of black people in white wars was something to be avoided at all costs if the processes of social change and evolving structures of social control were not to be threatened.

ATTITUDES TOWARDS BLACK INVOLVEMENT IN THE WAR

In October 1899 neither the British nor the Boers gave a formal undertaking that they would not employ black people as combatants during the war. Already in September, however, the issue had been discussed by Sir Alfred Milner, Joseph Chamberlain and officials at the Colonial Office. It was agreed that the conflict, on Britain's part, would be a 'white man's war'. Africans were to be instructed by magistrates to remain within the borders of their locations and not to become involved in military operations, though they would be entitled to defend themselves and their property against Boer aggression. The question of the role that was to be played during the war by black policemen appeared to those at the Colonial Office to be a more delicate issue: would they be permitted to defend the British colonies in southern Africa against a Boer invasion? The suggestion was advanced that all policemen other than white constables should be temporarily disbanded in the border areas, though the proposal did not appeal to Chamberlain, who minuted: 'I do not think it right or practicable to disband existing native police. As I understand the matter any offensive operations will be conducted by white troops . . . [and in defensive operations] the white troops will as a principle be placed in front of black police.'[21] Indeed, rather than being disbanded, the size of the African police forces in Basutoland, Zululand and Natal was increased during the war.

There were a number of reasons why at the outset of the war the British government decided that only white troops would be employed in South Africa. In the first place the War Office was confident that Britain's regular army and white volunteers would easily be able to overrun the Boer republics. Secondly, it was believed there was no group of indigenous collaborators in the region whose military assistance might be decisive in winning the war. Even after the British army had experienced important and unexpected military set-backs in South Africa, A. J. Balfour told the House of Commons, 'I need hardly say, there is no resemblance or analogy between the native tribes of South Africa and the native princes of India and their troops.'[22] The opposition spokesman, Sir Edward Grey, reiterated the theme later in the war when he argued that from a military point of view black South Africans could not be compared to the 'more highly trained and civilised' indigenous troops in India. Between them there was 'all the difference in the world', Grey confidently told the Commons.[23]

Finally, and this is much the most important reason, the British government had to take cognisance of the conviction in South Africa that the use of black soldiers in wars between the white communities was to be avoided at all costs. Balfour informed members of the House that in normal circumstances the government would have been proud to have accepted the assistance of the princes of India and their troops, and possibly also Hausa, West Indian and Chinese soldiers, but that 'the war in South Africa . . . [is] not to be carried out under ordinary conditions'.[24] The government based its decision not to use black troops in the war on grounds of expediency rather than principle, a view which was made abundantly clear in a statement on the subject made by Chamberlain in August 1901.

> There seems to be an opinion . . . that we have come to some sort of agreement with the Boers that natives are not to be employed in the war. There is no such agreement . . . The reason we have not employed natives is not because we do not think they . . . might fairly be placed in the field even against civilised nations, but because, in the peculiar circumstances of South Africa, we believe it would be bad policy. I want it to be clearly understood that it is not because we have any doubt about the morality of employing them . . . we are not creating a precedent to affect us in some other war. We should not hesitate to employ our splendid Indian troops; we should not hesitate to employ those magnificent soldiers who fought recently in Ashanti, providing they fought in accordance with the civilised usages of warfare – that is to say, were properly controlled by British officers. We should be perfectly justified in employing them in any war.[25]

The British government was fully aware that to arm Africans, or to bring into South Africa indigenous soldiers from elsewhere in the empire, would precipitate sharp criticism from the settler governments in the Cape Colony and Natal. In South Africa there was considerable anxiety among many colonists that a military encounter between the white communities would threaten the maintenance of structures of settler control. W. P. Schreiner, the Prime Minister of the Cape, agreed only reluctantly to the decision that black levies should be organised in the Transkei for the defence of the region.[26] Schreiner's successor, Sir Gordon Sprigg, told Milner that his government wished it to be 'clearly established that the rights and liberties of the people of this Colony are not dependent upon the support of the Native population'. During the same month, December 1900, the Cape government was informed that a volunteer force in New Zealand that was about to embark for South Africa included a group of Maoris. Sprigg protested to the Colonial Office that their entry into the country was unacceptable, and the Maoris were ordered to remain at home.[27] The government of Natal stated its opposition to black participation in military operations in some detail when a proposal was made that the Zulu might be organised into a force under white officers to defend Zululand. The Natal cabinet argued:

> (1) that the methods of native warfare are barbarous at all times . . . (2) that the Natives have been told that it is a white man's war . . . and that change of policy now would indicate vacillation and weakness and give the Natives an exaggerated idea of their own importance (3) that if the Natives should in

accordance with their methods of warfare mutilate the dead, kill wounded men, murder women and children and commit other atrocities, the condemnation would necessarily attach to the Government (4) that even if ordered by Europeans it would be impossible to restrain the Natives and keep them under control in accordance with the usages of civilised warfare (5) that inevitable slaughter of Natives would result from bodies of partially trained and unequally armed Natives against modern weapon precision in the hands of skilled marksmen (6) that if the Natives of Zululand are called out reasons quite as strong exist for calling out the Natives of Natal (7) that if the Natives are allowed to believe that their aid had become necessary . . . it would give them a false idea of their own powers and establish a sense of independence among them (8) that the employment of Natives would intensify the race feeling of the Dutch against the English . . . (9) that the employment of Natives . . . would be in opposition to the generally acknowledged trend of Colonial public opinion and would ultimately lead to the lessening of the prestige of the white man and the Natives' respect for the power of the British government.[28]

To Sir Hartmann Just at the Colonial Office these seemed 'very weighty reasons' against mobilising the Zulu or any other African group in the war.

The *krijgswette* (martial law regulations) of the two Boer republics held all inhabitants between the ages of sixteen and sixty liable for military service during the war. Nowhere is it stated that only whites would be mobilised, and indeed the *krijgswette* specifically state that Coloureds (*kleurlingen*) were liable to be called up.[29] At the same time there were laws in both republics that forbade Africans to possess firearms. The most detailed statement of the attitude of the Boers to African involvement in the South African War was made by J. C. Smuts, who at the age of only twenty-eight had been appointed State Attorney in the South African Republic in May 1898. Smuts conceded that it would not have been contrary to the rules of international law to have employed 'civilised' blacks under white officers in the conflict. This is an interesting point. In July 1899, barely three months before the outbreak of war, the first Hague convention, a statement on the customs of land warfare, was signed by the British government and the governments of twenty-three other states. Neither of the Boer republics was invited to attend the conference at the Hague, nor were they signatories to the convention, though the rules drawn up were clearly intended to apply to non-parties as well. The Hague agreement made no mention of customs relating to the roles that might be performed in military operations by black troops (or soldiers of any other race or nationality for that matter), and the convention certainly did not forbid the use of such troops.[30] Smuts maintained, however, that supplying black people with arms to fight alongside them in the war was unthinkable to the Boers in view of the tradition in South Africa of excluding subject peoples from actively taking part in conflicts between the settler groups.

> The peculiar position of the small white community in the midst of the very large and rapidly increasing coloured races and the danger which in consequence threatens this small white community and with it civilisation itself in South Africa, have led to the creation of a special code of morality as between the white

and coloured races which forbids inter-breeding, and of a special tacit understanding which forbids the white races to appeal for assistance to the coloured races in their mutual disputes. This understanding is essential to the continued existence of the white community as the ruling class in South Africa, for otherwise the coloured races must become the arbiters in disputes between the whites and in the long run the predominating political factor or 'casting vote' in South Africa. That this would soon cause South Africa to relapse into barbarism must be evident to everybody; and hence the interests of self-preservation no less than the cause of civilisation in South Africa demands imperatively that blacks shall not be called in or mixed up with quarrels between the whites. This tacit understanding . . . [is] the cardinal principle in South African politics.[31]

The unwillingness of the Boers to arm blacks in 1899 was also based on an awareness that to provide Africans with modern firearms in large quantities could increase the possibility of resistance to white control, especially in circumstances in which many white adult males had been called upon to leave their homes and fight beyond the frontiers of the Boer states. At the beginning of the war the republican governments could not take as a matter of course the subordination of all the African people living along their frontiers and within their borders. The independence of the Zulu and Pedi had been broken not by Boer commandos but by British arms only twenty years before; Venda power had not been finally overcome until 1898; and in the same year the Boers had moved a large number of men into Swaziland in fear of a Swazi rebellion.

In a number of regions of the South African Republic the practical powers of Boer landlords were weak. In some areas of the northern Transvaal farmers could not lay claim to all their lands, while in other parts of the republic a delicate balance frequently obtained between mobilising sufficient labour for farming purposes on the one hand and placing too great a burden on those who laboured on the other. Competition for labour with the mining industry, where higher wages were paid than on the farms, worsened the predicament of Boer households during the late 1880s and 1890s. Anti-squatter legislation, designed to redistribute African homesteads on white-owned farms in the interests of increasing the amount of labour available to Boer farmers, was first enacted by the Volksraad in 1887, and re-enacted in 1895, but achieved relatively little success because of the weakness of the state to implement it effectively. Officials in Pretoria, as well as local farmers, were aware that to have attempted to enforce the legislation rigorously, especially in the northern and eastern Transvaal, would have led to an exodus of tenants to the larger African locations and to the remoter areas of the republic. In consequence there was a heavy dependence by Native Commissioners and farmers in some areas on labour provided by collaborating chiefs and on coercive methods of worker recruitment for the farms. Such methods were the product of weakness rather than strength, revealing the inability of Boer farmers to mobilise workers by any other means. They resulted in brittle relationships between landlords and tenants in a number of localities, such as the Lydenburg district, the southeastern Transvaal and the Rustenburg–Marico area.[32]

It is significant that in such circumstances the republics only mobilised between 56 and 65 per cent of their burgher fighting strength in October 1899. Furthermore, during the initial Boer advances into Natal and the Cape Colony, a large number of men were deployed inside and along the borders of the republics to guard against African risings.[33]

BLACK PARTICIPATION IN THE WAR

Throughout the South African War the British and the Boers persistently accused each other of having abandoned the tacit agreement that blacks would not be permitted to participate actively in military operations. As early as 20 November 1899, little more than a month after the outbreak of war, President Steyn of the Orange Free State wrote to W. P. Schreiner to protest against the use by the colonial forces of armed Coloureds in the northwestern Cape. Steyn threatened that unless Cape Coloureds were withdrawn from participating with the colonial forces the Free Staters would make full use of Cape Afrikaners in their campaign.[34] In February 1900 a joint communication from Presidents Steyn and Kruger was despatched to Lord Roberts protesting against the employment of blacks by the British army and alleging that two armed Africans had been captured by the Boers at the Stormberg on 10 December, another later near Dordrecht, and that groups of armed blacks had been raised at Derdepoort, Mafeking, Tuli and Selukwe. The charges were rejected by Roberts, who maintained that 'No armed natives have been employed in our operations', though he did concede that a raid had occurred by the Kgatla on a Boer encampment at Derdepoort. But he insisted this had been 'contrary to the instructions of the British officer nearest the spot, and entirely disconcerted his operations'.[35]

The British government also received reports that the Boers were employing armed blacks in their military operations in Natal. Statements to this effect were made by black workers deserting from the Boers to the British army, and their stories appeared to corroborate eye-witness accounts provided by British soldiers. At first, officials in London were inclined to disbelieve the reports, and at the Colonial Office Charles Lucas minuted guardedly that 'Many of the Boers are very dark and might perhaps be mistaken for natives.' But only a week later, following the receipt in London of further reports of black involvement in Boer operations, Lucas became convinced of their authenticity, arguing that 'the use of natives by the Boers is beyond anything we have done because the Boers are not employed in defensive operations'.[36]

As the war progressed so the accusations of one side against the other continued. In March 1901 De Wet accused Kitchener of having armed blacks to such an extent that they made up 'a great majority' of his fighting men. In August of the same year General Ben Viljoen protested against the British army's employment of armed blacks and its use of African chiefs as military collaborators in the Transvaal. The protests of the Boers culminated in the despatch of a memorandum on the issue of black involvement in the war by

Schalk Burger and Frank Reitz, the Acting President and State Secretary of the South African Republic. The memorandum was addressed directly to Lord Salisbury.

> Whereas His Honour the Commandant General, and other commanding officers, have already more than once, without any result, protested to the Commanding Officer of your Forces in South Africa against the employment of savage aborigines in this War, and notwithstanding that we have repeatedly assured your military authorities here that on our side every effort is being made to keep kaffirs entirely outside this War, this Government is of opinion that it is its duty earnestly and solemnly to protest to your Government, as we hereby do, and at the same time to point out and direct its attention to the horrible and cruel consequences of this manner of warfare . . .
>
> These kaffirs, being ignorant of the rules of civilised warfare, have not hesitated on various occasions and even in the presence of your troops, to kill prisoners-of-war in a barbarous fashion . . . defenceless women and children have been made prisoners by these wild ruffians, and removed to kaffir kraals for detention until they were handed over to the British military authorities.

In reply to these and other accusations Kitchener and his officers accepted that black people were employed as non-combatants, policemen and scouts, but they denied that this involvement was contrary to the accepted practice of warfare in South Africa, and they went on to make counter-accusations of their own. In August 1901 Colonel A. Curran informed General Viljoen:

> In numerous cases armed natives have been employed by the burgher forces, particularly in the commando of General Beyers, and . . . armed natives have frequently been found in the commandos fighting against us.
>
> I have invariably told the natives that, although I could not forbid their defending themselves if attacked by burghers, they were on no account to attack. I am convinced but for the strict orders that I have issued on the subject . . . this war would have led to a native rising, with deplorable results to the Boer race.

During the same month Chamberlain addressed the House of Commons on the issue of black participation in the war.

> Throughout this war we have given instructions that natives should not be employed as belligerents. We have undoubtedly made a great and immediate sacrifice in doing that. We might have had, if we had lifted one little finger, 20,000 Basuto horsemen on the flanks of the Boers, and we might have had a large force of Swazis and Kaffirs in Cape Colony and elsewhere . . . On the other hand, again and again we have taken Kaffirs and found dead Kaffirs in the Boer ranks with arms in their hands and beside them.[37]

How far were the accusations of the British and the Boers justified? For purposes of defence the British army enlisted the active support of a number of blacks during the difficult first months of the war. To guard the frontier of the Bechuanaland Protectorate, and parallel to it the railway line that ran from Mafeking to Bulawayo, the Kgatla chief, Lentshwe, and Khama, the ruler of the Ngwato, were provided with 6000 and 3000 rounds of ammunition respectively. Khama mobilised between 800 and 1000 men to defend the border between the Ngwato reserve and the South African Republic.[38] In the Transkei 4000 Mfengu and Thembu levies were assembled to defend the region against possible Boer penetration. In the Cape Colony itself black people were occasionally mobilised to participate in the operations to halt the Boer advances beyond the frontiers of the republics. Alfred Harmsworth defended the magistrate's building at Klipdam with armed groups of Coloureds and Africans during the first week of the war, and the occupation by the Boers of Kuruman was initially resisted by a small force of local Coloureds and white policemen.[39] At Mafeking over 500 Barolong and contingents of other blacks took part in the town's defence system during the siege, while another 200 Africans were enrolled as special constables in Herschel to discourage incursions into the district by Free State commandos.[40]

From the beginning of the war the British depended upon black people for non-combatant duties. Transport-riding with the military was an almost exclusively Coloured and African occupation. 5000 Africans, most of them transport drivers and leaders, were employed by Lord Roberts's columns during the long haul to Bloemfontein in February–March 1900, and 7000 Africans similarly took part in General French's march to Machadodorp later in the same year. It has been estimated that at least 14,000 black transport drivers were in British military employment at any one time during the war.[41] The British army also depended on black workers for constructing fortifications, for loading and off-loading supply trains, for portering duties, for supervising horses in the remount and veterinary departments, and for sanitary work and other labour duties in the military camps. All these occupations could be defined without too much difficulty as non-combatant categories of military employment.

Other forms of work with the British army were not so easily defined. The military depended heavily on blacks for scouting and intelligence work. At the beginning of the war magistrates in the Cape and Natal were requested to provide reliable men for scouting purposes. R. C. A. Samuelson, a lawyer in Natal, raised a unit of men for intelligence work known as the Zululand Native Scouts, and other bodies of scouts were raised from among the Coloured people of the northern and western Cape.[42] The number of scouts employed by the army rose as the value of their intelligence work became recognised more widely. A circular was issued informing officers that 'For purposes of obtaining information, natives can be frequently employed with more success than patrols.' The circular continued, 'Natives work best at night, and when sent out should have some definite task assigned to them.'[43] Black scouts were used with particular success during the later stages of the war, when to counter the guerrilla tactics of the Boer commandos the army divided its men into smaller and more mobile columns, each of which depended upon reliable information about the enemy's movements for its success. Groups of black scouts, up to fifty in number, came to be attached to all the British columns, where their work was supervised by white intelligence officers. One of the most successful groups of black scouts was that led by Colonel Aubrey Woolls-Sampson, an eccentric former gold miner and ex-commander of the Imperial Light Horse. The main responsibility of Woolls-Sampson's men was the location of itinerant Boer guerrilla groups. So successful were the scouts that, during two weeks in December 1901, 300 of the 756 Boers captured by British forces throughout South Africa fell to the columns to which Woolls-Sampson's men were attached.[44] The Boers fully appreciated the value of African intelligence to the British army, and any black suspected by the guerrillas of working as a scout for the military, or of having supplied information about them to the British, was likely to be executed.

During the guerrilla stage of the war the British army also became dependent upon the active involvement of blacks in a number of other ways following the effective collapse of the structures of social control in a number of regions of the Transvaal. Blacks seized Boer livestock and brought the animals into the garrison towns in return for a share of the stock delivered. Black people participated in the destruction of farmsteads and crops, and in bringing into the concentration camps Boer women and children removed from the countryside. As a further measure to button up the movements of the guerrilla units and deny them access to supplies, a large number of blacks collaborated with the army of occupation to resist the encroachment of commandos into their localities, thereby seriously restricting the area over which the republican forces could operate and enabling the British army to concentrate its manpower elsewhere.[45]

During the first twelve months of the war strict instructions were issued by the army, at the request of the British government, that on no account were blacks to be furnished with weapons. In order that a clear distinction could be maintained between combatants and non-combatants, Roberts ordered in August 1900 that black people in army employment were forbidden to wear military uniforms, and that any person found infringing the order would be severely punished. Two months later Roberts made it clear that he did not favour the arming of black despatch riders, and in December it was decided that weapons could not be issued to black scouts.[46]

Already by the end of 1900, however, pressures were beginning to mount on military commanders to relax the official orders that debarred black people in army employment from carrying firearms. The number of casualties among unarmed black workers began to reach worrying proportions. Following the executions of five Africans by the Boers six miles west of Vredefort Road in the Orange River Colony, Roberts warned De Wet in September that unless such 'crimes' ceased he would consider it his duty to issue arms to all Africans in the territory. In December it was agreed that any black scouts who already possessed rifles when they entered army employment should not be disarmed.[47] By the end of the year it had become apparent, too, that the war was unlikely to come to a rapid end, and that the army's existing manpower resources would become stretched more and more as the months passed by.

Fatigue and ill-health among British soldiers had already accounted for many hundreds of deaths. In all during the war the British army lost 22,000 men, of whom 13,250 died from disease. Enteric fever accounted for most of the deaths and an additional 31,000 men suffering from the disease had to be invalided home. In October 1900 Roberts enquired of the War Office whether it would be possible for a West Indian regiment to be sent to the lowveld region of the northeastern Transvaal, where he believed the climate would take a heavy toll on European soldiers. In November Captain H. S. S. Hardan wrote to the Colonial Office to suggest that an African regiment should be established in South Africa, similar in organisation to those that had been raised elsewhere in the continent. The possibility of employing Indian troops in the fighting in South Africa began to be canvassed seriously in the British press, and in January 1901 Kitchener approached the government about sending a number of Indian cavalry regiments to the country.[48] St John Brodrick, the Secretary of State for War, and Roberts, however, believed that to send Indian soldiers to South Africa as combatants would appear as a confession of weakness, since the impression would be given that the army had no more white troops left. 'If only we had some native troops who could for one moment forget their stomachs and go for the enemy,' lamented Kitchener in reply.[49]

The new Commander-in-Chief's attitude towards black participants in the war was much less rigid than that of his predecessor, though during the first six months of Kitchener's command in South Africa it is impossible to tell how rigorously Roberts's order was observed that no arms be issued to black people. In July 1901, however, an important change of policy took place. In that month General P. H. Kritzinger warned Kitchener that any Africans or Coloureds employed by the British army, whether armed or unarmed, would be executed if they fell into Boer hands. Later this was extended to include any person who informed the British of Boer commando movements.[50] In these circumstances it was felt intolerable, both by the army and by the British government, that black scouts should continue to be denied weapons with which to defend themselves. During the latter part of 1901 most scouts attached to the British columns operating in the Transvaal and Orange River Colony were provided with firearms. Even the *Times History* acknowledged that these men could scarcely be classified as 'non-combatants'.

> As time went on most columns came to be accompanied by parties of armed native scouts, who did most valuable service; so valuable, indeed, that under exceptionally able direction, something like a tactical revolution was carried into effect, with not unimportant results. It would be an abuse of terms to describe these scouts as non-combatants . . . The only justification was sheer military necessity.[51]

The arming of scouts was criticised vigorously by pro-Boers in the House of Commons. Chamberlain found their objections utterly tiresome: it was irrelevant whether or not scouts were issued with weapons, he maintained,

23

because the Boers had said they would shoot all blacks assisting the British, whether they possessed arms or not. Later Brodrick told Lloyd George, who opposed the arming of blacks under any circumstances, that:

> the Boers [have] undertaken to shoot every native that they find, armed or unarmed. Are we, under these circumstances, to let these men, who are absolutely necessary . . . stand there in cold blood to be shot, as they have been shot, not in ones and twos, but in numbers that come to scores in the course of the war?[52]

Critics of British policy in South Africa recognised that having once accepted that black scouts might bear arms for the purpose of self-defence, this was likely to lead to other categories of blacks in military employment also being issued with weapons. This undoubtedly happened. Because of the strain on the manpower resources of the army, the military specially enrolled blacks and provided them with weapons ('to prevent accidents and for their own protection') to defend the lines of blockhouses established to restrict the mobility of the Boer commandos. There were other instances, too, of arms being issued to blacks in military employment. 'Kaffirs in South Africa have been armed by the British to such an extent that there is scarcely a camp . . . where a few natives with well-filled bandoliers may not be seen', asserted the Irish Nationalist John Dillon in the House of Commons in August.[53]

In view of the mounting criticism of the army's policy towards issuing arms to blacks, the War Office was naturally anxious to obtain reliable information from Kitchener on exactly how many blacks had been provided with weapons. The Commander-in-Chief at first told the government that it was impossible to obtain such information, which led to much embarrassment on the part of ministers when the issue was raised in Parliament, as it frequently was between August 1901 and the end of the war. Members found it difficult to believe that official replies such as 'No record could possibly be kept' and 'I have no information' represented the whole truth of the matter. At the beginning of March 1902 Brodrick asked Kitchener how many Africans were involved in guarding the blockhouses. Kitchener's reply was evasive.

> You have asked me a rather difficult question about black men who are stated to be actually garrisoning blockhouses etc.
> In Cape Colony, Cape Boys and Bastards are separated by Act of Parliament from natives. Of the latter we have none in the blockhouses, though we have some as watchmen between blockhouses. Of the former, Cape Boys, I believe French has recently allowed some to occupy intermediate blockhouses out west. Of the Bastards there has always been a corps at Uppington [sic] on the German frontier to guard roads and water holes; they may be said to be police. . . .
> In Orange River Colony and Transvaal and Natal, no natives are used otherwise than as watchmen, cattle guards, scouts, drivers and labourers. I will try to get accurate numbers, but it means a vast amount of telegraphing.[54]

Accounts by those who took part in the war make it clear that blacks were involved in guarding the blockhouses themselves, not merely the country between them, and that this happened in the Transvaal and Orange River Colony as well as in the Cape.[55] Whether the Commander-in-Chief was deliberately attempting to mislead the War Office is impossible to say; he may simply have been ignorant of the extent to which blacks had become directly embroiled in the war on the British side, and in any case found the whole issue thoroughly tiresome. His reply, however, did not satisfy Brodrick, who appreciated above all the political implications of the issue. He told Kitchener:

> One thing I am troubled about viz. employment of Kaffirs *as soldiers* . . . I can't help having a suspicion that on some lines of country, the CO's are so reduced in men that Kaffirs are possibly doing soldiers' work – I don't want – for your credit as well as my own – to go back on anything I may say in the H of C and though I have taken a pretty high line, the letters that come through hardly seem to square with our official assertions.[56]

Finally, Kitchener admitted to having provided firearms to 2496 Africans and 2939 Coloureds in the Cape, and 4618 Africans in Natal, Orange River Colony and Transvaal, 10,053 in all.[57] It seems doubtful whether this represented the total number since, as the Commander-in-Chief admitted himself, he did not have complete day-to-day control over all the actions of his subordinates. 'The temptation on the spot to relieve our men of hard work is no doubt very great', Kitchener confessed.[58] Furthermore, this figure does not represent the total number of armed blacks in British military employment, because many (especially scouts) brought with them their own firearms, which after December 1900 they had usually been permitted to retain. In March 1902 Lloyd George suggested in the House of Commons that there were as many as 30,000 armed blacks in British military employment in South Africa.[59] It is unclear on what basis Lloyd George arrived at the calculation, though the figure may not be wildly exaggerated.

Like the British army, the Boer forces depended on blacks to perform ancillary duties. At the beginning of the war men were conscripted to dig trenches, drive waggons, attend to horses and to perform other labour duties on campaign. For certain tasks, such as the destruction of railways and the attempted damming of the Klip river during the Ladysmith campaign (on which 500 labourers were employed), the Boers brought together large numbers of black workers. *Agterryers* again accompanied the commandos. The Boers relied on Africans for their intelligence, though black scouts employed by the Boers do not usually appear to have been armed.[60] According to the official German account of the war, the information conveyed to the commandos by black scouts was 'remarkably accurate and . . . transmitted with extraordinary rapidity'.[61] The assistance of black people was enlisted by the Boers in other ways as well. At the beginning of the war blacks were conscripted to work on farms in an attempt to maintain agricultural output in the absence of many farmers and servants at the theatre of war; oxen-teams and waggons belonging to black peasants were commandeered along with men to drive them; and during the war's guerrilla phase cattle and military supplies were sometimes left with Africans for safe-keeping (or, as it often turned out, not-so-safe-keeping) until they were needed by the commandos.[62]

Throughout the war the Boers consistently denied employing blacks as combatants in military operations. In January 1902 Smuts told W. T. Stead:

> The leaders of the Boers have steadfastly refused to make use of coloured assistance in the course of the present war. Offers of such assistance were courteously refused by the government of the South African Republic, who always tried to make it perfectly clear to the Natives that the war did not concern them and would not affect them so long as they remained quiet . . . The only instance in the whole war in which the Boers made use of armed Kaffirs happened at the siege of Mafeking when an incompetent Boer officer [Commandant P. A. Cronjé], without the knowledge of the Government or the Commandant-General, put a number of armed Natives into some forts.[63]

Although the arming of blacks was officially disapproved of by the Boers, there is evidence to suggest that on a number of occasions, other than the one at Mafeking mentioned by Smuts, black people fought alongside whites in the republican forces. Workers who defected from the Boers to the British military camps in Natal frequently stated that armed blacks accompanied the invading armies, and during the siege of Ladysmith it was reported that the Boers regularly employed armed blacks in their outposts at night.[64] A commissariat book relating to the activities of the Apies river commando, which was handed in to the prosecutor of the special treason court in Dundee in June 1900, purports to show that on one day during the Boer occupation of the town seventeen blacks were armed and each provided with thirty rounds of ammunition.[65] General French reported that during the army's march from Barberton to Heidelberg in October 1900 armed Africans were present among the harassing Boer units.[66] Later, Colonel H. M. Lawson stated that the Boer commando led by De Beer and Van Rooyen, which raided the Upper Tugela district of Natal from the Orange River Colony in July 1901, included thirty armed Basotho and twenty other armed blacks.[67] British soldiers, of course, may sometimes have mistaken *agterryers* for white members of the commandos, an understandable error, for in combat an *agterryer* loaded his employer's rifle, wore an ammunition belt, and was usually dressed in similar garments. However, it seems inconceivable that in exigent circumstances *agterryers* were prevented from engaging the enemy on their own account. Certainly this appears to have happened at the battle of Vaalkrans in Natal in February 1900. 'Prisoners say that Kaffirs were only used as after-riders,' General Buller told the Natal Governor, Sir Walter Hely-Hutchinson, 'but several officers saw Kaffirs, on more than one occasion, firing on our men.'[68]

On the part of both sides, therefore, a difference emerged between the precept and practice of black participation in the war. Both the British and the Boers depended upon black workers for the performance of tasks to which white participants were unaccustomed, and to enable a large number of white military personnel to serve actively in the field. Blacks provided much of the intelligence upon which military manoeuvres were based. Especially on the British side black people became more deeply involved in operations. Armed scouts and blockhouse sentries played an indispensable part in the prosecution of the war during its protracted guerrilla phase. Blacks helped to clear vast areas of the countryside of livestock and crops and to bring Boer civilians into the concentration camps. With British encouragement blacks closed their neighbourhoods to Boer penetration. The British army was largely composed of soldiers who previously had no first-hand experience of South African conditions or of colonial society in general, or men who had become accustomed to fighting in collaboration with indigenous troops in other parts of the empire. The army also had a specific military task to accomplish rather than the achievement of a general political objective. It is not surprising that British soldiers were much less influenced by the taboos in South Africa that were associated with the participation of black people in white wars than were the Boers or the settler governments in Natal and the Cape Colony. The ways in which black people perceived the war and became involved in military operations, on both a formal and informal basis, will be discussed in greater detail in the following chapters.

2

Mafikeng and beyond

During the final quarter of the nineteenth century both the British and the Boers sought to control the land of the Tswana peoples between the highveld and the Kalahari desert, the Boers to secure and extend the western frontier of the South African Republic, the British to control the route from the Cape to the interior of the continent. The colonial geography of the region was shaped in the mid-1880s when British forces overthrew the short-lived republics of Stellaland and Goschen, and Britain annexed the Bechuanaland Protectorate and the Crown Colony of British Bechuanaland (later incorporated in the Cape in 1895). The strategic importance of the land occupied by the Tswana determined that Bechuanaland, unlike Basutoland or Swaziland, became a theatre of military operations during the South African War, and that the administrative capital of the Protectorate (situated immediately beyond its frontiers), Mafeking, should become the most celebrated town associated with the war. Situated adjacent to it was the Tshidi-Barolong settlement whose name, meaning 'the place of stones', had been corrupted in the naming of the white town, *Mafikeng*.

The significance of Tswana country in British military planning has only recently been fully revealed. In July 1899 Colonel R. S. S. Baden-Powell was despatched to southern Africa to raise a force of 1000 men to patrol the northwestern borders of the Transvaal. It was hoped in some quarters that the presence of Baden-Powell's force would encourage Kruger to climb down in Britain's negotiations with the republic, and that in the event of war the force would invade the Transvaal, in much the same way as Jameson's men had done four years earlier, thereby drawing off large numbers of burghers and so protecting vulnerable parts of the Cape Colony and Natal during the first weeks of military operations before overseas reinforcements arrived. It was an optimistic scheme that stood little chance of success, though the plan played some part in drawing off a larger proportion of the Boer forces to the Transvaal's northern and western frontiers than might otherwise have been the case – 7700 men.[1] The posting of Baden-Powell to the Bechuanaland Protectorate, however, served other, rather more realistic, purposes, for it was deemed desirable to defend Mafeking as the principal colonial settlement in

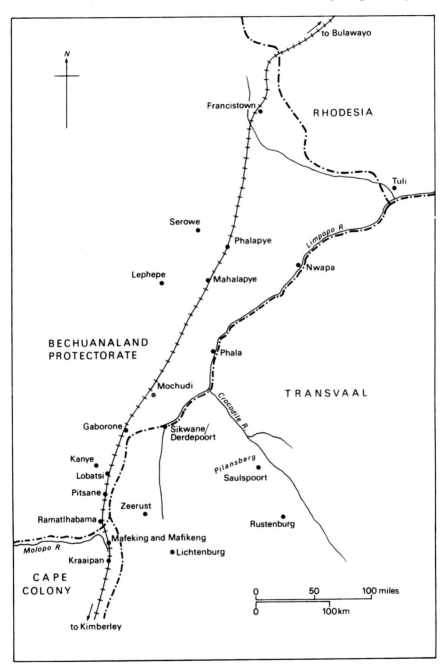

Map 2   The Bechuanaland Protectorate and Western Transvaal

the region, and on the eve of war it was also expected that the Boers were likely, ultimately, to be driven northward by advancing British forces from Natal and the Cape Colony and might seek to enter Rhodesia, either to escape from the invading armies or to create a military diversion. The possibility was viewed with some alarm, since it was feared that a Boer invasion of Rhodesia would be seized upon by the Shona and Ndebele to renew their armed resistance to white settlement of their lands following the unsuccessful rebellion in 1896–7. The defence of Rhodesia determined that the railway from Mafeking to Bulawayo, which ran through Tswana land almost parallel to the frontier between the Protectorate and the South African Republic, should be protected.[2] The scenario envisaged by Britain's military commanders never materialised, though the region along the northern and western frontiers of the Transvaal remained important to both armies. Three Tswana peoples became closely involved in the way military operations unfolded: the Barolong, Kgatla and Ngwato.

THE SIEGE OF MAFIKENG

On the eve of war Baden-Powell had raised two regiments of mounted infantry, a Rhodesian corps stationed in Bulawayo and led by Colonel H. C. O. Plumer, and a Protectorate corps under his own command based at Ramatlhabama, just across the border from Mafeking. On the outbreak of war Plumer's force moved south to Tuli and Baden-Powell's to Mafeking. On 13 October the siege of the town began. In fact it was really the siege of two settlements, the European town of Mafeking and the Tshidi-Barolong community of Mafikeng close by. Until detachments of Plumer's men could be moved further south, the Bechuanaland Protectorate, and in particular the Mafeking–Bulawayo railway, was left to be defended by only 142 British South Africa Company Police and sixty-one Protectorate Native Police (made up of four white officers and fifty-seven Basotho, recruited directly from Maseru). Before any significant number of Plumer's mounted infantrymen could move south, Commandant P. D. Swarts with a contingent of the Marico commando seized Lobatsi. A detachment of the Rustenburg commando under Piet Kruger moved from Derdepoort towards Crocodile Pools to destroy the railway bridge there and prevent the armoured train which patrolled the line to Bulawayo from travelling further south. To the north the Waterberg commando led by General Grobler established a camp close to Nwapa (Selika's) and advanced in the direction of Tuli. On 24 October Gaborone was evacuated and occupied by the Boers. By the end of the month British forces had been compelled to retreat as far north as Mahalapye, 200 miles from the besieged garrison at Mafeking. Only gradually were Plumer's men able to move southward through the Protectorate. In mid-November General P. A. Cronjé moved away from Mafeking to block General Methuen's advance towards Kimberley, leaving about 1500 burghers surrounding the town under the command of Commandant J. P. L. Snyman. Still the siege went on, much more of a military sideshow than before. The stalemate persisted for 217 days until on 17 May a relief column from the south led by Colonel B. Mahon, in collaboration with Plumer's force, reached the beleaguered garrison and liberated the town.

According to Sol Plaatje, who at the time worked as court interpreter to Charles Bell, the Resident Magistrate and Civil Commissioner in Mafeking, the Tshidi-Barolong took a keen interest in the negotiations between the British and Transvaal governments during the middle months of 1899. Tshidi councillors collected reports of Boer military preparations in the Lichtenburg district of the republic and presented their findings to the colonial administration in Mafeking, together with requests for rifles and ammunition with which to defend their villages should an assault from across the frontier be made. Bell steadfastly refused to entertain the notion that an invasion was likely and turned down all the Tshidi's requests for arms, his obduracy giving rise to 'some slight feeling of irritation' he reported to Cape Town. In fact the Tshidi were rather more experienced in these matters than Mafeking's colonial administrators, having themselves held out for two years against surrounding Boer and Barolong forces in the early 1880s. During an ill-tempered meeting between the Tshidi leaders and Charles Bell at the beginning of October, one headman, Motsegare, went so far as to pull off his coat and undo his shirt to reveal an old bullet-scar inflicted during the previous Boer invasion of Tshidi territory: 'Until you can satisfy me that Her Majesty's white troops are impervious to bullets', he told Bell forcefully, 'I am going to defend my own wife and children. I have got my rifle at home and all I want is ammunition.' Wessels, the Tshidi chief, meanwhile flatly refused to provide men for sentry duties around the white town until the Tshidi regiments received a share of the garrison's armaments.[3]

Upon the declaration of war, Mafikeng, the Tshidi *stad* (town), which normally housed 5000 inhabitants, was swelled by over 2000 arrivals – men returning from work in Kimberley, Johannesburg and other employment centres, families from outlying Tshidi villages in the locality, and groups of Shangane mineworkers fleeing the republic, who were allowed to take refuge in the town.[4] From the outset of the siege Baden-Powell planned to include the *stad* within the perimeter of Mafeking's defence works, for otherwise dangerous access would have been permitted to the heart of the town along the Molopo river and the outposts of the British defence system brought unacceptably close to the main area of white habitation. Baden-Powell also appreciated keenly the potential value of Tshidi help in defending Mafeking. Indeed, were it not for Tshidi assistance the siege would probably have ended in a matter of a few days, a forgotten episode in a drama played out elsewhere in South Africa.

Baden-Powell's force in Mafeking was made up of four contingents, numbering altogether some 750 soldiers and policemen. Before the declaration of war two more irregular contingents, the Town Guard and Railway Volunteers, numbering a little over 400 men, were raised from among the 1500

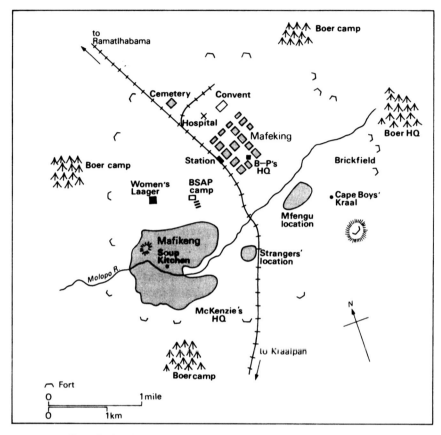

Map 3   Mafikeng besieged

white inhabitants of Mafeking. Three additional militia units were also created: a Coloured contingent of sixty-seven men led by Captain Goodyear and Corporal Currie of the Cape Police; the 'Black Watch', initially composed of about sixty men from the non-Barolong 'strangers' location', led by Captain McKenzie, and whose numbers swelled as the siege progressed; and a small unit raised from the local Mfengu community and led by Sergeant Webster. The Coloured contingent was armed with magazine rifles and Martini-Henrys, the others only with elephant guns or obsolete rifles. At first the Tshidi were not mobilised, though at the outbreak of war Wessels at last agreed to provide fifty mounted men for picket duties.[5]

From the outset the Boers appreciated the potential value to the town's defence of black assistance and, conversely, the way in which Tshidi resistance to Baden-Powell's force might play into their hands, and they almost immediately sought to create a breach between the British garrison and the local Tshidi community by shelling the *stad* of Mafikeng. In fact the strategy served only to cement a closer military alliance between the Tshidi and the British force, and following two particularly severe Boer attacks on the *stad* on 24 and 25 October the Tshidi were allowed to participate more fully in the British defence system.[6] By the end of the siege about 500 Tshidi had been permitted to take up arms. They were organised into regiments led by Motsegare, Badrile and other headmen under the general command of Lekoko and Sergeant Abrams, and were largely responsible for defending Mafikeng and the southwestern perimeter of the garrison's defence network.

As the siege progressed the black contingents played an increasingly important role in military operations. According to Major F. D. Baillie, the *Morning Post* correspondent in Mafeking, the Coloured contingent 'invariably opened the ball' in any exchanges of fire with the Boers: 'the Cape boys . . . are a most gallant race of men and good shots . . . very brave, and have accounted for quite a large number of Boers'. Edward Ross, an auctioneer in Mafeking, believed the Coloured contingent performed a 'wonderfully good service', and particularly singled out for praise one of the Coloured leaders, Sergeant-Major Taylor, who was two or three times mentioned in general orders and who died from severe wounds on 3 March 1900. The Coloureds and Mfengu operated especially in the district to the southeast of Mafeking known as the brickfields, and on 6 March the Coloured contingent was sent with bayonets into the advanced Boer trenches there, compelling the occupants to retire to more fortified positions. Five days later the Tshidi attacked the Boers occupying Fort Snyman, but with rather less success since their assault was handicapped by a shortage of ammunition. Throughout the final three months of the siege small Barolong and Mfengu guerrilla units, with Baden-Powell's approval, stole out of the town under the cover of darkness to harass the surrounding Boer forces, raid livestock and in some instances to ransack and burn neighbouring white farmhouses. In May, during the last determined offensive against the British garrison mounted by Kruger's grandson, S. J. Eloff, the Tshidi played a decisive role in capturing Eloff's party of 240 men who invaded and set fire to Mafikeng, and proceeded to the outskirts of the white town. It was the Tshidi who cut off Eloff's line of retreat and who 'bore the brunt of the fighting and saved the day'.[7]

The advance of General Cronjé's force to the outskirts of Mafeking had been achieved with the cooperation of the rival Rapulana-Barolong who, as they had done during the war of 1880–1, supported their traditional white allies. Cronjé's men first established a base at Lotlhakane, from where the Rapulana provided scouts, labourers and messengers to assist the Boers. Rapulana were also armed to raid and guard cattle and to participate in the manning of the Boer trenches and fortified positions around the town. Altogether some 300 armed blacks took part in the Boer force surrounding Mafeking. The Rapulana took the opportunity presented by the siege to settle old scores with the Tshidi. Chief Saane at Modimola was seized by the Rapulana, his cattle confiscated and held prisoner at Lotlhakane (from where, apparently, he was able to furnish the besieged garrison with intelligence reports carried by messengers through the Boer lines at night). According to two Tshidi who entered Mafeking in March, the Boers became so exasperated by the behaviour of the Rapulana, whose activities threatened to undermine white security in the region, that orders were issued threatening to disarm them completely unless the execution of blacks in the locality ceased.[8]

A series of charges and counter-charges concerning black participation in military operations took place between Baden-Powell on the one hand and Cronjé and his successor, Snyman, on the other. On 29 October Baden-Powell received a letter written on Cronjé's behalf by John Dyer, an American surgeon serving with the Boer forces. The latter accused Baden-Powell of creating 'a new departure in South African history':

> It is understood you have armed Bastards, Fingos and Baralongs against us. In this you have committed an enormous act, the wickedness of which is certain, and the end of which no man can foresee . . . I would ask you to pause and even at this eleventh hour, reconsider the matter, and even if it cost you the loss of Mafeking, to disarm your blacks and thereby act the part of a white man in a white man's war.

In reply Baden-Powell did not admit openly to having armed blacks, but he indicated that he could not prevent the Tshidi from defending the *stad.*

> The Natives are becoming extremely incensed at your stealing their cattle, and the wanton burning of their kraals . . . you thought it fit to carry on cattle thefts and raids against them, and you are now beginning to feel the consequences . . . please do not suppose that I am ignorant of what you have been doing with regard to seeking the assistance of armed Natives.[9]

A further exchange of letters occurred in January when Baden-Powell threatened that if Snyman continued to use armed blacks in his force it 'would justify the English in allowing the Basutos to join in the war, in bringing Ghoorka troops from India, in using "Dum Dum" bullets, and other such acts'. Furthermore, Baden-Powell told Snyman, 'I may add that the Baralongs have asked me to take them on as troops but I have declined to do so', a patent untruth.[10] On 28 February Baden-Powell threatened that if Snyman did not withdraw the Rapulana from participating with the Boer force, and restore chief Saane to his people, steps would be taken 'for carrying into an effect an invasion of the Marico and Rustenburg districts by Linchwe, Khama and Bathoen etc.'.[11]

Black military assistance helped the besieged garrison in a variety of other ways. African work parties were requisitioned daily during the siege and were responsible for constructing all the town's defences, sometimes under heavy fire from the Boers. The Shangane mineworkers were put to work digging the maze of trenches around Mafeking, which extended to four miles of covered ways. Edward Ross noted in his diary on 11 January:

> The stupendous work round and about the town, in the way of trench-digging, throwing up earthworks, making dugouts, etc. etc., is far more than one can imagine . . . Between two and three hundred in each gang have been at work

night and day for the past three months, and if the amount of work they have accomplished could be put into one length it would have formed a moat 7 feet deep totally surrounding Mafeking.[12]

Baden-Powell's local intelligence was almost wholly based on the reports of black scouts and spies. The regime was a stern one; scouts whose information turned out to be inaccurate were severely punished, and any black spy suspected of duplicity faced death by firing squad. All the information which reached the outside world about the plight of the town was carried through the Boer lines at night by black runners. Despatch running was not without risks, and a number of runners were killed or captured during the early months of the siege, though as time passed by circumstances eased, and for the besieged British journalists, taking part in the story of a lifetime, the payment of 2s 6d was usually sufficient to ensure their copy was safely carried beyond the town and eventually reached the breakfast tables and workplaces of an avid reading public in Britain.[13]

Baden-Powell first addressed himself in detail to the question of food supplies in November, when he calculated that black rations would not last beyond the end of the year and white rations would become exhausted by the end of February. He concluded that, somehow, changes to the system of food allocation would have to be made, and as a first step he forbade blacks to buy bread so as not to eat into the stocks of flour and meal assigned as white rations; instead he assigned part of the grain and oats allocated for horses to the stocks of black rations, and in this way, by the end of December, he calculated that sixty days of rations were left for both whites and blacks. During the final four and a half months of the siege further measures were taken to preserve food stocks by reducing rations, by issuing horseflesh as meat, by introducing into rations a kind of porridge made from oat husks, called sowen, and on 8 February by stopping the sale of rations to black refugees who were not needed for military duties (this now included the Shangane mineworkers, whose trench-digging work had been completed). The idea was to force the 2000 refugees to break out of the town and make their way to Kanye, where Plumer had laid down stocks of grain. Early in April Baden-Powell extended the strategy by trying to compel 2000 Barolong to abandon their homes and also attempt the journey to Kanye.[14]

Baden-Powell's measures to ration and preserve food stocks caused intense suffering among the black inhabitants of Mafikeng and led to a serious worsening of relations between the Barolong and the British garrison. Black rations were much more meagre, less varied and less nutritious than those for whites; blacks were made to pay, and pay handsomely, for their rations, including food commandeered from their own stocks; and the system of black rationing took no account of the number of dependents in a household. Baden-Powell handled the issue of rationing with as much delicacy as a sledgehammer. In January he suspected the Barolong, wrongly as it turned out, of hoarding grain in the *stad* and therefore stopped the sale of all rations to blacks, 'to see if there is any real want'.[15]

At a meeting of the Tshidi *kgotla* (council) on 31 December Baden-Powell suspended Wessels from his duties as chief, ostensibly for 'want of energy'. In fact the chief had expended rather too much energy in his opposition to Baden-Powell's ruthless prosecution of the food issue and high-handed attitude towards the Barolong leadership. Throughout the latter part of December he had actively discouraged his people from participating in work parties or collaborating in the town's defence. According to Angus Hamilton, the besieged correspondent of *The Times* (whose reports more often than not ended up in the Mafeking censor's wastepaper basket rather than in the hands of his subeditor), Wessels told his people that 'the English wished to make slaves of them, that they would not be paid for any services rendered; nor . . . would they be given any food, but left to starve when the critical moment came'.[16]

Although Baden-Powell succeeded in removing Wessels with the minimum of fuss, anger in Mafikeng did not wither away, and Lekoko and other Tshidi councillors, with whom the British authorities now dealt directly in their relations with the Barolong, persistently complained of the desperate position in which their people found themselves. Baden-Powell's insensitivity to the predicament of besieged blacks was shared by many of his subordinates responsible for administering food rations – 'young officers who know as little about Natives and their mode of living as they know about the man on the moon and his mode of living', Sol Plaatje commented dryly.[17] On several occasions workers in military employment went on strike in protest against conditions of work and rates of pay. The way in which the siege bureaucracy and Baden-Powell's incessant regulations bore down upon Mafikeng's inhabitants continued to arouse indignation and deep suspicion among Barolong households. When in March Plaatje was engaged in conducting a census of the *stad* he found many of the long-suffering inhabitants reluctant to cooperate in any way with the demands of the white town's authorities.

> The people are vexing me exceedingly; one would ask me what I wished to do with the name of the owner of the place . . . Another would say: 'no wonder the present, unlike all previous sieges of Mafeking, is so intolerable for the unfortunate beleaguered people are counted like sheep'. Another would stand at the door, empty herself of the whole stock of her bad words, and then threaten me to 'just touch my pen and jot down any numbers of her family'.[18]

The hardships endured by black people in Mafikeng from December until May is inestimable. Already by the end of 1899 the emaciated and diseased condition of many blacks had begun to cause serious concern to some of Mafeking's white inhabitants. On 30 December Ina Cowan wrote in her diary: 'The kaffirs dig up dead horses and eat them, and sit and pick on the rubbish heaps. Some of them are starving. I have seen as many dreadful things as I ever wish to see.'[19] The plight of the 2000 black refugees to whom in January the ration stores were closed was pitiful. Relations between them and the Tshidi were strained from the beginning of the siege and deteriorated with the increasing pressure on the town's food resources. They hunted for bones and scraps, dug up the corpses of dogs buried outside the town, and seized upon locusts whenever they swarmed inside the besieged area. At least one case of cannibalism was reported. Baden-Powell organised additional patrols to deter black refugees from stealing food from white households, and some of those apprehended were shot. Apart from the issuing of meat from ninety-four unlicensed dogs, the only official measure taken to alleviate the refugees' condition was the creation of kitchens to sell soup rendered from the carcasses of dead horses. White starch was added to the concoction to give the soup some thickness and to provide the recipient with the impression that a substantial meal had been taken, but hunger pains returned after little more than an hour. Ironically, and in keeping with Baden-Powell's obsession with garrison funds, the soup kitchens made a respectable profit.[20]

Sol Plaatje was appalled by the predicament of many of the black refugees in the town: 'it was a miserable scene', he wrote, 'to be surrounded by about 50 hungry beings, agitating the engagement of your pity and to see one of them succumb to his agonies and fall backwards with a dead thud'.[21] J. E. Neilly, the *Daily Telegraph* correspondent in Mafeking, was equally distressed by the scenes he witnessed.

> I saw them fall on the veld and lie where they had fallen, too weak to go on their way. The sufferers were mostly little boys – mere infants ranging from four or five upwards . . . Probably hundreds died from starvation or the diseases that always accompany famine . . . Words could not portray the scene of misery; five or six hundred human frameworks of both sexes and all ages . . . standing in lines, each holding an old blackened can or beef tin, awaiting turn to crawl painfully up to the soup kitchen. . . . It was one of the most heart-rending sights I have ever witnessed.[22]

The number of registered deaths among blacks during the siege was 478, but afterwards J. B. Moffat, Bell's successor, confessed that this represented 'only a portion of all the lives lost'. We shall never know how many deaths there were, but probably in all well over a thousand blacks succumbed to starvation in Mafikeng during the siege.[23]

Arrangements for the nightly exodus from the town of small groups of black refugees met with mixed success, and many of those attempting to pass surreptitiously through the enemy lines were cut down by Boer snipers. Parties of armed Barolong and Mfengu managed from time to time to raid cattle and return with them to the town, and one of the Barolong military leaders, Mathakgong, organised a number of successful sorties behind enemy lines to capture cattle. But the expeditions were filled with danger and often ended in disaster. At the beginning of April only one survivor returned from a thirty-three-strong Mfengu raiding party organised by Captain McKenzie of the 'Black Watch'. On 7 April 700 Barolong women were persuaded to attempt a mass break-out, but only ten got away, and the rest returned, some having been maltreated by members of the surrounding forces. On 13 April 200 women passed through the Boer lines undetected, but two nights later nine women from a party of thirteen were shot and killed, only four women returning, two of them wounded. During the final weeks of the siege, however, the Boers appear to have allowed large numbers of starving blacks to pass through their lines, for towards the end of the investment Bell calculated that almost three-quarters of the normal population of Mafikeng had left, and by the end of April Baden-Powell found that only 1600 units of Barolong rations were being issued each day. As the siege drew to its close he was even hopeful that white rations could be increased. Altogether 1210 blacks reached Plumer; many more must have escaped from the town and either sought food elsewhere or perished on the sixty-mile journey to Kanye.[24]

Immediately after the two relief columns entered Mafeking the Tshidi mobilised 300 men to overrun the Rapulana settlement at Lotlhakane and to rescue Saane, who was brought back to Mafikeng. The Rapulana regent, Mokgathu, was taken captive, and the leaders of the Rapulana community brought into custody and subsequently charged under the Indemnity and Special Tribunals Act of 1900 for their disloyalty to the Cape government. Paul Montshiwa was sent to take charge of the seized Rapulana lands. The humiliation of the Tshidi in the early 1880s was thereby avenged.[25]

Shortly afterwards General Sir Charles Parsons visited Mafeking at Lord Roberts's behest to thank the Tshidi formally for their assistance during the siege and for the creditable way Mafikeng had been defended. At the beginning of July Major Hanbury Tracey presented the Tshidi with a framed address in recognition of 'the loyalty to HM Queen Victoria, and the good behaviour of the Baralongs . . . throughout the long and trying investment'.[26]

ASSAULT ON DERDEPOORT

Before 1869 the Kgafela-Kgatla, one of the six branches of the Kgatla Tswana, lived entirely in the Transvaal. The seizure of Kgatla land by emigrant Boers and the demands for labour by Boer farmers eventually led to the Kgatla chief, Kgamanyane, accepting an invitation from Sechele, the Koena chief, to settle on the west bank of the Marico river, where the village of Mochudi was founded. However, neither Kgamanyane nor his successor, Lentshwe, acknowledged the Koena's claim to ownership of their new lands, and fighting broke out in 1875, continuing largely in the form of raids and counter-raids until 1883. The number of Lentshwe's people grew with the emigration of further Kgatla refugees from the Transvaal. In order to deal with the ever-present Koena threat and any attempt by the Boers to settle west of the Marico, the Kgatla during the 1880s became well armed, Lentshwe sending to the Kimberley diamond fields entire age-regiments whose wages were taxed on their return to raise revenue for the purchase of firearms.

For the first decade after the annexation of the Bechuanaland Protectorate relations between the independent-minded Kgatla and the new colonial administration were difficult. In 1889 Lentshwe refused to authorise the introduction of a hut tax among his people, and in the following year obstructed the construction of a telegraph line through his country. Relations began to improve, however, during the years immediately preceding the South African War as the economic independence of the Kgatla began to be undermined and Lentshwe's people became more integrated into the local colonial economy, first through the sale of produce and firewood, and progressively through the employment of Kgatla as wage labourers. Revenue earned in this way was vital following the ravages of rinderpest among Kgatla herds. Lentshwe also began to regard collaboration with the colonial authorities as a means of consolidating his own wealth and influence, and in 1897 he made a very favourable impression on Sir Alfred Milner during his visit to the Protectorate. In 1899 the chief agreed to the formal establishment of a Kgatla reserve and the introduction of a hut tax.[27]

In spite of Lentshwe's good relations with the Bechuanaland administration during the late 1890s, his loyalty to Britain was nonetheless a matter for close discussion among Protectorate officials on the eve of war. Shortly after the start of military operations reports began to circulate that the Boers had enlisted the support of a number of Kgatla communities in the Transvaal and were making preparations to occupy Mochudi. W. H. Surmon, the local Assistant Commissioner, immediately issued instructions to Lentshwe that any Boer encroachment into the Kgatla reserve should be repulsed by force, and on 20 October the chief warned a gathering of his people at Mochudi that they should be prepared to defend their villages and protect the Mafeking–Bulawayo railway line. Lentshwe also sent messages to a 200-strong Kgatla work party in Rhodesia to return home at once to help defend Mochudi. Lentshwe then applied to the British for a plentiful supply of ammunition for the 2000 rifles at his men's disposal; 6000 rounds were sent to Mochudi with the approval of J. S. Nicholson, the Commandant of the BSA Company Police.[28]

Lentshwe, however, almost at once changed his mind about resisting the Boers. Indicating that other Tswana chiefs had permitted the Boers to pass across their land unmolested, and arguing that the invaders were too strong to be repulsed successfully by his men alone, he returned the consignment of ammunition and requested that all policemen leave his territory forthwith. Nicholson accredited Lentshwe's *volte-face* to the influence of the Dutch Reformed Church mission community at Mochudi, whom he believed had encouraged the Kgatla to give assistance to the republican forces. (In January the staff of the Mochudi Mission were arrested, taken to Bulawayo, and returned to the Transvaal.) But it seems more probable that Lentshwe's resolve to go back on his earlier decision was based on sound military and political judgement. If the chief had accepted the ammunition, the arrival of which at Mochudi was known to the Boers, he would have placed himself in an unenviable position; the Boers would almost certainly have sought to punish the Kgatla, yet the number of British troops in the region was clearly insufficient to provide Lentshwe with meaningful military assistance – indeed, by the end of October the BSA Company Police had withdrawn completely from the Gaborone–Mochudi area. By his action Lentshwe ensured that the Boers satisfied themselves only with looting the stores in Mochudi and briefly occupying the railway station nearby.[29]

Events during November also suggest that Lentshwe's reluctance to resist the Boers was based on expediency. When the British returned south during the second week of the month, with fifty mounted infantrymen from Plumer's force designated to remain at Mochudi, Lentshwe's brother, Segale, led a regiment which participated in the reoccupation of the railway station. Shortly afterwards Lentshwe captured two armed Boers at his village and turned them over to the British forces. On 13 November Arthur Lawley, the Resident Commissioner at Bulawayo, informed Milner that the Kgatla had now accepted the ammunition which they had refused before, and reassured him that 'Linchwe is now with us and has turned out his men to protect the railway through his reserve.'[30]

Surmon stayed at Mochudi, and it was while he remained there that Segale, who appears to have appreciated more keenly the potential benefit to the Kgatla of unequivocal support for the British, proposed that the military, in collaboration with the Kgatla, mount an attack on the Boer encampment at Derdepoort, which was situated immediately across the Transvaal frontier. Surmon scotched the suggestion on the grounds that it would lead to the Kgatla crossing the border, that it would inspire Kgatla in the Transvaal to plunder Boer farms, and that such an uprising would probably involve the murder of women and children. However, when Colonel G. L. Holdsworth arrived in Mochudi on 23 November Segale again proposed the scheme. Between them a plan of attack was drawn up which accommodated Surmon's objections by providing for the Kgatla to remain at the frontier to prevent the Boers entering the Protectorate, while Holdsworth's force, now numbering 120 men, proceeded to Derdepoort. On 24 November three Kgatla regiments, the Makoba, Majanko and Mantwane, led by Ramono, Segale and Modise, started out with Holdsworth's force for Derdepoort. San were taken along as guides and messengers. When the column halted for water Surmon's ruling that the Kgatla regiments remain inside the Protectorate was set aside by Holdsworth, who feared that his men's heavy boots would betray the force when climbing up to the Boer laager. Holdsworth decided instead that the bare-footed Kgatla should secure the ground across the Marico river leading up to the Boer encampment, while Segale guided Holdsworth and his men to a place from which they could see the laager and open fire upon it. The clatter of the force's maxim gun would give the signal for a combined attack.[31]

On the following day the assault was executed with considerable misunderstanding. Under the covering fire of the maxim gun the Kgatla attacked the Boer position, while Holdsworth's force, rather than follow the Kgatla as arranged, did nothing and then retired to the railway station at Mochudi. In the attack on the Derdepoort encampment twenty Boers were killed, including two women and the local member of the Volksraad, J. H. Barnard, and seventeen women and children captured and taken by the Kgatla to Mochudi.

A German trader at the border village of Sikwane, Sidney Engers, was also shot when he attempted to escape after his house had been surrounded by the Kgatla to prevent him giving information to the Boers about the impending assault. More than 100 head of cattle were seized. The Kgatla, who had been left to extricate themselves from a difficult position, suffered fourteen men killed and sixteen wounded.[32]

Holdsworth attempted to justify his retreat by alleging that the Kgatla had crossed the border against his instructions, but this explanation cut no ice with Surmon, nor with his assistant, Jules Ellenberger, who had been present when the change of plan was made. Moreover, news of the Derdepoort assault caused deep concern in official circles in Cape Town and London. Milner admitted it was difficult to draw a distinction between self-defence, in which blacks might participate, and aggression, in which they might not; but of the events of 25 November he confessed, 'this incursion into [the] South African Republic certainly appears at first sight to bear [the] latter character'. Both Milner and Chamberlain noted that Holdsworth had acted contrary to the advice of Surmon, and officials at the Colonial Office were concerned that news of the Kgatla attack would be seized upon by anti-British newspapers on the continent. In fact the officials' worst fears were realised; early in 1900 one German periodical went so far as to print a story that the Boer women taken to Mochudi were subjected to communal rape by Kgatla and British soldiers. The allegation was investigated by Ellenberger, who found no evidence to substantiate the story.[33]

At first the Boers were unsure who had attacked the encampment at Derdepoort. A telegram sent by the landdrost of Rustenburg on the day of the assault suggested that those involved were 'Kaffirs of Linchwe, Segul and Khama', and an official Boer telegram of 28 November referred to an 'attack by Khama's Kaffirs and others'.[34] Once the identity of the Kgatla had been fully established, however, the incident prompted a spate of nervous rumours about possible future attacks on the local Boer farming communities. According to Commandant Kirsten the Kgatla had shot 'wonderfully well', in the same manner as the Boers; their aiming had been excellent, he reported, infintely better than that of the British.[35] The Kgatla were believed by some to be preparing to launch a large-scale invasion of the republic, and all burghers in the Rustenburg district were recalled for service at Derdepoort, and a number of men withdrawn from Mafeking to defend the Bechuanaland frontier. Official Boer sources claimed that the Kgatla had been compelled by the British to cross the Marico river under the threat of having the maxim gun turned upon them, and maintained that the assault on Derdepoort represented 'the most barbarous [deed] ever committed by a civilised government'. 'The Battle of the Second Blood River' is the subtitle of an Afrikaner account of the episode published in 1950.[36]

The incident at Derdepoort brought about a crisis in the relations between the Kgatla and the farming communities of the Rustenburg–Marico region. On 20 December Lentshwe complained bitterly to J. S. Nicholson of the ill-treatment which his followers were experiencing in the republic. On 17 December, having learnt of the arrival at Derdepoort of a further 500 men, Lentshwe began to make preparations for the defence of Kgatla villages along the Transvaal frontier; women, children and cattle were sent to Mochudi, and trenches dug around the perimeter of the largest border village at Sikwane. These precautions, however, were insufficient to withstand the 500-strong commando led by du Plessis, Louw and Swarts which on 22 December laid waste to the settlements at Sikwane, Malolwane and Mmathubudukwane in reprisal for the assault on Derdepoort. According to General van Rensburg three Boers died in the attack; 150 of those Kgatla defending their villages were slain.[37]

THE DEFENCE OF NGWATO COUNTRY

The Ngwato kingdom had its origins in the 1840s following the upheavals of the *difaqane* years. The first thirty years of its history were marked by acute political instability until the assumption of power in 1875 of Khama III. Khama's tenure of the Ngwato kingship lasted until his death in 1923, and was achieved by an economic and political revolution in which private property relations were liberalised, trading closely regulated by the king and Christianity encouraged as a catalyst of social and political change. Khama's reform programme in bringing the relations of production and trade in the kingdom under royal control coincided with the Ngwato state becoming an important entrepôt between southern Africa and the region beyond the Limpopo, and by the late 1870s goods to the value of £200,000 were passing south through the kingdom each year. With the opening up of 'the road to the north' the state prospered, especially the large cattle-owning Ngwato nobility, waggoners and cultivators. No-one prospered more than the entrepreneurial Khama, who sold livestock, hired out waggons and cultivated grain on a large scale, as well as growing tobacco and rearing valuable bloodstock of both horses and cattle.[38]

Khama's political authority grew, though his tenure of the Ngwato kingship did not pass unchallenged. In 1883 an attempt was made to usurp Khama's office by his brother, Kgamane, supported by the Koena chief, Sechele, who two years later again sought to remove Khama by placing a nominee, Kgari Matseng, at the head of the Ngwato state. In 1895 Khama faced a serious threat to his authority from a group of conservative Ngwato nobility led by Rraditladi. A crisis was averted by timely concessions and the agreement of the British to settle Rraditladi and his immediate followers in the Mangwe district of Rhodesia. Afterwards those who opposed Khama's revolution sought to gain the support of his son, Sekhoma. In reaction Khama disinherited Sekhoma, denied him the right to speak in the royal *kgotla* and, with the permission of the British administration, ordered the removal of his son and supporters from Phalapye, the Ngwato capital, to Lephepe, an isolated site on the southern border of his territory.

Following the creation of the Bechuanaland Protectorate, Khama built up for himself a reputation of being a strong, even overbearing, ruler profoundly loyal to Britain. Khama supplied workers to assist in both telegraph and railway construction, and in 1894 provided 2000 men to accompany Major H. J. Goold-Adams's contingent in the campaign against the Ndebele, though by doing so Khama appears to have been regarded by other Tswana rulers almost as a traitor, and the mobilisation of men was unpopular even among the Ngwato, since it disrupted the cultivation of maize close to harvest time. At the beginning of the war Khama was regarded by the British and Boers alike as Britain's most dependable ally among the Tswana rulers.[39]

Khama's first concern at the beginning of the war was to prevent the Boers making any encroachments into his country, in particular behind a policy of supporting a dissatisfied group within his territory. Khama knew that the Boers had already elicited support from the Seleka, whom he had expelled from Ngwato territory in 1887, and he especially feared that his son, Sekhoma, might conspire to remove him from Phalapye with Boer assistance. Two independent sources indicated that Sekhoma had been in contact with Boer emissaries in recent weeks. On 17 October Khama despatched his brother, Kebailele, with the Maolola regiment to Mahalapye to defend the railway bridge there and to resist any Boer advance towards Sekhoma's temporary settlement at Mohonono. Three days later news reached Phalapye that a large force of Boers under General F. A. Grobler intended to occupy the Ngwato capital in order to pin back further Plumer's isolated corps at Tuli on the Rhodesian frontier. Before the Boers had any opportunity to cross the Crocodile river, Khama at once sent a regiment to occupy Nwapa, the defence of which was regarded as vital to the maintenance of Plumer's communications with the south. At Khama's request 3000 rounds of ammunition were sent to Phalapye.[40]

At this time a letter was received by Khama from General Grobler.

> As you live beyond our boundary I have thought it good to warn you against taking part in the conflict between us and the English, and if you are not satisfied with this, you must take the consequences.
>
> Further, I wish to inform you, that, as you have allowed the English to use your ground for warlike operations, we shall also use it for that purpose, but without disturbing you, unless you help the enemy.

Khama's reply was immediate and unequivocal.

> If you do not intend fighting me what are you doing in my country with an armed force?
>
> If you enter with armed men into my country, and among my cattle posts, I shall fight you . . .
>
> You must not think that you can frighten me, and my people, with your war talk. You know that I am a Son of the White Queen.[41]

On 23 October 100 men from Plumer's force arrived at Phalapye, and with the assistance of the Ngwato and thirty whites the capital was fortified with obstacles and embankments. When news was received that Grobler's contingent on the frontier of Khama's country had been substantially reinforced, to bring the strength of the force there to 637 commandos and 750 Seleka auxiliaries, Khama ordered out a second regiment to Nwapa to increase the strength of his own contingent to between 800 and 1000 men. On 9 November an assault on Phalapye seemed imminent when the Boer force crossed the river and began firing from a long distance on the Ngwato position at Nwapa. The commando, however, soon afterwards recrossed the Crocodile river, and two days later most of the force moved either northward to reinforce the Boer unit near Tuli, or southward along the river, shadowed by Khama's men inside the Protectorate. On 3 December, the day on which Khama had been informed by J. H. Ashburnham, the Assistant Commissioner at Phalapye, that a simultaneous attack on Tuli and the Ngwato capital was likely to take place, the Boer contingent instead withdrew south to Crocodile Pools and Derdepoort.[42]

Between October 1899 and February 1900 Khama mobilised between 3000 and 4000 men to occupy Nwapa, guard the railway line at Mahalapye, Seribe, Macloutsie and Shashi, and patrol the length of the frontier from Tuli to Phala. Almost the whole of the scouting and intelligence work in the central and northern frontier regions of the Protectorate was performed by the Ngwato, and Khama also provided messengers who infiltrated the Boer positions around Mafeking and entered the besieged town to bring in Plumer's despatches. Khama's decisiveness and constancy during the difficult first months of the war were praised warmly by Ashburnham: 'The fact that not a railway-sleeper, or a telegraph wire in Khama's country has been damaged, and that the communication between Bulawayo and his southern border has never been interrupted for an hour is a great measure due to his firm and loyal support.'[43]

The Ngwato took no further direct part in military operations, though small groups of scouts continued to patrol the Rhodesian border and along the Crocodile river. In May 1900 a regiment was again mobilised to occupy Nwapa when a contingent of the Pietersburg commando was reported to be moving along the road towards the drift, but the Boer force instead turned southward. By the beginning of 1901 the guerrilla groups in the Waterberg district were faced with grave difficulties in obtaining food because of the collaboration with the British army of many of the African communities in the region, including the Seleka, who previously had guarded the Protectorate frontier for the Boers. In February General Grobler surrendered at Phalapye after having been sentenced to death for refusing to continue to serve on commando. In May a further 150 burghers crossed the frontier to surrender to Khama, who mobilised 200 Ngwato to guard the Transvaal border and so prevent the remaining guerrilla fighters under General Beyers from seizing the 2600 head of cattle brought into the territory by the surrendering families.[44]

KGATLA PARTICIPATION IN THE WAR, 1900–2

The breakdown in the relations between the Kgatla and the Boer farming community in the western Transvaal extended throughout the war. Disputes between Boer households and Kgatla farm tenants had a long history in the region. The land occupied by the Kgatla had been largely divided up for white farms in the mid-1860s, and from this time onwards Kgatla tenants complained bitterly of the excessive labour that was expected from them. It was the resistance of the Kgatla to the labour demands of the white farming community that prompted the exodus of Kgamanyane to Mochudi in 1869, and a regular flow of malcontent Kgatla continued to migrate across the frontier until the end of the century. At the outbreak of war the brittle relationship between landlord and tenant in the western Transvaal shattered. A large number of Boer families moved into laagers or fled to Rustenburg because of the hostility towards them of Kgatla rent-tenants living on land owned by the government or absentee landlords, the refusal of some Kgatla farm servants to continue to serve their employers after the start of military operations, and the fear that regiments from across the Bechuanaland frontier might come to 'liberate' their people. When Smuts entered the region in the middle of 1900 he found that almost all the farms had been deserted by their white occupants.[45]

Lentshwe's regiments from the Protectorate spearheaded the Kgatla campaign against the Boer 'landlords-in-arms'. In February 1900 Ramono, Lentshwe's brother, ambushed a Boer supply column guarded by forty-two commandos at Kayaseput, and seized six waggons fully laden with provisions. On 14 March the Kgatla captured thirty-six trek oxen from the Boers near Buffelshoek. In reprisal a number of raids were made by the Boers from their guarded encampments on Kgatla villages in the Transvaal to punish those whom they believed to be especially close adherents of Lentshwe and seize their livestock. At the beginning of May a particularly ruthless raid was made on the Kgatla settlement in Saulspoort, sixty miles to the southeast of Sikwane.[46]

Lentshwe protested that action should be taken by the British to protect his followers across the border since, he claimed, the Boers were 'cutting down his people in cold blood, stealing their cattle and sjambokking others'. The Kgatla tenants' revolt suited the purposes of the British army, and Surmon was able to tell Lentshwe with the consent of Colonel Plumer that he could take any steps in his power to defend his adherents in the Transvaal and to recapture the cattle taken from them by the commandos, in spite of protests from Sir Marshall Clarke, the Resident Commissioner at Salisbury, who argued strongly against such a departure from accepted policy. With official licence to protect the interests of his people in the Transvaal, Lentshwe organised a series of raids on Boer farms around the Pilansberg, and to the south as far as Rustenburg. The Kgatla also seized livestock belonging to the chiefs Magato and Ramakok, who were known by the Kgatla to be supplying scouts and giving sustenance to the Boer commandos, in addition to protecting the cattle of landlords actively engaged in the war.[47]

So intense became the Kgatla campaign against Boer households that affairs in the western Transvaal became a matter of some concern to Lord Roberts and Baden-Powell, promoted after the siege to Major-General and given command of the newly created South African Constabulary. According to Baden-Powell the breakdown of military and civil authority in the northwestern Transvaal had reached very worrying proportions by the end of June 1900: 'The Natives are armed and in many places are active in hostility against, and a standing danger to, the Boers. Last week four Boers were wounded and one killed by Natives at different places about the Pilansberg; most of the Boers from that neighbourhood have come to live under our protection.'[48] Both Roberts and Baden-Powell sought to enforce the disarmament of the Kgatla, but in the Transvaal the uncertainty of affairs and the strained manpower resources of the British army made this almost impossible to achieve, and in the Protectorate Kgatla disarmament was strongly opposed by local officials, Sir Alfred Milner and Lord Selborne at the Colonial Office.[49]

The Kgatla campaign therefore continued. Indeed following Roberts's replacement by Kitchener the military role of the Kgatla was enlarged with the new Commander-in-Chief's approval. It was not long before the British army could concentrate its manpower resources elsewhere in the Transvaal because of the collaboration of Kgatla regiments. After the war the Native Commissioner in the Pilansberg, F. Edmeston, described how the British army had been 'relieved of all anxiety as to this district, which was held by these people as far north as Phala'.[50] The Kgatla were also encouraged to raid Boer cattle, 30 per cent of the animals captured becoming Lentshwe's property. In one daring raid at Moreeletse a Kgatla regiment led by Kgari seized 300 oxen and two waggons from a Boer commando unit passing through the district. In September 1901 a Boer force of 400 men advanced upon Lentshwe's border in a final attempt to defeat the Kgatla, but Lentshwe's regiments successfully repulsed the commando at the Crocodile river. On 12 December an estimated 2000 head of cattle were seized by General Kemp from the Kgatla at Saulspoort; Lentshwe at once despatched a force of 1000 men under Segale to recover the livestock.[51]

REWARDS OF COLLABORATION

The British administration's indebtedness to Khama for his loyalty and support during the war strengthened the ruler's bargaining position in his dealings with the colonial regime. Before the war Protectorate officials had been largely sympathetic to Sekhoma in his dispute with Khama and had agreed to him settling at Mohonono rather than the isolated and arid site at Lephepe. It was recognised, however, that little could be done when in November 1899 two regiments led by Kebailele, while patrolling the railway line through Ngwato territory, removed the fences from Sekhoma's fields and destroyed all his adherent's crops. Shortly afterwards officials reluctantly agreed to the final removal of Sekhoma and his depleted followers to Lephepe.[52]

It was at this time, too, that the Ngwato capital at Phalapye was relocated to the west to Serowe for ecological reasons. Milner was at first reluctant to approve such a move because of the additional administrative costs that would result from the relocation of government buildings and other facilities, expenses which he urged should be met by increased Ngwato taxation if the move took place at all. The tone of the reply from Ralph Williams, the new Resident Commissioner, giving his support to Khama's application, aptly conveys the stronger bargaining power that the ruler was able to command in his dealings with the colonial administration as a consequence of his contribution to the British war effort.

> The chiefs have been singularly loyal to us. It may be that it suited them to run with what was likely to be the winning side but . . . Linchwe and Khama have spared neither men nor money in aiding us by rendering an immense frontier practically safe against Boer inroads and by furnishing us with constant intelligence . . . I cannot but think at this moment it is reward rather than increased taxation that they might expect, and that . . . the present move offers us an opportunity of making Khama some return for what he has done.

The relocation of the Ngwato capital was duly approved and the move from Phalapye to Serowe took place between February and August 1902.[53]

The war ushered in a period of unprecedented prosperity among the Ngwato. As a result of the wartime curtailment of competition from Boer households in the western Transvaal, the disruption to railway communications between Rhodesia and the south and the plentiful harvest in Ngwato country in 1899, large amounts of grain were sold by the Ngwato to the British army and to white settlers north of the Limpopo, where prices soared. The livestock market was also buoyant; in 1900 £25,000 was paid to the Ngwato for cattle to supply Plumer's force moving southward towards Mafeking. The interruption of railway services and the demand for vehicles to transport local produce enabled waggon-owners to accumulate cash by hiring out carts to traders and to the military. Khama was paid £1727 for the assistance of the Maolola regiment in defending the Protectorate's frontier with the Transvaal. The money was used to build a new church at Serowe. Tax receipts increased from £3816 in 1899–1900, to £5024 in 1900–1, and to £5300 in 1901–2. Despite high consumer prices because of the dislocation of the war and the shortage of transport, the Ngwato bought so many imported goods in 1899 and 1900 that some traders ran short of cash and offered reduced prices in exchange for bank notes and premiums of up to 15 per cent on silver and gold currency. In 1902 Kebailele informed Khama that God had helped the Ngwato 'wonderfully': 'this war has not hurt us at all . . . no dead or wounded to lament, as in former wars. Instead we have made much money.' However, as Neil Parsons has indicated, the period between 1896 and 1902 witnessed not only 'the flower of past Ngwato development' but also 'the seeds of its future underdevelopment' as a result of the transit victualling trade being removed by the railway, the incidence of drought and disease, the lack of real economic growth at this time and the consumption of grasslands and rapid deforestation.[54]

The collaboration between the Kgatla and the British during the war brought some tangible benefits to Lentshwe's people. The question of the ownership of cattle raided by Kgatla regiments became an important issue during the later stages of the war and immediately afterwards. When in October 1901 Ralph Williams visited Mochudi, Lentshwe complained of the Transvaal government's policy of restoring stolen livestock to those burghers who had surrendered, claiming that he was in danger of having to hand over all the cattle that his men had acquired.[55] Milner, however, accepted a recommendation by Williams that the Kgatla be allowed to retain all the livestock taken from the Boers while defending their reserve, and that unless surrendered burghers could prove to the Resident Commissioner their right to cattle that had been stolen from farms in the Transvaal, Lentshwe should also be permitted to keep these animals, both in recognition of his services during the war and as compensation for the Kgatla's own losses. Milner's ruling was naturally disliked by Boer farmers who had been the victims of livestock raiding during the war, and who had already begun mounting raids in the Rustenburg district with the object of recovering cattle stolen from their farms by local Kgatla. Indeed in order to prevent further bloodshed between the Boer and Kgatla communities at Saulspoort, the South African Constabulary was instructed to patrol constantly between the two settlements.

In June 1902 Lentshwe placed a large body of men on the Protectorate frontier when a rumour circulated that General Kemp was planning to mount a raid into the Kgatla reserve to recover cattle seized from the farms of his burghers. Largely as a result of petitions from Boer farmers in the region, the government in Pretoria in 1903 agreed to allow Boers entry into the Protectorate in order to identify their cattle and begin legal proceedings for their recovery, but only on condition that they in turn provided the Kgatla with reciprocal access to their own farms. Very few Boers appear to have taken advantage of the procedure.[56] It has been estimated that the war enabled the Kgatla in the Protectorate to acquire sufficient cattle to make up for the enormous losses suffered during the rinderpest epidemic in 1896–7.[57]

In 1902 Lentshwe requested that the land occupied by the Kgatla in the Protectorate and in the Transvaal be amalgamated into one common reserve. Shortly afterwards a petition from the Kgatla living in both Bechuanaland and the Crown Colony was forwarded to Sir Arthur Lawley, the Lieutenant-Governor of the Transvaal, requesting that the two groups be joined together and that the laws relating to passes, which were needed to travel between the two territories, be abolished.[58] The implications of the request were far-reaching, since the Kgatla petitioners wished Lentshwe to be recognised officially as the chief over all the Kgatla communities living within the Transvaal, and, more importantly, desired their wartime occupation of white farms to be acknowledged as permanent by the authorities. Although it was generally recognised that the land possessed by the Kgatla before the war had been insufficient for their needs, to have reinstated them as an independent peasantry on their former lands would have set an unacceptable precedent in a settler colony. (The Kgatla clung tenaciously to the occupied farms and even by October 1902, four months after the conclusion of peace, none of the local white families from the Pilansberg had dared to return.) The Kgatla request was not unexpectedly turned down, and the farms gradually restored to their former white owners, with the assistance of the South African Constabulary. However, Lentshwe was permitted to appoint his brother, Ramono, as his deputy at Saulspoort, where he received tribute and recognition as chief from the Kgatla inhabitants. Ramono remained at Saulspoort in this capacity until his death in 1917. While Lentshwe was not recognised officially as chief over the Transvaal Kgatla, he was nonetheless allowed to visit his people there on a number of occasions after the war.[59] There can be little doubt about the new authority he possessed among all the various Kgatla communities on both sides of the frontier. 'Since the war', wrote a member of the British administration in the Transvaal, 'the Bakgatla look upon Lintsue as a very important personage indeed and consider his authority here almost supreme.'[60]

Cordial relations continued between Lentshwe and the Bechuanaland administration. The frequent complaints of the Koena ruler, Sebele, concerning his boundary with that of the Kgatla reserve were no longer paid serious attention to by colonial officials. Most of the grievances relating to the welfare of the Kgatla in the Protectorate which Lentshwe brought to the notice of the government were dealt with sympathetically. In 1913 Lentshwe was described as the 'best' chief in the Protectorate after Khama, and during the First World War Kgatla recruits accompanied the South African forces to Europe and donated £365 'to help their King in waging a great war'.[61] Louis Truschel has argued that Lentshwe's loyalty during the South African War, and his participation in military operations, 'led directly to a reversal of . . . [his] former isolation from the network of British–Tswana relationships and eventually to [Kgatla] participation in the new nation of Botswana.[62]

Immediately after the war, however, there was also considerable disquiet among leading members of the Kgatla community that their claim for an enlarged reserve 'by right of conquest' had not been granted, and that their kinsmen in the Transvaal had not been allowed to reclaim their former lands from Boer farmers. Ramono told W. J. S. Driver in the Pilansberg that 'he could not understand why Lintsue's aid should have been accepted as it was during the war in this district and that he was then recognised as Chief of the Bakhatla in Rustenburg, if now that the war is over he is to have no voice in the settlement of the affairs of the tribe'.[63] A social revolution of the kind envisaged by the Kgatla formed no part of Britain's post-war design, and it was inevitable that the tenants' revolt in the western Transvaal was doomed to failure once the Boers had been defeated and peace signed.

Disillusionment set in too among the Barolong following their sacrifices during the siege of Mafeking. Their immediate disarmament once the town had been liberated caused a good deal of consternation, and when early in 1902 a Boer raid was made on Mafikeng the Barolong inhabitants were unable to prevent the commando seizing hundreds of cattle. In Britain a relief fund for the white town of £29,000 was raised, but none of the money went towards the rehabilitation of Mafikeng or Tshidi villages in the locality destroyed at the time of the siege. Indeed the Tshidi had to fight hard for the little compensation they received, and it was only following the visit of a deputation to Cape Town in 1903 that the issue received the attention it deserved. Promises of land made at the time of the siege were never fulfilled, and even Joseph Chamberlain turned a deaf ear to Tshidi requests for the issue to be reopened when he visited Mafeking early in 1903. A farm promised to Mafeking's Mfengu community remained little more than a pipe-dream to those who had fought so tenaciously on Britain's behalf. The Rapulana, meanwhile, who had collaborated with the invading Boer forces and had been responsible for much devastation to Barolong homesteads, were restored to their former lands at Lotlhakane.

The participation of the Barolong in the military operations around Mafikeng was concealed as much as possible by the British – and especially by Baden-Powell. In May 1900 the press censor in the town would not allow the publication of an account of the important role played by the Barolong in resisting the final offensive against the besieged town by S. J. Eloff. It was not until the day following Baden-Powell's departure from Mafeking that the description of Barolong participation was eventually published. In his evidence to the Royal Commission after the war Baden-Powell admitted only to having armed 300 Africans 'to look after cattle and prevent them being looted when they were out grazing'. When asked whether the Barolong had been involved in military operations, Baden-Powell denied it: 'No, we tried to make them defend their own town, but on the first attack . . . they all ran away, so we did not rely on them at all.' Unlike the Coloured contingent and the Mfengu, the Barolong did not receive war medals in recognition of their contribution to the defence of Mafeking. An article which appeared in the *Mafeking Mail* during the week after the medals had been presented in the town advocated that the Barolong should be put 'at least on an equal footing with other natives employed in the operations . . . none of them were wounded in the back through running away, as would be, if the statement of "B.P." were true. They got their wounds fighting face to face and not so very far away from the enemy either.' Even the Mafeking Municipal Council was moved to send a memorandum to the Royal Commission to set the record straight about the role of the Barolong in the fighting and to correct other distortions and half-truths contained in Baden-Powell's account of the siege.[64]

Social and political relations between the Tswana communities and the British and Boers were therefore shaped in a variety of ways by the war. The close pre-war relations between Khama and the British colonial administration in the Bechuanaland Protectorate were consolidated, and the Ngwato ruler and Ngwato nobility were able to gain significant political and economic benefits from their active support for the British side in circumstances when the imperial authorities were dependent upon Ngwato assistance and in conditions of military upheaval across the Protectorate's frontiers. Meanwhile across the Protectorate's southern border in the settler state of the Cape Colony the Tshidi-Barolong were unable to gain any advantages of substance from their assistance to the British. Although their support for Baden-Powell's force was crucial to the British army's success in holding Mafeking against all odds, they received almost nothing in return. They lost property, cattle and their firearms, hundreds of Barolong lost their lives, they received only minimal compensation, and were never granted land or any other tangible economic rewards for their participation in the struggle. After the war ordinary members of the Barolong community were less able than before to withstand pressures to work for white farmers or to enlist as migrant labourers on the Rand.

The Kgatla in the Protectorate, once Lentshwe threw his weight behind the British, were able to gain substantial plunder in cattle from Boer farms across the Marico river, and Lentshwe, like Khama in similar circumstances, drew closer to the Protectorate administration. In the Transvaal Kgatla squatters and tenants, supported by regiments from Bechuanaland, were able to liberate themselves from the control of the local Boer farming community. The success of their campaign reveals the brittleness of pre-war relationships between landlords and tenants in the area and sheds light on the very real difficulties that confronted the Boer state in the Transvaal in mounting a war against an external enemy and at the same time maintaining order within its own frontiers. As soon as local military forces were withdrawn the system of social control in the Rustenburg–Marico region collapsed, enabling the Kgatla to entrench themselves on white farms and effectively closing down the land area over which the guerrillas could operate and safely draw supplies. Once the war was over, however, the power of the new British-controlled state in the Transvaal was put behind the Boer farming community in re-establishing families on their former lands. Kgatla hopes were dashed of permanently securing more land by right of conquest to cultivate on their own behalf.

3

An encircling struggle

When war was declared on 11 October 1899 the potential military importance of Basutoland could scarcely have been doubted. The colony possessed a 200-mile frontier with the Orange Free State, and its southern and eastern boundaries gave access to the Cape Colony and Natal. Basutoland was also integrated closely into the southern African regional economy. Grain exports and the sale of wool from Basotho homesteads were substantial in value, and in 1880 had been worth almost half a million pounds; although the volume and value of exports decreased during the closing years of the nineteenth century, Basotho cultivators still produced over 50,000 bags of maize each year for export throughout the 1890s. Large numbers of Basotho workers regularly migrated to the Kimberley diamond fields, some travelled further afield to the Rand gold mines, while Boer farmers in the Free State were accustomed to recruiting seasonal labour from the colony. Thousands of Basotho also resided as labour tenants, sharecroppers and squatters on Free State farms. The response of the Basotho to the war was therefore a matter of importance to both sides in the conflict, and it was recognised too that in the event of a prolonged struggle Basutoland's resources of labour, grain, cattle and horses would become extremely valuable assets.

BASOTHO SOCIETY BEFORE THE WAR

Basutoland had become a colonial possession in 1868 following a request to Britain for protection from the ageing Moshoeshoe to prevent further inroads being made into the Basotho's lands by the military forces of the Orange Free State. The Boers' eagerness to claim the fertile lands of the Basotho on the western side of the Caledon river had led to a series of armed conflicts during the middle years of the nineteenth century, culminating in the wars between May 1865 and April 1866, and July 1867 and February 1869. Upon annexing Basutoland, however, the British government had no wish to undertake direct responsibility for the new colony's administration, and in 1871 the authority for its government was transferred to the governor of the Cape Colony. Relations between the Basotho chiefs and the Cape authorities began inauspiciously. The formal terms of annexation approved by the Cape legislature gave to the administration in Basutoland complete civil and criminal jurisdiction, which was fiercely opposed by many Basotho chiefs, who objected in particular to the withdrawal from their authority of criminal jurisdiction and the right to allocate land. In 1878 legislation was approved providing the Cape government with the authority to disarm those African peoples within its jurisdiction, and in April 1880 an order to carry out the Basotho's disarmament was issued. Disarmament struck at the heart of chiefly power in Basutoland, and the proclamation led to resistance by a substantial number of Basotho communities. The ensuing conflict between September 1880 and April 1881, known as the Gun War or *Ntoa ea Lithunya*, was described by Theal, the early historian of South Africa, as 'the most formidable attempt ever made by natives in South Africa to throw off European supremacy',[1] though from a strictly military point of view its outcome was indecisive. The Basotho were nonetheless permitted to retain their arms, and in 1884 imperial rule was established in Basutoland to replace the authority previously exercised by the Cape Colony, whose system of direct rule was abandoned in favour of a procedure which recognised the Basotho chiefs as agents of the administration. Chiefs were permitted to adjudicate in civil and criminal cases involving their own people, and the authority to allocate land, vested in the governor under the previous regime, was relinquished. The new Resident Commissioner, Sir Marshall Clarke, and his successor in 1894, Sir Godfrey Lagden, worked closely with the Basotho paramount chief, who was encouraged to extend his influence and authority.

The implications of the Gun War played an important role in shaping white attitudes towards the Basotho at the outbreak of the South African War. The Basotho were regarded as probably the best armed of the African peoples of southern Africa, having accumulated firearms largely as a result of working on the Kimberley diamond fields. During the 1880–1 conflict the large number of breechloading rifles possessed by the Basotho had been much more effective than the Sniders and carbines used by the Cape forces, and although the superior quality of the Basotho's firearms was gradually being undermined by the introduction of more modern guns firing smokeless powder (which they were unable to obtain in significant numbers), the military potential of the Basotho at the end of the nineteenth century could not be ignored. It has been estimated that in 1898 some 35,000 Basotho possessed firearms, of whom 30,000 could be mounted in the event of war.[2] From a military point of view at least, there was a core of truth in Lagden's remark made early in the South African War that the Basotho were 'the only unbroken tribe' of the region.[3]

The system of administration inaugurated by Britain in 1884 paved the way for closer collaboration between the colonial authority and the Koena royal lineage in both the economic and political spheres. Between 1884 and 1899 economic inequality in Basutoland grew and Basotho wealth became even more concentrated into the hands of the Koena rulers. During the last forty years of the nineteenth century the contraction and stabilisation of the

Basotho's frontiers, the loss of the fertile lands to the west of the Caledon river, the rapid increase in the population of the colony, and the opening up of new markets for Basotho grain, brought about a remarkable increase in the area of land under cultivation. More and more land was cultivated along the western boundary of Basutoland, and the colony's winter grazing on the slopes of the Maloti mountains was taken into permanent occupation. In 1873 the Basotho exported 100,000 bags of grain and 2000 bags of wool; in the same year manufactured goods to the value of £150,000 were imported into the colony. The royal lineage especially benefited from participation in the commodity markets through its control over the distribution of Basotho livestock and its right to tribute labour, which enabled chiefs to plough considerably more land than others. Furthermore, chiefs retained part of the money collected in hut tax from their people and also received money from the earnings of migrant workers.[4]

Commercial grain production, however, began to be handicapped by restrictions first imposed by the Free State government in the early 1870s on the passage of Basotho grain exports through the republic, and later by the arrival of cheap imported Australian wheat in Kimberley in the mid-1880s, made possible by the coming of the railway. Commodity production also brought difficulties for Basotho cultivators and pastoralists, since soil and pastureland deteriorated from erosion on marginal slopes, fertile land did not receive regular fallowing for the recovery of the soil, and overstocking occurred on grazing land. All these factors, together with the rapidly expanding Basotho population, combined to increase the demand for even more land, and the situation soon became serious indeed. 'The population is rapidly increasing, the fields are becoming exhausted, the pastures diminishing; stock farming yields more disappointments than profits . . . Money is scarce', commented one missionary in 1887.[5] According to Lagden, by 1895 all the land suitable for cultivation had been allocated and occupied: 'the rising generation of men are no longer able to support themselves upon it'.[6] Increasingly, Basotho participation in the labour market was based less on the desire to acquire cash to purchase guns, ploughs, livestock and manufactured goods than on the need for wages with which to buy food and pay taxes. The rinderpest epidemic in 1896–7 destroyed perhaps 90 per cent of Basotho cattle and drove many more men on to the labour market. The number of Basotho seeking work outside the colony rose from about 15,000 in the late 1870s to over 20,000 by 1893–4, and to 37,000 by 1898–9. The Koena rulers, meanwhile, suffered less severely from the economic difficulties of the late 1880s and 1890s and benefited most from the stability engendered by colonial rule, the collection of colonial taxes and the organisation of a regular outflow of agricultural commodities and labour.[7]

Competition for land played an important and sometimes disruptive role in Basotho politics, largely as a result of rival claims for upland pastures which in the past had been used on a communal basis when competition for grazing land had been less intense. Claims were put forward vigorously, especially following the death of an important chief. Land disputes occurred annually and from time to time resulted in armed skirmishes and cattle raiding, such as that between Lerotholi (pronounced in Sesotho, Lerothodi), the Basotho paramount, and his brother Maama in 1893, which formed part of a wider scramble for the inheritance of Lerotholi's father, Letsie, who had died in 1891.[8]

Between the Gun War and the outbreak of the South African War politics in Basutoland revolved around the division of the Basotho polity into three groups. First, there were those Basotho who had disarmed voluntarily and had remained loyal to the Cape authorities throughout the Gun War. Prominent among them was Jonathan, the heir of Moshoeshoe's son, Molapo, who had died on the eve of the war. Jonathan was a shrewd businessman, a wealthy producer of grain for export, and an Anglican Christian. He was held in high esteem by members of the colonial administration. His sons, Majara and Setsomi, attended Zonnebloem School in Cape Town. Jonathan was supported by some of the sons of Moshoeshoe's junior houses who were working for the colonial administration in official posts (most of the Basotho collaborators with the authorities of the Cape Colony came from this group). Secondly, there were those Basotho who had fought against disarmament in 1880, but who had become reconciled to imperial rule once the new terms of colonial rule had been agreed and the retention of their weapons had been guaranteed. Foremost among them was Lerotholi. Thirdly, there were the independent-minded Basotho chiefs who had fought in 1880–1 for complete autonomy, and who had accepted the advent of direct imperial administration only with great reluctance. They included among their number Moshoeshoe's son, Masopha, and Joel, Molapo's son and half-brother of Jonathan. Both Masopha and Joel refused to attend the *pitso* (public assembly) in November 1883 at which the terms of imperial rule were discussed.

Throughout the period from 1884 the influence of the Koena paramountcy grew in collaboration with the British administration, though the trend towards greater centralisation of authority was not welcomed by all members of the royal lineage. Foremost among the critics of Letsie and Lerotholi was Masopha, who enjoyed considerable influence among conservative-minded Basotho and those chiefs who adhered to the principle of local autonomy in the affairs of their own territory. In 1891 Masopha supported one of Letsie's younger sons in challenging Lerotholi as the new paramount. In 1898 persistent difficulties between Masopha on the one hand and Lerotholi and the British administration on the other led to the paramount mobilising an army against him. Masopha was defeated, heavily fined, deprived of his district chiefship and forbidden to reoccupy his village at Thaba Bosiu. He died in the following year, a broken man.[9]

Political tension arose, too, from the consolidation of Koena authority over other chiefdoms in Basutoland. Moshoeshoe and his descendants made it their policy to place members of the royal lineage in charge of troublesome communities, and following the unsuccessful rebellion of the Phuthi chief, Moorosi, in 1879, Letsie had settled his son, Nkoebe, in Quthing district with authority over the Phuthi and Thembu peoples. Relations between the Basotho and Phuthi again became difficult following the coming of age of Moorosi's grandson, Mocheka, who petitioned Sir Alfred Milner for permission to be released from Lerotholi's control and allowed to settle in Herschel district in the Cape Colony. In May 1899 Lerotholi responded by appointing his son, Griffith, as caretaker over the Phuthi, a provocative step since in the previous year Mocheka had complained bitterly that Griffith had made a series of threats against his life. The *pitso* arranged to discuss the issue had scarcely begun when the Phuthi chief called on his people to leave the assembly in protest against the new appointment, and an immediate escalation of the dispute was prevented only by Lagden's mediation.[10]

An important source of political unrest in northern Basutoland after 1879 was the feud between Joel and Jonathan, the sons of Molapo. Jonathan was a progressive-minded entrepreneur who was popular with the administration; Joel by contrast was a traditionalist who was discontented with the trend of Basotho affairs and who was consequently looked upon by the colonial authorities as jealous, ambitious and 'less enlightened and amenable to reason' than most other Basotho chiefs. In 1882 the antagonism between them led to three years of sporadic fighting concerning their rival claims to the considerable cattle inheritance from their father. In 1888 Jonathan attempted without success to persuade Letsie to do away with the boundary between himself and Joel in order that he might deal with affairs directly in all parts of Leribe district. In 1890 fighting between the two chiefs again seemed imminent when 12,000 of their followers assembled fully armed at Leribe, and bloodshed was only averted by the intervention of Lerotholi and the Resident Commissioner. Throughout the 1890s the dispute between the two brothers continued to simmer.[11]

THE BRITISH, BOERS AND BASUTOLAND

As in a number of other regions of southern Africa,[12] the rinderpest epidemic in 1896–7 was accompanied in Basutoland by a wave of political unrest, in which Lerotholi's sons, Letsie and Makhaola, and a number of conservative Basotho chiefs, including Masopha, came together to represent to their people that the British administration was using the cover of the epidemic to make new boundaries along the southern border of Basutoland with the intention of introducing white farmers to the zone. The crisis reached its climax in December 1896 when Makhaola placed a large body of men on the Griqualand frontier to stop the construction of a fence designed to prevent the movement of infected livestock from Basutoland into the Cape Colony. In the midst of the political crisis in southern Africa engendered by the Jameson Raid, the reactions to the rinderpest emergency of a number of Basotho chiefs were not encouraging to colonial officials, and in Lagden's view the activities

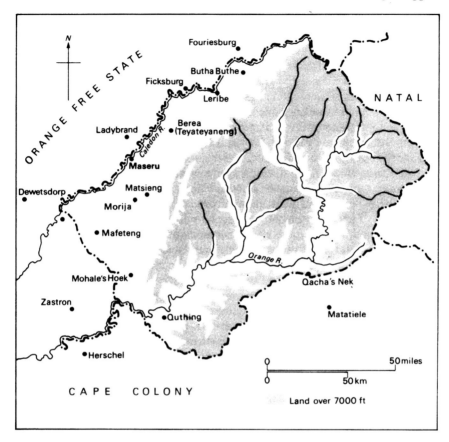

Map 4 Basutoland

of Lerotholi's sons did not auger well in the event of a further and more serious crisis occurring in relations between Britain and the Boer republics. Lerotholi's reluctance to admonish his sons for their behaviour made the Resident Commissioner deeply anxious about the future: 'these sons of yours will make you mad unless you suppress them and they will kill the country . . . they are choosing a bad time for their stupidity', Lagden told the paramount shortly before the outbreak of war.[13]

Throughout 1899 Lagden's policy was to instil confidence in Lerotholi that should war occur the British army would easily defeat the forces of the republics and so would not require the armed assistance of sympathetic African peoples. Although he believed the Basotho to be more favourably disposed towards Britain than towards the Boer states, he appreciated that most chiefs were aware that it would be inexpedient to support the losing side.[14] At the very least, therefore, Lagden believed the loyalty of Lerotholi and other Basotho would depend on a swift military victory by the British forces. In July

57

Lagden travelled to Cape Town to confer with Milner and to urge that an extension of telegraphic communications be undertaken in Basutoland, since there were only two telegraph stations in the colony, at Maseru and Mafeteng, and these formed part of the Orange Free State's communications network. Arrangements were hastily made for the construction of a telegraph line linking the main settlements in Basutoland to the Cape Colony's communications system, so that Lagden could keep in close touch with all his Assistant Commissioners and with the High Commissioner in Cape Town.[15]

Almost immediately upon his return to Maseru Lagden's sudden uncertainty about Basotho affairs was heightened by the activities of a number of neighbouring Free State farmers who spread reports through workers returning to the colony that the Boers would soon be the undisputed masters of southern Africa. Another rumour which officials in Leribe and Berea (present-day Teyateyaneng) found to be widespread was that the troops recently despatched from Britain were intended to coerce the Basotho people. Lagden reported that 'So much had the impression grown that many Basuto believed a force of British soldiers had actually arrived in South Basutoland by way of Herschel and Pathlala Drift on the Orange River.'[16] During August 1899 stories also began to reach Maseru that Joel had come to an agreement with the landdrost at Fouriesburg in the event of military action taking place. Joel was to hand over two of his sons as hostages in return for the assistance of 500 commandos, with whose help he undertook to defeat Jonathan and take over control of the whole of Leribe district. As a reward Joel was to receive a large part of Basutoland once the British army had been defeated. At first Lagden dismissed the rumour as 'a wild idea circulated with the intention of bluff, for the purpose perhaps of deterring Basutoland Government from making a general raid on the OFS', which some Boer farmers popularly believed to be planned. The reports continued to be received nonetheless, and the Assistant Commissioner in Leribe, J. Macgregor, for one became convinced of their authenticity.[17]

A new difficulty over taxation also arose on the eve of war. During a visit to Basutoland in 1898 Milner had arranged that the annual hut tax be increased from 10s to £1, but it was not until the following year, when diplomatic tension between the British and Boer governments was at its height, that a concerted attempt by the Basotho to prevent the increase emerged. In September Jonathan held a *pitso* among his people in Leribe which urged that the tax be maintained at the 10s rate, and Jonathan invited Lerotholi to repudiate his pledge to implement the new tax. Other protests followed and it was Letsie, the paramount's son, who emerged as the main public spokesman for the movement to stop the increase. The introduction of the new rate of tax could not have come at a worse time for Basotho homesteads in view of the economic difficulties following the rinderpest epidemic, and some kind of protest was therefore inevitable. But Lagden at least did not regard the occasion of the protest as entirely coincidental.

It is natural . . . that some of the chiefs should have regarded a serious misunderstanding between the English and the Dutch as the opportunity to shake free of any fetters that were uncongenial, and to embarrass the Government. The question of taxation was seized upon by one or two men of rank . . . whose example to Lerothodi's son and heir, Letsie, had the effect of inducing the latter to constitute himself a leader of opposition.[18]

Once war in South Africa seemed unavoidable, the role conceived for the Basotho by the British government was explained by Lagden to the chiefs at a *pitso* held in Maseru on 3 October. Lagden told those assembled that the conflict would be 'a white man's war' in which black people were not to take part. 'If Basutoland were invaded by the Boers it could be defended in the Queen's name; beyond that, there must be no aggressive movement or violation of the border.'[19] The precise nature of British policy towards Basutoland became clearer as the war progressed. During the first week of military operations many Basotho workers returning home through the Free State were apprehended by commandos and railway officials and their money and most of their clothing and belongings taken from them. Lagden telegraphed Milner: 'It appears to me that a diversion in the Imperial favour might be created if you could inspire newspapers that Basutos are incensed by this treatment, and are agitating to resent it.' Milner agreed, and Lagden circulated reports in the Free State of Basotho indignation: 'Our interest no doubt is that the OFS should continue to fear Basuto attack, but that such attack should not be made', he told the High Commissioner.[20]

The task of preventing armies from spilling over Basutoland's western and southern frontiers was made more difficult by the way military operations unfolded. Kimberley was swiftly besieged by Boer forces, and in November Aliwal North, Lady Frere and Burghersdorp were occupied. On 5 November, because of the advance of Boer forces into the Cape Colony and the cutting of the telegraph wire between Burghersdorp and Aliwal North, Basutoland's communications with Cape Town were temporarily suspended, and an alternative system of communication had quickly to be organised with the help of Basotho runners through the Drakensberg and East Griqualand. Following Lord Roberts's occupation of Bloemfontein on 13 March 1900 the southern Free State became an area of regrouping for the republic's forces, and when Roberts immediately began making secure the British line of communications and supply in preparation for the northward advance across the Vaal river, the region was contested by both armies. Thaba Nchu, Ladybrand, Dewetsdorp and Ficksburg all changed hands on three occasions. Wepener, on the Mafeteng border of Basutoland, was besieged by De Wet from 9 to 25 April 1900.

Lagden's first priority was to organise the defence of Maseru. The Basutoland Mounted Police was made up of only ten white officers and eight constables, together with six Basotho officers, seven sergeants, nine corporals, and two hundred and four privates. Thirty-seven whites and fifty regular

Basotho policemen were maintained in Maseru, and sixty armed men were provided by Lerotholi's brother, Mojela, and his son, Api, to supplement the force until 23 May 1900. Two stone forts were hastily constructed, and Basotho pickets posted around the settlement at all times. To guard the frontiers of the colony men were enrolled by chiefs to supplement the police force, and a chain of patrols was extended along Basutoland's borders.[21]

From the outbreak of war Basotho scouts began to be recruited for work with the British army, and some of the most reliable information about Boer troop movements received by the British forces were the reports conveyed from the republics by Basotho scouts and spies, whose information was then passed on to the Cape by whatever means were available. Basotho intelligence was especially valuable to the British army when in February 1900 Lord Roberts began the long haul into the Orange Free State.[22]

At the beginning of April, 1850 troops of the Cape Mounted Rifles and Brabant's Colonial Division commanded by Colonel E. H. Dalgety, advancing behind the main columns of the British army, occupied Wepener and took up a position at Jammersberg Drift on the Caledon river. The isolated position of Dalgety's force was quickly appreciated, and on 6 April Milner contacted Lagden about their exposure to Boer attack: 'In case they cannot fall back on Colony but retire into Basutoland, I trust you can rely on Paramount Chief and Basuto to protect their retreat and resist invasion of territory.' The plight of the force at Wepener provided the first occasion when military expediency appeared to threaten the neutrality of Basutoland's terrain. Milner argued that the Basotho would be justified in resisting any invasion by the forces of the Free State whether it was to pursue a retreat by the colonials into Basutoland, or to outflank their position on the Caledon river. The next day De Wet, with 6000 men, attacked the colonial force, and shortly afterwards laid siege to the encampment. Lagden, who was privately convinced that De Wet would attempt to enter Basutoland, completed arrangements for a Basotho frontier guard of 3000 men to resist any Boer encroachment. On 12 April an attempt was made by the Basotho to smuggle into Wepener a number of sheep and goats and 30,000 rounds of ammunition, and during the siege 100 sick and wounded soldiers were brought over the Basutoland border at night to receive medical attention at Mafeteng. The Basotho frontier guard was maintained for the duration of the siege, until on 25 April Dalgety's men were rescued by a relief column from Bloemfontein. In spite of the atrocious conditions in the encampment and instructions from Roberts to retire into Basutoland if necessary, no retreat across the border was made.[23]

A similar situation to the one which had developed at Wepener emerged four months later when a force of 123 regular soldiers and 30 local volunteers, commanded by Major F. White, were invested at Ladybrand from 1 to 5 September by Commandant Piet Fourie. On 29 August Roberts informed Lagden that he had advised White to withdraw into Basutoland should he be attacked. Lagden saw no reasonable alternative but to concur reluctantly with

Roberts's decision, though he was enraged by the Commander-in-Chief's lack of consultation, and when General Bruce Hamilton enquired whether it was in order for his relief column to enter the colony, Lagden tartly told him it was not. Milner considered Lagden's response 'too categorical'.

> Surely you do not mean that troops are not to retire into Basutoland if hard-pressed or not to enter it for strategical purposes, in order to surround or cut off the enemy? Of course in such cases you should be informed beforehand to enable you to cooperate and prepare the minds of the people so that the object of [the] movement may not be misunderstood.

Lagden nevertheless remained adamant that if for strategic reasons British troops were permitted to enter Basutoland the neutrality of the colony would become meaningless, since the Boers would be encouraged to take up a position within its frontiers to anticipate such a movement. Lagden argued that if this happened he 'could not justly regard such action as an invasion and resist it by the natives'.[24]

The conflicting views of the British high command on the one hand (with whose opinions Milner, on this subject at least, was sympathetic) and the colonial administration on the other concerning the role to be played by Basutoland in military operations, were at no time properly resolved. Both parties at least agreed that Boer infiltration into Basutoland should be resisted at all costs, and in July 1900 and again in February 1901 Basotho forces were mobilised to prevent any attempt by De Wet to enter the colony to evade capture by pursuing British columns. In September 1900 General Sir Leslie Rundle wrote to Lagden to inform him that he would do all in his power to prevent any strategic movement of British troops across Basutoland since, he believed, 'the Basuto would consider it weakness on our part if we did so'. But this did not represent official military policy. Lord Kitchener ordered General Hector Macdonald to march his men from Wepener, through Basutoland, to Aliwal North in January 1901, and he was stopped from doing so only by the protest of Herbert Sloley, the Acting Resident Commissioner in Maseru, who argued that such action would lead to 'complications'. A request soon afterwards by Colonel Pilcher for 500 Basotho to cross into the Orange River Colony to destroy crops under the cover of his forces was turned down when Sloley again intervened. When in June 1901 J. W. Bowker, the Assistant Commissioner at Mohale's Hoek, sent a party of Basotho into the Orange River Colony with the agreement of the local military commander to bring back to Basutoland as many carts as possible from deserted Boer farms, Sloley suspended him from duty.[25]

At the beginning of the war the border between the Orange Free State and Basutoland was guarded by over 1000 burghers from Ficksburg, Bethlehem and the Wittebergen. When in November the Ficksburg commando, which made up a substantial part of the frontier force, was ordered by the Free State government to join the main body of commando units, the local commandant argued that to do so would be to expose Boer families in the region to Basotho raids, and the commandos were therefore maintained close to the frontier until after Roberts's forces entered the republic.[26] In part to prevent the possibility of immediate large-scale raiding, on 30 October the pont hauser on the Makhaleng river between Zastron and Mohale's Hoek had been cut by commandos, and threats also made by the Boer guards on the Free State border near Maseru to destroy the pont on the Caledon river.[27]

On 18 October a proclamation from President Steyn, printed in Sesotho and English, was circulated in Basutoland and addressed to the 'Chiefs and Nation of the Basutos'.

> Be it known that the English Government have forced a war upon the Transvaal. The real cause of the war is that there are gold-fields and diamonds in the Transvaal which certain English people covet. The Free State is helping the Transvaal in this unjust war that the English Government have brought about. As the Free State is liable to be attacked by the British Government on all sides, it has sent commandos of burghers to the neighbourhood of its several borders in order to defend this country in case of attack. The Free State has stationed such commandos in the neighbourhood of the Basutoland border.
>
> Be it known, however, that the Free State is at peace with the Basutos and has no quarrel with them. No harm will be done to Basutos who remain quiet and take no part in the assistance of the English.[28]

The Boers also communicated directly with some of the most important Basotho chiefs. The first contact was almost certainly with Joel, who was approached by Veldkornet Michael Rautenbach from Fouriesburg. At a meeting of commandos, Rautenbach assured those assembled that 'if there would be fighting on the Basuto border, which he did not for a moment expect, their neighbour across the river [i.e. Joel] would give them timely warning and would be found fighting alongside them'. During the first week of the war two officials of the Free State made contact with Jonathan, who reported to Lagden that the message had instructed him to choose his side, and had threatened that if he did not assist the Orange Free State he would be treated by the Boers in the same manner as an Englishman. Letters to Letsie and Lerotholi were sent by Commandant Diedricks, who requested a meeting with the paramount or one of his representatives, and pointed out that during the Gun War the Free State had not assisted the Cape forces against the Basotho and that therefore the time had come for the republic to count upon Basotho neutrality in its struggle with Britain. Further messages were sent to Maama, to the sons of Masopha and to the Basotho chief Mallbanye. Further messages were intercepted by the British administration and several Basotho arrested as Boer agents.[29] In November a messenger was apprehended carrying a letter to Jonathan from Solomon Raads, a farmer in the Free State. The message demanded that 'Jonathan must state his position plainly, whether he was an Englishman, a Dutchman or a Mosuto . . . First, he must allow his people to come and go freely into Orange Free State. Secondly, he must drive away his Magistrate, as the Boers would not have an Englishman there.[30]

On 12 December a message to Letsie from H. Potgieter, the new landdrost of occupied Aliwal North, was intercepted, in which 100 Basotho reapers were requested to help farmers in the district in return for high wages.[31] The dependence of the farming communities in the locality of Basutoland on Basotho harvesters was of particular concern to the Boers, who were anxious to overcome the difficulty of maintaining agricultural production when large numbers of men had been drafted into military service. When De Wet later captured 280 Basotho working with the British army between Kroonstad and Viljoen's Drift the men were made to work on farms nearby for fourteen days before being allowed to return to Basutoland.[32] A number of Basotho, mostly from Leribe, Butha Buthe and Mohale's Hoek, crossed the border to work on farms in the Free State. Colonial officials believed they were tempted by high wages, and punished those whom they found returning to the colony.[33]

Narratives of Boer victories in the war were printed in Sesotho and circulated in Basutoland, and in November false reports were issued telling of a capitulation by the besieged British force at Ladysmith.[34] Direct Boer intervention in the affairs of Basutoland, however, did not take place on a large scale. Although immediately before the war Lagden feared that farmers across the Free State border contemplated bringing arms into the colony for the Basotho to use against the British, no indiscriminate issuing of firearms appears to have taken place, though a small consignment of rifles was given to Mocheka, and probably also to Joel.[35]

Some Boer cattle and sheep were brought secretly into Basutoland when the British columns began sweeping through the southern Free State in April and May 1900. During the guerrilla stage of the war Boer units made a small number of raids into Basutoland to drive off horses belonging to refugees and in March 1902 four Basotho were convicted of stealing horses in Berea for the Ladybrand commando, but generally the Boer guerrillas operating in the region appear to have been able to purchase food, clothing and horses from Basotho across the colony's frontier with little difficulty.[36]

BASOTHO REACTIONS TO THE WAR

Following his meeting with the Basotho chiefs on 3 October 1899 Lagden was sure that Lerotholi would give Britain his unconditional support during the difficult months ahead, writing in his diary that he was confident after all that Basutoland was 'off the HC's shoulders and that we have relieved him of a great burden'.[37] But the outbreak of war appears to have caused Lerotholi a good deal of anxiety. His own personal wealth and influence in Basotho affairs, as well as the prosperity of close-related members of his family, had grown under British rule, and he feared that if the territory were overrun by Boer forces his own position, as well as that of the British administration, would be undermined. On 18 October Lerotholi therefore urged Lagden to allow him to defend the colony in force.

> I say to you Chief you are dangerous, you wish to kill me and get me into trouble
> . . . I am alarmed at my hearing that this unrest is increasing Chief, especially in

the matter of Maseru being attacked cruelly. I asked to be allowed to come with force to Maseru but you prevented me . . . Chief according to our Sesuto custom a man is never without a gun; now I have just sent my gun to you; and now I beg you Chief to send it back to me . . . I beg you to send me cartridges.[38]

Lerotholi continued for some time to request ammunition so that if necessary he could deal quickly with any threat either to his own authority or to that of the British administration. A second *pitso* was held on 24 October at Motseki's near Maseru when Lerotholi again demanded that the Basotho be armed and permitted to fight with the British army. Lagden's conviction of the paramount's loyalty was reinforced, and he wrote in his diary that the occasion 'went off well . . . I feel sure of the Basuto'.[39]

The relations between Lagden and Lerotholi during the early stages of the war can be traced through the unfolding of events in Basutoland. The fifteen months between Masopha's defeat and the outbreak of war had been a period of relative calm in Basotho politics, interrupted only by the dispute between Griffith and the Phuthi chief, Mocheka. The beginning of the war, however, foreshadowed a period of intense political activity as a number of chiefs attempted to achieve the most possible benefit from the threatened disruption to the established system of colonial authority. The difficult relations between Mocheka and Lerotholi, who was becoming increasingly frustrated by the activities of the Phuthi and was anxious to assert his full authority in Quthing district, was the first political issue to be influenced by the changed circumstances. Mocheka was nonetheless the first to act and during September and October he obtained rifles and ammunition from a border farmer in the Free State, threatening that the Boers would help his people to free themselves from Koena control. Since the actions of the Phuthi clearly could not be ignored by Lerotholi, the paramount persuaded Lagden to allow him to send men to bring Mocheka to Matsieng in the traditional way of taking livestock belonging to the Phuthi, which the owners were obliged to follow. Chief Seiso was despatched with a body of men to accomplish the task, but when the party was returning home it was ambushed at Quthing by a Phuthi force led by Mocheka and Semenekane, a chief suspected of collaborating in the illicit arms traffic. Lagden had no alternative but to issue a warrant for the arrest of the two Phuthi chiefs, but he was angry at the behaviour of Lerotholi's men. 'I don't know the orders you gave your messengers . . . [they] went beyond what was necessary when they seized such a quantity of stock and especially small stock . . . all the mischief and alarm created in Quthing and along the Orange River was due to the loud and loose threatening talk of your messengers.'[40] Mocheka reacted by crossing with 250 armed men into the Herschel district of the Cape, at the time threatened by Boer invasion. Here he proclaimed Moorosi's former settlement at Letuka's Kraal, near Palmietfontein, to be the new home of the Phuthi community, beyond the control of the Koena paramount. Later in the month the Thembu chief, Stokwe Tyali, followed Mocheka's example and crossed from Quthing district into the Tella and Blikana valleys. Having arrived in Herschel,

Mocheka claimed that he had been driven out of Basutoland, all his livestock seized and taken to Matsieng, and that his people were starving. He elicited some sympathy from W. P. Schreiner, who attributed the exodus from Basutoland of both the Phuthi and Thembu to the disposition of the Basotho to use the occasion of war to 'eat up' other chiefdoms within the colony. Milner and Lagden, however, believed that the two leaders, possibly encouraged by emissaries from the Free State, had taken the opportunity to free themselves from the control of Lerotholi and Griffith by removing their people beyond Basotho jurisdiction. On Milner's instructions the government in Cape Town ordered that the Phuthi be returned to Basutoland where Mocheka, Semenekane and another Phuthi chief, Tsehla Khorlenya, were immediately disarmed and imprisoned. Tyali's attempt to take the Thembu beyond Lerotholi's control, and to reclaim the land from which his people had been expelled after supporting the Phuthi rebellion in 1879, also ended in failure.[41]

In Leribe district the close relations that Joel Molapo maintained with a number of Boer farmers in the Free State was a matter of concern to Jonathan even before the outbreak of war. Jonathan's mistrust of Joel's intentions was heightened by reports that Veldkornet Rautenbach had supplied him with a consignment of Mauser rifles, which Jonathan feared would be used in some design against himself. Every able-bodied man was called upon to take part in sentry duty around all his people's homesteads, and even the local mission schoolmaster, Andrew Makhobotloane, was not exempted from night duty. The war in South Africa offered each brother an ally in their long-standing feud concerning Molapo's inheritance. In response to Joel's contact with the Boers, Jonathan pledged his unconditional support to the British government, and at the *pitso* on 24 October he agreed, after weeks of opposition, to abide by the decision to collect the new rate of hut tax.[42]

Joel soon afterwards settled Qhobela, his son, close to the village of his brother, Hlasoa, who in the disputes in Leribe had increasingly identified himself with Jonathan. Relations between the two immediately became difficult, and on the night of 18 November Qhobela attacked his neighbour, killing five men, destroying his homestead, and driving Hlasoa's people from their land. The refugees fled to a cave near Kokolosameng where mealies were issued to them by Jonathan and subsequently by the colonial administration. On 24 November Jonathan organised a *pitso* at Leribe which demanded that Joel be removed from office. Four days later Joel retaliated by seizing a large number of Jonathan's sheep, after which Jonathan requested that a detachment of the colony's mounted police apprehend his brother. Macgregor, the Assistant Commissioner at Leribe, mollified Jonathan by convincing him that he had the support of the Basutoland administration and that Joel would be made to answer for his actions in due course. Joel meanwhile evidently felt unable to press matters further without the active support of the Boer farming community across the Caledon river. According to reliable intelligence reports, Qhobela visited the Free State on two occasions, but he appears to have been unsuccessful in mobilising support. The delicacy of the situation, however, made it inexpedient to reprimand or arrest Joel since, as Lagden wrote later, neither he nor Lerotholi 'knew what power they could command when opinion was so much divided; a false move might have ended disastrously, have suited intrigues and sorely embarrassed the Government'.[43]

The dispute between Joel and Jonathan, coming as it did at a time of Boer successes in the war, ushered in a period almost of crisis in the relations between Lerotholi and the Resident Commissioner. When Lerotholi first became acquainted with the trend of events in Leribe he suggested to Lagden that neither of them should intervene. 'If the sons of Molapo have a plan let us stand aside, let it be their own doing because if we work this matter strongly now at present, and if they should do something it will be said that we have caused this difference.'[44] Lerotholi's own relations with Jonathan were poor, and had been ever since the Gun War when Lerotholi had fought alongside Joel while Jonathan had disarmed. At the time of Lerotholi's dispute with Masopha, Jonathan had threatened to assist Masopha with 1000 men. Jonathan also exercised almost complete autonomy from Lerotholi's control in his own district. When reports reached Maseru in September that Joel and his brother, Khetisa, were prepared to join the Boers, Lerotholi had protested to Lagden that this was 'a false charge that Jonathan is charging them with'.[45] Two months later, when reports were received of the conflict in Leribe, Lerotholi's advice, that neither he nor Lagden should intervene, almost certainly sprang from the paramount's satisfaction that Joel appeared to be challenging Jonathan's authority with some success. Lagden interpreted Lerotholi's plea for inaction not only as support for Joel, but for his agreement with the Boers as well. 'Lerothodi does not seem much concerned about Joel's conduct and disturbance in Leribe. I cannot help suspicions that Lerothodi may have had a hand in Joel's coquetting with the Boers and does not know how to get out of it. I suspect that the future of Basutoland hangs upon this incident.'[46]

The continuing uncertainty of events beyond Basutoland's frontiers, together with the uneasy aftermath of Joel's activities, caused Lagden much renewed anxiety. In Berea a *pitso* was organised by the sons of Masopha at which the local Assistant Commissioner reported that 'everyone shouted in favour of siding with the Boers', largely at the instigation of Fako, a minor son of Masopha, and Mhlonhlo, the Mpondomise chief who had taken refuge with Masopha after the Transkeian rebellion in 1880–1. 'So far as the episode has gone it in no way shows openly any trace of extra-territorial politics . . . but I am personally inclined to think that it is Dutch influence on both Fako and Mhlontlo: they are fools, they are simply throwing their district into Lerothodi's hands.'[47] The worries of officials in Basutoland at this time were compounded by the only half-hearted efforts in some areas, notably in Joel's ward and in Berea, to collect the increased rate of hut tax.[48] On 3 December Lagden wrote to Milner that 'some of our chiefs have secretly disapproved of

Lerothodi's pronounced loyalty unless and until Boers were being soundly beaten . . . We cannot expect the people to be unanimous nor forget that every course in guiding the mass offers alternative difficulties.'[49] Lagden even feared that perhaps Lerotholi himself was contemplating using the occasion of war in South Africa to liberate the Basotho completely from colonial control. Later he wrote that during the early weeks of the war Lerotholi had been 'tempted by his own people to throw off the yoke of Government, and generally taunted by all those who saw a favourable opportunity for gaining points out of the white man's struggle'. Lagden also apparently began to muse with the idea that the Basotho might be encouraged by other African communities to spearhead a concerted black uprising in South Africa.[50]

At the beginning of December Sir Henry Elliot in the Transkei received information 'from good sources . . . that Lerothodi's son Griffith was bent on mischief and joining the Boers'.[51] This news alarmed Lagden, who believed the paramount was always 'liable to be swayed by his children if they forced his hand'. On 14 December he sent Mojela to ask Lerotholi why he was 'sleeping'. The message was indignantly received:

> You say you are talking to a person who is sleeping. I say tell me what is my sleep whereas I say I am following you and working with you . . . even the hut tax I am ordering about it, and it is paid and even the people on the border I am calling them to instruct them as to how they will watch the border.
>
> Chief it is not law to drive people from your court before they have given account of themselves. This is a thing which you frequently do.[52]

Lagden's pessimism was reinforced by the knowledge that a number of Basotho from Letsie's ward had illicitly crossed the Basutoland border to work as harvesters on Boer farms, and by the discovery of correspondence between Letsie and the landdrost at Aliwal North.[53] According to S. Barrett, the Assistant Commissioner at Quthing, Letsie 'was furious at his letters being opened and . . . sent to all his brothers and males to ask what was the use of a Government which doubled their taxes and interfered with their private correspondence'. Lerotholi, too, was uneasy about the arbitrary interception of letters addressed to members of his family.[54]

Lagden's anxiety about affairs in Basutoland did not end until the British occupation of Bloemfontein. On 13 March he confided to his diary: 'We little know how near we have been to a Basuto rising against us. It becomes more apparent to me every day. The natives have time after time very nearly deserted and joined with the Boers to cut our throats.'[55] Yet Lagden's view of events is seriously open to question, and perhaps reveals more about his neurotic temperament and self-delusion than about the realities of Basotho affairs. It is true of course that during the early months of the war some Basotho appear to have recognised the imprudence of identifying themselves too closely with the British side until the probable outcome of the conflict was more apparent. Both Joel and Mocheka elicited support from neighbouring Boer farmers. Griffith and Letsie, Lerotholi's sons, became frustrated by the constraints imposed by wartime conditions and sought to maintain normal economic relations with Boer farmers across the colony's frontiers, but even during the weeks of Boer pre-eminence in the war at no time did they openly support the republican side. The pro-Boer sympathies of Masopha's sons were not transformed into a concerted movement of resistance in Berea. Lerotholi, though he found the methods of the British administration irksome and Lagden's lack of confidence in his loyalty irritating, cooperated fully in the arrangements for the defence of the colony, and regularly sent messages of congratulation following news of victories by the British army.[56] In short, although some of the traditionalists in Basutoland may have flirted with the Boers, the loyalty to Britain of the wealthy and powerful Basotho, men such as Lerotholi and Jonathan and the leaders of the Christianised peasant communities in the colony, could at no time be questioned.

Lagden, therefore, almost certainly exaggerated the perils that confronted the Basutoland administration. He nevertheless received Chamberlain's warm approval for the way affairs had been managed during the difficult early months of the war, and largely on the basis of his administrative record at this time Milner first considered him as a possible Lieutenant-Governor for the Orange River Colony and eventually selected him to head the Native Affairs Department in the Transvaal Crown Colony.

THE IMPACT OF WAR

Almost from the first days of military operations Basutoland afforded a haven to refugees, both white and black. The pace of refugee arrivals quickened following the British occupation of Bloemfontein, and even more so after the beginning of Kitchener's scorched earth campaign in the republics in December 1900. Already in May Basotho from the Free State had begun crossing into the colony with their herds to prevent livestock being requisitioned by the British army. The refugees were allowed to enter Basutoland provided they could show that the cattle were their own property. In March 1901 Africans uprooted from the land by Kitchener's forces were permitted to settle temporarily in Basutoland in order to alleviate pressure on the black concentration camps in the republics. Altogether 12,000–15,000 African refugees entered the colony. About 2000 Boer refugees were also afforded asylum, though they were not allowed to settle within five miles of the frontier to lessen the possibility that they might give sustenance to the guerrilla units remaining in the field.[57]

In addition to the recruitment of scouts and spies from Basutoland, which had begun early in the war, the British army soon began to hire Basotho workers. At the end of March 1900 arrangements were made with various chiefs for the supply of 2000 men to travel to Bloemfontein to undertake railway repair work. Although recruitment initially met with some resistance, by the end of May the workforce had been assembled, and a further 1000

Basotho workers were recruited by the army during the following two months. The employment of Basotho workers by the military continued to increase, and in the following year over 11,000 workers from the colony were employed by the army. Precise statistics of the number of men recruited were not maintained, though correspondence between military recruiters and colonial officials during the latter part of 1901 makes regular mention of the growing strains on the colony's labour resources.[58]

Army pay was generally good (up to 110s a month for an experienced transport driver and even higher for some groups of scouts), and large numbers of Basotho regarded military wages as a means of replenishing herds depleted by rinderpest three years earlier. Cattle stocks were also rebuilt by livestock rustling in neighbouring districts of the Free State and the Cape Colony, and by the sale of horses to the remount department of the British army. Although the incidence of cattle rustling was moderated by frontier police patrols, looting across Basutoland's borders nonetheless took place regularly and to an extent which could not be fully controlled because of the constant movement of people and livestock through the colony. In May and June 1900 it was reported in Leribe that 'cattle were stolen right and left from across the border'; in December 1900 Basotho from Quthing took part in extensive stock thefts from rebel farms in Barkly East; and throughout the war almost all the Basutoland officials complained of the unacceptable amount of cattle thieving practised by the Basotho.[59] Parties of men were organised by Lerotholi, at the request of the Resident Commissioner, to recover stolen livestock, and many Basotho were arrested for cattle rustling, so much so that the colony's gaols teemed with such offenders.[60] But the difficulties confronting the administration were made clear when in June 1901 one of the best organised looting expeditions into the Orange River Colony was initiated by a group of border guards. The loot taken from Boer farms consisted not only of livestock but of household goods too, including a piano; the items eventually recovered by the authorities filled thirty waggons and three smaller carts. Twenty-four men were held responsible for the expedition and fined a total of 443 cattle, 30 horses and 681 sheep and goats.[61]

During the 1890s the stocks of horses owned by the Basotho had begun to be transformed from a valuable military asset into an important source of cash wealth. Large-scale purchasing of Basotho horses began in 1890 when the British South Africa Company bought animals for the Pioneer Column's trek into Mashonaland, and afterwards 500 or more horses were exported annually from the colony. During the first six months of the war the Basotho were reluctant to sell horses to the British army, probably because of the uncertainty of affairs in the region, but following Lord Roberts's occupation of Bloemfontein sales of horses began to be made on a considerable scale. In May 1900 General Rundle's division was re-equipped with horses almost entirely from Basutoland, and horses continued to be purchased from the colony in very large numbers for the next eighteen months. The Basotho sold

4419 horses in 1900 to the value of £64,032 (an average of £14 10s for each animal); in 1901 15,684 horses left Basutoland worth £262,991 (an average of £16 15s each).[62] Sometimes up to £50 was paid for the best animals. Horse trading was entered into by the Basotho at a time of depression in commercial grain production, brought about by the dislocation of the Basotho's grain markets and the scarcity of waggon transport. An intelligence officer in Bethulie reported in June 1900 that many Basotho employed by the British army in the Orange River Colony were deserting their picket duties to return to Basutoland under orders from their chiefs 'to get their horses fat'. In many cases horses could only be obtained by the army in exchange for cattle. Confiscated stock from the Orange River Colony was brought to the drifts on the Caledon river for bartering purposes, and district commissioners at Smithfield, Ladybrand and Wepener were requested by the military to procure as many cattle as possible since it was often the case that four or five cattle were needed to exchange for one horse.[63]

Throughout the war British officials commented upon the prosperity of the Basotho. The Assistant Commissioner at Berea reported in 1900 that money was plentiful everywhere. Sir Herbert Sloley, Lagden's successor as Resident Commissioner, wrote in the following year that the Basotho had 'shrewdly extracted every possible advantage from the situation by carrying on a brisk trade in ponies, cattle and produce at war prices'.[64] Undoubtedly for those Basotho who participated in the lucrative trade in livestock the period between 1900 and 1902 was one of great commercial opportunity. The war also helped numbers of homesteads to replenish their herds after the devastating losses from rinderpest. But the extent to which the prosperity of the war years percolated through to all sections of Basotho society should not be exaggerated. Basotho communities were highly stratified, and it was the chiefs in particular who were in the best position to exploit the wartime livestock market. Army wages were high but commodity prices were equally inflated. Between 60,000 and 70,000 Basotho migrated from Basutoland to find work in 1902–3 compared to 37,000 in 1898–9.[65] Furthermore, the remarkable increase in the scale of livestock trading brought with it some damaging economic consequences.

It is evident from the almost immediate decline after the war in the quality of the Basotho's stocks of horses that the best animals were sold to the military (indeed only the larger animals were suitable for remounts). The breeding stocks of the Basotho were irreparably damaged, and in 1903 Arab stallions were imported by the Basutoland administration in an attempt to arrest the decline. Livestock diseases were brought into the colony by cattle bartered for horses by the army's remount department. The worst affected areas were those in the eastern region of Basutoland along the valley of the Orange river. In March 1901 cattle with lungsickness already breaking out among them were sent into Qacha's Nek, and the Assistant Commissioner claimed that the remount department 'knew full well the cattle they were swopping for horses with the Basuto were infected'. Cattle losses from pleuropneumonia were severe. Rinderpest was introduced into Basutoland by trek oxen from the Orange River Colony and again spread through the Basotho's herds, though its impact was much reduced by the lesser virulence of the disease, by more widespread acceptance of preventive inoculation, and because some of the older animals were still immune from earlier treatment. Diseases were also spread to Basotho horses and the incidence of scab accounted for the loss of thousands of animals, further depleting breeding stocks. In 1902 Sloley regretted that 'the necessary introduction of herds of cattle and horses for military purposes has been accompanied by every variety of equine and bovine disease in South Africa. This is an unpleasant legacy of the war, and has occasioned much loss.' Basutoland was regarded by the military as a safe highway for sending captured cattle from the north to the Cape Colony, and the movement of livestock through the colony not only helped to spread disease but also caused damage to pastures and gardens. Overstocking in Maseru, Berea and other districts was made more acute by the influx of refugees with their cattle.[66]

The dislocation of markets for wheat, maize and sorghum was at first caused by military operations and the commandeering by the army of all available waggons. But the problem was made more acute by the reluctance of traders to purchase grain when the trade in livestock offered such lucrative returns. Thousands of bags of grain remained in the colony awaiting purchase and export, and as late in the war as August 1901 the problem of transporting grain to its markets had still not been fully overcome.[67] Nevertheless when convoys were arranged to transport produce they were an impressive sight. A visitor to Thaba Nchu in March 1902 described 'an immense convoy coming from . . . Basutoland . . . the oxen are splendid and the waggons very fine and painted'. In 1903 Basutoland was described as the 'great granary of South Africa', but in the same year, with the collapse of the wartime boom and the onset of drought, the colony was obliged to import North American wheat to feed its people.[68]

The economic difficulties experienced by many Basotho during the war produced tense relations with remount officers and white traders. In February 1901 the Assistant Commissioner at Qacha's Nek reported that horse trading was 'not popular with the Natives'. Earlier Lagden had prevented the entry into Basutoland of a large number of white refugees with their herds of cattle on the basis that 'the seizure of pasture is resented by the natives whose pasture is now terribly short'. The increase in the price of consumption items and the low price offered for grain because of the dislocation of trade and high transport costs created tensions between Basotho peasants and white traders. Sloley turned down most of the applications for new trading stores during the later stages of the war and immediately afterwards because each one had become, in his words, 'a possible point of friction between the natives and the European residents'. Following complaints about the prevailing prices at trading stores, Maama forcibly closed those at Mokema and Roma in June 1902. Sloley accused the chief of acting against the best interests of his people, but Maama disagreed: 'I say Chief it is the people who are speaking these words they say they work hard to get this grain and it is taken away by the shopkeepers for nothing.'[69]

By the end of the war perceptible political as well as economic changes had taken place in Basutoland. In July 1902 Joel was eventually summoned to Maseru to explain his wartime conduct. Joel had maintained close relations with the Boers, sold horses to the commandos, permitted his men to enrol as servants with the guerrilla units, harassed Jonathan and Hlasoa, and made only a token gesture of collecting the hut tax in his district in 1900.[70] The chief was imprisoned for a year and fined 500 head of cattle. The dispute between the sons of Molapo nonetheless lingered on until Joel's death after the First World War.

During the war Lerotholi and his family continued to consolidate their authority over the Phuthi and Thembu communities in Quthing and Mohale's Hoek. After Mocheka's arrest Griffith immediately began looting large numbers of Phuthi and Thembu livestock. In 1901 the Assistant Commissioner at Quthing reported a growing number of complaints against Nkoebe, Griffith and other Basotho chiefs for their harsh and arbitrary treatment of the local communities, and suggested that 'their intention is to drive these aliens to remove out of the territory and leave Basutoland for the Basuto'. The Phuthi responded by refusing to attend courts and pay their hut tax to Lerotholi's agent, Griffith. Angered by such resistance, Lerotholi threatened he would 'punish the Phuthi severely without sending messengers', maintaining they were taking advantage of wartime conditions, when his own attention was diverted elsewhere, to challenge the authority of the paramountcy: 'the Baphuti wish to destroy peace – as they have stated we killed Moorosi and that they will catch me by the leg when matters are as they are now – and now when they see this war between the Boers and the Government they catch me by the leg'. It seems equally clear, however, that Lerotholi and his family did not miss an opportunity during the war to attempt completely to subordinate the Phuthi to their authority.[71]

Mocheka and Semenekane remained in gaol for almost the whole of the war, and were brought to trial only in April 1902. Mocheka argued without success that 'Moorosi . . . was an ally but not a subject or vassal of Moshesh . . . that they [the Phuthi] were, or ought to be, independent and not subject to the control of Moshesh's descendants.' As punishment for his wartime behaviour Mocheka was no longer recognised by the Basutoland administration as the Phuthi chief, and was forbidden to return to the location he had previously occupied. In 1902 the subordination to Koena control of the Phuthi and Thembu communities in southern Basutoland was more complete than ever before. In June 1902 Mocheka, accompanied by the Thembu chief, Stokwe Tyali, again crossed over into Herschel district and requested permission from the local magistrate to travel to Cape Town to put their case before the High Commissioner. The two men were handed over to the Basutoland Police and returned to the colony. Again in March 1904 Mocheka left Basutoland without permission with the intention of gaining an interview with the High Commissioner, but was intercepted at Lady Grey and brought back to Basutoland.[72]

Although Lerotholi was in poor health for most of the war,[73] he nevertheless appears quickly to have realised that the Basutoland adminstration's dependence on the prestige and authority of the paramountcy to maintain the tranquillity of the colony, the benevolent neutrality of the Basotho people and access to their produce and resources, was likely to provide him with opportunities to consolidate his influence. Lagden was aware that his dependence on Lerotholi served both their interests, and as early as 1900 he wrote that the paramount had taken advantage of wartime circumstances to enhance the wealth and authority of loyal members of his family. On a number of occasions Lerotholi was given responsibility for tasks such as raising auxiliaries to defend Basutoland's frontiers and providing men to search for cattle stolen from across the Free State and Cape borders. Lerotholi invariably entrusted these duties to his dependable brothers and sons. These parties of armed men, close adherents of the paramount and led by loyal members of his immediate family, were sent to the more remote border regions of Basutoland where in the past chiefs had often resisted the right of Lerotholi and his father, Letsie, to interfere in any way in the internal affairs of their own locality. The despatching of armed men throughout the colony enabled Lerotholi to express tangibly his power and authority, much to the dislike of some prominent chiefs. Jonathan, for example, who had consistently prevented Lerotholi from interfering to any great extent in the affairs of Leribe, unsuccessfully sought to stop a group of Lerotholi's men led by Api from searching in his district for stolen livestock; the party returned having seized 112 cattle and 20 sheep.[74]

The close relations which had been forged since 1884 between the British colonial administration in Basutoland and the Koena paramountcy were therefore consolidated by the circumstances of war. The uncertainty of events in 1899 and Britain's dependence on the assistance and resources of the Basotho shifted the balance of political power in Basutoland during the war perceptibly in the direction of the Koena. This was recognised immediately by the Resident Commissioner and was the cause of some anxiety on Lagden's part, albeit exaggerated and misplaced. The authority and prosperity of the paramountcy had grown in collaboration with the British, and Lerotholi and close members of his family recognised the dangers inherent in a British defeat. Lerotholi and other wealthy and powerful Koena chiefs committed to the colonial system may have found events early in the war irritating and worrying, but their loyalty was never seriously in question. As the conflict progressed Lerotholi used the opportunities presented to him to extend his immediate family's wealth and influence in Basotho affairs with British approval. He nonetheless remained watchful of his position, and a major reason that lay behind the establishment of a National Council in Basutoland a year after the war ended was Lerotholi's concern to ensure the orderly succession to the paramountcy of his son, Letsie, who succeeded as Letsie II upon his father's death in 1905.

4

The Zulu's war

The essence of the military campaign in Natal was the siege and relief of Ladysmith. At the outbreak of war the colony was invaded by commandos of the Orange Free State, pouring in through the Tintwa, Van Reenen and Bezuidenhout passes, and the Transvaal forces of General Joubert, who by the end of October 1899 had captured Charlestown, Newcastle and Dundee. Between 29 October and 2 November Joubert laid siege to Ladysmith, where the British and colonial forces from the frontier region had retired. Although advanced Boer patrols reached Mooiriver, only fifty miles from Pietermaritzburg, Joubert's commandos concentrated around Ladysmith rather than advance in force towards Durban and the sea. Three attempts by General Buller to relieve Ladysmith ended in defeats at Colenso (15 December), Spion Kop (24 January) and Vaalkrans (5–7 February). After four months the town was eventually relieved on 28 February. Thereafter the Boer forces were pushed back to the colony's frontiers. Dundee was entered by imperial troops on 16 May and Newcastle two days later, and by the end of May the whole of Natal and Zululand was once again under British control.

Events in Natal are especially interesting from the point of view of black involvement in the war. In the first place Natal was the settler colony in South Africa in which the proportion of colonists to black people was smallest; whites were outnumbered 10:1 in Natal. Secondly, the colony was the scene of some of the most intense fighting in the war. Thirdly, for a number of months of the war Boer forces occupied the northern divisions of the colony and two districts of Zululand, setting up rudimentary regimes of occupation in areas predominantly inhabited by black people. Finally, the reactions of the Zulu to the war, and the roles they might perform in military operations, were issues which frequently engaged the attention of both the Natal and British governments.

THE ADVENT OF WAR

At the beginning of September 1899 preparations began to be made by the Natal government for the defence of the border divisions of the colony. A communication to all chiefs and *induna* (headmen) was drawn up and transmitted through magistrates stating that in the event of war black people were to remain within their borders and to take no part in the fighting, though they would be allowed to protect themselves and their property against attack or seizure by the enemy.[1] The number of black policemen in the border divisions was increased; on the upper Tugela river 200 men were recruited by chief Ncwadi to be enrolled as constables and provided with firearms with the intention of deterring an invasion of the colony from the Witzie's Hoek district of the Free State.[2] The Natal government was determined that firearms or ammunition should not be supplied to black civilians, whose protection, ministers considered, should be organised under the umbrella of the police force, and not carried out on an irregular basis by chiefs themselves. The government's military preparations elicited little confidence among many Zulu communities close to the frontier;[3] the decision not to supply firearms to those chiefs especially vulnerable to attack was criticised with some vigour.[4] A mood of considerable anxiety on the border was revealed in the movement of some blacks away from the frontier, and in the slaughter and sale of a number of livestock in the belief that animals were likely to be seized by invading Boer forces or commandeered by the British army.[5]

The defence of Zululand was entrusted to the Zululand Native Police, whose complement was raised to 400 men immediately before the outbreak of war. The inability of the force to defend the region successfully against a determined Boer invasion was nonetheless recognised, for Eshowe was not in heliographic communication with Nkandla, Nquthu, Nongoma, Ubombo and Melmoth, and the Chief Commissioner of Police advised that in Nkandla, Melmoth, Mahlabathini and Hlabisa there existed no defensible positions sufficient to withstand an attack for any length of time. Preparations were made for magistrates in these districts to retire in an emergency to Eshowe or Nongoma. In the event of an invasion it was envisaged that Zulu leaders would at once place themselves under the orders of the police.[6] Sir Charles Saunders, the Chief Magistrate and Civil Commissioner in Zululand, believed there was little danger of a Boer raid into the province or an attack on Natal through Zululand, though he was concerned that law and order might be threatened by Zulu 'restlessness' inspired by an aggressive movement of British troops through the region or by a build-up of commandos in the New Republic, the region of Zululand lost in 1884 and subsequently incorporated in the South African Republic. The protection of Zulu herds was a matter of concern both to the administration and to homestead-heads in view of the social and economic importance of cattle in Zulu society. The 2000-head of cattle on the Mahlabathini frontier were moved away from the border, and orders issued by magistrates throughout Zululand that resistance to cattle raids by Boer forces would be conducted by the Zululand Police.[7]

Rivalry between the emigrant Boers and the Zulu state had deep roots, extending to the time of the Great Trek, the assassination of the trekker leader Retief and the battle of Blood River in 1838. The loss of the New Republic to white freebooters under Boer leadership in 1884 was followed by the subdivision of the area into white farms and the transformation of thousands of Zulu into tenants and squatters. The partition of Zululand was a bitter blow, for the annexed region contained valuable grazing lands, many important homesteads and the burial sites of the pre-Shakan kings at Emakhosini. On the eve of war Boer leaders in the New Republic were concerned that some attempt might be made by the Zulu to reclaim the region while their attention was diverted elsewhere. Boer farmers around Melmoth retreated with their livestock, and families living close to the Zululand border moved further away from the frontier, concentrating close to laagers.[8] During the two months before the outbreak of war a number of prominent Boer leaders from Vryheid district visited Dinuzulu, the head of the Zulu royal lineage who had been permitted to return to the province as an ordinary petty chief from detention on St Helena in 1898.[9] At the time Dinuzulu told the magistrate at Nongoma, J. Y. Gibson, that the visitors had given no reason for their calls other than a desire to see him, though once the war was over Dinuzulu was more explicit about his contacts with emissaries from the Transvaal.

> I remember receiving a message from Coenraad Meyer, [a border farmer with a long record of involvement in Zulu affairs] soon after the war began, telling me we were to take no part in the war; that we natives were to leave the white peoples to fight their own battles. A short time before the commencement of the war, Coenraad Meyer came to see me, personally, at my Osuthu kraal, and told me that there would be war between the Boers and the English; that we natives were to remain perfectly passive and take no part in it . . . When the Boers started for Dundee, Lukas Meyer sent me a similar message to the one I had received from Coenraad Meyer.[10]

One of the main fears of the Natal government and many colonists was that the outbreak of war would be accompanied by conflicts between various black groups, precipitated by the diversion elsewhere of the colony's military resources or by Boer intrigues designed to broaden the front of military activity in Natal. J. R. Bennett, the magistrate at Alfred, implored the government not to call out volunteers for the war because of the threat of 'native trouble', and similar warnings were voiced by other officials. Many settlers feared that conflicts between African groups would almost inevitably lead to the destruction of white property. In Dundee division farmers warned the local magistrate that if war broke out blacks would begin looting and destroying their farms, and on 18 October a public meeting of mostly Boer farmers in Kranskop demanded of the government that it was imperative 'to provide substantial aid in the shape of Police in this Division for the protection of property'. There was alarm at the gathering that livestock on white farms in the neighbourhood of African locations would be plundered, a register was opened for the names of those settlers willing to enrol in a local militia, and arrangements made for improving the defences of the local laager.[11]

In the light of fears such as these F. R. Moor, the Secretary for Native

Affairs, began to take action. As much information as possible was to be collected by magistrates and intelligence officers about rivalries between African groups. Accordingly, instructions were issued that black people should be 'invited or induced to volunteer information on matters generally . . . [with] pointed reference to the present political crisis'.[12] The information collected was wildly inaccurate and exaggerated, but sufficiently worrying to provoke Moor to warn a number of magistrates that 'From confidential reports received there seems to be a possibility of inter-tribal disturbances to avenge old-standing mutual grievances. Be on your guard, and if you have a laager you should see that it is put into a good defensible condition as a rallying point in the event of panic.'[13] It is interesting to note that only 2410 men from Natal were recruited for military service – less than one in five of whites of military age – even though during the early stages of the war Natal was the theatre of the most intensive military operations.

If some colonists feared that the outbreak of war was likely to usher in a new period of hostility between black and white, then equally many Zulu distrusted the intentions of both the Boers and the British, and also other Zulu groups. In August Dinuzulu applied for 500 rounds of ammunition because he had heard reports that the Boers intended to kidnap him. However, most concern was directed towards the intentions of the Usuthu, the followers of the Zulu royal lineage, and the Mandlakazi, the principal opponents of the Usuthu during the civil war between 1879 and 1884. Mandlakazi forces had been routed by Dinuzulu with Boer help in 1884 and defeated once more in 1888. The roots of conflict ran deep between the Usuthu and Mandlakazi, whose interests were supported unswervingly by the Natal administration. The conflict in 1888 had led to the enforced exile of Dinuzulu to St Helena in the following year. In essence, as Jeff Guy has shown, the conflict between the Usuthu and Mandlakazi was a struggle between 'representatives of the old Zulu order working for the revival of the kingdom, and those trying to ensure political division as a prerequisite for subordination to capitalist production'. The years between 1888 and 1899 had witnessed the further undermining of the economic self-sufficiency of the former Zulu state.[14]

On the eve of war the magistrate at Hlabisa noted that ever since the return of Dinuzulu there had been 'a steady growing unsettled feeling amongst the people . . . one tribe is afraid that the other at any time may make a surprise attack and kill their Chief'.[15] The magistrate at Nquthu suggested that the Zulu were talking openly of revenge and an attempt being made by the Usuthu to reclaim lost territory in the New Republic should war with Britain engage the attention of the Boer settlers there. In Emthonjaneni information circulated that Zibhebhu, the Mandlakazi chief, had signified his intention to remove with his followers into the Transvaal where a location had been set apart for him, and that the Boers were prepared to assist him in 'wiping out' the Usuthu.[16] The most articulate expression of the rumour was recounted to the magistrate in the Lower Tugela division by Martin Luthuli, who in the 1880s had been Dinuzulu's secretary and was the uncle of Albert Luthuli.

Quite recently the Chief Sibepu [Zibhebhu] of Zululand had taken a number of young cattle into the Transvaal for the purpose of exchanging them for heifers, and whilst he was in the Transvaal he conferred with the Amabunu [Boer] authorities with a view to helping them in the event of trouble arising. Sibepu's people now style him as an 'Isiula' [fool] . . . In the course of conversation with the Chief Magidi of this District, the Chief said it is quite true what is said about Sibepu. Quite recently Sibepu sent over his induna named Skizana to confer with the Amabunu with a view to overthrowing Dinuzulu.[17]

Such stories may have been spread by the Usuthu to discredit Zibhebhu. Certainly nothing came of any Boer–Mandlakazi plans that might have been made. Indeed, at the beginning of November Zibhebhu reported to the magistrate at Ubombo that he feared an imminent Usuthu–Boer attack on the Mandlakazi, and he was reported to have moved some of his cattle eastwards into the location of a neighbouring chief for safety.[18]

The commandeering by the Boers in Vryheid district of Zulu cattle and horses, and the taking away of Zulu adolescents as servants to accompany families on their journey from isolated farmsteads into Vryheid, worsened relations between the Boer farming community and Zulu in the New Republic. Further unrest was caused by the conscription of Zulu labourers and cattle-guards to accompany the local commando. The methods of Boer mobilisation became an issue which the Natal government could not choose to ignore, since a number of Zulu crossed the frontier to lay their grievances before Dinuzulu, which immediately called into question the practicality in time of crisis of denying Dinuzulu's followers from outside his district access to him without official consent, one of the conditions laid down for his return to Zululand. As early as September Zulu from the New Republic had begun entering the province to seek protection from Boer recruiters. Dinuzulu on a number of occasions drew the attention of the Zululand administration to the maltreatment of his people in the Vryheid district, indicating that 'although [their] country was given to the Boers they consider themselves as much subjects of Her Majesty the Queen as any Englishman resident in [the] Transvaal Republic'.[19] On 18 October a deputation of eight Zulu representatives from different parts of Vryheid district, accompanied by Dinuzulu, visited Gibson at Nongoma to seek the advice of the Zululand administration on the issue of Boer oppression. Dinuzulu was especially concerned because cattle belonging to the Qulusi, one of the most important royal sections, had been confiscated by commandos. Saunders was impressed by the restraint shown by the Zulu towards the Boers, and in a letter to Sir Albert Hime, the Prime Minister of Natal (1899–1903), he suggested this was attributable to Dinuzulu's calming influence.

Nothing could have been more calculated to goad these Zulus into open rebellion than the treatment they have been subjected to at the hands of the Boers who have seized their children and cattle and flogged the people when they remonstrated, but notwithstanding this, they have, on Dinuzulu's advice, remained perfectly quiet . . . For this reason, apart from any other, I think

Dinuzulu's case is worthy of special consideration with a view to his receiving compensation for any loss he may have sustained when hostilities cease.[20]

At the Colonial Office Sir Frederick Graham minuted that when the war was over Dinuzulu's loyalty and discretion should not be forgotten.[21]

THE BOER INVASION OF NATAL AND ZULULAND

The movement of Boer forces into Natal in October 1899 and the occupation of the northern divisions of the colony caused a tide of refugees to sweep towards the coast, mostly workers from the coal-mining industry of Newcastle and Dundee. Above all, however, the Boer invasion created circumstances in which the neutrality or partisanship of the black communities in the occupied divisions would be tested. At Pomeroy the evacuation of the town immediately before a Boer raiding party entered the locality brought about a temporary breakdown of authority. The scene when the Boers had departed was described by the Rev. James Dalzell.

About 3 [o'clock] word was brought to me that the Boers had left and that natives were looting the stores at Pomeroy. At once we saddled and rode over . . . On the way I saw dense smoke rising from the government buildings, but on arrival my attention was first taken up by the looting of the stores by the natives, especially young men and lads and women old and young . . . Ultimately I found four native policemen – they had their badges off and were standing looking at the looting, not one of them doing anything to prevent it . . . The Post Office was in such a state that I knew nothing of it. The natives have done the rest. Young men were heard shouting 'Burn the tronk: that's where they imprison us.'[22]

Helpmekaar nearby was occupied by the Boers and its stores looted. The invaders sent for Kula, a government-appointed chief, to make it known that he and his people were answerable not to the government of Natal but to the Boers. Kula fled.[23]

In the occupied divisions the Boers generally took every precaution to maintain authority over the local African communities. In Newcastle the Rev. J. J. A. Prozesky of the Dutch Reformed Church Mission Station at Muller's Pass was appointed superintendent over the black population, and notices were issued under his signature that the division had been incorporated into the South African Republic. (Afterwards he was fined £500 and sentenced to twelve months' imprisonment by the Natal government.[24]) Stern action was taken by the Boers against Africans who took up arms against other black groups, or who were suspected of passing on intelligence to the British. A system of forced labour was introduced to recruit workers for service with the commandos or with the occupying administration. In Dundee a meeting of chiefs and *induna* was called on 3 December to instruct them that burghers who required remounts should be provided with fresh horses; oxen, needed by the Boers for draught purposes, were to be exchanged for two head of cattle. In January the Boers announced their intention of doing away with existing

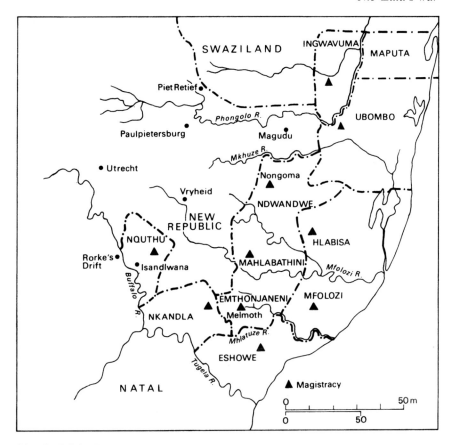

Map 5 Zululand

taxation and instead imposing a poll tax of £1 per homestead-head, which, it was pointed out, was lower than the tax levied by the Natal government, and thereby represented proof of the Boers' intention to deal with Africans more leniently (the Natal government levied an annual tax of 14s payable on each hut in a homestead and on any wife who did not possess a hut of her own).[25]

The Natal government feared that the loyalty of Zulu in those areas occupied by the Boers would be placed under considerable stress. At the beginning of 1900 Moor wrote to the Prime Minister,

> I am of opinion that the allegiance of many of the natives in this Colony cannot be relied on when once the enemy has occupation of the country they occupy; and I am also of the opinion that this is owing to fear on the part of the natives, and a desire to ingratiate themselves with the Dutch for their own safety.[26]

However, of the major chiefs in the Dundee–Umsinga region – Dumisa, Sandanezwe and Bande – only Sandanezwe appears to have given substantial

81

support to the Boers. Dumisa charged him with volunteering to provide scouts for the occupying forces, and having signed an agreement of friendship with the Boers,[27] though it is possible both Dumisa and Bande may have attempted to discredit Sandanezwe by portraying him to the Natal government as a 'collaborator'. Nevertheless it was widely rumoured that Sandanezwe had been provided by the Boers with a European's house in Dundee and, unlike Dumisa and Bande, he did not send secret reports of events in the occupied districts to the government through the magistrate's office at Weenen.

Dumisa's intelligence work was regarded as reliable and valuable. The chief's reports, usually written by one of his aides, Z. M. Masuku, were passed on by the magistrate at Weenen to F. R. Moor, who then forwarded the information to the military authorities. Dumisa also kept a diary of events, which after the Boer withdrawal from Dundee was sent for perusal to the Native Affairs Department in Pietermaritzburg, and the governor even offered to send a copy to the Colonial Office for Chamberlain's inspection. When the invasion was eventually repulsed Dumisa requested that he be allowed to take over a number of abandoned Boer farms in the region in return for his intelligence work. The request was turned down.[28]

The letters of Dumisa and other Zulu to the Natal government during the Boer occupation suggest that the Boers' policy of living off the land in the invaded territories, and the commandos' arbitrary methods of maintaining law and order, gave rise to widespread disenchantment. Untiloyi, one of Bande's followers in the Umsinga division, complained that his people were greatly in want of food since the Boers had commandeered grain supplies. The Boers were also accused of 'taking horses cruelly'.[29] Sayimana complained that many atrocities against blacks had been committed by the occupying forces; 'Natives are thrashed without cause,' he noted, 'going to court for a native simply means going for a thrashing.' He alleged, too, that black workers who had come with the invading forces had stolen mealies and illicitly sold them to people from neighbouring homesteads. By February and March many Zulu were said to be refusing to provide labour for the Boers, or deserting on a large scale from their service.[30]

Although Saunders had argued before the beginning of the war that a Boer invasion of Zululand was unlikely, officials in the province could not close their eyes to the possibility that a movement of Boer troops in their direction might take place, and during the first week of the war intelligence sources warned of the intention of the Boers to move across Zululand from Vryheid in order to raid Pietermaritzburg and Durban. The threat of a determined Boer invasion was made to appear more of a reality following a lightning strike by the Boers on a trading store at Mhlatuze in Nkandla district, and by the burning on 29 October of the magistrate's office at Ingwavuma, evacuated only ten minutes before. On 3 November the Ingwavuma district was taken possession of by 400 commandos led by Commandant Ferreira. The magistrate, B. Colenbrander, and his staff, together with ten white constables and twenty-five Zulu policemen, retreated to Ubombo, having initially fled into the Nhlati forest, where for a week they depended on the hospitality of chief Sambane and his people, who had provisioned their strongholds in anticipation of an attack from across the Transvaal frontier.[31]

Throughout the final weeks of 1899 the Zulu lived in expectation of a Boer invasion. On 30 November a deputation of Nquthu chiefs warned the magistrate that should a Boer sortie be made into the district their men would attack the invaders, since in the absence of troops they considered it their duty to protect the Queen's property. Chief Mehlokazulu spent the night of 13 December on Nquthu hill with 250 armed men, prepared if necessary to defend the magistrate's building. Rumours that the Boers planned to take Dinuzulu hostage for the good conduct of the Zulu during the war encouraged many men to travel to the Osuthu, Dinuzulu's headquarters at Nongoma, to take part in its defence. By 24 December Saunders reported (with some dismay) that 500 Zulu from the Transvaal were dispersed in the neighbourhood of Nongoma.[32] Many of those who came were followers of Kambi, the son of the Ngenetsheni chief, Hamu, who had defected to the British in 1879 and had supported the Mandlakazi against the Usuthu during the civil war, but much of whose lands had been incorporated in the New Republic.

At the end of December and beginning of January two more Boer raids into Zululand were made when trading stores at Rorke's Drift and Vaant's Drift were looted. On the first occasion Tlokoa from Nquthu assembled at the magistrate's office and pursued the raiders out of the district.[33] These incursions prompted the military to send into Nquthu a force of Colonial Scouts under Colonel R. H. Addison, the former Resident Magistrate of the district, a move that was also designed to serve as a diversion to assist the forces of General Buller, who was preparing to mount an assault on Boer positions on the lower Tugela river. The decision to send Addison into Nquthu was taken without consulting either the Hime ministry or the administration in Zululand, and the arrival of the force immediately drew protests from ministers and from Saunders at Eshowe, who suggested to Hime that Addison's men ran the danger of being mistaken by the Zulu for a Boer contingent, and that their presence in Zululand would encourage a build-up of Boer forces on the border and make it even more likely that there would be further raids into the province, and perhaps even an occupation. This in fact happened. During January Boer troops amassed on the Nquthu border. On 31 January 600 commandos led by Ferreira invaded Nquthu and moved on to occupy Nkandla as well.[34] Nkandla was recaptured on 24 February; Nquthu was not finally cleared of republican forces until May.

The Boer invasion of Zululand strained relations between the Natal and British governments. On 8 February the Natal cabinet issued a warning to the government in London through the governor, Sir Walter Hely-Hutchinson, that ministers could no longer hold themselves responsible for the continuation of the peaceful attitude of the Zulu, whom, they believed, would rapidly become disillusioned with the measures taken for their protection, and were likely, therefore, either to come to an understanding with the occupying forces, or, more probably, take into their own hands the defence of the remaining districts of Zululand.[35] Events at once took a new turn when a letter from Kruger to Dinuzulu was revealed and a copy sent to Saunders and eventually to the Colonial Office. The letter read:

> I have understood you have taken weapons in your hands fighting against the Boers and as this war is not between black and white or civilised against uncivilised it is not right of Her Majesty's Government to cause you to fight against us . . . If commandos require food or anything else from blacks and take it, Field Cornets must give owner, or person from whom he takes it, receipt; then owner can obtain payment for it from Government, for it is not promised by an individual but by a Government. And now the war is not to cause injury to black or white but to maintain rights of people of Transvaal Republic and Orange Free State: as soon as Her Majesty's Government are prepared to acknowledge those rights and no longer to try to oppress us and drive out African Boers as they have hitherto done, then there will be peace on African soil and there is room enough for all as well for whites as for blacks so long as English leave us alone, but so long as English aim at being masters of the whole world, so long will there be no peace on earth . . . If you keep quiet and at rest and do not involve yourselves in this war then all others of your people will be released but if you go forth to fight against us then they shall bear the burden, I have tried to make it all clear and to warn you.[36]

Chamberlain suggested that in those districts not under Boer occupation it would be of benefit to organise the Zulu into military units led by British special service officers, similar in purpose and organisation to the groups of African levies mobilised to defend the Transkei.[37] The Hime ministry, however, opposed this because it would represent a departure from the principle of excluding blacks from taking part in military operations. Instead ministers advocated that a despatch be sent to the Boer governments warning that any aggressive action taken by the Zulu would be entirely the republics' responsibility.[38] In March the Natal government urged that a military force be sent to Zululand to drive out the Boers from Nquthu district and restore the confidence of the Zulu in the British army.

Although a despatch to Kruger was drafted and discussed at the Colonial Office, the communiqué was not sent because, according to Graham, 'It would not keep the Boers out of Zululand and it may give them an excuse to attack the natives and commit the depredations which in their message to Dinuzulu they say they will not commit.'[39] General Buller also refused to send a detachment to the province on the basis that he had no men to spare and that 'the Zulus should be encouraged to defend themselves'. Instead a system of espionage was established in Ndwandwe and in the valleys of the Mkhuze and Phongolo rivers under the supervision of Colenbrander working with ten Zulu spies, since Buller feared that when the Boers were eventually driven out of Natal contingents of the Vryheid and Piet Retief commandos might attempt to create a fragmentary republic with a port at Kosi or St Lucia Bay. The Natal government considered the possibility remote.[40]

The responsibility for the administration of the occupied districts of Nquthu and Nkandla was entrusted to Veldkornets I. J. van den Berg and H. Potgieter. Although widespread looting occurred during the Boer invasion, Van den Berg and Potgieter attempted rapidly to restore normality to the region. Van den Berg announced that the districts had been annexed by the South African Republic; that chiefs were to exercise the same authority under the new regime as under the old one; that he wished Zulu policemen who had fled to return to perform their normal duties; and that Zulu having claims against others could sue before him at once. It was made known that in March taxes would be collected at the rate of 7s a hut, half the existing rate.[41] According to Maxwell, the magistrate at Melmoth, the Boers made every effort 'to conciliate the natives so as to prevent them rising to defend themselves'.[42] Zulu were permitted to buy mealies and meat brought into the occupied districts from the Transvaal, to share in some of the spoils of the looting during the initial invasion, and food was distributed to those in need.[43] Van den Berg is reputed to have announced to the Zulu at Nkandla that

> the Boers proclaimed Mpande king, and he reigned in peace, and died of old age, whereas Cetshwayo, who was crowned king by the English, was very soon destroyed by the English, and they the Boers intend to crown Dinuzulu king over the whole native population, and there would be only two kings in the whole of the land – Paul over the whites, and Dinuzulu over the blacks.[44]

Unlike in the occupied divisions of Natal, the Boers in Zululand appear to have been much more cautious about commandeering livestock and conscripting men to perform military labour.

Chiefs Mehlokazulu, Nongamulana and Sitshitshili fled in the wake of the Boer invasion: Mehlokazulu since he was suspected of arming his men to withstand the occupation; Nongamulana because he had arrested a Boer spy in Zululand at the beginning of the war; and Sitshitshili on account of having warned J. L. Knight at Nkandla of the movement of Boer troops in his direction, thereby enabling him, unlike C. F. Hignett at Nquthu, to avoid capture by the commandos. With these major exceptions, however, most Zulu remained peacefully at their homesteads (though a regular system of intelligence soon developed between the occupied districts and Eshowe). When the occupation was over Nongamulana described how he had been informed at his place of hiding that the Zulu were going in large numbers to the Boers in both Nquthu and Nkandla to receive gifts of grain, beef and looted goods.[45] Hignett believed the Zulu's readiness to cooperate with the Boers stemmed from the scarcity of food in Nquthu, since 'at the time they came . . . [the Zulu] were suffering from the pangs of hunger'.[46]

The Boer occupation came at a time of crisis in food production and supply throughout most of Zululand, and the reaction of the Zulu both to the war and to the Boer invasion must be seen against this backcloth. By the close of the century the economic foundations of the Zulu homestead system of production had begun seriously to crumble as a consequence of the imposition of colonial rule and the introduction in 1888 of an annual hut tax. Throughout the 1890s labour migration from Zululand increased on a large scale, economic wealth and power in Zulu society grew more unequal, and it became progressively more difficult for young men to obtain sufficient *lobolo* cattle to marry and establish independent homesteads. The decade was one, too, of damaging natural disasters from which the ailing Zulu economy was unable fully to recover. Locusts almost entirely ruined the 1894–5 grain crop; in the following year drought conditions produced a serious short-fall in homestead production; and in 1897 rinderpest entered Zululand and destroyed about 85 per cent of Zulu cattle. The number of labour migrants leaving the province rose sharply, and further difficulties emerged in the collection of the annual hut tax.[47]

Against this background came war, the dislocation of the migrant labour system and another poor harvest in 1899–1900. By the turn of the century grain was especially scarce in the Nkandla, Nquthu and Emthonjaneni districts. In Nquthu the Rev. Charles Johnson described a 'terrible famine', caused at first by a disappointing harvest but exacerbated by 'having so many more people to feed' in view of the large number of younger men who had re-turned home from the gold mines (an indication of the extent to which the Zulu economy had come to depend on the absence of migrant workers and the cash they earned).[48] The situation was made more serious still by the inability of storekeepers to obtain supplies of grain from outside Zululand because of the cessation of work by Boer transport-riders, and by the British army's commandeering of waggons and draught animals. Some traders were also reluctant to purchase grain from outside in case their stores were raided by the Boers.[49] In Britain the Aborigines' Protection Society established a Zululand Relief Fund which raised £500 to buy food for distribution in the province, and the Native Affairs department of the Natal government set up a relief committee to purchase mealies and transport them to the areas where food was especially scarce.[50] Many homesteads had insufficient cash to pay for relief and had little choice but to buy grain on credit. When a consignment of mealies arrived at Nkandla on 19 December the hundred sacks were distributed in only an hour.[51] At the beginning of 1900 Dinuzulu warned Saunders that his people would have great difficulty paying their taxes because of widespread unemployment and because the Zulu's need to purchase additional food had eaten away their financial resources.[52]

For many ordinary Zulu in Nquthu and Nkandla the Boer occupation, the distribution of food by the invading forces, the opportunities for sharing loot and the promise of a halving of the annual hut tax, must have seemed a godsend. Nongamulana noted that 'People seem to have settled down quite comfortably under the Boers and are happy.'[53]

The good relations between the Zulu and the occupying Boer forces was little more than a marriage of convenience, however. In the wake of the commandos' retreat from Zululand and vacation of large areas of Vryheid district in May and June 1900, Zulu from Nquthu and Nkandla, as well as from other districts of Zululand bordering on the Transvaal, took part in swiftly organised and well-executed cattle-raiding expeditions into the New Republic. Cattle-rustling from Boer farms in Vryheid district occurred on an unprecedented scale, and prompted strict instructions from Saunders that on no account were raiding parties from the province to cross the Transvaal border.[54] Hely-Hutchinson cabled General Buller at the end of May to inform him that the Zulu were 'getting out of hand', and urged that troops be moved quickly into the area. To Sir Alfred Milner he wrote that if the widespread looting of cattle by the Zulu continued 'we might find it difficult to restore and keep order amongst them after the war'. It would not be the last time during the war that dire consequences were predicted if Zulu cattle-rustling from Boer farms in the New Republic was not brought to an end.[55]

THE ZULU AND THE GUERRILLA WAR

Once the Boer occupation of Natal and Zululand was over Dinuzulu furnished the British army with an ever-increasing number of scouts and guides. Some men worked locally, reporting on events in Vryheid district and relaying their information through the offices of government officials in Zululand. The effectiveness of the Zulu intelligence network was founded upon the cooperation of Zulu in the Transvaal, who provided spies with information and gave them shelter and food while they remained in potentially hostile territory. Other Zulu were sent directly to the British army in Natal. After despatching a group of scouts to Buller's camp in May 1900 Dinuzulu wrote to the general, 'If you continue your good treatment you will find no better men to act as scouts as these . . . they know the country well and are brave men.' Buller was evidently impressed by the Zulu, and in July Colonel H. E. Sandbach wrote to Dinuzulu on Buller's behalf that 'Your men are excellent scouts and do very good work.'[56]

Dinuzulu's close relations with the military soon became an important source of friction between the Natal government and the British army. Early in 1901 a large British column led by General French began moving through the southeastern Transvaal, destroying farm buildings, burning crops and seizing Boer livestock. It was appreciated that the frontier between Zululand and the Transvaal would need to be sealed if Boer farmers were to be prevented from driving livestock into the province to avoid capture, and on 3 February Kitchener authorised Colonel H. Bottomley to raise a small body of men to assist the Zulu to accomplish this. His instructions, however, went further. Dinuzulu and other chiefs were also to be encouraged to provide men whose responsibility it would be, under military supervision, to drive into Zululand cattle which might otherwise supply the guerrillas with animals for slaughter and draught purposes. Bottomley's force was to operate for three months; it was to act independently of the General Officer Commanding Natal, General Hildyard; and it was to be self-supporting, its principal objective the seizure of Boer cattle. Of the animals captured 65 per cent would become the property of Bottomley's force, 10 per cent would be retained by the Zulu in return for their cooperation, and the remaining 25 per cent handed over to the British army.[57] On 26 March Bottomley arrived in Zululand and at once assigned military agents to the border districts to organise the operation.

The freedom of action given to Bottomley and the planned role of the Zulu in the scheme were bitterly criticised by Saunders and ministers in Pietermaritzburg. According to Hime, the course being pursued by the military was 'fraught with dangers; it will result in complications the full extent of which it is difficult to foresee, and it can only have been adopted in ignorance of the antecedents of the Zulu people, of the delicate and diplomatic handling they require, and of their intricate and complicated inter-tribal relations.'[58] General Hildyard believed Bottomley was 'going too far' in not planning to issue orders through magistrates, and he appreciated that the Zulu would probably be provided with opportunities to raid cattle in the Transvaal on their own initiative, as they already had done on a number of occasions. But he wrote to Hime, 'I am satisfied Bottomley may be trusted to carry out his instructions to the best of his power. Interference with him now can lead to no good results.'[59]

Even before Bottomley's scheme was planned to commence, on 4 April, groups of Zulu again began to cross the frontier to raid livestock from the New Republic. On 1 April chief Nqodi, with a party of armed men, crossed into Vryheid district under the cover of darkness and returned with 500 cattle and 600 sheep, some of the cattle belonging to a German settler in the district. On the following night a Buthelezi force made a similar foray across the border. Dinuzulu responded to Bottomley's operation with considerable enthusiasm. A 1500-strong *impi* (regiment) was formed that became known as the 'Nkomindala' and was based at Nongoma. By 4 April Dinuzulu reported the *impi* had already raided 200 cattle, and on the same day he informed Bottomley's agent at the Osuthu that he wanted British troops 'to work down towards Magudu and engage the enemy so as to give me a chance to raid their stock'. In spite of Bottomley's cheerful zeal that the Zulu should give the Boers 'a hot time', Dinuzulu's men showed great reluctance to engage the enemy, probably because the *impi* was not well-endowed with firepower. The most significant engagement took place at a hill known as the Dhleke, where quantities of firearms were seized from the Boers with the loss of only two men. Other Zulu chiefs also participated in Bottomley's enterprise; Mehlokazulu, Sitshitshili, Nongamulana, Zibhebhu and Kambi all organised sorties into the Transvaal to bring back livestock from Boer farms. Under the cover of the operation small-scale cattle-raiding also occurred between the Usuthu and Mandlakazi.[60]

The unfolding of events in Zululand during April and May seemed to confirm the worst fears of officials in Zululand. From the beginning of the operation magistrates had sought without success to frustrate Bottomley's scheme by ordering that no *impi* was to cross the frontier. 'Let no person under me dare any longer to set foot across the boundary', the magistrate at Nongoma told Dinuzulu on 6 April, 'you are to obey the orders *of me only*.'[61] Saunders was convinced Dinuzulu would seize the opportunity of sending bodies of armed men into the Transvaal to resume effective control over Zulu homesteads there, people over whom, according to the conditions laid down for his return from exile, he was to have no authority whatsoever. Saunders was suspicious, too, that Dinuzulu was covertly extending his authority in the province as well, and when Bottomley contacted the magistrate in Mahlabathini to request that he send an armed group of Tshanibezwe's Buthelezi to form part of Dinuzulu's force, he interpreted this as yet 'another attempt on Dinuzulu's part . . . to assume control over people under other chiefs'. The implications of Bottomley's activities so alarmed Saunders that, in protest, he proposed withdrawing magistrates from the border districts of Zululand altogether.[62]

Pressure on the British army to withdraw Bottomley's force quickly built up, not only from the Natal government but from the Colonial Office as well. Kitchener was enraged. He possessed little respect for civilian sensibilities, still less for those of Natal settlers, and pointed out that it was only by such methods that the war would be brought speedily to an end.

> The military position is that it is necessary to clear the country of stock and that troops are very much hampered in their operations in doing so. Moreover the help of Natives for this purpose is valuable and I would request all Magistrates to give their utmost assistance and encouragement to help to terminate the war.

He continued by claiming that those Zulu who had crossed the border had done so unarmed and under close supervision (though this was patently untrue), and that ministers in Natal had 'apparently taken civil statements as accurate without as far as I know any proof, and have entirely ignored denials'.[63]

On 6 June Bottomley's enterprise was nonetheless brought to an end. By this time British columns had left the region, and during the three weeks preceding the order there had been only a small number of Zulu expeditions into the Transvaal. Bottomley remained in the area to supervise the allocation of livestock to the Zulu and to send the remaining cattle to market at Durban and Pietermaritzburg. Estimates vary widely about the number of livestock taken from the Transvaal. Barnabas Brecher, a settler in Vryheid, later testified that it was common talk the Nkomindala had raided 48,000 cattle during April, while Coenraad Meyer put the figure at only 1200 cattle and 2000 sheep.[64] From the very limited evidence available it seems likely that at least 10,000 cattle were brought back to Zululand, together with a few thousand sheep. According to the terms of the scheme the Zulu should have been allowed to retain only 10 per cent of the seized livestock, but it is evident they received a rather more generous share, especially since some of the cattle taken were never formally declared to the military. Officials in Zululand urged that the cattle kept by the Zulu should be converted into cash to avoid giving

Boer farmers the opportunity to contest their ownership once the war was over. The cattle acquired by the Zulu were of value in helping to replenish herds devastated by rinderpest, though some of the seized animals were infected with lungsickness and had to be destroyed.[65]

In October Bottomley prepared finally to leave the region, sending back to the Osuthu those Zulu who remained directly under his command. Dinuzulu was bitterly disheartened.

> I am very much disappointed and if a column was sent up this way the war would soon be brought to an end, but . . . it appears that you do not wish this war to come to an end which will cause great oppression on the Natives in the SAR Dist. General Botha has two farms in this country . . . he is very much acquainted with the country as he was once Field Cornet. Some of my scouts report that General Botha is still in the Vryheid Dist. as he has been seen by Natives who report that he sent message calling all the Boers together, he has not left the country as it is thought. If a column was sent this way which would connect with the troops operating at the Pongola . . . Botha could be cornered . . . I beg that you should have an interview with General Commanding troops and point this to him, so as also to save the Natives from destruction.[66]

The Zulu forces on the frontier were disbanded except in Ndwandwe, where Dinuzulu and Zibhebhu were instructed to keep small bodies of men on patrol. Dinuzulu was officially requested to disband the Nkomindala, though the magistrate at Nongoma told him that if it was found impossible to disperse members of the force immediately he would 'just keep silent'.[67]

THE HOLKRANS INCIDENT

The southeastern Transvaal and Zululand remained relatively quiet between the end of September 1901 (when a force led by General Botha was defeated by the British at Itala close to the Nkandla border) and March 1902. New efforts were then made by Kitchener's forces to root out the 500 guerrillas led by Botha who at the end of February returned to the Vryheid district, an area described after the war as 'the despair of British generals' because of its hilly and wooded terrain which permitted small bands of Boers to evade even the most intensive drives of the British columns. On 5 March General Bruce Hamilton arrived at Vryheid with a large force. At once he contacted Dinuzulu to send 250 men to join his column at Ngenetsheni to help in the work of capturing Boer livestock. With Saunders's permission an *impi* led by Ndabuko, Ndabankulu and Gilbert, Dinuzulu's secretary, was sent to Bruce Hamilton, though the force exceeded the number of men requested since, Dinuzulu explained, it was to operate in Boer country and therefore needed to have the strength to withstand a determined attack. The Zulu were armed with assegais, and a number carried firearms, though neither arms nor ammunition were supplied by the military. When the force reached Ngenetsheni the *impi* was placed under the general command of a British intelligence officer, F. J. Symmonds. The Zulu were instructed to march alongside the British column, collect livestock and take prisoner any guerrillas they intercepted. During operations the regiment was joined by a Qulusi *impi* of between 700 and 800 men. By the end of the month, however, it was evident that the exercise had been no more successful than earlier attempts to clear the region of guerrilla groups. The Zulu were instructed to return to Vryheid, where they were accommodated in the station buildings before being ordered to travel back to Zululand with a gift of 100 cattle that were described by Ndabuko as 'thin and mangy oxen . . . no longer fit for transport work' (in fact most of the animals were infected with rinderpest and had to be disposed of for slaughter at once). The failure of the operation and the refusal of the army to pay the Zulu individually for their work added to the general mood of disappointment and frustration felt by Zulu on both sides of the border.[68]

The operations during March precipitated a complete breakdown in the relations between the Vryheid guerrilla bands and the Qulusi, who had provided valuable intelligence to Dinuzulu's spies throughout the war and had joined his force accompanying Bruce Hamilton's column. Relations between the Boer farming community and the Zulu in Vryheid district had been strained from the beginning of the war as a result of the conscription of Zulu to accompany the republican forces (in June 1900 Dinuzulu had presented J. Y. Gibson with a report listing the names of 226 Zulu aged between six and twenty-five who had been forced to join the Vryheid commando);[69] the seizure of Zulu livestock and grain; and the ruthless intimidation of homesteads to counter the intensive intelligence network controlled by Dinuzulu from inside Zululand. The Zulu reacted by occupying farms, closing their neighbourhoods to guerrilla penetration, and cooperating with British troops in the area. Not surprisingly vendettas developed between individuals over which the commando leaders had almost no control. Relations were especially difficult between Veldkornet J. A. Potgieter and the Qulusi chief, Sikhobobo.

At the end of April the greater part of the Vryheid and Utrecht commandos, on the orders of General Botha, razed Sikhobobo's homestead at Qulusini, seized 3800 head of cattle and 1000 sheep and goats, and drove the chief and his people to seek shelter and protection with the British garrison at Vryheid. It was only a matter of days before the Boer assault on the Qulusi was avenged. On the evening of 5 May Sikhobobo informed the magistrate at Vryheid, A. J. Shepstone, that he was taking a party of men outside the town to attempt to recover some of the stolen cattle. That night a Qulusi *impi* of 300 men fell upon the Boer encampment at Holkrans (Ntatshana), twelve miles from Vryheid, killing fifty-six of the seventy guerrillas, most of them local farmers, and driving off the cattle at the camp. Fifty-two members of the *impi* were killed and forty-eight wounded. It was afterwards rumoured that the body of Veldkornet Potgieter had received forty-five assegai wounds.

Botha subsequently referred to the Qulusi assault as the 'foulest deed of the war', and an account of the episode that appeared many years later in the *Natal Mercury* described it as 'one of the darkest tragedies ever enacted on

South African soil' and compared the incident to the assassination of Retief's party by Dingane.[70] The assault at Holkrans was followed by an enquiry conducted by Colonel G. A. Mills on the orders of the British government. A large volume of evidence was collected about the ways in which the war had borne down upon Zulu homesteads in Vryheid district. Receipts had rarely been given for horses and cattle requisitioned by the commandos; frequent raids had been made on Zulu livestock in reprisal for cattle-rustling, desertion from Boer service and supplying livestock to the British forces; and many Zulu had been executed without trial either for carrying weapons or on suspicion of being British collaborators. General Emmett testified that the commando leaders had found it impossible to control effectively the actions of their men, some of whom had raided Zulu cattle either to exercise revenge on individual chiefs or to enrich themselves at the expense of the Zulu. Mills's report concluded: 'The war has undoubtedly pressed very heavily on the Kaffirs, as they have had to practically feed the Boer commandos . . . Enormous numbers of cattle and stock have been taken, and many Zulu, particularly Sikhobobo's tribe, are practically destitute of stock through no fault of their own.'[71]

It is not immediately clear why Botha ordered the destruction of Qulusini in the almost certain knowledge that it would bring about an escalation of existing tensions. The attack took place only three weeks before the end of the war, at a time when arrangements were already being made for the meeting of Boer representatives to discuss the possibility of accepting peace terms, and when an informal truce between the British and guerrilla forces existed in the Vryheid district (which possibly explains why no sentries were posted by the Boers to guard the encampment at Holkrans). Botha himself testified that the operation had simply been in retaliation for frequent attacks made on his men by the Qulusi, and he described how it had 'become very dangerous for despatch riders to pass along the road without a strong escort because they were continually being fired on by Kaffirs hidden among the rocks'.[72] Another reason appears to have been the pressure on Botha from some of his subordinates, especially Veldkornet Potgieter, for action to be taken against the Qulusi. Settlers in Vryheid probably argued that it would be expedient finally 'to teach the Qulusi a lesson' before the opportunity was lost when the war was over. A more intriguing explanation was put forward by some Boers at the time, namely, that Botha had razed Qulusini 'to incite the Natives to rise in order to frighten the Boers of the Vryheid District into surrendering'.[73] Since Botha could not have expected that the assault on the Qulusi would end in the manner that it did at Holkrans, it is conceivable (though only just) that he may have wished to draw attention to the difficulties of the Boers in their relations with black communities. This was certainly a powerful argument that Botha (and others) used to persuade the republican representatives at Vereeniging that the time had arrived for their forces to accept a negotiated peace settlement.

Boer suspicions of Shepstone's complicity in Sikhobobo's assault were not allayed by Mills's report, which concluded there was 'no doubt that Mr

Shepstone knew late on the evening of the 5th May, that Sikhobobo meant to go to Holkrans to try to retake his cattle and that he did not tell the OC Vryheid that Sikhobobo meant to go out'.[74] Botha demanded to know why Shepstone had not tried to prevent the Qulusi from leaving Vryheid, and made a number of efforts to have an exhaustive and impartial commission appointed to reinvestigate the whole affair. The British government, however, was satisfied that Shepstone could have had no idea that Sikhobobo intended to go out in such force, nor that the chief contemplated an assault on a large number of Boers in close attack. Furthermore, the government endorsed Mills's opinion that it was questionable whether the OC Vryheid would, or indeed could, have prevented the exodus of the Qulusi even if he had been informed by Shepstone of the chief's intentions.[75]

Wartime events in the New Republic show some similarities with events in other regions of the Transvaal. The Boer mobilisation of labour and resources bore down heavily on the black inhabitants of the area, as they did elsewhere in the republic. Once the bulk of the commandos withdrew from the region in mid-1900 those Boers continuing the struggle experienced grave difficulties in their relations with African homesteads, in much the same way as the republican forces encountered problems in the western Transvaal and in the Lydenburg district (as we shall see in the next chapter). In a similar way to which tenants in the Rustenburg–Marico region were given support by Kgatla from the Bechuanaland Protectorate, so the Zulu in the New Republic received encouragement and assistance from Zululand in their resistance to the local white farming community. Boer cattle were plundered, many white farms were abandoned and left in the occupation of tenants, commando supplies had to be seized, the guerrillas had to operate in the knowledge that the British could rely on Zulu intelligence to monitor their movements, and burghers were on occasions harried by Zulu snipers. The breakdown of Boer–Qulusi relations was particularly marked, culminating as it did in the virtual wiping out in a single Qulusi assault of the Vryheid commando.

The material impact of war in Zululand was two-edged. On the one hand the flow of cattle into the province during the final two years of the war helped to replenish herds devastated by rinderpest in 1897. Military wages were good, and grain prices soared to the benefit of those with sufficient productive capacity to produce a surplus for sale. On the other hand the dislocation of the migrant labour system at the outbreak of war, coinciding with the poor harvest of 1899–1900 and escalating food prices, plunged many more families into a cycle of indebtedness, especially in the Nkandla, Nquthu and Emthonjaneni districts. As in other regions of South Africa, one of the most important influences of wartime conditions and the war economy seems to have been the acceleration of growing inequalities of wealth within African society.

By the end of the war Dinuzulu had exercised a degree of influence in Zululand and the New Republic that went far beyond the role formally set out in the terms for his return from St Helena. This was acknowledged by all the

Zululand officials. He had been permitted to organise the Usuthu for the defence of the Zululand border; he had assembled men to raid cattle in Vryheid both on his own initiative and in close collaboration with the British army; Zulu from the Transvaal (including at one time, Dinuzulu claimed, 'nearly all the headmen of the SAR') had taken refuge at the Osuthu when their lives seemed in peril across the frontier; and he had acted as an intermediary through whom Zulu in the New Republic had brought their grievances to the attention of the Natal and British governments.

Dinuzulu had little direct control over the wartime circumstances that thrust responsibilities upon him. He exercised remarkable skill nonetheless in playing off the military against the civil administration. To the military he consistently portrayed the Zulu in the Transvaal as his own subjects.[76] When Saunders admonished him for receiving too many unauthorised visitors from the Transvaal, Dinuzulu pointed out that he was 'one of the chief scouts doing good service to the government' and that many of those who came furnished him with intelligence reports.[77] At other times Dinuzulu attempted to create the impression to civil officials that he was cooperating only reluctantly with the military, yet his private correspondence reveals that he gave army officers his enthusiastic support. Later Dinuzulu tried to exploit the division between the civil and military authorities to obtain permission for a visit to Vryheid, and to recover cattle herds originally seized by the Boers during the 1880s. On both occasions he was chastised for having written directly to the military on civil matters without first seeking the approval of the magistrate at Nongoma.[78] Strained though the relations between the Natal government and the army undoubtedly were, they were sufficiently close for any correspondence to the army not directly concerning military affairs to be communicated to the civilian administration. Dinuzulu's influence was generally regarded with apprehension by whites in Zululand and Natal. The sentiments of many settlers were expressed by an anonymous correspondent, purporting to be 'a well-known Zululand resident', to the *Natal Mercury* on 15 October 1902. 'First, we are told, on Dinuzulu's return, that he was no longer Chief of the Zulus, but the same as other Chiefs – head of a tribe. But what are the facts? We find Dinuzulu today with far greater power than he ever had, extending not only in Zululand, but into Swaziland, Transvaal and Natal.'

Some interesting contrasts and comparisons with circumstances in Bechuanaland and Basutoland emerge from events during the war in Zululand. It is clear that the relationship between Dinuzulu and the Natal administration underwent some wartime changes. As in the cases of Khama and Lerotholi, the balance of power in Dinuzulu's relations with the colonial authorities shifted during the war to Dinuzulu's advantage because of the disruption to the peacetime system of colonial authority and because of the need for Zulu assistance in the British war effort. Dinuzulu was therefore able to demonstrate in a tangible way the important position he retained in Zulu society, regardless of the terms for his return from exile. Unlike the British-administered territories, however, Zululand since 1897 had been incorporated into a settler colony, Natal, whose government planned to open up the province to white settlement, and did so in the years after the war (in 1905, 2.6 million acres of Zululand – 40 per cent of the province's land area – were demarcated for white settlement). Another important difference, too, was that while Khama and Lerotholi had allied themselves with the colonial authorities as a means of maintaining and consolidating their dominant role in society, Dinuzulu's position in Zulu affairs was of a different nature. His influence was exercised in spite of the colonial administration not with its approval or support. Unable to come to terms with the enduring allegiance to the royal house of the majority of Zululand's population, colonists persisted in accounting for Dinuzulu's influence in a sinister way.[79]

The war was followed in Zululand and Natal by a period of intense suspicion between Africans and settlers about the intentions of the other. Rumour spread of an impending concerted black uprising on the one hand, and on the other that, with the war over, the whites were going to join forces to launch an offensive against the black population. Fuelled by post-war troop movements and economic depression, the prevalence of rumour was a sensitive barometer of group tension. It was in this atmosphere, and in the circumstances of the progressive impoverishment of large numbers of Zulu homesteads, that a £1 poll tax on all men not already paying hut tax was promulgated in Natal and Zululand in September 1905. Resistance to the tax followed early in 1906, and unrest continued into 1907. It was a complex rebellion in which between 3500 and 4000 Zulu lost their lives. A number of those who conducted guerrilla warfare against the colonial forces used Dinuzulu's name as their authority and employed the war-cry and war-badge of the Zulu kings. A large number of rebels sought shelter at the Osuthu. At the end of 1907 Dinuzulu was arrested on suspicion of being behind the disturbances and later twenty-three charges of high treason were brought against him. Much of the prosecution evidence presented in court, though voluminous, was confusing and based on hearsay and the testimony of witnesses whose motives were questionable. Dinuzulu was eventually found guilty on three charges of harbouring rebels, sentenced to four years' imprisonment and fined £100. Released by the Union government in 1910, the son of the last Zulu king died in exile three years later on a lonely farm near Middelburg in the Transvaal, still a comparatively young man in his mid-forties.[80]

5

Allies and neutrals

During the war black resistance to the Boers was not confined only to the western and southeastern Transvaal. In other regions, too, the pre-war state effectively collapsed from wartime pressures from within. Throughout many rural areas of the Boer republics the war generated new circumstances in which the established system of state authority was overthrown, and in which the republics' forces were increasingly hindered from operating over African-controlled terrain and were compelled more and more to live off land whose use and products were controlled by others.

For black communities in the countryside the war opened up new possibilities as well as posing new difficulties. In the larger locations in the northern Transvaal many homesteads prospered largely untroubled by direct interference from officials of the colonial state. The absence of Boer landlords and the evacuation of white farms, especially during the final two years of the war, enabled many African peasants to cultivate more land on their own behalf, and so long as fields and crops could be protected from guerrilla raids, and provided produce could be safely transported to market, excellent prices were to be obtained for grain, tobacco, vegetables and livestock. In many of the areas of the republics where 'scorched earth' was never truly attempted or effected by the British forces, the interests of agrarian communities coincided closely with those of the army of occupation. Both wished to see the Boer forces defeated and both wished to deny the commandos access to supplies. The measures taken by peasants to close their neighbourhoods to guerrilla penetration were directed as much towards the hope of regaining farms and protecting the produce of the soil as to assisting the British army.

In the eastern Transvaal the Pedi, who had twice resisted Boer commandos sent against them in 1852 and 1876 before being finally defeated by British force of arms in 1879, took advantage of wartime conditions to attempt to reshape the pattern of colonial relations in Lydenburg district. During the war supporters of the Pedi paramountcy successfully liberated themselves from the control of the republican government and local Boer officials, re-established much of their former influence in Pedi affairs, and then sought to renegotiate more favourable terms for their participation in the post-war colonial state. In rather different circumstances the Dlamini in Swaziland achieved a measure of independence during the war and sought to take advantage of their wartime status to influence the settlement of Swazi affairs once the struggle was over.

THE PEDI

Following the overthrow of the Pedi state in 1879 and the assassination of Sekhukhune I in 1882 the economic and political foundations of the Pedi polity had begun seriously to crumble. Indeed land shortage in the Pedi heartland between the Olifants and Steelpoort rivers appears to have been a problem even in the early 1870s. In the train of the collapse of the Pedi state more land was demarcated for white farms (many of which were in fact bought up by land companies), and an oppressive regime of tax collection, labour recruitment and control over Pedi affairs instituted by the local Native Commissioner, J. A. (Abel) Erasmus. A succession of regents, all deeply committed to collaboration with the colonial state, were appointed for Sekhukhune's heir, a small child of the same name: Kgoloko, a junior son of Sekhukhune's father, Sekwati, 1882–93; Nkopodi, 1893–4; and Kgolane, Kgoloko's son, after 1894. All were little more than mouthpieces for Erasmus, especially in his efforts to exact taxation and conscript Pedi labourers for work on neighbouring farms and railway construction. The appointments of Nkopodi and Kgolane, who were in effect government-appointed chiefs, were particularly unpopular among the Pedi, and in 1896 order had to be restored between Kgolane and prominent leaders of the 'Sekhukhune' or 'Mokatela' party, who rose in opposition to the labour demands being made by the regent on Erasmus's behalf. A new settlement was made by General Joubert whereby the largest area of Pedi habitation, the Geluks location (created in 1885), was divided into two portions, and Thorometsane appointed regent on behalf of her son Sekhukhune in the northern half and Kgolane recognised as chief of the southern half, the most densely populated, best watered and most fertile area. The followers of each faction were ordered to remove to their respective part of the location, though very few Sekhukhune supporters moved north because of the lack of water there. Kgolane's followers were in the minority but were supported by Erasmus, his sub-commissioner at Schoonoord, W. R. van der Wal, and by the Rev. J. A. Winter of the Bapedi Lutheran Church (established in 1889), who was also agent for the Consolidated Land and Exploration Company which owned farms adjacent to the Geluks location.[1]

Concern for the security of the white farming community in Lydenburg district was revealed by the government in Pretoria on a number of occasions at the beginning of the war, and in October 1899 a strong force under Commandant Klaas Prinsloo was posted to the Pedi heartland to deter resistance, control cattle-rustling from farms in the neighbourhood, conscript workers for Boer households whose labour force had been depleted by the mobilisation of the Lydenburg commando, and discourage any attempt by the Sekhukhune party to re-establish its control over Pedi affairs. The regime of occupation was an oppressive one. Young men were taken away to Boer farms in the locality, and to provide the commandos with food, clothing and forage a tax of 2s 6d was imposed on every taxpaying Pedi in the Geluks location. The levy was collected on two occasions, and each homestead was also ordered to provide the occupying force with an ox. Arrangements were also made for collecting a £1 poll tax.[2]

The Boer-occupation continued until the fall of Pretoria, when almost all the guards in the Geluks location were withdrawn to join the main Boer armies. The evacuation of the area was followed by a determined campaign on the part of Sekhukhune's followers against the principal Pedi collaborators with agents of the colonial state. In the early morning of 11 June a regiment of 140 men was sent by the Sekhukhune party to seize Kgolane and his followers at Masehleng. Kgolane and most of his supporters escaped, but eight headmen were killed. The chief fled across the Leolu mountains, later returning to Schoonoord to accompany Prinsloo, Van der Wal and a number of members of the Bapedi Lutheran Church to Rietfontein, half-way between Schoonoord and Lydenburg. Three days later Kgolane's followers led by Ihgolani were attacked by Kgobalale, the military leader of the Sekhukhune party, and their homesteads incinerated. Van der Wal's office and house at Schoonoord were then destroyed, and on 19 June a regiment led by Kgobalale accompanied Asaf, Sekhukhune's secretary, to visit J. A. Winter, who was ordered to surrender any ammunition in his possession and to return all the cattle he had received for his work as Erasmus's interpreter. Winter's house was searched and the missionary forcibly disarmed, as were two local traders, one of whom, like Winter, acted as a land company agent and rent collector. Asaf presented Winter with a letter bearing Sekhukhune's signature.

> You know, that 9 years long I do not live well in this land, which had been ours. I only see it, when it leaves me and belong to other people. Now, I will have it to be as in the old times. Again this has been said by God: you want an eye. From 1892 . . . I was like a thief and evil-doer in this land.[3]

Having ousted Kgolane and his most important followers from the Geluks location, the Sekhukhune party set to work to re-establish its authority over all Pedi in neighbouring locations and on farms in the region, where most of the Pedi lived as tenants and squatters. Mafefe, the Magakala chief, was attacked and driven out of his location across the Olifants river.[4] Instructions were issued that all Pedi policemen were to be executed, and any Pedi who were known to have been loyal to the Boer administration were ordered to send immediately to Sekhukhune either cattle or a young girl as a symbol of their submission to his authority. When Winter protested that the Sekhukhune party had no right to interfere with those Pedi living on white-owned farms, he was told that, although the ground had been alienated to land companies and farmers, the people living there still owed allegiance to the paramountcy.[5]

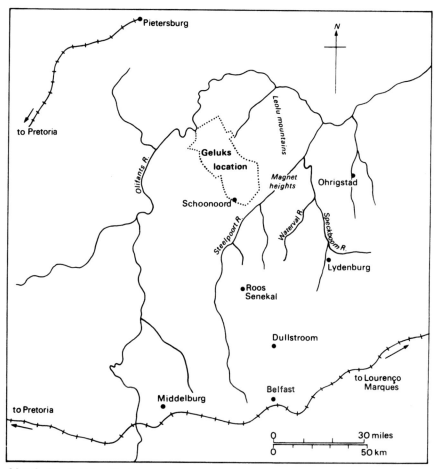

Map 6 The Pedi heartland

Kgolane, meanwhile, fled to Erasmus at Krugerspost and requested a commando to help him resist the Sekhukhune party. Erasmus, however, appreciated the inability of the government to spare men to regain control over the land between the Olifants and Steelpoort rivers, and provided Kgolane with only a small number of rifles and ammunition. Anxious to avoid widespread alarm that might encourage Lydenburg farmers serving on commando to return home, and under pressure from those with farms along the Steelpoort river (such as Veldkornet David Schoeman), Boer officials recognised the Sekhukhune party as undisputed master of the Pedi heartland and again defined the Steelpoort river as the eastern dividing line between Pedi and Boer territory. Those farms adjacent to the Pedi locations owned by land companies were thereby looked upon by the Boers as having been restored to the Pedi. By regarding the territory in the neighbourhood of the main

99

locations as a 'no go' area, the Boers evidently hoped to appease the Sekhukhune party and safeguard the farms to the east of the Steelpoort river. Moreover, the landdrost at Lydenburg is reputed to have sold a horse to the Sekhukhune party in exchange for ten cattle, provided them with ammunition and promised that Kgolane would be surrendered to the Pedi if apprehended by members of the commandos.[6]

Unable to elicit Boer help in Lydenburg district, Kgolane fled to Malekutu at Mamone in Middelburg, where he gathered around him a force some 300 strong. The Sekhukhune party demanded that Malekutu, the son of Sekhukhune I's rival half-brother and assassin, Mampuru, should deliver Kgolane to them: when the order was not acknowledged preparations were made to take Kgolane by force. The Sekhukhune party assembled a large army composed of men not only from the Pedi locations but from beyond the Leolu mountains and from white-owned farms across the Steelpoort river. With this force Malekutu and Kgolane were attacked, but the army was eventually repulsed with the loss of at least sixty men when a commando led by C. Fourie, the Native Commissioner of Middelburg, came to the defenders' rescue. Sporadic fighting between the two factions continued until the British occupation of Lydenburg at the beginning of September 1900.[7]

Both Pedi groups at once made contact with the British army, each providing its own version of the recent upheavals. Winter forwarded a report of the fighting on behalf of Kgolane and Malekutu, while the Sekhukhune party sent Asaf to Lydenburg. On 4 October instructions were issued by the army that all fighting was to cease, and an intelligence officer, Richmond Haigh, was sent to Magnet heights as Acting Commissioner. Haigh's task seemed a difficult one, for he had on the one hand to prevent further bloodshed between the rival factions and prepare the way ultimately for a settlement of Pedi affairs when the war was over, and on the other hand to mobilise Pedi support for the prosecution of the war against the Boer guerrillas in the eastern Transvaal. Haigh created a small force which included leading members of both Pedi factions; Kgobalale and Mateu, a prominent supporter of Kgolane, were both enlisted in the contingent. Some of the most important Pedi chiefs were also encouraged to participate more informally in intelligence work and in the arrangements for hunting down Boer guerrilla groups.[8] Indeed, Haigh found few difficulties in obtaining the enthusiastic support of both the Malekutu–Kgolane and Sekhukhune factions for the army's campaign against the guerrillas.

Anxious to restrict as much as possible the area of potential Boer operations and to deprive the guerrilla groups of the grain and livestock resources of the northern and eastern Transvaal, the army readily enlisted black support to disrupt Boer communications and close large areas of the country to guerrilla activity. In June 1900 Steinacker's Horse was formed to patrol the Transvaal border with Mozambique and prevent arms shipments reaching the Boers from Lourenço Marques. The corps was composed of 450 whites, together with numbers of Pedi, Swazi, Shangane and Thonga, and was based at Komatipoort. In August 1901 a detachment of the force was defeated by General Viljoen and Commandant Moll in the lowveld near to the village of the Shangane chief, Mpisana. Fifty blacks (reported by the Boers to be supporters of Sekhukhune) were taken captive and executed.[9] The region north of the Blood river in Middelburg district was defended against the guerrilla fighters by Malekutu, who on military orders concentrated his followers into closely guarded settlements and organised intensive patrols, thereby preventing any Boer incursions into his territory.[10] Micha Dinkwanyane completely closed the strategically important Waterval valley to guerrilla penetration. By his action he blocked all the waggon routes which the Boers could have used to transport grain from the Ohrigstad valley to Dullstroom and Roos Senekal, and from there to the commandos on the highveld. 'Chief Michal [sic] . . . has been quite invaluable to us, worth a whole column really', Captain A. W. Baird at Middelburg told the Director of British Military Intelligence in South Africa, David Henderson. 'The importance . . . of holding Waterval valley cannot be overrated. Two attempts have already been made to turn him out . . . and both unsuccessfully.'[11] No commando dared to move westwards beyond the Steelpoort river into the Pedi heartland controlled by the Sekhukhune party.[12] In April 1901 General Walter Kitchener arranged with the paramount to take over all the Boer cattle driven by the British troops in his direction and to round them up into the Geluks location. In return the Sekhukhune party was permitted to retain half the animals their men captured. A similar arrangement was agreed with Malekutu and with Mpisane.[13] In July 1901 three members of a commando were murdered by the Pedi near Lydenburg,[14] and around Ohrigstad Pedi farm servants and tenants led a determined campaign against employers and landlords. R. W. Schikkerling, a young diarist serving with the Boer forces, noted in November 1901 that 'a bitter war is raging between master and servant in which quarter is unknown. The domestics, knowing the locality well, come forth at night to plunder and murder, and many comparatively innocent people have been the victims. The natives are frequently barbarous.'[15]

But it was not only the activities of the Pedi outside the locations that began to cause the military serious concern during 1901. Haigh quickly appreciated that the cooperation in military operations elicited from the Sekhukhune party was looked upon by the Pedi less as a symbol of allegiance to the new British regime than as a marriage of convenience against a common enemy, the Boers. Following the fighting with Malekutu and Kgolane, members of the Sekhukhune party had been consolidating their influence among the Pedi. In 1901 a shilling was demanded from all Sekhukhune's followers as proof of their allegiance, a move that appears to have been designed to establish that the Pedi owned financial tribute to the paramountcy and not to white landlords or government tax collectors.[16] The Sekhukhune party demanded of Haigh that the new government acknowledge the reversion to the Pedi of the farms between the Olifants and Steelpoort rivers alienated to land companies before the war, and that Winter, Kgolane's political benefactor and agent of one of the most powerful land companies with interests in the locality, be compelled to leave Pedi territory.[17] In September 1901 Haigh told Henderson that Sekhukhune 'simply wishes to be independent . . . although he will acknowledge England as a suzerain power. This may sound strong, Sir, but it is quite correct.' E. H. Hogge, the new Native Commissioner at Lydenburg, afterwards wrote that the Sekhukhune party desired 'entire independence from the Government, Sekhukhune paying tribute only in the form of a Hut Tax to be collected by him and handed over in a lump sum to the Government' (an indication that the Sekhukhune party did not wish to separate the Pedi from all the instruments of the colonial state).[18] When in October Sekhukhune informed Haigh that he intended to visit Pretoria with his advisers to lay the Pedi's grievances before the Secretary for Native Affairs, Lagden prevented him from travelling by military order and recommended that the paramount be detained until the end of the war and Kgobalale appointed as caretaker ruler. Lagden's recommendation was not, however, acted upon.[19]

Increasingly the sympathy of the British administration was extended to Malekutu and Kgolane, who provided valuable assistance to the army with fewer complications. Haigh arranged for grain to be distributed among Kgolane's supporters who had no land to plough and no cattle to barter for food. He also urged the Sekhukhune party to permit the wives of those of Kgolane's warriors driven from the location to go to their husbands with food, and requested them to provide Kgolane with land on which he and his followers could settle permanently.[20] The Sekhukhune party steadfastly refused to entertain Haigh's suggestions, believing he was meddling in internal Pedi affairs.

Members of the Sekhukhune party supported their claims for more land and less colonial interference in Pedi affairs by arguing that they were allies, not subjects, of the new government; that they had ousted the Boers from their country before the arrival of British troops in the Lydenburg district; and that they had provided the British army with valuable military assistance that merited generous compensation.[21] Once the war was over and a civilian administration was established in Lydenburg, they turned to another method of bringing pressure to bear on the government: the Sekhukhune party sought to enforce an embargo on the supply of Pedi workers to local farmers. Commenting on the labour difficulties in the region, Hogge told Lagden that many Pedi workers refused to return to their former employers because 'they have instructions from Sekukuni not to work till he gives them the orders to do so'. It was not until the end of 1902 that some Pedi again began to resume work with local farmers.[22]

At no time do members of the Sekhukhune party appear to have contemplated using force against the new regime to support their demands, almost certainly because they were aware of the number of Pedi followers of Malekutu and Kgolane whom the British army could have deployed against them. In any case they did not wish to reject all aspects of the colonial order. Furthermore, as all the British officials concerned with Pedi affairs soon realised, the Sekhukhune party did not represent a cohesive political force. Thorometsane, Kgomani, and Pasoane, all of whom had exercised influence in the days of Sekhukhune I, defended the principle of Pedi autonomy much more fiercely than some of the younger members such as Asaf, Kgobalale, Mogas and Petedi.[23] Sekhukhune himself was only a young man and lacked political experience (though Hogge's belief that 'left to his own devices he would be perfectly satisfied with plenty Kafir beer and numerous wives' appears to be an exaggeration, for the paramount spoke with some force at a number of meetings with British officials during 1902).[24]

After the war the Sekhukhune party placed less emphasis on claims for complete internal autonomy than on the need for the redress of specific economic grievances. At a meeting with the Native Commissioner at Schoonoord in August 1902 every Pedi speaker referred to the subject of more land and the extension of the Pedi locations. Pasoane in particular drew attention to the overcrowding in the Geluks location, while Asaf and Sekhukhune demanded that the nearby territory alienated to land companies be restored to them as an extension of their locations. Members of the Sekhukhune party were also adamant that in the future missionaries and traders should not be permitted to interfere in Pedi affairs in the interests of the government. New demands were made that Winter should be compelled to leave Pedi territory – 'Mr Winter is worthless and not suitable to act as a clergyman' – and Asaf demanded of Hogge that a local storekeeper, Hannan, a supporter of Kgolane, should also be removed.[25]

The resistance of the Sekhukhune party to the British regime quickly crumbled away. By the end of 1902, 4321 firearms had been reluctantly surrendered by Sekhukhune's followers. Hogge had at first believed the Pedi would rise rather than hand in their weapons, and had arranged for 100 members of the South African Constabulary to be on hand when the disarmament order was issued.[26] Kgolane was brought back to the Geluks location in August 1903 with 780 followers and restored to his pre-war position. He abandoned Masehleng and founded a new settlement at Madibong on the western side of the location, further away from Sekhukhune's homestead at Mohlaletse and closer to his ally, Malekutu. Two headmen who refused openly to recognise him as chief were removed to the northern half of the location, but most supporters of Sekhukhune, including Pasoane, declined to leave the south for the paramount's less fertile and badly watered district.[27]

THE SWAZI

Throughout the nineteenth century the Swazi state, founded by the Dlamini in the 1820s, pursued a policy of collaboration rather than confrontation with the settler polities of the region. The first important phase in the incorporation of Swaziland into the colonial system of the subcontinent was marked by the signing away by Mbandzeni (1874–89), especially during the last five years of his reign, of almost the entire resources of the state to unscrupulous concessionaires. Monopoly grants eventually encompassed almost every conceivable activity of an agricultural and industrial country, such as the right to use land, extract minerals, create and operate industries, collect customs revenues, build railways and operate a postal service, and in 1889 a concession was even granted that gave the holder the right to collect the king's private revenues, including concession revenues, in return for an annual payment of £12,000. The wholesale granting of monopolies enabled the Transvaal government, by acquiring vital concessions, to extend its influence over Swazi affairs, culminating in 1894 in Swaziland, with British approval, becoming a 'political dependency' of the South African Republic.

The Dlamini aristocracy, whose control over Swazi production survived the concessions era largely intact, was unable to make any significant impact on the external decision-making that settled the future of the Swazi state. A number of appeals by the royal family for British protection against Boer encroachment were turned down, and when in 1894 the Dlamini sent a deputation to London to protest against the terms of the third Swaziland convention, which they refused to sign, their appeals fell on deaf ears. It was not long before the conditions of Swaziland's new colonial status began to undermine the structures of the Swazi social system. In 1898, only a year after the Swazi herds had been ravaged by rinderpest, colonial taxation was introduced. In the same year, too, formal Dlamini authority within Swazi society was threatened when Bhunu, Mbandzeni's successor, was held responsible by the Transvaal government for the death of a senior *indvuna*, Mbhabha Sibandze, at the royal homestead at Zombodze. The king was eventually found guilty of tolerating public violence, fined £500, made to pay £1146 to defray the expenses of the enquiry, and the Dlamini's rights over criminal jurisdiction in Swaziland circumscribed.

Although the Swazi possessed no tradition of military resistance to colonial penetration (unlike the Zulu, Basotho and Pedi, for example), both the British and Boers seriously believed on the eve of war that a Swazi rising was likely. As early as May 1899 Sir Alfred Milner warned the British Consul in Swaziland, Johannes Smuts, that reliable information had come to light that 'the Swazis are watching events and are determined to rise if there is any rupture between us and the South African Republic'.[28] Smuts was optimistic that any resistance would not be directed towards Britain, but noted there was a general feeling not confined exclusively to whites that because of opposition to taxation, and the harsh methods of its collection, in the event of war it would mean 'an assegai for each Boer unless Swazis forbidden to take part'.[29] Smuts informed the queen mother, Labotsibeni, that the Swazi were to remain 'absolutely still and neutral', and implored her to continue to submit to the authority of the Boer administration. At the beginning of the war the British and Transvaal governments agreed that both sides would evacuate Swaziland

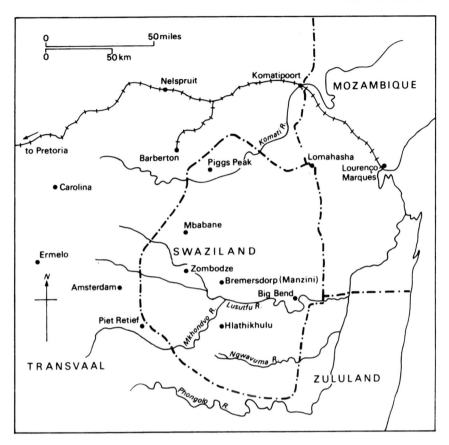

Map 7   Swaziland

and respect its neutrality, though the republic reserved the right to raise a commando from among the country's 1400 white settlers and to employ members of the Swaziland police force in military operations.[30]

The Boers, meanwhile, were unmistakably apprehensive. Only a year before, at the time of the dispute with Bhunu, it had seemed possible the Dlamini would take up arms against the Transvaal in defence of their authority within Swazi society; to deter resistance Bremersdorp (Manzini) had been fortified, 2000 men with artillery brought into the country and the strength of the Swaziland police force raised from 100 to 300 men. In October 1899 between 800 and 1000 burghers mostly from the Lydenburg commando under Schalk Burger were posted to guard the Swaziland frontier, and a small commando from Swaziland led by Chris Botha remained for a while at Bellskop before pressing on to the Natal front. Thys Grobler was instructed to liaise closely with the Swazi, and a letter outlining Boer policy was sent to Bhunu by the Commandant-General, Piet Joubert.

105

> Boers and not the English made Umbandine [Mbandzeni] King. They saved him from the Zulu King. Boers never make a man King and then kill him. Paramount Chief or his predecessors never tried to fight Boers, who have always lived in peace with Swazis. English always intervened, and peace is at an end . . . English wish also to send a Commando to Swaziland . . . we prefer not to fight English in Swaziland, for by doing so some Swazis might be killed. South African Republic Government therefore says to all Europeans in Swaziland and to all Government officials and police, close your houses and take your cattle . . . The Government buildings and houses will be without a single white man, and *you, Bunu, are the only person who, as long as the war lasts, has power in Swaziland over everything.* For so long you can do as you like, and it would be very good if you guarded and took care of every house and work, so that no damage is done . . . you can tell all the remaining whites to go. If any woman, child or defenceless person, black or white, is injured or marauded, South African Republic Government will be dissatisfied.[31]

The letter had far-reaching implications, for it effectively restored to the Swazi their independence, albeit for the duration of the war. An early indication that the Dlamini no longer regarded the authority of the Transvaal government as absolute was the refusal of Bhunu in November to provide Schalk Burger with 100 Swazi porters, the king replying that 'his men had been so heavily taxed they had to go out to work, and had not yet returned'.[32]

At the beginning of December Bhunu died. His heir, Mona (Sobhuza II), was but a small child, and effective power passed to the Swazi Council, and in particular to Labotsibeni and her son, Malunge. Labotsibeni had been the most influential figure in Swazi politics since the death of Mbandzeni, and was later described as 'a woman of extraordinary diplomatic ability and strength of character'. J. C. Krogh, the Swaziland Special Commissioner, brought the queen regent a small herd of cattle in lament for Bhunu's death, and later J. Ferreira presented her with three sheep. Labotsibeni, however, declined to accept the gifts, and since Krogh refused to take them back they remained at Zombodze. In March 1900 the British held an audience with Labotsibeni at which a petition was presented to the delegation requesting protection, though the queen regent made no reference to the precise arrangements the Dlamini had in mind other than a reduction in taxation. It is evident, however, that Labotsibeni intended renegotiating new conditions of colonial protection in which Dlamini control over Swazi society would be guaranteed, rather than simply having Boer officials replaced by British ones under the existing system, and that new terms would need to be approved by the full Swazi Council before any arrangement was finally agreed.[33] According to David Forbes, General Manager of the Swaziland Coal Mining Company,

> As far as the Queen and Council and Chiefs are concerned they hate any white authority and interference as they consider it, they only prefer the British to the Boers because they think they will get more freedom under the former when once they are forced to come under white rule . . . They are, I believe, taking the stand that they are independent, as the Boers handed back the country to them when they left.[34]

106

For most of its duration Swaziland remained much less affected by the war than many other regions, and the Swazi much more reluctant to become embroiled in the conflict than most other African peoples. Some Boer farmers from the eastern Transvaal retired into the country with livestock to evade the drives of the British columns, and guerrillas occasionally conscripted Swazi servants for their campaign. The British army, with Milner's approval, gave Labotsibeni permission to resist any Boers who entered Swaziland, but with the exception of an attack in February 1901 by Thintitha Dlamini on a small party of thirteen members of the Piet Retief commando near Hlathikhulu, all of whom perished, the Swazi made few efforts to prevent groups of guerrillas entering Swaziland for provisions and recuperation.[35]

For most of the war the only British force to maintain a presence in Swaziland was Steinacker's Horse, the irregular unit of mercenaries and local whites led by a German soldier of fortune, Ludwig Steinacker, whose main task was to seal the border between Mozambique and the Transvaal. The force employed about 300 blacks, mostly Thonga, in intelligence work inside Swaziland and along its borders, and maintained a small garrison of fifty men in Bremersdorp. Members of the unit spent at least as much time enriching themselves by looting Swazi homesteads, ransacking abandoned white property and gun-running to Mozambique as they did resisting the Boers. The Swazi Council declined to recognise the force as a legitimate British unit, refused to cooperate with its members and pressed for its withdrawal from Swaziland. Johannes Smuts sympathised with the Council's request.

> I don't wonder at it for they know many of them as well as I do. Lieutenant Marsden was barman at the Bremersdorp Hotel, Captain Holgate was a dweller on the Lubombo, Sergeant Wilcoxson did six months' hard labour in Bremersdorp for gun-selling, and so on. Sandy McCorkindale, a burgher, and a notorious drunkard and bad character, seems to have charge of the Piggs Peak district and if reports are true has been indulging in looting and gun-selling.[36]

Kitchener, however, refused either to disband or withdraw Steinacker's men; 'No one thinks S. an angel but he has his uses', noted one of his aides.[37] When the unit imprisoned Prince Mancibane Dlamini on suspicion of Boer sympathies this was the final straw for the Swazi Council. Labotsibeni contacted General Botha through Thys Grobler and informed him that a group of British 'robbers' were operating in Swaziland without her consent. On 21 July 1901 the Ermelo commando led by Tobias Smuts crossed the Swazi border and surrounded Bremersdorp, where Steinacker's men were billeted. The commando soon overpowered the unit, took forty-one prisoners, captured a haul of firearms, seized four hundred cattle and fifty horses, liberated Mancibane and incinerated the town (thereby ending Bremersdorp's period as the administrative capital of Swaziland). Tobias Smuts was given an audience by Labotsibeni before an assembly of the Swazi Council and thanked for his efforts; in return Smuts presented the queen regent with some of the seized cattle.[38]

Labotsibeni skilfully remained aloof from the war, maintaining cordial relations with both sides and preserving Swaziland's neutrality and nominal independence for the duration of the struggle. With the exception of the burning of the colonial town of Bremersdorp and the looting of some European property, little devastation occurred in Swaziland, in spite of the intense guerrilla war carried on beyond the country's frontiers. Few Swazi lost their lives, colonial taxation was suspended between 1899 and 1902, those Swazi who enrolled as workers with the British army earned good wages (between £3 10s and £6 a month, according to Johannes Smuts[39]), and a small amount of cattle-rustling from the eastern Transvaal also took place (with British approval).[40] The signing of peace in Pretoria at the end of May 1902, however, created new circumstances much more inimical to Swazi interests.

Following the British annexation of the Transvaal the affairs of Swaziland were placed under the nominal control of the High Commissioner, but in May 1901 it was decided the country should once more revert to its pre-war status as a dependency of the Transvaal. The constitutional status of Swaziland, however, still had to find practical expression, and after the signing of peace Labotsibeni sent two deputations to Johannesburg to discuss, and to attempt to influence, the nature of the new British administration. The Dlamini advanced a number of arguments for a more equitable colonial relationship and to support their case for greater internal autonomy: first, they argued that their independence in internal affairs had been guaranteed by the earlier Anglo-Boer conventions, and that rather than having been annexed by the South African Republic they had agreed only to its protection; secondly, they maintained that since the Boers had restored to them their independence at the beginning of the war they had been allies of the British, and should not be treated as a conquered people simply because the Transvaal had come under British control; and thirdly, they suggested in view of Britain's annexation of the Transvaal those concessions granted to citizens of the South African Republic should be annulled. They were anxious, too, that the rate of colonial taxation should be reduced.[41]

The Dlamini, however, were unable to make any impact on Britain's plans for the government of Swaziland, contained in the Swaziland Order-in-Council of 25 June 1903, by which the governor of the Transvaal was empowered to legislate by proclamation and to administer the country through a Resident Commissioner. According to the order-in-council the governor was to 'respect any Native laws by which the civil relations of any Native chiefs, tribes or populations are now regulated, except in so far as may be incompatible with the due exercise of His Majesty's power and jurisdiction or is clearly injurious to the welfare of the said Natives'.

The opposition of the Dlamini to the post-war constitutional arrangements was intensified by the legislation subsequently enacted. The Swazi were disarmed; the private revenues concession was cancelled and all rents, royalties and other payments made under it became part of the revenues of the colonial state; trading monopolies were expropriated through a loan charged on the country's revenues; and most important of all, in order to solve the problems created by Mbandzeni's large-scale granting of land concessions and to regularise private property relations for encouraging commercial agriculture, a programme of land apportionment was carried out whereby one third of the country was reserved for the exclusive use of the Swazi, and two-thirds alienated to land concessionaires who were given freehold rights over their awarded land. Although the Swazi were granted those areas of the country where the largest number of homesteads were situated, in time the fertility of the land diminished because of overcrowding, overstocking and soil erosion. Indeed, evidence of growing impoverishment in Swazi society was already apparent during the first decade of the century.[42] For the Swazi people the aftermath of war signified an era of more intensive subordination to the forces of a rapidly developing capitalist system in the subcontinent.

The Dlamini campaigned vigorously for the maintenance of the king's private revenue and were fiercely opposed both to the principle and methods of land partition. In 1907 a delegation again visited London to protest against land apportionment; to argue that the introduction of an appeal from the king's court to that of the Resident Commissioner was an invasion of Dlamini rights; and to press for the creation of a court of chiefs, or similar institution, so that the Dlamini would have to be consulted formally before legislation that affected their interests could be introduced.

The activities of the Dlamini were not entirely fruitless. Their dominant role in Swazi society was maintained and has continued to the present day. In 1906 annual taxation was reduced from 40s to 30s, and their opposition to the government's intention that Swaziland be eventually incorporated into a self-governing Transvaal encouraged Britain to disannex Swaziland from the crown colony in 1906, the country thereafter becoming for all practical purposes a British protectorate, though its precise constitutional, if not economic, status remained ambiguous until the eventual achievement of Swazi political independence in 1968. Once the war had ended, however, the Dlamini had no longer been able to play off the British and Boers and they rapidly lost the freedom of action they had exercised during the war.

6

The war in the Cape

The coming of war between Britain and the Boer republics elicited considerable interest among members of the small, articulate, predominantly mission-educated and politically conscious groups of Africans and Coloureds in the Cape. Members of the black elite prospered as peasant farmers, taught in mission schools or preached as clergymen, or lived and worked in the towns of the colony as traders, craftsmen and journalists, or as interpreters, clerks and messengers in the Cape civil service. Dedicated to education as a means of self-improvement, and seeing their own social progress and achievements in colonial society as an example of the possibilities that were open to their own people, members of the elite embodied many of the traditional virtues of the mid-Victorian age. Small in number though they were, they formed a closely-knit segment of public opinion that was of by no means negligible importance and influence in the colony. Members of the elite were able to bring their point of view to bear on white opinion and the colonial government through letters and petitions to officials and white newspaper editors, through representations to government and political organisations, through the medium of sympathetic white politicians and other 'friends of the natives' and through the columns of African newspapers such as *Imvo Zabantsundu, Izwi Labantu* and, a little later, *Koranta ea Becoana*, all of which contained sections in both English and the vernacular. At election times politicians of all persuasions could be approached much more forcefully and directly, for a 'colour-blind' franchise operated in the Cape whereby any adult male, irrespective of the colour of his skin, was entitled to register as a voter provided he could pass a simple literacy test and either owned property to the value of £75 or possessed an annual income exceeding £50. The franchise was looked upon by members of the black elite as the corner-stone of their liberties and opportunities in Cape society, and though the number of black voters was never large and the proportion of the total black population enfranchised was small, in at least seventeen constituencies candidates were obliged to make some gesture towards black voters to ensure success at the polls.[1]

It was natural that the conduct of diplomacy between Britain and the

110

government of President Kruger should attract a good deal of attention among the members of this elite, and that educated men who took pride in their knowledge of the larger political questions of the day should have decided views about the outcome of any move towards war in South Africa and the possibilities that would be created by such a train of events. As war drew near it was widely believed that the defeat of the Boers by the British forces would be accomplished without undue difficulty, and that once the republics had been overthrown the liberties and opportunities afforded to black people in the Cape might then be extended to the Transvaal and Orange Free State. In particular, the hope was generated that once these territories were administered directly by Britain, whose record in matters of liberal reform and liberty of the individual was generally admired, the Cape's franchise system would be extended throughout South Africa.

Such optimism on the part of members of the black elite was encouraged by the course of diplomacy before the outbreak of war and by the character of British propaganda during the months immediately after hostilities began. During the late 1890s pressure was brought to bear on Kruger's government to alleviate some of the grievances of British Coloured citizens in the South African Republic. In 1897 Milner approached the Pretoria government on the question of Cape Coloureds living in the Transvaal being subject to the provisions of the Pass Law approved by the Volksraad (law 31 of 1896). The legislation was accordingly amended in order that Coloureds carrying on a business or practising a skilled trade might purchase certificates of exemption. In October 1898 the South African League took up the issue of police brutality against Coloureds in Johannesburg, a question which Milner also raised at official level with the Transvaal government.[2]

Once the war had begun the argument was advanced both by prominent English churchmen and by leading members of the British government, as part of their case for justifying the declaration of war, that the time had arrived once and for all to put an end to the oppressive treatment of black people in the South African Republic. 'The treatment of the natives [in the Transvaal] has been disgraceful; it has been brutal; it has been unworthy of a civilised Power', Chamberlain told the Commons in October 1899. The Colonial Secretary implied that affairs would be run very differently under British administration. The Prime Minister, Lord Salisbury, informed Parliament in February 1900 that following victory in the South African campaign, 'There must be no doubt . . . that due precaution will be taken for the kindly and improving treatment of those countless indigenous races of whose destiny I fear we have been too forgetful.' Later, Milner told a Coloured deputation in Cape Town that he 'thoroughly agreed . . . it was not race or colour, but civilisation which was the test of a man's capacity for political rights', a statement widely interpreted as an assurance that once the war was over the political rights enjoyed by black people in the Cape would be extended to those in the Boer republics.[3]

The expectation that a British victory would bring about an extension of political, educational and commercial opportunities for black people led many members of the elite to endorse Britain's military intervention with enthusiasm, and to give unreserved support to the British war effort. As early as September 1899 a large meeting of Coloureds in Cape Town chaired by H. J. Gordon passed resolutions applauding Milner's diplomacy with the Transvaal government, those present expressing hope that 'no basis for peace will be accepted . . . that does not secure Equal Rights for all civilised British subjects irrespective of colour'. A month later a petition was drawn up by a large meeting of Africans in Cape Town which described the signatories' 'warm and loyal devotion to Her Majesty the Queen' and approval that 'the Chief Minister of the Queen has mentioned the welfare of the Native people as one of the things he is bearing in mind'.[4] Later during the war another petition was presented to Milner which assured him of the 'firm and unalterable' loyalty of the Coloured population of South Africa, adding: 'We trust that everything will be done . . . [in the Transvaal and Orange River Colony], to secure liberty and freedom for all civilised people . . . we feel that only under the British flag and British protection can the Coloured people obtain justice, equality and freedom.'[5] Following the lead of those in the Cape, a Natal Native Congress was founded in Pietermaritzburg in June 1900, passing resolutions of 'devotion and loyalty' to Britain and approving a motion that 'this meeting earnestly prays that Her Majesty's Government will in arriving at the settlement of South African affairs safeguard Native races from restrictive legislation in regard to (1) education (2) a certain amount of direct representation in the Legislatures of the different states (3) freedom of trade (4) acquisition of land.'[6]

The support of the black elite for the British side in the war was not universal, however. Most significantly, John Tengo Jabavu, the influential Mfengu editor of the newspaper *Imvo Zabantsundu*, which was founded in 1883 and published in King William's Town in the eastern Cape, remained critical of British policy in South Africa throughout the war. Jabavu, who was never afraid to speak out against the views of the majority of his people, argued in a long editorial in *Imvo* during the first week of the war that the British government had succumbed to the influence of an irresponsible war party in Britain and South Africa, and that meaningful negotiations could have taken place with the Boers if only the government in London had not been persuaded that a military solution was the only alternative to a complete surrender by the Transvaal government of its internal autonomy. Jabavu concluded, 'without any notice the present unexampled crisis is forced on [the Transvaalers] . . . and they are called upon at a moment's notice in one day to make their conservative state as liberal as any Utopia'. The war, in Jabavu's estimation, represented 'the very quintessence of unfairness'.[7]

Jabavu's reaction to the war stemmed from his own pacifist inclination; from his rivalry with the Rev. Walter Rubusana and A. K. Soga, the founder and editor of *Izwi Labantu*, which was established in 1898, published in East London, financed by the Argos newspaper group, and gave its support to the

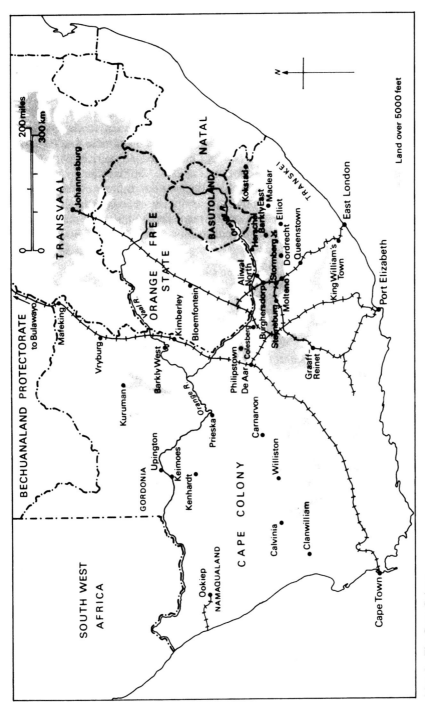

Map 8 The Cape Colony

Progressives in Cape politics and to the British military intervention in South Africa; and from Jabavu's political loyalty to the South African Party in the Cape, and in particular to John X. Merriman and J. W. Sauer, who advocated Anglo-Boer conciliation. The uncomfortable position of these men, who on the one hand advocated a more enlightened management of African affairs and on the other hand criticised the British government for going to war against the Boer republics, whose policies towards Africans they were unable to defend, was a position which Jabavu took upon himself to share – and shared all the more uncomfortably because of his own black skin. The *Eastern Province Herald* accused *Imvo* of having 'embraced Krugerism with both arms' and converted itself into a 'Pretoria organ': 'To find the docile *Imvo* now turning to lick the hand that wielded the sjambok is more amazing than amusing.' Jabavu's erstwhile reputation as the most influential leader of opinion among the black elite was swiftly tarnished by his stand on the war. Especially scathing was a correspondent to *Imvo* who addressed his remarks directly to the editor.

> Have you read Livingstone's Mission story? Has the Boer changed, think you?
> . . . Is there not an internal hatred in the heart of the Boer towards the aborigines of this country? Are the Natives allowed to own and possess land in the adjoining states? Are there Native institutions there? Is there a Native editor of a newspaper in either state? Would it be allowed, think you? Would you like such a state of things here?[8]

Jabavu persistently argued in the columns of *Imvo* that condemnation of the war did not imply approval of the circumstances of black people in the Boer republics. To add weight to his arguments Jabavu regularly printed extracts from speeches made by prominent members of the anti-war movement in Britain, and cited such names as Jesus Christ, the Apostles, Wesley, Bunyan, Ridley and Latimer as examples of people who had defended uncomfortable truths in an unapproving climate of opinion. Many people, both white and black, however, were unsympathetic to the finer points of the 'pro-Boer' case. *Imvo*'s circulation declined, a number of prominent white supporters publicly withdrew their subscriptions, the Mercury Printing Company terminated its contract to produce the newspaper, and although Jabavu prudently trimmed his sails following the introduction of martial law in the King William's Town district in January 1901, the military authorities brought the publication of *Imvo* to a halt in August of that year. It did not reappear until 8 October 1902, its financial position much weakened.[9]

The reactions to the war of the black elite were set against a shifting scenery of military operations in the Cape, which form the main subject of the rest of the chapter.

THE DEFENCE OF THE TRANSKEI

During the months of political uncertainty that followed the Jameson Raid a series of rumours had circulated in the Transkei that some black groups were making preparations for armed resistance in the event of a complete breakdown of Anglo-Boer relations. Though such fears were largely unspecific in form, and subsided as both sides pulled back from what seemed the brink of war, the conviction that there might be serious trouble in the region (a conviction seemingly held both by whites and blacks) re-emerged in 1899. Fears were heightened by reports that individual Boers were conspiring to win black support and encourage rebellion against the Cape government. 'Agents and emissaries from the enemy were at work amongst all the tribes, and at every kraal where the chief or headman was supposed to have influence', wrote Sir Henry Elliot, the Chief Magistrate of the Transkei, and in November 1899 three Afrikaners, Bosch, Reunders and Coetzee, were arrested at Penhoek in the Ciskei for encouraging African sedition. During the first weeks of the war the government received numerous petitions from whites requesting protection against possible black unrest and lawlessness.[10]

It was in this environment of rumour and anxiety that decisions had to be taken about the measures necessary to protect the eastern Cape, whether against enemy incursions, or sedition from within, or both. Milner was eager that Sir Walter Stanford should leave his post as head of the Native Affairs Department in Cape Town to organise a black force for the defence of East Griqualand and to supplement the white contingents in the region, the Cape, Transkei and East Griqualand Mounted Rifles.

The Cape Prime Minister, W. P. Schreiner, demurred, however, arguing that an invasion of the Transkei was unlikely, that the white forces in the area were sufficiently strong to deter an occupation or rebellion, and that to arm blacks would serve only to heighten white anxieties.[11] Schreiner's views were understandable enough in the context of Cape politics, for his ministry depended on the cooperation of the Afrikaner Bond, whose members were vigorously opposed to the idea of arming African levies; because of the fear of a full-scale white rebellion in the colony Schreiner was especially anxious to remove any further sources of Afrikaner discontent. To Milner, however, Schreiner's attitude was somewhat less comprehensible, the High Commissioner interpreting his views as tantamount to arguing that 'it would be a less serious matter to lose the Territories than to arm natives against the white man, even in the defence of their own district against wanton aggression'.[12] The issue was settled, temporarily at least, by both men agreeing that responsibility for the Transkei's defence should be placed in the hands of General Buller, who was left to give Sir Henry Elliot the necessary instructions for defending the region. Buller initially saw no reason to supplement the white forces in the eastern Cape by raising a contingent of black levies.

No sooner had this arrangement been made than further pressure began to build up for some positive action to be taken to secure the defence of the colony's eastern regions. Magistrates in the western districts of the Cape had already recognised the necessity of arming small numbers of Coloureds and Africans in trying to stem the Boer invasion. Both Elliot and J. H. Scott, the

Chief Magistrate of East Griqualand, became convinced that in the light of continuing Boer penetration into the colony the best way of defending the area was to involve as many blacks as possible on the side of the government.[13] Pressure was exerted too on the government by Africans themselves. Chiefs in Mount Ayliff district told Scott they considered local stocks of firearms to be 'shockingly low'. Sigcawu, the Mpondo chief, warned R. W. Stanford at Lusikisiki that if the Boers came into contact with Transkeian Africans 'matters would be very bad' because they were so inadequately armed. Sam Majeke, a Bhaca headman, suggested that 1000 armed blacks should be raised to join the Cape forces at the front since attack was the best method of defence.[14]

Among members of the black elite there seems to have been somewhat less enthusiasm for a black combat force to be raised. *Imvo*, for example, believed that little point would be served by permitting blacks to take part in military operations: 'if the Natives in the British possessions had been let loose on Dutchmen, they on their side would probably have commandeered the heaps and heaps of blackmen within their territories and we should have had a welter of chaos and confusion, such as it would have been very difficult to imagine'. *Imvo* nonetheless believed that Africans should be allowed to defend their property against Boer aggression, and should be actively encouraged to do so.[15]

The issue of raising black levies in the Transkei was ultimately settled by rapidly changing military fortunes in the region following the rebellion in, and Commandant J. H. Olivier's occupation of, Barkly East, adjacent to East Griqualand, and by the defeat of General Gatacre's force at the Stormberg at the beginning of December. It was generally surmised that these developments would have a deleterious effect on the confidence of Africans in the British army's capability of affording them protection. It also appeared unlikely that the Boer forces would of their own accord refrain from attempting to commandeer grain and livestock from blacks in those areas of the Transkei close to the occupied districts. Preparations were therefore quickly made with Buller's authority to mobilise black levies for the defence of the region. Schreiner reluctantly agreed to the decision.

During December black levies were mobilised and encamped close to the Transkeian frontier. The recruits were led by white officers and supplemented by small detachments of the Cape Mounted Rifles and white volunteers. The force eventually grew to 4000 men and was divided into two groups. The Griqualand Field Force had its headquarters at Mount Fletcher and consisted of 200 whites and 2000 levies commanded by Sir Walter Stanford. The Thembuland Field Force under Elliot's command comprised 180 whites and 1100 levies stationed at Engcobo, another 500 men between Cala and Indwe, and advanced detachments close to the Wodehouse and Barkly East frontiers. For each one hundred levies one captain and two lieutenants were appointed (whites), and four sergeants and eight corporals (blacks). The levies were paid daily 3s (sergeants), 2s 6d (corporals) and 2s (privates);

the wage was increased by 1s a day if a recruit provided his own horse.[16]

Most of the men recruited were Mfengu and Thembu. By the end of December 2500 Mfengu had been mobilised, many of whom were reported to have volunteered to serve, if necessary, without pay and only in return for their keep. Mfengu levies made up almost the whole of the East Griqualand Field Force, and another 500 men joined Elliot's contingent at Engcobo.[17] The rest of Elliot's force was made up of Thembu recruited under chiefs Dalindyebo, Mgudlwa and Mvusu. Dalindyebo also ran an Intelligence Corps, was given the rank of captain, and paid 20s a day. Elliot was enthusiastic about the intelligence work performed: 'Dalindyebo has kept me fully and constantly informed of the actions and feelings of every tribe throughout the Native Territories. He has secret agents here, there and everywhere, and supplies me with the fullest and most minute information.'[18]

The readiness of the Mfengu and Thembu to volunteer for military service was interpreted at the time as evidence of their profound loyalty to the government, a continuation of the people's tradition of collaboration. This is certainly a significant point to make, but equally importantly account has to be taken of the prevailing socio-economic circumstances. During the final years of the nineteenth century, and especially after the rinderpest epidemic, a more unequal distribution of wealth and resources had taken place in both Fingoland and Thembuland. During 1899 and 1900 not only were many Thembu and Mfengu thrown out of work, along with large numbers of other Transkeians (the loss of wages from the Transvaal mines alone to workers from the region was estimated to total £300,000[19]), but the dislocation of the labour system at the beginning of the war also coincided with a period of prolonged drought and in some areas the almost total ruination of the harvest in an already seriously overpopulated region. The final weeks of 1899 and early months of 1900 were a period of economic crisis for the majority of people in such districts as Butterworth, Willowvale, Engcobo and Xalanga, from where many of the levies were drawn. The attraction of military employment – relatively close by, with rations provided and good wages paid – was overwhelming, and many enthusiastic volunteers had to be turned away, so numerous were those who came forward to enrol.

The mobilisation of levies was regarded both by the military and by local magistrates and officials as an unqualified success, for on no occasion during the first phase of the war did the Boers attempt to cross into the Transkei. The levies were mostly disbanded on 19 March 1900.

Schreiner was described as being 'very sick about the arming of the natives'. He was obliged nonetheless to defend the decision to Bond critics, many of whom had been denied the right themselves to purchase weapons and ammunition. A Bond public meeting in Elliot passed a resolution protesting 'most strongly' against the action of the government. From Graaff-Reinet J. F. du Toit informed Schreiner that the confidence of the Bond in the government had been 'severely shaken'. The renewed circulation of rumours of impending conflict between black and white, which appear in some way to

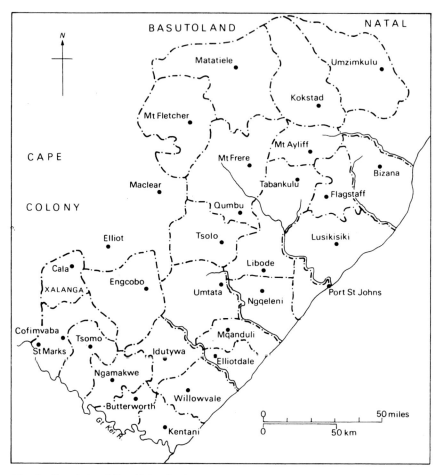

Map 9   Transkei and East Griqualand

have been inspired by the mobilisation of levies, threatened further to undermine the already strained allegiance to the government of Cape Afrikaners. The Rev. W. P. de Villiers told Schreiner from Carnarvon that it was 'whispered our towns and villages will be garrisoned by Indian Sepoys . . . and that the alleged attack at Derdepoort by Kaffirs is . . . an example of what is coming'. 'We are in great danger', D. W. Schoeman of Maraisburg wrote to the Prime Minister. 'It is unsafe to arm the Kaffirs, and arms and ammunition are forbidden us. Sir, I ask you, if matters go thuswise, is it possible for us to remain loyal?' Schreiner's customary reply to letters such as these was to point out that the mobilisation of black levies had not been his direct responsibility, and that if only the Boers would withdraw from the colony the levies could be disbanded.[20] But his role as mediator between imperial and Afrikaner interests in the Cape was becoming almost daily more hopeless, and on 13

118

June 1900 Schreiner resigned from office over the question of the disfranchisement of Cape rebels.

GUERRILLAS, REBELS AND PEASANTS

The political crisis in the Cape Colony, of which the issue of mobilising black levies in the Transkei formed a part, had begun from the onset of war, when Boer forces had struck across the colony's frontiers and found widespread sympathy and a strong measure of active support among Cape Afrikaners in the countryside. Free State commandos, with local support, annexed the frontier districts of Colesberg, Aliwal North, Albert, Dordrecht and Barkly East during November 1899, while to the west commandos captured Vryburg and later advanced through Kenhardt, Gordonia and Prieska.

The districts invaded were predominantly agricultural in character and Afrikaner in settler origin. A number of mission stations were located in the region where independent peasant communities prospered, providing cereals and other produce for the Cape markets. In the small market towns dotted over the region Coloured and African artisans such as blacksmiths, farriers, wheelwrights and carpenters serviced the agricultural communities. Close economic relations with local merchants, the support of missionaries and access to the Cape's franchise gave citizens such as these a not insignificant role in local affairs. In a number of areas, meanwhile, white agriculture was under some pressure at the close of the nineteenth century from the damaging effects of the progressive subdivision of farms, competition from black peasant producers and a shortage of workers. Among Afrikaner farmers labour scarcity was a recurrent theme. Not only was their supply of labour adversely affected by the presence of thriving mission stations and other peasant communities, but farmers had to compete for workers with the diamond fields and other industrial centres, where more attractive wages were on offer.

In the occupied districts of the northeastern Cape it is clear that the invading forces and Afrikaner rebels conceived their role as extending beyond simply that of an army of fleeting occupation with local support. As in the occupied districts of Natal, measures were taken to establish a new administrative structure in which local rebels played a key role as newly constituted veldkornets, landdrosts and other officials. For the local black population, and especially for the more prosperous and enfranchised peasantry, a much more oppressive order followed, in which passes were rigorously enforced, labour disputes summarily resolved by landdrosts, and workers conscripted to perform duties for the occupying forces and to provide labour on Afrikaner farms. Since the districts were deemed to have been annexed and therefore had become subject to republican jurisdiction, the disfranchisement of black voters was authorised, and in some areas steps were taken systematically to enforce this.[21] In essence, the dismantling of the social and political structure of the Cape, based on the converging interests of peasant producers and mercantile capital, was begun to be effected and replaced by a regime founded upon the harmony of interests between the invading commandos and the local Afrikaner farming community.

News of the events taking place in the annexed districts spread rapidly through the region, and in some of the areas adjacent to the occupied districts blacks began to organise themselves to resist enemy encroachments, in some instances independently of local officials. Threats were issued that if the invaders moved further into the colony Afrikaner farms would be raided and livestock looted. In the no man's land districts of Molteno and Steynsburg, scoured by patrols from both sides and in which no regularly enforceable authority prevailed, a good deal of raiding and counter-raiding took place between local Afrikaner farmers and black peasants. Once the military tide turned and the republican forces withdrew, there were further retaliatory peasant raids on the farms of rebels and collaborators.[22]

A similar pattern of activity occurred in the northwestern Cape, where rebels joined with the invading forces to control occupied districts according to republican law and to plunder the resources of peasant holdings. Resistance to the mobile commandos and rebels was necessarily dependent on Coloureds and Africans in view of the widespread local sympathy with the occupying forces. The magistrate at Kuruman was able to count on the active support of only twenty loyal whites (including police officers), and hastily made plans to raise a force of 200 Coloureds. Further west in Gordonia the magistrate at Upington was given consent from Cape Town to raise a Coloured defence force but was told by a deputation of Afrikaner farmers that if Coloureds were armed the district was likely to rise in protest. Similarly, local Afrikaners at Kenhardt threatened to rebel if any Coloured contingent was mobilised and armed. In the event small numbers of Coloureds were armed in both Kenhardt and Calvinia but were unable to halt the towns' occupation. At Calvinia the Chief of Police, suspected of issuing arms to local Coloureds, was immediately thrown into gaol by the invading forces.[23]

By the end of March 1900 most of the commandos had been cleared from the Cape, though it was not until the end of May that the last major rebel force, in the Prieska area, was defeated. Throughout the remainder of the year the Cape lay outside the main theatres of military activity. However on 16 December, Dingane's Day, P. H. Kritzinger and J. B. M. Hertzog crossed into the colony with 1700 Free State guerrillas and Cape rebels and rapidly occupied Philipstown. By the end of the month fourteen districts of the Cape had been placed under martial law, and by the end of January 1901 martial law had been extended to the whole of the colony except the seaports and the Transkei. Local forces were quickly assembled and despatched to protect the railways and principal towns. The Cape remained a theatre of Boer operations until the end of the war. Incursions into the colony to encourage an Afrikaner rebellion were made by De Wet, briefly, in February, by Van Reenen in April, and by Smuts from September. Smaller groups of burghers and rebels led by Scheepers, Lötter, Kritzinger, Myburgh, Maritz, Fouché, Wessels and

Bezuidenhout operated in the Cape almost continuously throughout 1901 and the first months of 1902. Already by the middle of 1901 much of the northwestern Cape had fallen under republican influence, and later Boer operations extended throughout almost all the colony's western districts. Though the scale of guerrilla activity was never allowed to get too much out of hand, the petty and sporadic warfare remained to the last a thorn in the side of the British army. Moreover, the implications of the guerrilla war determined that for the inhabitants of the colony, both black and white, the war had entered upon a new and ruthless phase.

From mid-1900 the defence of the western districts of the Cape, from the Cape Town–Kimberley railway route to the Atlantic Ocean, was largely entrusted to Coloured contingents mobilised from the region. In May the Border Scouts regiment was formed at Upington. Initially composed of 200 Coloureds under Major J. Birbeck, the official strength of the force was raised to 500 men in January 1901, and eventually to almost 800. During 1901 a Coloured corps of 600 men, the Bushmansland Borderers, was mobilised by Major Soames, and in July 1901 the Namaqualand Border Scouts was raised, with 362 Coloured members. Unofficially the number of Coloureds armed was almost certainly higher than these figures suggest, for men designated to perform support roles invariably came to carry firearms for their own protection. Armed men also patrolled other principal towns, and at Ookiep, the most important copper-mining settlement in Namaqualand, a town guard was established of 206 white miners and 661 Coloureds. Between 4 April and 3 May 1902 the force was besieged by Smuts's commandos following the fall of the neighbouring settlements at Springbok and Concordia. When Smuts had originally entered the colony in September 1901 a brief skirmish had taken place between his guerrillas and a detachment of the Herschel Mounted Police, a force of 200 Basotho under white officers that had been formed to deter cattle-raiding and to protect the district from guerrilla incursions.[24]

The use of Coloured and African troops, armed scouts and informers became a constant source of dispute between the British and the Boers in the Cape. Any Coloured or African carrying a firearm whom the Boers apprehended was invariably shot. In July 1901 Kritzinger informed Kitchener that any blacks employed by the British army, whether armed or not, would be executed if they fell into Boer hands; in November this threat was extended to include anyone who informed the British of guerrilla movements without their employer's consent.[25]

Rural violence in the western Cape became endemic as bands of guerrillas and rebels roamed the countryside, often seizing peasant produce and livestock for their supplies and in some cases for redistribution among local Afrikaner farmers. For their own security Coloured communities sometimes organised themselves into irregular and unofficial defence units. Particular targets for the guerrillas were localities from where Coloureds had been recruited for the defence forces of the region and for work as non-combatants with other British military units, and areas in which peasant produce promised an especially attractive reward. Such guerrilla activity was a necessary military pursuit, but cannot be separated from existing social relations in particular localities, where prosperous, independent peasant communities were sometimes prime targets for rebel guerrilla bands composed largely of younger men and poor white *bywoners*. Areas occupied by guerrillas, however temporarily, were invariably made subject to republican native law.

Mission stations tended to be well-defended but promising prey for the guerrillas, and a number were brutally attacked. When the Rev. C. Schröder of the Rhenish Missionary Society returned to Gordonia after the war he found remaining only a small portion of his former congregation.[26] The Methodist mission station at Leliefontein in Namaqualand, a thriving community of independent peasants that served as a valuable source of British military labour and a haven for deserters from neighbouring Afrikaner farms, was ruthlessly razed and plundered by guerrillas and local rebels led by S. G. Maritz in 1902, its resources either expropriated or destroyed, and many of the survivors conscripted to work on local white farms. The brutality of the attack sickened even Smuts and Deneys Reitz, who arrived at Leliefontein shortly afterwards. 'We found the place sacked and gutted, and, among the rocks beyond the burning houses, lay twenty or thirty dead Hottentots, still clutching their antiquated muzzleloaders . . . Maritz [had] wiped out the settlement, which seemed to many of us a ruthless and unjustifiable act We lived in an atmosphere of rotting corpses for some days.'[27]

The agrarian violence of the time was amply recorded by military and civilian officials and considerable documentation exists of the murder, execution and ill-treatment of peasants and artisans. A case typical of the period, and one that was used extensively for British propaganda purposes, was that of Abraham Esau, a Calvinia blacksmith, prominent Coloured community leader and a fiercely patriotic British agent for local intelligence, who in early 1901 was tortured and executed by Free State guerrillas following the occupation of the town.[28] Those accused of executing Coloureds and Africans were brought to trial by the British wherever possible, but this was no easy matter, and men apprehended were not easily proven guilty. The use in such cases, and in other treason trials, of black witnesses became yet another matter for local white grievance and a further source of intimidation. The execution and ill-treatment of loyal blacks was nonetheless one of the charges made against most of the prominent guerrilla leaders who were captured and brought to trial, including Johannes Lötter and Gideon Scheepers, both of whom were executed, in October 1901 and January 1902 respectively.

In the eastern Cape the Transkeian levies that had been mobilised in December 1899 were mostly disbanded in March 1900, with the exception of 350 men in East Griqualand and 110 in the Transkei who were maintained to control cattle-rustling. By the end of 1900 the implications of severe famine in a number of districts of the Transkei and Ciskei had begun to cause the authorities serious concern. In Peddie and Butterworth the local supply of grain by the close of the year was reported to be 'practically nil', and between 400 and 500 paupers received daily rations of mealies in Willowvale. Several cargoes of American wheat were imported through East London but did little to alleviate the problem in the most distressed areas.[29] The famine was accompanied by a bout of stock thieving described as reaching 'epidemic proportions'. Afrikaner farmers, especially in those districts from which a number of men had left to join the rebels, were frequently the victims. W. T. Brownlee, for one, believed the trend was directly related to food scarcity, since stolen cattle were often bartered for grain.[30] The Transkeian administration, alarmed by the scale of livestock thefts, was concerned too that in the environment created by the renewed guerrilla incursions and rebellion in the colony the desperate circumstances of many blacks might assist the work of Boer agitators. Thembu and Mfengu levies were quickly brought into Engcobo district when Boer emissaries were reported to be orchestrating discontent among the impoverished inhabitants. Later it was rumoured that the guerrillas were drawing sustenance from the Coloureds of the Kat River settlement.[31]

On 31 December 1900 an additional 500 Mfengu and Thembu levies commanded by Colonel F. W. Armstrong were called out on active service. On 13 January the force arrived at Maclear to prevent guerrillas entering East Griqualand. On 14 June, however, a small force led by Fouché moved into the Maclear district, where they remained for over two weeks before retiring into Barkly East with 200 fresh horses. The incursion drew attention to the difficulties of preventing guerrilla groups from penetrating the region and led to more levies being raised. On 18 July fifty Africans were enrolled and armed, and on 3 September called up to join Armstrong's force at Lehana's Pass in Mount Fletcher district. On 6 September 500 Bhaca and 500 Basotho were mobilised by H. P. Leary and posted to Katkop. On 23 September additional levies were mobilised from Tsolo and Qumbu.[32] A Griqua detachment was also raised. Interestingly, during the first phase of the war the defence of East Griqualand had been entrusted to the Mfengu, largely because of memories of the activities in 1897 of the Griqua rebel, Andries le Fleur. By 1901, however, it was apparent that the Griqua did not contemplate resistance. The detachment was made up of 250 men, some of whom had earlier fought in the frontier wars and in Rhodesia, and who collectively made a favourable impression on a local newspaper correspondent, who noted that it was 'a revelation to see what a well set-up and serviceable body of men they have turned out . . . It would seem as though the Griquas had found a vocation at last.'[33]

Small guerrilla groups led by Myburgh, Fouché, Wessels and Bezuidenhout continued until the end of the war to conduct almost an independent campaign in the northeastern Cape, but only one significant confrontation took place with the levies in the neighbourhood of East Griqualand. On 19 November Bezuidenhout with fifty-three men invaded Maclear district and moved towards Gatberg where, on the next day, he was met by Captain Herbert Elliot, the son of the Chief Magistrate, with 300 black levies. A brief engagement followed, in which Elliot was killed, before the Boer force withdrew with the loss of six men.[34]

The eastern regions of the Cape, where there were the largest concentrations of the African population, were therefore successfully defended against guerrilla penetration; indeed, no determined efforts were made by the republican forces to enter East Griqualand or the Transkei. However, it was a different story elsewhere in the colony. In the rural areas of the northeastern and northwestern Cape guerrillas and rebels launched a ruthless campaign against the property, civil liberties and in some cases lives of black peasants and artisans. The Boer forces were concerned with activities beyond living off the land and extending the theatre of operations; they were intent, too, upon reshaping social relations in the interests of the predominantly Afrikaner farming community, which before the war had been under some pressure from the success of black peasant agriculture and a scarcity of farm labour. The eager participation of black peasants and artisans in the British war effort was closely related to defending their roles as citizens with control over their own skills, produce and labour.

7

Black workers

The development of diamond mining in Griqualand West from 1867 and gold mining on the Witwatersrand from 1886 produced far-reaching changes in the South African economy. Minerals attracted capital and immigrants from overseas; new markets for food were created in the thriving towns of Kimberley and Johannesburg; railways were built with revenue derived from the mining industries; the seaports developed; and manufacturing and service industries also began to grow because of the demands of the mining sector and the expansion of the domestic economy. The mining industry required capital, imported technology and skilled workers from overseas; but above all it needed a cheap and assured supply of black labour. In the gold-mining industry the price of labour was of paramount importance, especially to those mining concerns that became involved in the mid-1890s in the capital- and labour-intensive deep-level extraction of gold.

The mineral revolution in South Africa led to a growth in the demand for black labour in all industries – in mining, manufacturing, on the railways, in commercial agriculture and at the seaports. The migration of Africans to work in industry was determined by the fiscal pressures placed on them to obtain cash for taxes and rents and to provide for new consumption requirements, and by the increasing difficulties experienced by many peasants of meeting their cash needs through the sale of agricultural produce and livestock because of land shortage, soil deterioration, changing patterns of production and the pressure of population on the cultivable land available.[1] Livestock losses from the rinderpest epidemic in 1896–7 effectively terminated many Africans' independence from the labour system and provided a fresh incentive to accumulate capital with which to rebuild depleted herds.

The gold-mining industry was the most rapidly expanding employer of labour during the years before the South African War. In 1890 the number of Africans employed on the gold mines was 15,000; by 1895 the labour force had risen to 50,000, and by 1899 it had risen to almost 100,000.[2] The migration of workers to the gold mines was stimulated by the increased intensity of recruitment, especially following the establishment in 1896 of the Rand Native Labour Association, and by the conclusion of an agreement with the

Governor-General of Mozambique in 1897 which permitted licensed agents for the industry to recruit workers from the southern region of the Portuguese colony, which was a less competitive recruiting area than most other parts of southern Africa and was capable of providing large amounts of relatively cheap labour for longer periods than anywhere else. By 1899 workers from Mozambique made up almost two-thirds of the entire black workforce on the gold mines.[3] During the first half of the 1890s the average monthly wage of black mineworkers rose from 42s to 63s 6d. However, in 1895, and again in 1897, wage reductions were enforced so that by 1899 the average monthly rate had fallen to 49s 9d, though the reductions were not of the order the mining companies hoped for because of administrative difficulties, continuing inter-company competition for workers and fluctuations in the labour supply. The general increase in the supply of workers nonetheless remained largely unaffected because of the impact of colonial taxation, agrarian poverty, the developing cycle of debt among hard-pressed blacks in the countryside, and the effects of the rinderpest epidemic, which pushed peasants into wage employment throughout southern Africa in almost unprecedented numbers.[4]

Africans did not respond passively to the prevailing conditions of work. The strategy of black workers can be seen in the first stage of the migrant labour system, for some workers refused to be recruited by labour agents, instead making their way independently to employment areas to avoid the deception frequently practised by recruiters.[5] The patterns of labour migration in southern Africa were largely determined by the rates of remuneration available in the various regions. In particular the higher wages offered to workers on the Rand produced a southward migration of labour from south-central Africa. Migration patterns determined by wage levels developed between the different states of South Africa and also within them. The higher wages available on the gold mines and diamond fields drew workers considerable distances, while dock employment at the seaports, which was more remunerative than farm labour or unskilled work in the small market towns, attracted migrants from the rest of the Cape Colony and Natal, and even from further afield.

The careful selection of an employer by workers occurred when men arrived at a particular labour centre. Their choice was based on the desire to procure the highest available wage and the most congenial conditions of work and employment. On the South African gold mines the quality of accommodation, the reputations of overseers, compound managers and mine police, and the physical conditions at the labourer's place of work, all were important criteria of selection. Desertion was usually the means by which workers were able to exercise choice once contracted to a particular mine. In spite of the introduction of a pass law in 1896, and efforts to administer labour more rigidly by the mining companies themselves, desertions reached such a scale on the gold mines in 1898 that in one month the number of deserters reported by companies affiliated to the Chamber of Mines exceeded the number legitimately discharged.[6] Workers were able to exploit the inconsistencies and maladministration of the pass regulations by applying for new passes immediately outside the mining area, or by representing themselves as new arrivals to the Rand by purchasing travelling passes from unscrupulous labour recruiters.[7] Furthermore, many mining companies systematically recruited workers from nearby locations and neighbouring compounds by employing labour 'touts' who encouraged desertion by promising workers better pay and conditions.[8] The failure of mining companies to counter successfully the strategies practised by black workers to protect as much as possible their own interests was one of the factors that convinced the mining industry in the late 1890s that to achieve optimum conditions for the successful development of the industry, it required the full collaboration of a state that was not only more amenable to mining interests than the South African Republic, but also one that possessed the capacity to implement effectively the legislation that the industry needed.

MINEWORKERS AND THE OUTBREAK OF WAR

The black labour force on the gold mines began to become depleted some months before the beginning of the South African War. As early as June 1899 labour representatives were obliged to send messengers along the line of reef to allay the anxiety of workers who feared they would be prevented from returning home by seemingly imminent military operations. A similar exodus of workers had taken place in 1896 immediately after the Jameson Raid, when thousands of workers returned home from the Rand as a result of reports that war between Britain and the South African Republic was impending. At the beginning of October 1899 the departure of workers from the industrial region gathered new momentum. On one day, 9 October, 3000 workers from Mozambique were despatched by train to Lourenço Marques, and a further 1316 labourers were issued with travelling passes to return home by whatever means they could. The arrival of so many workers in Lourenço Marques caused the Portuguese administration difficulties in accommodating the migrants; temporary camps were established and troops held in readiness to deal with any signs of disorder. Altogether between 1 September and 19 October some 78,000 blacks left Johannesburg by rail for destinations beyond the frontiers of the Transvaal. As well as workers, those who left included pimps, prostitutes, criminals and illicit liquor sellers, many of them taking refuge in the coastal towns such as Cape Town and Durban. In Johannesburg general confusion prevailed, with thousands of workers carrying blankets and cooking utensils coming into the town from the mines and the Witwatersrand region generally. Crime increased as Africans raided stores and broke into houses and removed furniture. Bands of armed workers moved around the mining area with knobkerries and a number of storekeepers were murdered, the confused state of affairs offering opportunities for recrimination against individuals and their property. There was also a groundswell of anger brought about by the failure of some *uitlanders* to pay the wages of their African servants and employees in their haste to leave the Transvaal.[9]

The lawlessness that prevailed in Johannesburg and its environs spurred the government into introducing special legislation to control those blacks – estimated to number about 35,000 – who after the beginning of the war remained in the industrial region.[10] A curfew was introduced on the Rand from 7 p.m. to 5 a.m. (9 p.m. to 5 a.m. for whites), and all gatherings of blacks, whether in the streets or on private property, were prohibited. Police activity was stepped up considerably, and more African agents enrolled (at £8 a month) to report on the activities of workers in the compounds and to ascertain the number of guns, rounds of ammunition and other weapons concealed there. Particular attention was also paid to rooting out criminals and illicit beer manufacturers. Both F. P. Joubert, Inspector of Passes, and Commandant Dietzsch, Chief of the Peace and Order Commission, organised lightning strikes on suspected operators.[11]

At the beginning of October the office of J. S. Marwick, the Natal Native Agent in Johannesburg, was surrounded by thousands of Zulu workers, unable to leave the Rand by rail because of the suspension of passenger trains to Natal, and concerned lest their earnings be confiscated before they left the republic. Since one of Marwick's main responsibilities was to ensure that Zulu workers' wages were safely and regularly remitted to the colony (tracing tax defaulters and debtors was another of his assignments), it is scarcely surprising that he was prepared to go to some lengths to secure the safe passage of Zulu workers and their earnings back to Natal to avoid any possible shortfall in hut tax revenues (already between 28 September and 6 October £9877 had been remitted by Marwick's office). Aware of the serious threat to law and order posed by the Zulu, the Boer authorities eventually granted permission for Marwick to march the 7000–8000 workers to the Natal frontier. By 7 October the multitude, containing criminals and petty thieves as well as migrant industrial workers, reached Heidelberg, marching thirty abreast and headed by musicians performing traditional Zulu songs. As the march continued the procession lengthened as stragglers fell further behind, and a number of deaths from exhaustion occurred. By 13 October the Natal frontier was reached, and two days later the Zulu entered General Penn Symons's camp close to Dundee, though only after 400 workers had been commandeered by General Joubert's invading force to drag its siege guns up to the summit facing Majuba. Once in Natal workers were charged £1 per head to continue their journey by rail. In a state of exhaustion, and anxious to leave the theatre of war without delay, most men were easily persuaded to surrender almost two weeks' wages for a ticket.[12]

Although the seven-day, 240-mile trek to Natal was an arduous journey, the Zulu marchers were more fortunate than many other workers. Labourers from all regions of southern Africa were compelled to leave the Rand by the Delagoa Bay railway route, wherever might be their ultimate destination, and a number of men perished on the journey home on foot from Lourenço Marques.[13] As an additional measure to discourage further unrest on the

Rand, the Kruger government mobilised men to round up blacks without a job or any visible means to support themselves and to march them out on to the veld. Seventy-nine prisoners from the Boksburg gaol were escorted all the way to Ressano Garcia on the Mozambique frontier.[14]

The Boer authorities were concerned to ensure that as little money as possible left the Transvaal, and intensive efforts were made to seize the wages being carried to the frontiers by departing black workers. There are many reports of workers who left the industrial region having their earnings confiscated by commandos and railway officials. Some Africans were apparently deprived too of most of their clothing because it was customary for them to conceal wages in their garments.[15] As a result workers devised a variety of ways to hide their cash, either about their person or in everyday objects that were unlikely to arouse suspicion. One worker purchased a bar of soap, used it a little, then formed a cavity in the block into which he placed his money. His companion bought a loaf of bread, cut off the top, and concealed his money inside, hoping that the Boers would not be interested in looking for money in an old dry crust of bread. But all their efforts were in vain, for the soap was confiscated and the bread crumbled away. The men eventually arrived home in East Griqualand penniless and exhausted.[16] In the Transkei workers were described as having returned to the region from the Rand 'in a state of absolute destitution, great numbers having walked from inability to pay railway fares, and emaciated from want of food'.[17]

Meanwhile in Kimberley those workers employed on the diamond fields faced the threat of almost immediate encirclement by Boer commandos at the beginning of the war. Although many successfully escaped from the area before the siege began, over 10,000 workers were compelled to endure the subsequent five-month investment. At first an attempt was made by the British forces to expel 3000 Basotho workers from the town, but most of the men were turned back by the Boers and a number shot by the garrison in the confusion that followed.[18] Workers were conscripted to build all the town's fortifications, and when these had been completed De Beers employed men on maintenance work, stone-breaking and on the construction of a road designed to 'afford a pleasant drive from Belgravia to the Racecourse'. Because the company's supply of fresh vegetables was taken over by the military for general white consumption, scurvy soon spread in the compounds. There were over 2000 reported cases of the disease among Africans during the siege, of which more than 250 eventually proved fatal. Typhoid and dysentery also spread, with the result that a death rate among blacks of 252 per thousand per annum was recorded in January 1900. Altogether there were 1500 deaths during the siege, almost all of them blacks. According to official figures, during 1900 only two out of every ten black children born in the Kimberley area survived.[19] Resistance by workers to the appalling conditions of the siege rapidly emerged. Men refused to return to the compounds, declined to work and none volunteered to risk their lives further by acting as runners to pass through the Boer lines with despatches.[20] The Basotho chief, Jonathan, demanded an investigation of the 'brutal' way in which workers were being treated in Kimberley when he was given an account of conditions there by one of his men who managed to escape from the town.[21]

The disruption of the migrant labour system at the outbreak of war increased the pressure on food resources in the rural areas, especially in districts of the Transkei, Zululand and parts of Natal where the unprecedented influx of people was accompanied by disappointing harvest yields. Supplies of food were particularly short during the first year of the war in the Emthonjaneni, Nkandla and Nquthu districts of Zululand, and in some areas of northern Natal, where the laying waste of crops by military operations was an additional cause of distress. Both the Cape and Natal governments administered relief in hard-pressed districts in the wake of the migrants' return. Food consignments were rapidly distributed on their arrival in Zululand, and in the Willowvale district of the Transkei between 400 and 500 Africans received daily rations of 1 lb mealies during 1900.[22]

LABOUR MOBILISATION

The labour policies of the Boer republics at the beginning of the war were designed not only to satisfy the manpower needs of the commandos but were also related to the measures taken to preserve law and order among the black population, especially on the Witwatersrand. Another consideration to be taken into account was the need to provide additional labour to maintain agricultural output, which was made difficult by the absence on commando of farmers, their sons and some of their regular servants. At the outbreak of war blacks in the republics were conscripted to work on farms and forbidden to leave their employers for its duration, to collect firewood for the commandos and to accompany the Boers as labourers, waggon-drivers, leaders of oxen, *agterryers*, guides, scouts and as members of an ambulance corps.[23] To refuse to serve with the Boer forces was punishable by a fine of £5, by imprisonment or by twenty-five lashes, and the methods of conscription did not err on the side of leniency.[24] In October 1899 the *Standard and Diggers' News* protested:

> It is time the attention of the authorities was drawn to the inhuman treatment meted out to the natives in town by some of the so-called commandeering officers. Lashes are quite common, and, while we are not ultra-sentimental, and believe in the native being firmly treated, we cannot allow cruelty to go by unnoticed.[25]

Many workers recruited by the Boers were paid no wages, but given daily rations and permitted to retain a limited amount of loot (in practice often taken from other Africans). Conscription frequently took the form of raids into mine compounds and the Witwatersrand locations, and served the additional purpose of intimidation following the introduction by the government in January 1900 of a maximum monthly wage for all black workers of 20s (the 20s maximum wage had been applied to black mineworkers a month earlier).[26] Commandos also made raids on railway stations and halted trains carrying migrant workers to the republics' frontiers. Those workers detained were either put to work immediately by the commandos, or else sent to Pretoria, from where men were allocated to various Boer units.[27] Landdrosts made a careful check on the movement of migrants to ascertain where the largest concentrations of returning workers were situated, and the labour requirements of the Boer units were monitored by the Native Affairs administration.[28] Commandos also entered locations to procure labour for military and domestic duties, and in the occupied districts of Natal and the Cape commandos brought together Africans and Coloureds to work in their camps, in the occupied towns and on the farms of Boer rebels.[29] In many cases it seems such labour was unpaid. It has been suggested that during the first phase of conventional military activity the Boer forces directly employed about 10,000 Africans, a conservative estimate.[30]

Among those blacks conscripted into employment by the Boers there was an understandable groundswell of dissatisfaction. A regular stream of deserters sought the protection of the British army, and so common was the crossing over of blacks from the Boers to the British that officers found they could glean useful intelligence from the deserters.[31] So desperate were some workers to get away from the Boers around Ladysmith that several black workers made their way *into* the besieged town, in spite of the dreadful conditions that were known to prevail there.[32] When the British columns entered Pretoria Lord Roberts received a petition from two black clergymen, who on behalf of the inhabitants of the town requested relief to alleviate the distress brought about by the Boer conscription of labour.

> A very large majority of us were commandeered for Government and private work, such as rendering of menial services at the front, at the Artillery Camp, in the town, and even at private farms, without any remuneration whatsoever; and in consequence whereof, many of us find ourselves quite destitute and on the brink of starvation.[33]

In the countryside, too, the conscription of labour and expropriation of African livestock to feed the commandos caused hardship and resentment, especially since some black agriculturalists were compelled to work on the farms of neighbouring whites. Nor did all the seized livestock find its way to the commandos.[34] There can be little doubt that some of the seeds of the agrarian unrest that followed the British invasion of the republics were sown at this time.

On the Rand labour was mobilised and rigidly controlled to maintain gold production at nine of the most important mines, whose output was taken over by the state. Pumping operations were also continued on other mines whose production was suspended. Labour was strictly supervised and in some cases the duration of underground shifts increased by one hour.[35] From the time of its introduction the maximum monthly wage of 20s was rigidly enforced. Not surprisingly resistance by workers occasionally erupted against the more oppressive wartime system of worker control. As early as in October 1899 two workers at the Dreifontein Mine had 'occupied' the underground section armed with Martini-Henry rifles; in January 1900 between thirty and forty workers at the George Goch location attacked a group of white policemen; and during March mine constables all over the reef engaged in disarming workers of knobkerries and assegais, which on some mines were reported to have been found in large quantities.[36] When Roberts's troops entered Johannesburg in mid-1900 some black workers jubilantly burned their passes in relief at the apparent passing of the harsh wartime regime on the Rand and the danger of being conscripted by the Boers to perform unpaid military duties at the front.[37] It is clear, too, that their action symbolised an expectation that the British would introduce a new, more flexible and remunerative labour system on the Rand. (Earlier, when Boer prisoners were marched into Pietermaritzburg in Natal they were jeered by Africans shouting 'Where are your passes?'[38])

The earliest recruitment of workers by the British army was undertaken in the locality of military camps and through magistrates in those areas of the Cape and Natal that had become associated with the supply of labour for the mines and transport work – in particular the African locations in the Ciskei, Thembuland, Fingoland and northern Natal, and among the Coloured communities of the western Cape. Most of the men were enrolled in the remount and transport departments. In Natal, the main theatre of the earliest and most intense military operations, the government instructed *isibalo*[39] work parties that had been ordered out for road building to proceed to the front to construct fortifications and perform other labouring duties for the army. The government's directive, however, was strongly resisted by many workers. Almost the whole of a party of labourers working near Pietermaritzburg deserted home to Victoria County when the men received word they were being moved up-country. At the beginning of November desertions by *isibalo* workers were reported by the Chief Engineer, J. F. E. Barnes, to be 'increasing dangerously'. The Public Works Department at first attempted to override the objections of workers: police constables were hired to watch over labour parties; the number of African overseers was increased by requesting chiefs to provide the department with additional *indunas*; and orders were issued that all deserters were to be arrested by magistrates the moment they returned home. But the depletion of the labour parties continued, so strongly did workers object to moving to the front where, they believed, men would be expected to perform dangerous and unpleasant tasks for an uncompetitive wage of only 20s a month.[40]

In these circumstances a new labour policy was formulated in Natal. At the beginning of December it was decided that a Native Labour Corps should be created and administered by the Public Works Department, but with the important difference that the labour employed would be – nominally at least – voluntary. Barnes was appointed to supervise the general arrangements for the corps, and J. S. Marwick given responsibility for mobilising workers. Within a short period Marwick had recruited over 1000 men, supplied largely by chief Ncwadi and indirectly by the magistrates in Weenen and Estcourt. The men were usually engaged for three months and paid 40s a month, double the rate for *isibalo* labour. A small number of Indians were also enlisted, some of whom acted as overseers and were paid 60s a month. As the war progressed the corps gradually became dispersed throughout northern Natal, the Orange River Colony and the southeastern Transvaal.[41]

During the early engagements in Natal an Indian Ambulance Corps was also established consisting of 300 'free' and ex-indentured Indians – professional men, artisans and labourers – and 800 indentured workers, mostly from the sugar estates, who were despatched to the front by their employers. The men were paid 20s a week and sirdars 25s. M. K. Gandhi played a prominent role in encouraging free Indians to enrol in the corps, which he also joined himself. The Ambulance Corps was active in a number of the most important engagements on the Natal front, in particular at Spion Kop, where Indians entered the firing line on General Buller's instructions to remove wounded soldiers. The corps was disbanded in the middle of 1900 when Red Cross units from Britain arrived in South Africa.[42]

In November 1899, in expectation of the growth in the army's labour requirements, the military appointed Colonel E. P. C. Girouard, an officer with experience of recruiting and organising indigenous labour in the Sudan (and later to become Director of the Imperial Military Railways), to establish labour depots for the supply of black workers to all the departments of the army except the transport department, which continued to enlist in-dependently its own drivers and leaders and many of its unskilled workforce. The first labour depot was established at De Aar, an important railway junction in the northern Cape inhabited mainly by railway employees and 'well-known in South Africa as being unhealthy, very hot, and frequently subject to red-dust storms'.[43] Recruitment to the De Aar depot was initially entrusted to magistrates in the Transkei and Ciskei. Workers were enlisted for three months and paid 60s a month with free rations. After the British occupation of Bloemfontein in March 1900 another depot was organised there. Here the monthly wage was fixed at 40s with rations, and recruitment placed largely in the charge of Sir Godfrey Lagden in Maseru. A third labour depot at Johannesburg was established in July following the occupation of the Rand. At this site the monthly wage with rations was fixed at only 30s. The number of men registered at the labour depots and supplied to military departments was maintained at about 8000. Each worker was issued with a distinctive metal badge bearing his number.[44]

After the occupation of Johannesburg and Pretoria the labour policy of the British army became linked first of all to the need to maintain law and order in the industrial region and its environs, where there were about 35,000 blacks, including 14,000 still on the gold mines. Many workers on the Rand, as we have seen, evidently expected that immediate and substantial changes would take place in the system of labour relations. Two days after the army's entry into Pretoria the Italian consul informed General Maxwell, the Military

Governor, that all the members of the consular corps had remarked upon 'the growing arrogance of the natives, and . . . the insubordination towards their masters, which is already showing itself everywhere'. The army was alarmed to find widespread 'looting and . . . depredations'.[45] Those blacks working in municipal employment in Johannesburg demanded an immediate return to their pre-war rates of pay, and the payment of wage arrears. On being told that the old system would remain in force – including for the time being their wartime monthly wage of 20s – some of the municipal workers refused to continue in their occupations, and troops were called in to arrest the leaders of a strike among employees of the town's lighting department.[46]

In these circumstances it was not unexpected that, in spite of African hopes to the contrary, the harsh republican laws relating to the control of the black population were maintained in force by the British army. Military police rounded up hundreds of blacks and removed the bulk of remaining liquor sellers and prostitutes. On 7 June a notice was issued that 'with a view to the maintenance of order amongst the native population . . . the provisions of the Pass Law of the South African Republic, will, pending further arrangements, continue in force'. Africans arrested for failing to produce a pass were immediately sent to the compound of the Ferreira Deep Mine, where they were compelled to break stones in order to earn the 5s necessary to pay for a pass. Between 21 June and 31 October 1900 some 3990 blacks were sent to the compound. From there almost all went into some form of employment. 2190 were employed by the railways, 366 by the mines, 740 by private individuals and the rest – with the exception of 31 deserters – were put to work by the army.[47] A court to deal with breaches of the pass laws and disputes arising out of masters and servants legislation was organised by the military, and during the course of the war almost 1400 cases brought before it.[48] Additional regulations were later issued by the army in the Transvaal forbidding blacks to be in towns or on white men's farms unless they possessed a pass showing they were in the employment of a white person. Those blacks whose employers were absent had to obtain a certificate from the police commander in their district. Failure to produce a pass on demand rendered a person liable to be treated as a prisoner of war. During the war the pass laws can be said to have been relaxed somewhat in only one respect: in July 1901 the penalty of lashing was abolished for certain offences.[49]

It was the existence of a reservoir of unemployed mine labourers after all gold production had ceased that the army believed posed one of the greatest threats to order in the industrial region. The solution proposed by the army was that, with the exception of those men required by the mines for pumping and necessary maintenance work, blacks should be put to work by the military authorities to earn their subsistence and to discourage lawlessness. The Imperial Military Railways conscripted 8000 men to work on the construction of a new line for transporting coal along the gold reef. The men were paid 10d a day plus rations. Another 4000 workers were drafted to form the initial recruitment to the Johannesburg labour depot, at the rate of 1s a day plus rations. Since the number of blacks detained in gaol had grown so much during the first months of the war, pressure on prison accommodation was relieved by sending some detainees to work for the British army in Natal. Forced labour was also adopted as a method of discouraging lawless behaviour elsewhere in the Transvaal. When 400 blacks at Balmoral were reported by General Pole-Carew to be 'getting out of hand', General Maxwell arranged for them to be transported by rail to Johannesburg to be enrolled at the labour depot.[50]

The employment of black workers by the army on the Rand was looked upon favourably by the mining industry since it avoided the further dispersal of workers back to their homes. Because of the suspension of gold production it would have been impossible otherwise for the industry to have kept together the nucleus of a black workforce, since the mines could not have afforded to pay and ration labourers until such time as production was restarted. Milner was especially anxious that the labour requirements of the army and the mining industry be harmonised as much as possible, for he appreciated that the successful resumption of gold production depended on a regular supply of black labour. And it was the wealth to be derived from the mining industry that formed the keystone of his design for the reconstruction of South Africa when the war was over. When in February 1901 the Imperial Military Railways began to reduce its workforce on the Rand, and many blacks began either to return home or to seek work elsewhere in South Africa, Milner urged General Kitchener to make arrangements for workers to be transferred from military to industrial employment.

> If they could be engaged by the mines as the IMR dismisses them, they would suffice to commence work on two or three of the central mines along the outcrop. Not only would this mean a certain amount of business, a certain amount of revenue at once, *but it would keep the natives on the spot.* One of the greatest difficulties, when tranquillity is finally established, will be to get back a sufficient number of natives to work the mines. It is a thousand pities to let any go who are already on the spot.[51]

The army kept the mining industry informed of its demobilisation of labour from the railways in the industrial region, and efforts were made to encourage workers to make themselves available again for work on the mines. During the first week of May milling operations began at four mines – the Robinson, Meyer, Charlton, and Treasury; during the next four weeks the May Consolidated, Geldenhuis Deep and Wemmer mines resumed work. In order that more gold production might take place it was necessary that additional black workers resumed employment in the industry, and in order that this might proceed smoothly it was believed that measures were needed to minimise competition between the military and the mining industry in the labour market.[52]

For both parties concerned an ideal solution appeared to lie at hand in the form of the growing black refugee problem in the Transvaal and Orange River Colony. In June 1901, the same month that Kitchener ordered the release from military employment of the 4000 mine labourers conscripted to the Johannesburg labour depot, a Native Refugee Department was created with responsibility for mobilising labour for the army from among the refugees who were brought into camps established for those blacks whose livelihood had been destroyed by military operations. By April 1902 over 13,000 Africans had been enlisted from the camps for military employment, thereby making possible the run-down of the labour depots. While the arrangement was of benefit to the army, because it made available a regular flow of workers who possessed very little bargaining power in the labour market, the mining industry was unable to recruit as many blacks released from employment as it wished. Some workers either did not wish to enter into any new contract at all, wishing only to escape from the harsh wartime regime on the Rand until peace was restored and more certain conditions again prevailed, or else they were not attracted by the 30s–35s monthly wage introduced by the Chamber of Mines, and chose instead to seek more remunerative employment elsewhere. By December 1901 only fifteen of the seventy-seven gold mines that had been in production in August 1899 were operating again.[53]

The labour system described above represented the most centralised, and best documented, method of mobilising labour by the army. The workers conscripted by this system, however, made up only a part of the total recruitment. Very large numbers of blacks were employed locally in all the regions of South Africa. Scouts and guides were recruited by officers from local chiefs. The transport department, by far the largest single employer of labour within the British army, continued to enlist workers independently throughout the war. Transport workers were mobilised by magistrates, army recruiters and labour agents, and were drawn from locations, white farms and mission stations. Peasants possessing waggons and teams of mules and oxen, many of whom had a long history of involvement in the transport sector of the economy, hired themselves out to the military in large numbers. The opportunity to accumulate capital was too good to miss, for attractive contracts could be negotiated. The monthly wages of unskilled and skilled workers varied from as little as £2 to as high as £4.10s and £5.10s, and in the Cape, Coloured blacksmiths, wheelwrights and farriers could sometimes earn £10 a month. At least 14,000 Africans and Coloureds were at any one time employed in transport work, and probably many more, far outnumbering the Madras, Bengali and Punjabi cavalrymen brought to South Africa to perform non-combatant assignments in the remount department.[54]

Unfortunately, no comprehensive statistics of the total number of black workers in military employment were kept. When in the House of Commons the Under Secretary of State for War, Lord Stanley, was asked how many Africans were employed by the army and what were their terms of pay, he replied that 'No such record could possibly be kept.' It is impossible to use civil government statistics of the numbers of military workers leaving particular districts because the army regularly enlisted labour independently of magistrates and employed many men on a casual basis. It seems probable that the British army employed at least 100,000 black people in various capacities throughout South Africa, though this can only be a very rough estimate in view of the absence of complete documentation.

WORKERS IN BRITISH MILITARY EMPLOYMENT

Black people took up employment with the British army for a variety of reasons. Many white observers believed workers were attracted to the army simply by the availability of high wages. Some contemporaries were astounded by the levels of wages paid to Africans, and all kinds of exaggerated stories spread about the high remunerations on offer. It was noted that the wages of black skilled workers, such as transport drivers, exceeded those earned by agricultural labourers in Britain, and the journalist, J. Ralph, summed up the view of many when he commented, 'the British everywhere demoralise the blacks with too generous treatment, which is as bad for them as Boer unkindness'. The wages paid to certain categories of workers, especially skilled and semi-skilled labourers, were indeed high; drivers, leaders, scouts, blacksmiths and others with skills in demand were able to command wages of at least 60s a month, with rations generally included and additional payments for overtime and length of service. Throughout most of the Cape and Natal an experienced and industrious skilled man could expect to earn in a month not less than 90s. Unskilled workers could generally command wages as high as those obtainable on the Rand before the war, and in some cases up to 60s a month. However, wages paid to black workers by the army were not uniformly high, and were generally lower, especially for the unskilled, in the Transvaal and Orange River Colony, where the mobilisation of refugee labour helped to keep down wage levels. Some departments, such as remounts, paid their workers particularly badly in view of the hazardous tasks employees were expected to perform and the poor conditions in which they were obliged to work. The Methodist missionary, the Rev. George Lowe, felt moved to write home that press statements about workers being paid almost as a matter of course 80s a month were completely false.[55]

For more prosperous peasants, especially those who themselves owned waggons and draught animals, work for the military was attractive because of the exceptionally good money that could be earned. In the Cape ox-drivers possessing their own carts and oxen could earn up to 15s for each 100lb of produce transported eighty miles, and in the eastern Cape some contractors were prepared to pay hire fees of 35s a day. The 20,000 Tlhaping of the Taung reserve were paid a total of £25,490 by the military for the hire of waggons and as wages to drivers and leaders. Providing transport was by tradition an effective way of accumulating cash, and in view of the rinderpest losses of 1896–7 the wartime demand for transport and skilled drivers came at a particularly opportune time for replenishing herds. There are many reports of those blacks engaged by the military using their wages to purchase cattle, sheep and goats.[56]

One of the most attractive features of skilled and semi-skilled occupations with the army was the relatively short contracts that could be obtained. A contract for three months (compared to a six-month contract, customary for industrial labour at the time) made it much easier within the system of agricultural production to accommodate a period of absence engaged in transport riding. The military authorities were quick to realise the benefits of a short contract in attracting skilled peasants, especially from mission stations, and without it serious difficulties would undoubtedly have emerged, for during the war there existed in all but the most remote regions a remunerative market for produce and livestock. Peasant producers immediately took advantage of the army's demand for agricultural and animal products, grain, tobacco, vegetables, draught animals, cattle and remounts, for which they received considerably inflated prices. Peasants most able to benefit were those who already produced a substantial surplus for sale on the market and therefore were in a position to gain most from the inflation of grain and other prices; those who farmed close to garrison towns and camps, or who possessed the means to transport produce to the areas where troops were quartered (and who thereby cut out the system of local entrepreneurs and military contractors); and those who were in a position to extend significantly their area of cultivation.[57]

Other aspects of work with the army were attractive. For some, military employment was regarded as a prestigious and educative experience, calling upon a sense of patriotism and of 'belonging', sentiments especially common among the black elite and the better-off peasant farmers. Military *esprit de corps* was eagerly pursued; transport riders proudly wore brightly coloured clothing as a symbol of a common profession and to distinguish themselves from unskilled workers; military uniforms (though forbidden to be worn by workers) covertly changed hands at high prices; and skilled workers especially were always keen to acquire guns, whether officially or illicitly, and to drill regularly, thereby in their own eyes reducing the social distance between themselves and the fighting troops.[58]

The possibility of acquiring loot and joining in the spoils of war had its attractions too. In the Cape, raids on the livestock of Afrikaner farmers by military workers were not uncommon occurrences, and during the British advance through the northern Cape into the republics in 1900 loot auctions were almost a regular feature of army life. Blacks played an important role in the Transvaal and Orange River Colony in denuding the countryside of cattle and grain, and during the scorched earth campaign numerous opportunities were presented for quietly disposing of goods and livestock without recourse to official army records.[59]

There were perceived benefits too in the army for labour tenants and farm servants. The chance simply to get away from relationships of debt or to abscond from the service of over-zealous or cruel employers encouraged men to join up, and in the Cape many Afrikaner farmers, in particular, found their workforces seriously depleted. Clothing and blankets were sometimes supplied to workers by the military, and regular rations were generally available. Some workers received daily rations of meat, a practice that James Weir, chairman of the Indwe Mining Co., blamed above all for the movement of some of his company's workers into military employment. Although conditions of work varied a great deal between departments and between different areas, the impression appears to have become current in some districts that military employment involved duties that were less onerous than those on the mines. The magistrate in Albany reported in 1901 that workers who had returned from the army expressed themselves 'well satisfied and loud in their praises of the way they were treated by the military authorities', though this was by no means a unanimous opinion among all returning workers.[60]

Above all, many unskilled and semi-skilled workers had little choice but to look to the army for employment in view of the disruption of the migrant labour system at the outbreak of war, which temporarily deprived many blacks of an income upon which they depended to buy food and pay taxes and rents. The return to the rural areas of thousands of men normally absent at work increased the pressure on food resources, and in some of the already overpopulated and impoverished districts of Natal and the Cape the beginning of the war was followed by serious harvest failures. Grain prices soared and famine conditions rapidly developed. In order to alleviate the destitute circumstances of their families many men enrolled as ancillary workers with the army. In the Bathurst district of the Cape, where crop yields in 1900 were especially poor, 72 per cent of the adult male population enlisted with the military. The initial recruitment to the De Aar labour depot was concentrated largely in the King William's Town district, one of those worst affected by harvest difficulties, and from where over 3000 Africans left to join the army. In 1901 it was reported in Peddie that the local food supply was 'practically nil, and many families have been put in dire straits'. So many men left the district to work for the military that apparently few able-bodied men remained.[61]

Labour relations in military employment were not always harmonious, nor working conditions idyllic. Recurrent sources of grievance among workers emerged. Discipline was sometimes harsh, and stories of beatings, floggings and fines were regularly carried in the columns of *Imvo*. Relations with British working-class soldiers were at best ambivalent, as William Nasson has noted.

> It was inevitable that British troopers would seize opportunities to assert their muscle over those even lower in the army pecking order, and the actions of Tommies at camps ranged from beatings and stabbings of labourers to the forcible drowning of an African mule-driver in a pig trough at Green Point Camp in October 1901. Black mule-drivers resorted to indirect verbal retaliation, yelling 'Englishman' at their animals when whipping them . . . [But], as the war progressed, Tommies and blacks became increasingly involved in close personal relationships . . . Tommies were far more inclined than the officer elite to view blacks as fellow *men*, hostile and devious perhaps, but nonetheless inhabitants of a recognisable world. More than one soldier saw analogies

between black labourers and Irish navvies, and between malnourished black children and Glaswegian urchins.[62]

Colonial troops, especially Australians, seem to have played a prominent part in some of the day-to-day violence directed against black workers, while the high-handedness and cruelty of 'poor white', often Afrikaner, overseers frequently became sources of protest, desertion and even violence.

Other sources of grievance included lack of rest days, irregular rations, long working hours without overtime pay and the regular performance of hazardous and unpleasant tasks. Workers were sometimes reluctant to expose themselves to overt military danger, not considering that the endurance of excessive personal risk formed part of their contract with the military. Living accommodation was often poor, and alongside labour depots and remount stations insanitary and overcrowded shanty villages sprang up, housing single men, some workers with their families, the dependents of other workers absent with the troops and refugees. More often than not workers' settlements became a magnet for traders, petty criminals, prostitutes and liquor sellers, all anxious to relieve men of their army pay.[63]

Wage consciousness was well-developed among black workers. Chiefs and headmen who accompanied work parties, though sometimes siding with their charges in disputes, nonetheless vigorously upheld their own pay differentials, often thought by those concerned to be insufficient or less than promised; skilled and semi-skilled workers aggressively protected their status and higher rates of pay. The wages paid by different departments of the army, and even by different camps and depots within the same department, sometimes varied, and news of this soon spread. Military labour centres that paid inferior wages found it extremely difficult to recruit a full complement of men.

Protests by workers erupted from time to time and took a variety of forms, though strike action was relatively rare, largely because of the unpropitious military environment. Desertion, however, was a common phenomenon and a serious difficulty for the army even from the intensively policed compounds housing conscript workers on the Rand.[64] Workers' grievances were sometimes articulated through headmen hired as overseers, and traditional rulers intervened with the authorities on occasions on behalf of their people. It was largely through the lobbying of Lerotholi in 1900 that the wage paid at the Bloemfontein labour depot was increased from 40s to 60s a month, the rate being paid at the De Aar depot.[65] Later in the war Lerotholi brought to the attention of Sir Herbert Sloley the complaints of Basotho workers that they were being compelled to stay longer with the army than their contracts prescribed by being made to work an additional month's notice. Lerotholi also told Sloley that workers were 'sending their cries to me saying that they are working hard and are placed in the charge of Boers [i.e. Afrikaner "poor whites"] to make them work and the Boers are handling them without feeling'. An army circular was thereafter issued warning military departments that 'any report of ill-treatment seriously affects the labour market, and makes it difficult to obtain labourers'.[66]

Much of the dissatisfaction among workers centred upon those employed by the remount department, who were generally paid lower wages than voluntary workers employed by other departments of the army, and many of whose tasks, such as the breaking-in of horses, were dangerous and led to frequent serious injuries, sometimes resulting in loss of life. Workers at the Pietermaritzburg remount depot, paid only 30s a month, refused to work in the areas where military operations were taking place unless they were paid 40s. The army relented, but when these workers returned to the depot from up-country, having won their case, those that remained also struck successfully for a wage of 40s a month.[67]

Disillusionment with military employment became widespread among workers at the seven major remount depots in the Cape, at Queenstown, Port Elizabeth, Stellenbosch, Worcester, Naauwpoort, Bowker's Park and De Aar. In May 1901 a worker at the Naauwpoort depot, David Mokuena, complained bitterly of the high-handed treatment meted out by the chief conductor, Mr Gott, 'a great enemy of Natives'. Mokuena continued: 'We do not live in tents . . . but in very dirty places, we get very scanty rations and generally go to sleep without food, we work with spades, we carry bags etc., we work by day as well as by night without any mention of overtime pay, we also work on Sundays.'[68] Complaints by workers against conditions at the remount depots at Bowker's Park and Worcester prompted the Cape government to order an independent investigation. The report submitted revealed that the workers' principal grievance was their low rate of pay, though the report also drew attention to the men's inadequate diet, which did not include vegetables because of scarcity, and the fact that money was owed to the dependents of workers who had died while in military employment.[69]

THE WARTIME LABOUR MARKET

The outbreak of war and subsequent suspension of gold production on the Rand stemmed the southward migration of black labour from south-central Africa, and to some extent the flow of migrant workers in the subcontinent was reversed. Mining companies in Southern Rhodesia (Zimbabwe) sought to take full advantage of the temporary closure of the Rand mines and the prevailing uncertainty in the south to recruit labour from a wide area. Already in November 1899 large numbers of Africans were reported passing through the Bechuanaland Protectorate to work on the Rhodesian mines, and during the war workers from Basutoland, Bechuanaland and the Transkei were to be found employed there, as well as large numbers of men from Mozambique. At the beginning of 1901 the Labour Board of Southern Rhodesia planned a recruiting drive in the northern Transvaal, but the British administration, mindful of the need for military labour and workers for the impending resumption of gold production on the Rand, refused passports to the appointed labour agents (officials were aware, too, of the difficult relations that existed between the new regime and the black population of the region).[70]

141

Following the British occupation of the Transvaal the labour agreement with Mozambique had been abrogated by the Portuguese, and mining companies were especially concerned about the wartime migration of semi-skilled Shangane workers to Rhodesia. Although a few hundred workers were supplied to the British army as a personal favour by the Governor-General of the colony, a new agreement for supplying labour to the mining industry was not successfully renegotiated until late in 1901. However, workers from Mozambique did not immediately begin migrating again to the Rand in substantial numbers because of the absence of men on the Rhodesian mines, the wage reduction enforced on the Rand and the conscription of workers in the industrial region both by the Boer and British administrations, news of which circulated in Mozambique and made workers reluctant to enter into new contracts until all their people had returned. After the war Mozambican workers resumed large-scale migration to the Transvaal, but many more than in the late 1890s did so clandestinely and independently of recruiting agents for the gold-mining industry.[71]

During the war and immediately afterwards there was an enormous increase in the demand for labour in South Africa – in military employment, on the railways, at the seaports, in construction work, on white farms, in service industries and in manufacturing. Almost all industries experienced labour shortages. Labour was scarce on the Natal coalfield; the Indwe mines in the Cape were able to recruit a workforce only half the size of that which they had employed before the war; road-building budgets remained unspent for want of labour; and in some areas agricultural production was cut back because white commercial farmers could not recruit the workers they needed. Even De Beers, which before the war had experienced few difficulties in recruiting workers, was compelled to hire agents on a large scale and found particular problems in enlisting semi-skilled workers for drilling.[72]

The increased demand for labour that accompanied the expansion of economic activity during the war had a number of important consequences. First, government officials in Natal and the Cape Colony assumed an even more active role than hitherto in the direct mobilisation of labour. In the Cape so important did the function of magistrates as providers of labour become that *Izwi Labantu* accused the Native Affairs Department of having 'converted itself into a Labour Bureau'.[73] Workers were recruited by magistrates for military and government employment, and some men were supplied directly to private companies. Great efforts were made to enlist labour for dock work and to encourage workers to return to Kimberley after the siege. In May 1900 magistrates in the Transkei were instructed to send to the De Beers convict station all prisoners with six months or more of their sentence still outstanding. In Natal magistrates made a particular effort to encourage chiefs to supply additional workers. Though the recruitment of labour in this way was ostensibly voluntary, the practice was compared by some to an extension and intensification of the methods of *isibalo*.[74]

The period of the war and its immediate aftermath witnessed a remarkable growth in the operations of private labour recruiting agencies. Large companies, such as the South African General Agency Ltd, expanded and prospered, while smaller agencies and individual recruiters, both white and black, proliferated. Problems concerning wages and working conditions arising from the deception of workers by recruiting agents increased as well, adding to labour difficulties at employment centres and helping further to consolidate the already highly developed wage consciousness among black workers. In order to alleviate recurrent problems caused by false promises being made by recruiters to workers, and to seek to maximise the supply of labour with a view to enforcing wage reductions, a movement emerged in the Cape to lobby the Native Affairs Department to set up a special government recruiting agency, though the proposal was not taken up in spite of strong pressure from such organisations as the Table Bay Harbour Board.[75]

There was a generally modest, though in some cases much more pronounced, rise in the money wages of black workers outside the gold-mining industry. In Natal the wages of dock labourers at Durban harbour rose from 30s–35s to 30s–40s a month, and the wages of the most highly skilled workers from 2s 6d to 3s a day. Dock workers at Cape Town during the war were able to command wages of between 3s 6d and 4s 6d a day, even for unskilled work. On the coal mines in Natal the monthly wage of surface workers rose from 33s to 43s, and of underground workers from 43s 6d to 50s 4d. At Indwe the average daily rate for underground men rose from 1s 7½d to 2s, and the Indwe Company in 1901 extended its programme of offering allotments at a low rent to workers who entered into contracts in the hope of encouraging more men to enrol. The wages of domestic servants also increased. In the Orange River Colony members of the colonial administration petitioned for an increase in salary because of the higher wages demanded by domestic workers. After the war the magistrate at Richmond in Natal was surprised to find that domestic servants who had earlier been content to receive 25s a month were asking for 40s. The increase in money wages, of course, did not automatically mean a rise in real incomes for those wholly dependent on wage labour; the prices of food, cattle and manufactured goods also increased, in some areas much more than the increase in workers' wages.[76]

In some industrial sectors, such as in dock employment and work on the railways, where the demand for general labourers rose enormously during the war, pay differentials between skilled and unskilled workers became eroded, and in September 1901 the *Cape Times* remarked pointedly that the prevailing wages offered to black workers by the Harbour Board exceeded the pay of poor whites in other industries.[77] Above all else, employers blamed competition from the military in the labour market for the scarcity of workers, and companies resented having to offer three-month contracts and pay higher wages to compete.

Workers not uncommonly took advantage of their strengthened bargaining position in the labour market to counter duplicity practised by recruiters and to attempt to increase wages and improve conditions of work. Because wages on the farms remained low, a number of workers demanded more land for their use, while others refused to engage in farm labour until they had received their wages in advance. In Natal some farmers reluctantly agreed to such demands in the interests of maintaining a stable workforce, though their action was strongly disapproved of by the government.[78] In November 1901 the Cape Town docks were brought to a standstill by a strike in protest against the deduction of travelling expenses from workers' wages, and to draw attention to the 'wretched housing and general discomfort' of life for workers. In April 1902 a Mpondo work party contracted to the Cape railways refused to commence work for the wages offered, 3s 6d a day for labourers and 4s 6d for headmen. Instead they demanded rates of 4s 6d and 5s in view of workers being expected to pay for food and accommodation while at work.[79] Discontent prevailed, too, among *togt* labourers at the docks in Durban (i.e. those workers hired and paid on a daily basis). Here workers struck for a pay rise of 6d a day in June 1902, though after all the strikers had been dismissed on the recommendation of the local Superintendent of Police, most of the men returned to work under the existing regime.[80]

The increase in the number of black workers employed in industry and transport services during the war brought hundreds of additional workers to the seaports of Cape Town, Port Elizabeth, East London and Durban. Accommodation for workers in such numbers was simply inadequate, especially in Cape Town and Port Elizabeth, and many African migrants were obliged to find shelter where and how they could. When late in 1900 a shipment of forage for the British army arrived in Cape Town, the rats and fleas that accompanied it carrying plague bacillus, it was only a matter of time before the first human cases of bubonic plague occurred, and the infection began to spread through the crowded districts of the town that housed Coloured and African workers. By September 1901 the plague had claimed 389 victims.[81] The coming of plague was the final straw for many workers, already deeply dissatisfied, and angry about rigidly controlled working conditions and expensive, overcrowded and insanitary living quarters. The regulations introduced to isolate contacts and inoculate black migrants before they returned home were vigorously resisted by workers who argued first, that everyone was capable of catching plague and therefore it was unfair that only blacks should be inoculated by compulsion, and second that the introduction of yet another procedure to go through before being able to return home was unacceptable, since workers already had to obtain a pass from their employer and a travelling permit from the military. The largest protest against compulsory inoculation in the Cape seaports took place at Port Elizabeth in June 1901, when the port was brought to a standstill for two days by a strike of black workers that was so well organised that assistants in shops and stores and some domestic servants also stopped work.[82] The arrival in South Africa of bubonic plague, the concern of whites for public health, and the wartime overcrowding of white refugees and black workers at the seaports, all combined to accelerate the establishment of separate locations for black workers outside Cape Town and Port Elizabeth, at Ndabeni and New Brighton.[83]

8
Refugees

Between June 1901 and May 1902, 27,927 Boer refugees perished in British concentration camps in South Africa, a death toll of extraordinary proportions that probably amounted to twice the number of men killed in action during the war on both sides, and represented perhaps 10 per cent of the Boer populations of the two republics. In October 1901 the annual death rate in the camps reached 344 per thousand. More than 22,000 of those who died were children under the age of sixteen, and more than 4000 victims were adult women.[1] The hardships endured by Boer women and children in the camps aroused a storm of criticism in South Africa, Britain and indeed throughout the world, and became an issue around which opposition to the war in Britain crystallised. The Liberal leader, Sir Henry Campbell-Bannerman, described the army's policy of clearing vast areas of countryside in the Boer republics of livestock and crops, burning farmsteads, and removing the civilian population into concentration camps, as tantamount to 'methods of barbarism'. Lloyd George likened the army's methods to those of Herod, who had also 'attempted to crush a little race by killing its young sons and daughters'.[2] The suffering and humiliation of women and children in the concentration camps have become implanted indelibly on the collective memory of the Afrikaner people.

Yet it was not only Boer civilians who were compelled to endure the hardships of life (and death) in British concentration camps. By the end of May 1902, 115,700 Africans had also been settled temporarily in sixty-six refugee camps: 60,004 in the Orange River Colony, and 55,969 in the Transvaal. 14,154 black refugees are recorded as having lost their lives in the camps, and in December 1901 the annual death rate reached 380 per thousand (436 per thousand in the Orange River Colony camps), a rate of mortality more severe than that in all the white camps in any one month.

Contemporaries generally paid little attention to the black refugee problem and the suffering endured by those Africans brought into the camps. Napier Devitt, writing on the concentration camps in 1941, noted that while the Dutch Reformed Church took part in compiling the lists of lives lost in the white camps, it took no interest in the losses suffered by Africans, even though the Church had black members.[3] Emily Hobhouse, whose reports on conditions in the white camps played such an important part in drawing public attention to their maladministration, never visited an African concentration camp.[4] Indeed, those who either commented upon or investigated the predicament of black refugees were rarely critical of the administration of the camps. In March 1902, three months after the worst casualties had been recorded, the Aborigines' Protection Society requested of Joseph Chamberlain that 'such inquiries may be instituted . . . as should secure for the natives detained no less care and humanity than are now prescribed for the Boer refugee camps'; but the Society added the rider that its members recognised that 'the conditions of native life inevitably render the concentration of large numbers within limited areas extremely insanitary'.[5] William Alexander and Lawrence Richardson, who reported on the black concentration camps on behalf of the Society of Friends in 1902, found conditions to be generally satisfactory and in some respects laudable:

> At one time there was much illness and many deaths in the camps, but lately the health was much better. The people were encouraged to grow crops where they settled, and thus were not only able to provide their own food, but to hand over quantities to the military. The men were able to get plenty of work as drivers, scouts, servants etc., at even higher wages than they were accustomed to. The children were given the chance of attending school. It seems possible that this experience may have far-reaching effects on the natives.[6]

In a statement issued by the executive committee of the Cape-based South African Native Congress in 1903 the authors thanked Lord Milner for his 'able administration' of the black refugee problem and for 'the great work of repatriating the Native refugees, and for all that has been done in protecting, housing and feeding them in the Concentration Camps'. The statement continued: 'The cause of the sufferers can be confidently left in the generous hands of the Imperial Government in its anxiety to do the best for all classes.'[7] The confidence of the Congress, however, was sadly misplaced, and the neglect of the black refugee problem during the war and its aftermath concealed a story of profound misery and inhumanity.

THE EMERGENCE OF THE REFUGEE PROBLEM

Following the British annexation of the Transvaal and Orange River Colony and the beginning of the guerrilla war, the military administration was faced with two immediate problems concerning black refugees: first, to alleviate hardship and destitution among those Africans whose livelihood had been destroyed by military operations; and secondly, to give protection to black communities in danger of suffering at the hands of the Boer commandos for the assistance they had given to the imperial forces. Already by the end of July 1900 groups of blacks had begun entering the British lines and garrison towns to seek protection from military operations and punitive raids on their settlements. At Vryburg, where a large number of refugees with their livestock entered the town, the local newspaper suggested that 'A stranger . . . passing through the streets for the first time might be excused . . . for supposing that he had stumbled into a large native location.' In an attempt to enforce the dispersal of the refugees the municipal council decreed that they should all pay grazing fees, but few Africans were persuaded by the measure to leave.[8] In the western Transvaal many blacks with herds of livestock numbering several thousands sought military protection with the British columns operating in the region.

Though some refugees arrived with cattle and flocks of sheep and goats, others came in a starving and destitute condition. Some Africans in the latter category received help. The inhabitants of Zwaartboys, their *stad* having been destroyed by General Grobler, were permitted to settle close to Wolmaransstad and some assistance given them. In garrison towns relief was occasionally dispensed through the offices of the District Commissioners, though when Karl Kekane, a chief from Hamanskraal, requested permission to bring into Pretoria some 800 followers, mostly women and children whose menfolk were absent in military employment, General Maxwell considered it undesirable that they should be given protection in the town and provided with food.[9]

By the end of 1900 the need for a coherent policy towards black refugees had become apparent. Simply to turn them away from the garrisons threatened either to create a climate of opinion among Africans hostile to all white authority, or to force back the refugees on to the favours of the guerrilla fighters, who depended upon black informants to monitor British troop movements. Yet no arrangements had been made to accommodate African refugees for any length of time. The solution proposed by the District Commissioner of Heidelberg, that refugees be sent to Johannesburg and 'kept in compounds out of mischief', carried with it the danger they might become influenced by the disillusionment with the new military regime that was already prevalent among blacks on the Witwatersrand.[10] The question of how black refugees were to be accommodated assumed new importance when it became clear that if the policy of destroying farm buildings, livestock and crops, and concentrating Boer families into supervised settlements, was to be an effective way of combating the guerrillas, then blacks would also have to be removed from the countryside.

The question of precisely which groups of Africans should be removed was not one that could be regulated closely, and military expediency often took precedence over prescribed orders. In December 1900 a directive was issued which stated that it was 'not intended to clear Kafir locations, but only such Kafirs and their stock as are on Boer farms'.[11] This meant that rent-tenants and sharecroppers, as well as labour-tenants, were liable to removal. In the Rietfontein valley in Middelburg district 500 Africans were cleared from the neighbourhood of Boer farms because it was believed 'as soon as the Dutch families have left . . . these people will plunder their homesteads'.[12] The possession by Africans of grain supplies and appreciable herds of livestock was often an important factor in determining whether they were removed from the land, for in addition to the possibility that their produce and stock might fall into enemy hands, they were of direct benefit to the supply services of the British army.[13] When the commandos became more daring in their raids on cattle and grain supplies, blacks were cleared from locations and even from mission stations. Such actions were not always approved of by members of the administration responsible for African affairs. The suggestion made by Major J. Weston Peters, the assistant to the Military Governor of the Transvaal, that 'The orders of the Commander-in-Chief are that all stads are to be destroyed', was repudiated by J. S. Marwick, by this time the Superintendent of Native Affairs in the colony, who minuted 'It is to be hoped that there will be no attempt to carry out this order . . . the disquieting effect of such measures will become very widespread.' Sir Godfrey Lagden, the Commissioner for Native Affairs, agreed: 'I think a disastrous state of things will arise if Intelligence and other Officers are allowed to order the removal of native tribes from their locations . . . If the tribesmen are hustled about it may make them desperate and drive them into the enemy's hands.'[14]

Initially, blacks capable of work were handed over to the nearest military department, their wages being used not only to support themselves but also their refugee dependents, who were accommodated alongside the settlements established for Boer refugees. These rapidly grew in size and number during the first half of 1901 when intensive manoeuvres were begun to clear the countryside of African as well as Boer crops and livestock. The camps provided accommodation too for the black domestic servants of Boer women, many of whose husbands had accompanied their employers on commando, and for the dependents of other blacks already working for the British army as labourers, scouts and messengers. African and Boer refugees were intended to be separated in the camps, but servants were allowed to attend their employers during the day, and blacks were used for sanitary work and other labour duties in the camps, and even for guarding the settlements. Emily Hobhouse observed that at the Bloemfontein camp a white woman, her five children and a black servant were all living in one tent. At the Barberton camp it was reported: 'There are over a hundred native servants, principally with their families, who have accompanied their employers . . . There appears to be undue familiarity; some native sleeping, eating and drinking in the same tents as whites.'[15]

During the first six months of 1901 a small number of completely separate camps for black refugees were begun to be established. Sometimes this was in the belief that the concentration of blacks in too close proximity to the white camps adversely affected sanitary conditions. Often, however, they grew up simply as a result of the grouping of refugees in the neighbourhood of garrison towns. In the Orange River Colony 12,043 refugees had been concentrated in eight separate camps by the end of April 1901, and by the beginning of June this number had risen to 20,590. The largest camps in the territory were situated at Brandfort, Vredefort Road, Heilbron, Kroonstad and Edenburg.

In the Transvaal little is known about the number of black refugees before the end of June 1901, when 11,570 had been concentrated.[16]

During the first half of 1901 the black refugee camps were administered by the superintendents of the camps set up to accommodate white refugees. In June, however, a Native Refugee Department was established in the Transvaal under the command of Major (later, Colonel) G. F. de Lotbinière, a Canadian officer serving with the Royal Engineers. On 1 August De Lotbinière took over the responsibility for black refugees in the Orange River Colony. The creation of a separate department to deal with the black refugee problem was brought about in part by the recognition on the part of the military government of the hitherto inadequate and uncoordinated administration of black refugees. There can be little doubt about the neglect of some of the camps for Africans that had been set up. At Heidelberg, for example, refugees were reported to be subsisting only on the carcasses of diseased cattle; when two water carts were sent to the camp to improve the supply of water, these were soon afterwards commandeered back again by the army. Africans assembled at Heidelberg were consequently dying at the rate of about one a day.[17] It was recognised that as the scale of the black refugee problem grew – as it was certain to do with Kitchener's more intensive prosecution of the scorched earth campaign – concentration camps for blacks could only be administered satisfactorily by a separate department. Another, more important, reason for the establishment of the Native Refugee Department was the need to create a full-time staff with responsibility not only for supervising black refugees but also for recruiting workers from among them to release those mineworkers in military employment. On Kitchener's instructions these labourers were discharged from the army in June 1901 in order that gold production on the Witwatersrand might be resumed. The Native Refugee Department thus came into existence, its 'first consideration . . . the supply of native labour to the Army'.[18]

The organisation of the black concentration camps was based on two principles: to ensure that sufficient labour was forthcoming for the army; and to make the camps as self-supporting as possible. The settlements were situated along the lines of rail in easy communication with bases of military operations and centres where labour was required. The wage of 1s a day plus rations that was paid to refugees who accepted military employment was inherited from the army's labour depot at Johannesburg. Workers were enlisted for three months to enable them to return at intervals to their families in the camps. Farm tenants and sharecroppers possessing quantities of grain were allowed to bring only a small amount to the camps, ostensibly because limited transport was available for its carriage. It is unlikely that this was the most important reason for the decision, however, since the dependence of refugees on the camp authorities for food was exploited in order to encourage

Table 1. *Adult male workers recruited from the black concentration camps in the Transvaal, June 1901–June 1902.*

Month	Popula-tion of camps	Adult male popula-tion of camps	Men in employ of army or govern-ment	Men in private employ-ment	Men em-ployed in camps	Total adult male popula-tion in employ-ment	Propor-tion of adult male popula-tion at work/%
June 1901	11,570	1,728	195	40	17	252	14.6
July	14,759	2,278	1,146	154	50	1,350	59.3
August	22,795	3,942	1,951	385	106	2,442	61.9
September	28,491	5,187	2,343	583	194	3,120	60.2
October	32,006	6,032	2,597	337	370	3,304	54.8
November	39,323	7,427	3,254	654	681	4,589	61.8
December	43,420	8,496	4,100	750	736	5,586	65.8
January 1902	48,932	9,634	4,814	875	688	6,377	66.2
February	52,139	10,674	6,314	1,039	699	8,052	75.4
March	52,606	10,678	5,912	1,006	722	7,640	71.5
April	53,198	11,164	6,503	1,028	801	8,332	74.6
May	55,696	11,563	6,438	1,023	746	8,207	71.0
June	55,910	11,499	6,421	914	768	8,103	70.5

Source: Transvaal Administration Reports for 1902, *Final Report of the Work Performed by the Native Refugee Department of the Transvaal from June 1901 to December 1902*, p. 2.

men to accept work. Those in employment, and their families, were permitted to buy mealies at $\frac{1}{2}$d per lb, or 7s 6d a bag; Africans who objected to working, or who possessed cash or saleable commodities which enabled them to decline, were asked to pay double this price – 1d per lb in the Orange River Colony and 18s a bag (or more) in the Transvaal.[19]

The number of refugees who took up military employment rapidly grew. In addition, refugees – both men and women – were supplied to private employers in the neighbourhood of the camps. In Johannesburg an agency was opened to employ refugee children in domestic work and 276 boys and 133 girls found work in this way. Those refugees whose labour was not demanded either by the military or by employers in the locality of the camps, or who were physically unfit to perform strenuous labour, were provided with jobs as sanitary workers, cultivators and watchmen. Judged by its own principles – in January 1902 De Lotbinière wrote that supplying workers to the army 'formed the basis on which our system was founded' – the Native Refugee Department's mobilisation of labour was immensely successful. By the end of 1901 over 6000 workers had been supplied to the army, and by the end of April over 13,000 refugees from the camps were to be found working for the military.[20]

Table 2. *Death rates in the black concentration camps, June 1901–May 1902.*

Month	Orange River Colony			Transvaal			Total		
	Number of refugees	Deaths	Death rate per 1000 p.a.	Number of refugees	Deaths	Death rate per 1000 p.a.	Number of refugees	Deaths	Average death rate per 1000 p.a.
June 1901	20,790	No return	—	11,570	No return	—	32,360	—	—
July	22,713	256	135	14,759	No return	—	37,472	(256)	—
August	30,359	430	170	22,795	145	76	53,154	575	130
September	37,098	287	93	28,491	441	185	65,589	728	133
October	43,944	640	175	32,006	687	257	75,950	1327	210
November	45,791	1356	355	39,323	956	291	85,114	2312	326
December	45,987	1671	436	43,420	1160	320	89,407	2831	380
Jan. 1902	49,054	1542	377	48,932	992	243	97,986	2534	310
February	49,205	936	228	52,139	530	121	101,344	1466	177
March	48,693	555	137	52,606	417	95	101,299	972	115
April	55,188	333	72	53,198	297	66	108,386	630	70
May	60,004	233	47	55,696	290	62	115,700	523	54
Total Deaths		8239			5915			14154	

Sources:

a. Transvaal Administration Reports for 1902, *Final Report of the Work Performed by the Native Refugee Department of the Transvaal from June 1901 to December 1902.*

b. OFS Archives, CSO 86, 358/02, report of the development of the Native Refugee Department from August 1901 to December 1901.

c. CSO 90, 586/02, report on Native Refugee Camps for January 1902.

d. CSO 104, 1254/02, Native Refugee Department, report for March 1902.

e. CSO 108, 1493/02, report on Native Refugee Camps for April 1902.

f. TA, SNA 12, 1411/02, Refugee camp returns for May 1902, Orange River Colony and Natal.

g. *Statistics of the Refugee Camps in South Africa*, Cd.939, 1902.

h. *Statistics of the Refugee Camps in South Africa*, Cd.1161, 1902.

CONDITIONS IN THE CAMPS

The concentration of blacks in hastily organised and frequently insanitary camps unavoidably produced many deaths. By the close of 1901 the death rate among black refugees had reached alarming proportions. In all there were 14,154 recorded deaths in the camps, or more than one in ten of those assembled. This figure certainly underestimates the number since the recorded statistics of deaths in the black camps are even more incomplete than those in the white camps, and no reliable returns are available for the deaths which occurred before the establishment of the Native Refugee Department and during its first two months of administration in the Transvaal. Similarly there is no evidence of the death rate for refugees in transit to the camps and for deaths among workers recruited from them. Many deaths probably occurred within the camps that were not officially recorded. Half of the fatalities took place during the three months of November and December 1901 and January 1902; in December, the worst month, the annual death rate reached 436 per thousand in the Orange River Colony camps and 320 per thousand in the camps in the Transvaal. The overwhelming number of deaths occurred among children (81 per cent).[21]

The Native Refugee Department claimed that most deaths were brought about by the epidemics of chicken-pox, measles, dysentery and other diseases that swept through the camps. The extant documents from the camps shed little light on the matter because the cause of death of individual refugees is rarely given. It is interesting, however, that an incomplete set of returns indicating the causes of death of black refugees at the Bloemfontein and Vredefort Road camps between May 1901 and April 1902 reveals that the overwhelming number of recorded deaths resulted from pneumonia (60 per cent), followed by dysentery (26.5 per cent) and 'natural causes' (7 per cent).[22]

The conclusion arrived at by De Lotbinière after considering the high mortality rate among Africans in his charge is illuminating only in so far as it reveals the outlook of the man with responsibility for black refugees: 'natives do not thrive under abnormal conditions and sudden changes; if transplanted to new conditions, water, soil, food, etc., they appear to require time to become acclimatized'.[23] It is clear that the main causes of death derived from the appalling conditions of life in the overcrowded camps. Huts and tents were placed too close together and did not afford sufficient protection against the weather. Materials for roofing were scarce and fuel scanty. Water supplies were often insufficient and sometimes contaminated, and the diet of the refugees, who were usually in a poor physical condition when they arrived in the camps, lacked fresh vegetables and milk. The situation was not helped by deplorable medical facilities. In the Orange River Colony military doctors visited the camps only twice a week, and at Rooiwal it was reported in February 1902 that refugees had not been visited by a doctor for over a month.[24]

The alleviation of hardship in the African camps took second place to the improvement of conditions in those for whites. The peak death rate in the white camps of 344 per thousand per annum was recorded in October 1901, but the highest African casualties did not occur until December, and the abnormal death rate was not brought fully under control until March 1902.[25] The rations allocated to whites were larger, more varied and more nutritious than those provided for blacks. In the Orange River Colony, while the black camps were still administered by the Burgher Refugee Department, a contractor was engaged to ration black inmates at a cost per day of $4\frac{1}{2}$d for adults and $3\frac{1}{2}$d for children. At this time the cost of supplying white refugees was $8\frac{1}{2}$d per head per day. In practice many more blacks than whites worked, and more blacks were required to pay for their own food. At the time of the worst casualties among refugees in the black camps in the Orange River Colony less than a third of those detained in the settlements received free rations. The final financial statement of the Native Refugee Department shows that in the Transvaal the cost of the black concentration camps worked out at less than a penny per day for each refugee. Arrangements were made to enable Boer refugees to supplement their diet with so-called 'luxuries' such as tinned food, coffee and sugar; for a long time this privilege was denied to blacks, except when these items were prescribed to individual refugees as 'medical comforts'. The publicity given by the anti-war movement in Britain to conditions among Boer civilians helped to persuade the military to relinquish overall control of the white camps; black concentration camps remained under military supervision throughout the war.[26]

By the beginning of 1902 changes were being made to effect a reduction in the death rate in the black concentration camps, which were gradually broken up into smaller settlements and dispersed over a larger area. Most attention was given to improving the diet of those interned. Milch cows were purchased or hired to supply fresh milk to the refugees, and the system of free rationing was extended. More nutrients were introduced into the diet of refugees through the issue of tinned milk, bovril and cornflour. In spite of delays caused by transport difficulties, stores were gradually opened to sell 'luxuries' – flour, sugar, coffee, tea, syrup, candles, tobacco, clothing and blankets. These were found to be of benefit not only in helping to bring down the number of deaths, but in acting as an incentive to labour. In the Transvaal Africans spent £33,063 on 'luxuries', including £14,415 on cereals and £5500 on clothes and blankets.[27] These purchases became an essential part of the refugees' system of survival.

Greater emphasis, too, was placed on the need for Africans to cultivate land in the immediate neighbourhood of the camps. Arrangements for the cultivation of land by refugees had already been made before the death rate in the camps had manifestly got out of hand. Originally this had simply been in keeping with the department's principle of self-sufficiency and the intention to provide refugees with food when the time came for their eventual repatriation. It was quickly appreciated, however, that cultivation by blacks could provide a greater variety of food for the refugees, especially fresh vegetables and mealies. The splitting up of the settlements was therefore designed not only to improve sanitary conditions and prevent the unmanageable spread of disease, but also to provide sufficient cultivable land in protected zones close to the railway system. Because crops might afford cover to commandos crossing the British lines of defence, Kitchener issued instructions that land within a mile of a blockhouse was not to be cultivated. But cattle for draught purposes were scarce and ploughs even more so; in the Transvaal only 150 ploughs were

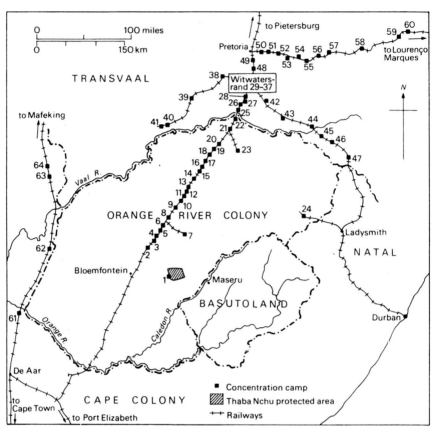

Map 10   Distribution of the main black concentration camps, 1901–2

Key

Orange River Colony
1   Thaba Nchu
2   Allemans Siding
3   Houtenbeck
4   Eensgevonden
5   Vet River
6   Smaldeel
7   Winburg
8   Welgelegen
9   Virginia
10 Rietspruit
11 Ventersburg Road
12 Holfontein
13 Geneva
14 Boschrand
15 America Siding
16 Honingspruit
17 Serfontein
18 Rooiwal
19 Koppies
20 Vredefort Road
21 Wolvehoek

22 Taaibosch
23 Heilbron
24 Harrismith

Cape Colony
(administered by ORC)
61 Orange River
62 Kimberley
63 Taungs
64 Dryharts

Transvaal
25 Vereeniging
26 Meyerton
27 Witkop
28 Klip River
29 Klipriviersberg
30 Natal Spruit
31 Bezuidenhout Valley
32 Boksburg
33 Rietfontein West
34 Bantjes
35 Brakpan
36 Springs

37 Nigel
38 Krugersdorp
39 Frederikstad
40 Koekemoer
41 Klerksdorp
42 Heidelberg
43 Greylingstad
44 Standerton
45 Platrand
46 Paardekop
47 Volksrust
48 Olifantsfontein
49 Irene
50 Van Der Merwe Station
51 Elandsriver
52 Bronkhorstspruit
53 Wilge River
54 Balmoral
55 Brugspruit
56 Groot Olifants River
57 Middelburg
58 Belfast
59 Elandshoek
60 Nelspruit

available for the cultivation of 9000 acres. The earth was often broken up only with the assistance of picks and hoes, a back-breaking exercise which to their surprise the camp superintendents found the refugees unaccustomed to, most of them being used to ploughing their land. Cultivation was practised mostly by older men, women and children so that the supply of labour to the army was unaffected. Crop production was also designed to provide oat forage and potatoes for the military; 32 per cent of the camps' yield was supplied to the army.[28]

A system of armed pickets was organised to defend the black refugee camps at night from raiding parties of Boer commandos, though in practice their duties were extended to protect crops and livestock and to collect firewood during the day. The groups were closely supervised and ordered to maintain a low profile, since in a war which was ostensibly – though not in fact – confined to white participants, it was feared by the military that their presence might attract, rather than prevent, commando raids. Orders were issued that on no account were the pickets to fall back on military camps or blockhouses if attacked.[29] There were some attempts by the Boers to infiltrate the African camps. During the early months of 1901 three successful raids were made by commandos on refugees at Potchefstroom; 258 cattle and 400 sheep were stolen, and one refugee killed.[30] The most spectacular incident occurred at the Taaibosch camp in the Orange River Colony on 29 December 1901 when an eighty-strong commando under Commandant Piet Lombard, led by a Coloured guide, quietly made its way into the settlement under the cover of darkness and looted money and clothing before being driven off by the forty pickets at the camp. The incident persuaded the department to increase the force of pickets to 100 men. A month later a second, less successful, attack was made on the Taaibosch camp, and a party of thirteen pickets shot by a guerrilla group three miles from the Geneva camp.[31] This last incident brought about a reassessment of the role of pickets, since it was suggested 'The fact of [blacks] being armed only invites attack.' The pickets were not disbanded, but afterwards permission to collect firewood was withdrawn and instructions issued that when refugees were obliged to escort livestock they should be accompanied by a white person. By the end of the war there were 850 pickets engaged in guarding the black concentration camps, 600 in the Orange River Colony and 250 in the Transvaal.[32]

The reports made by staff of the Native Refugee Department present a picture of undismayed refugees, grateful for the protection afforded in the camps against starvation and Boer assaults. In January 1902 Capt. F. Wilson Fox, the Superintendent of Native Refugees in the Orange River Colony, suggested that 'the natives seem generally contented', and in February, following a tour of inspection, he added, 'so much so that large numbers stated they want to stop in the camps for the rest of time if they should be allowed'.[33] G. B. Beak, a member of the Orange River Colony administration and later Assistant Director of the Government Relief Department, wrote of the black concentration camps: 'In a spirit differing vastly from that which prevailed in the concentration camps [for whites] they realised the situation, and accepted all that was done for them as partial compensation for the loss of their stock and crops, and for the hardships inseparable from a state of war.'[34]

The picture painted by some of the missionaries who visited the camps is a very different one. The Rev. E. Farmer, who visited black refugees at Krugersdorp, found acute pessimism and misery prevalent among those with whom he spoke: 'The natives I have talked with . . . tell me that cattle, gardens, houses have gone – that families are separated, that there is no knowing if fathers or mothers, sisters and even wives, certainly many husbands, are alive or safe. I have been told of many who have been brutally murdered by Boers.'[35] The Methodist Hugh Morgan wrote that he had heard stories of suffering, personal injury and oppression that had astounded him,[36] and the Rev. W. H. R. Brown, who visited the camp at Dryharts, was dismayed by the dreadful physical condition and low spirits of those whom he found there.

> They are in great poverty and misery, and our visit was a comfort to them. Many are dying from day to day – what is to become of the survivors I cannot think. Between the Dutch and the English they have lost everything, and there being no political party interested in their destiny, they 'go to the wall' as the weakest are bound to.[37]

While some of the less crowded camps do seem to have been relatively well run and formed thriving units of agricultural production, it is clear even from its own administrative records that the impression the Native Refugee Department attempted to create of universal contentment and tranquillity in the camps was some way from the truth. In November 1901 a meeting of refugees at the Harrismith camp complained bitterly of the lack of medical supplies, of accommodation which often consisted only of a few grain bags tied together (which they had themselves provided) and of their failure to receive satisfactory compensation for wasted crops and livestock commandeered by the army. The refugees were aware of the different organisation of the white camps: 'They receive no rations while the Boers who are the cause of the war are fed in the refugee camps free of charge . . . they who are the "Children of Government" are made to pay', the Magistrate of Harrismith reported the refugees' grievances.[38] Two refugees at the Honingspruit camp, Daniel Marome and G. J. Oliphant, lodged their protest with the Deputy Administrator of the Orange River Colony, Major Hamilton Goold-Adams.

> We have to work hard all day long but the only food we can get is mealies and mealie meal, and this is not supplied to us free, but we have to purchase same with our own money.
>   Meat we are still not able to get at any price, nor are we allowed to buy anything at the shops at Honingspruit . . .
>   We humbly request Your Honour to do something for us otherwise we will all perish of hunger for we have no money to keep on buying food.[39]

Fox himself reported that 'the people seemed altogether out of hand' at the Rooiwal camp, and found a general anxiety among refugees concerning compensation for their crops destroyed by the military.[40] Another form of protest was understandably less articulate. The precise statistics of black desertions from the camps are unavailable, but by the end of 1901, in spite of the careful supervision of those interned, 149 refugees had disappeared from the Transvaal camps and 136 from those in the Orange River Colony, where in the following month a further 117 desertions were recorded. The department speculated that many of the deserters joined up with the Boer commandos.[41]

REFUGEES OUTSIDE THE CAMPS

The magnitude of the black refugee problem extended beyond the concentration camps. An exodus of farm tenants and squatters into municipal and government locations and even beyond the frontiers of the annexed colonies also took place. In the Orange River Colony approximately 10,000 black refugees settled in the locations at Thaba Nchu, Bloemfontein and Kroonstad, and refugees were sometimes brought into these areas in preference to detaining them in the already overcrowded and insanitary concentration camps. In the municipal locations blacks were conscripted to perform general labour duties in the towns, and in the rural areas they were encouraged to take up arms as cattle guards on stock farms and to act as scouts with the military forces. The largest area where refugees were permitted to settle for the duration of the war was the Thaba Nchu district in the Orange River Colony, which was administered by the Native Refugee Department as a protected area. Thaba Nchu was planned by the military as an extensive farm for the production of grain, forage and potatoes. In return for providing the cultivators of the region, and the many refugees who sought a haven there, with picks, hoes and a small number of ploughs mostly taken from deserted white farms in the area, together with 6000 bags of seed oats and seed potatoes, the department reserved for itself the right to purchase the communities' surplus production. This was to be used to supply the black concentration camps and to sell to other military departments. The department estimated in January 1902 that the crops produced would be 'sufficient to feed all the refugees for a year – two bags per head for the population will suffice. The revenue derived from the sale of oats and potatoes should be sufficient to pay a considerable portion of the expenses incurred, including Staff.'[42] The project was something of a success, and many peasant families prospered, though the crop yields fell short of those hoped for, and the protection given to the Thabu Nchu communities did not prove complete. In February 1902 a Boer raiding party stole from the area 590 cattle, 32 horses and 6625 sheep and goats.[43]

In March 1901 Goold-Adams enquired whether in view of the difficulties of accommodating the growing number of black refugees in the colony some might be settled for the duration of the war in Basutoland. Sloley, the acting Resident Commissioner, agreed that some refugees could enter the territory, provided they arrived in small numbers, carried passes and were accommodated within the economic system of the Basotho communities without the issuing of government relief. By the end of the war some 12,000–15,000 African refugees had settled temporarily in Basutoland.[44]

A movement of Africans from the Orange River Colony and the Transvaal into Natal also took place. Over 6000 refugees with their livestock were permitted by the Natal government to settle on farms (some of them deserted) and in locations and reserves along the foot of the Drakensberg from Witzie's Hoek to Botha's Pass.[45] The Natal government appointed a Superintendent of Refugees, Arthur Leslie, who worked in close collaboration with magistrates and farmers in the border divisions who required temporary labour. Only a small amount of relief was dispensed by the Natal government, though arrangements were made for mealies to be sold to refugees at 10s a bag when they were selling for 17s at Harrismith. In Natal, therefore, where the number of refugees to be accommodated was smaller than in the annexed colonies, and where Boer raids on African pastoralists and cultivators were less frequent, a

Table 3. *Black refugees in Natal, December 1901–June 1902*

Division	Month	Men	Women	Girls	oys	Origin	Total
Klip River	December 1901	185	154	229	192	ORC	
	January 1902	16	62	74	71	ORC	
	June 1902	37	54	58	61	ORC	
	(Total)	238	270	361	324		1193
Estcourt	December 1901	15	23	36	25	ORC	
	February 1902	57	72	57	46	ORC	
	June 1902	19	13	19	10	ORC	
	(Total)	91	108	112	81		392
Upper Tugela	December 1901	625	243	262	245	ORC	
	February 1902	63	58	58	60	ORC	
	June 1902	57	51	45	46	ORC	
	(Total)	745	352	365	351		1813
Newcastle	January 1902	514	741	586	604	ORC	
	June 1902	158	145	124	117	ORC	
	June 1902	81	14	11	11	Transvaal	
	(Total)	753	900	721	732		3106
Dundee	February 1902	1	—	—	—	ORC	
	February 1902	44	14	33	25	Transvaal	
	June 1902	14	2	3	6	Transvaal	
	(Total)	59	16	36	31		142
	Total						6646

Source: NA, SNA 1/1/296, 1963/1902, encl. in Moor to McCallum, 19 June 1902, return of Native refugees.

different system of accommodating those blacks displaced by military operations emerged, one that fulfilled the perceived needs of economy and the mobilisation of refugee labour, but one which in practice preserved with greater success the interests of the refugees themselves. After the war De Lotbinière conceded that the refugees in Natal 'may be considered, comparatively speaking, well off compared to the bulk of the refugees in the camps in the Orange River Colony and Transvaal'.[46]

THE REPATRIATION OF REFUGEES

From the first days of the Native Refugee Department's existence, plans had been prepared for the rapid repatriation of refugees to white farms so that the agricultural recovery of the annexed colonies could be achieved in the shortest possible time. According to De Lotbinière, the objective of his department had been 'from the beginning to look upon the natives as an asset of the farming industry, and to preserve them . . . for this industry'.[47] Once the peace was signed the difficulties facing the administration were considerable: only four months were available for refugees to rebuild their homes and prepare land for cultivation before the onset of the rains; very little transport was available for the resettlement of refugees; only a limited supply of grain was on hand for purchase so that families might not be without food until the next season's crop could be harvested; and large numbers of men remained in military employment who could not be repatriated until their labour was dispensed with by the army. Arrangements were nevertheless made for an exodus of refugees from the camps on a large scale. Initially farmers were obliged to apply directly to the camps for labour, but this process was speeded up by allowing blacks to make their own arrangements with employers. Refugees were permitted to buy up to three months supply of grain at 7s 6d per bag, though this was clearly insufficient to last until the next season's crops were harvested. The system of repatriation was assisted by the rapid demobilisation of black labour by the army. Ironically this resulted immediately in a temporary increase in the number of refugees in the concentration camps. In June the population of the camps in the Orange River Colony rose to 60,604, and in the Transvaal to 55,910. Resettlement was accelerated, too, by farmers loaning waggons for transporting workers back to the farms. In the Transvaal over half the refugees had been repatriated by the end of August 1902, and by November only 3000 remained to be resettled. The repatriation of refugees from camps in the Orange River Colony was completed in January 1903.[48] Greater difficulties were experienced by the Refugee Department in Natal. In order to prevent an unmanageable movement of Africans into the Orange River Colony, the administration in Bloemfontein insisted that employers made applications directly to the Native Refugee Department for the return of individual blacks to the colony. Because refugees were thereby denied the opportunity to make their own arrangements with employers, the repatriation of blacks from Natal proceeded more slowly than in the Orange River Colony. Also, unlike most of the refugees concentrated in camps in the former republics, those in Natal had sometimes been able to cultivate land on their own initiative, and many refugees refused to return until all their crops had been harvested. At the end of 1902, 1149 refugees still remained to be resettled, and the complete repatriation of black refugees was not achieved until almost a year later. Indeed, a number of refugees appear to have settled permanently in Natal.[49]

To imagine, as Beak wrote in 1906, that 'The natives went forth from the camps as they had come in, with no cares and few wants, unambitious and happy-go-lucky', was wholly unrealistic.[50] Since it was known by refugees that blacks working for the British army had generally been shot by commandos when captured, there was a general anxiety among those waiting for repatriation that a hostile reception awaited them on their return home – some even feared execution.[51] Though there is no evidence that such an occurrence took place, some Boer farmers did apply financial sanctions against their tenants and workers by demanding rents for the period of their absence. Disillusionment with British policy also appears to have been commonplace in the camps. Some refugees refused to leave until they had been compensated in full for the grain and livestock commandeered by the army, and the Native Refugee Department was obliged to dispel the aspirations of others who hoped that by remaining in the camps the government would be persuaded to grant them land and thereby ensure their independence from the Boer farming community. De Lotbinière reported that black refugees 'were quick to see that although the British had conquered, they intended to restore the burghers to their farms, and they hoped that they too might receive equally liberal treatment'.[52]

Of more immediate concern to many refugees was their ability to subsist during the difficult months that followed the war. Although the run-down of the camps took place with great haste, many refugees missed the opportunity to cultivate enough land for their needs during the season ahead. The difficulties of cultivation were worsened by the shortage of seeds and even the most rudimentary implements such as picks and hoes.[53] Of greater long-term importance was the scarcity of draught animals. Livestock in the possession of refugees had mostly been taken from them when they entered the camps and receipts issued; many of those animals that had been brought into the settlements were destroyed by cattle diseases such as rinderpest and lungsickness.[54] There was little chance of livestock at a reasonable price coming on to the market until the farms of Boers and British settlers had been restocked.

The question of compensation for African losses during the war was fraught with difficulties. Because many claims had begun to be dealt with by unscrupulous legal agents who took the largest share of the money owed to Africans, the Native Refugee Department organised a system to pay compensation directly to blacks who held receipts. Military officers were appointed whose responsibility it was to forward all military receipts to the district paymasters at Pretoria and Bloemfontein. In each district one day during the month was fixed when blacks could claim their compensation and bring in additional receipts. By the end of January 1903 £163,109 had been distributed in the Transvaal and £100,000 in the Orange River Colony. Receipts, however, had been carelessly and haphazardly issued. In July 1902 Milner admitted:

> Compensation to natives must needs be a very rough and ready affair. Great thing is to give them something quickly to restart them as they are fearfully destitute . . . I fear army receipts as regards natives have been given so casually or not given at all that it is hopeless to expect them to get compensation from that quarter . . .[55]

De Lotbinière conceded in October 1902 that 'few men have taken the trouble to give the natives proper acknowledgements for their receipts'.[56] The Native Commissioner in Waterberg believed that 'for every receipt produced, three other receipts were due', and in Heidelberg district African losses were calculated to amount to at least £150,000, but military receipts accounted for only £4733.[57] Receipts were handed in by some blacks whom it was found impossible to identify afterwards.[58] In some regions the payment of compensation to blacks proceeded so slowly that as late as June 1905 it was reported that some men, after waiting three years in vain for payment, had gone to the gold fields.[59] As a result of the scarcity of livestock generally in South Africa, and in the former republics in particular, the inflation of cattle prices precluded refugees from using the money they received as compensation to purchase livestock equivalent in number and value to those that had been either destroyed or commandeered during the war.

In the aftermath of the war the rehabilitation of white agriculture was given first priority in the programme of rural reconstruction. Altogether £14.5 million was spent by the British government on resettlement after the war, but almost all this sum was devoted to Boer farmers and British settlers.[60] In the Transvaal £1,183,594 was spent by the Repatriation Department to supply seeds, implements, livestock and transport to white farmers; £16,194 was spent on African repatriation by the Native Refugee Department. In the Orange River Colony £27,652 was expended on the repatriation of African refugees.[61] In November 1902 £2 million was granted by the British government to supplement compensation in the annexed territories. Of this £300,000 was specially apportioned for the compensation of Africans; £15,000 for those in the southeastern districts of the South African Republic that were ceded after the war to Natal, £114,000 to Africans in the Transvaal Crown Colony, and £171,000 to those in the Orange River Colony. In the Transvaal alone compensation to Africans was officially assessed at £661,106.[62]

Some assistance to blacks was provided by the Native Refugee Department, which organised regional grain depots where repatriated refugees, and others in difficult circumstances, could buy mealies at £1 per bag. Because of the prolonged droughts of 1902 and 1903 the depots were kept open after the formal closure of the department in December. For blacks without any cash or saleable goods the depots provided no solution to pauperism. In the regions of the former republics where the activities of the

British army had been concentrated, and from where many blacks had been uprooted from the land, evidence of impoverishment after the war is overwhelming. In the neighbourhood of Amsterdam in the Transvaal it was reported that black communities everywhere were close to starvation: 'They are now living principally on roots; rats also form a large part of their diet.' Sheep-stealing from white farms in the district occurred on a large scale and was attributed almost entirely to hunger.[63] De Lotbinière conceded that the Piet Retief, Wakkerstroom, Standerton, Ermelo, Bethal, Carolina and Heidelberg districts were all bordering on famine six months after the conclusion of peace.[64] A similar situation existed in parts of the Orange River Colony. The Resident Magistrate at Senekal admitted that he could not see how local black communities would survive if the supply of rations issued by the administration were suspended, and in September 1903 it was reported from Lindley that 'large numbers of natives in this district are without food to supply their wants'.[65]

While a limited amount of relief was dispensed to destitute refugees, the British administration generally encouraged those in difficult circumstances to alleviate their condition by seeking employment. When in October 1902 the Rev. C. Poulsen reported from Volksrust that 'the people are starving yea dying of hunger' in the Wakkerstroom district, he was told by Sir Godfrey Lagden:

> In the event of any natives being in needy circumstances I am to suggest that you should point out to them that there is a very large market open to them for their labour and that you might encourage them to take advantage of this market, instead of asking for pecuniary assistance from the Government.[66]

In December E. H. Hogge, the Native Commissioner of Lydenburg district, wrote that blacks were 'constantly being encouraged to go and seek work and this is done more especially in districts where food is not too plentiful'.[67]

It is clear that the implications of the scorched earth campaign and the nature of the arrangements made for the reconstruction of the most devastated areas of the former republics extended beyond the temporary impoverishment of many of those blacks uprooted from the land. The destitute condition in which many refugees found themselves at the end of the war, the shortage of seeds, implements and draught animals, the inadequacy of military compensation, and the difficulties of the drought years of 1902 and 1903, made it impossible for large numbers of blacks to withstand the fiscal pressures to sell their labour in order to raise cash for taxes, rents and food. In this respect De Lotbinière believed the performance of his department had been salutary: 'On the whole I consider our refugees have been fairly treated . . . the natives have been made to work while in our camps . . . and still further they will feel the necessity of work for the next few years.'[68]

9

Aftermath

SEEDS OF UNREST

The military successes of the British army early in 1900, followed by the annexations of the Orange Free State and Transvaal, generated among many black people a mood of optimism that a new future was dawning, a future in which their interests would be safeguarded, and in which their status and influence in South African society would be progressively advanced. The expectation that a British military victory would be followed by an extension of political, educational and commercial opportunities for black people, especially for those living in the Boer republics, determined the support for the war of the vast majority of members of the black elite.

Before the end of the war, however, some blacks had already begun to argue, on the basis of the measures enacted during the early period of British administration in the Transvaal, that progress towards reform might not be as smooth as had earlier seemed possible. One of the first signs of a new, rather more pessimistic, mood among some members of the black elite was the publication of a series of short articles in *Ipepa lo Hlanga*, a newspaper controlled by men prominent in the Natal Native Congress, warning against the excessive influence exercised by leaders of the Transvaal mining industry. In December 1900 a contributor warned that:

> At the end of the war the whites will all unite to formulate some scheme by which they may make the Native industrious, so they say, and though we are rejoicing over the defeat of the Boers, the truth is that it will be fortunate for us if for three years we obtain the same wages from the English as we got in the past at Johannesburg.[1]

The consolidation rather than amelioration of the grievances of black industrial workers in the Transvaal led *Izwi Labantu* to warn that pressures from industrialists and financiers might preclude the reforms in the north they wished to see.

> Whilst we recognise the advantages of capital so long as it is subservient to the interests of the state, we are equally alive to the terrible consequences of its unrestricted power which threatens to monopolise all the humbler trades and smaller industries, to rig the markets, raise and depress stocks, to control the

163

liquor and similar great interests, to enslave people by the sweating process, to undermine the stability of governments, and to dictate the policies of States.[2]

The worst fears of those who looked forward to the beginning of a new and more liberal age seemed confirmed by the clauses of the peace agreement, signed in Pretoria on 31 May 1902. By the Peace of Vereeniging the representatives of the republics agreed by an overwhelming majority to surrender their independence in return for a general amnesty and the repatriation of prisoners of war; the limited protection of the Dutch language in the courts; various economic safeguards such as the maintenance of property rights, protection against punitive taxation, the honouring of the republican war debt up to £3 million and generous relief for the victims of war; and the promise of eventual self-government. Most significantly, by clause eight of the peace agreement it was resolved that no decision would be taken on the question of extending political rights to black people until self-government had been restored to the former republics, thereby effectively preventing the introduction of a non-racial franchise in the foreseeable future, and casting to the wind the earlier promises of reform seemingly made by Chamberlain, Salisbury and Milner. Left to their own devices neither the British settlers nor the Boers were ever likely to agree to political rights being extended to black people in the Transvaal and Orange River Colony.

From the outset Britain planned to reconstruct the Transvaal in order that the interests of mining capital and the state were harmonised. This was to be achieved by the creation of an efficient and professional bureaucracy, uncorrupt judiciary and effective police force; by the promotion of modern commercial agriculture in order to provide inexpensive locally produced foodstuffs; by encouraging the creation of a plentiful supply of cheap black wage labour for mining, manufacturing and agriculture, and ensuring its effective direction and control; and by legislating to minimise competition between mining capital, commercial capital and commercial farming. It was intended that rapid and sustained economic growth, large-scale British immigration and a policy of anglicisation would help to destroy the basis of Afrikaner nationalism, so that direct British control of Transvaal affairs could be relinquished, and the way ultimately paved for the creation of a stable federal dominion in South Africa in which British interests would be safeguarded. Although some of the means of achieving this goal quickly went awry, the object of British policy was achieved with spectacular success.

For black people a new era had indeed begun with the end of the war and the beginning of resettlement and reconstruction; but it was an era whose character was rather different from that anticipated by most members of the black elite, and by many other black people in South Africa, at the onset of war.

UNREST IN THE COUNTRYSIDE

The occupation of white farms by blacks in the Transvaal during the war was looked upon by many of those Africans concerned as a permanent phenomenon. 'The natives emerged from the war . . . with the idea that the object of the war had been to return them to their old lands, and that white owners had been expelled forever from their farms and habitations', it was reported from the Zoutpansberg.[3] According to S. W. Scholefield, Native Commissioner in Waterberg, who after the war interviewed Africans from the district at Warmbaths:

> The spirit engendered in the native mind was most marked at the meeting. The native generally thought that after the war it was the intention of our Government that all their engagements to their landlords would be cancelled, and it was further the intention of Government to practically divide the Boer farms among them, at least in so far that each native would receive the holding he then rented from his landlord from Government in fee simple.[4]

In the districts of Vryheid and Utrecht (which along with Paulpietersburg were ceded to Natal by the peace agreement) many Zulu believed that since Britain had not annexed their land immediately after the Zulu War, those settlers who had taken over land in the New Republic would be obliged to return it to its original owners. Colonel T. Roch, Mills's successor as Commander of the Vryheid column, wrote that among Kambi's people especially, 'many of them [possess] a strong feeling that the land ought to revert to them'.[5]

On African-occupied farms abandoned during the war by white landlords a good deal of economic activity had taken place in many instances, especially in those districts relatively immune from 'scorched earth'. Africans had established new gardens, planted crops, built new homes and generally prospered from the increased area of land under their cultivation and the rise in the market price of the produce they sold. Difficulties naturally arose when attempts were made to remove them after the war. In the Rustenburg, Waterberg and Vryheid districts peasants and tenants forcibly resisted the return of Boer families to their homes.[6] Even prominent military leaders were not exempt from trouble. Returning to his farm in Vryheid district, Louis Botha, the Transvaal Commandant-General no less, was run off his own land by former tenants, telling him he 'had no business there, and I had better leave'.[7] Some surrendered guerrillas were almost immediately permitted to take up arms again in order to repossess their farms, and after the conclusion of peace much of the work of the South African Constabulary during 1902 was devoted to making possible the resettlement by Boer families of their lands.

The British administration pressed ahead without delay to enforce the complete disarmament of black communities in the Transvaal, and under the provisions of Ordinance 13 of 1902 all black people were called upon to surrender their arms and ammunition. Altogether 50,488 weapons were surrendered. The value of the arms and ammunition handed in was assessed at £60,990. Some compensation was made, though the money paid out for firearms was much less than the weapons' market value, and some categories of guns were then sold to whites at the surrendered prices. Disarmament was pursued with great vigour but met with little active resistance. In Waterberg district the proportion of arms surrendered to the total black adult male population was slightly over one firearm to every three men. But undoubtedly some blacks successfully concealed their weapons, and among the well-armed Kgatla in the Rustenburg–Marico region large numbers of firearms were simply transported covertly across the Bechuanaland frontier.[8]

The issue of Boer cattle which during the war had come into African possession was another issue that embittered relationships between landlords and local black communities immediately after the peace. In some instances Boers had deposited cattle with blacks for safe-keeping until the end of military operations. When the war ended, however, some blacks refused to return the animals because they claimed their own herds had been persistently raided by the commandos. Others were unable to do so because those cattle in their possession belonging to whites had been confiscated by the British army, or had died from disease.[9] The redistribution of livestock occurred in other, more important, ways too. A number of British officers had permitted blacks to raid cattle from Boer farms in return for a proportion of the animals handed over to the military; sometimes blacks were furnished with cattle removed from white farms in return for services rendered; and when opportunities had arisen blacks on their own initiative had seized livestock from neighbouring farms. In the war's aftermath the possession of as many cattle as possible, especially for draught purposes, was of great importance to both black and white cultivators, since livestock were in considerable scarcity in the former republics and much inflated in value. 'The effect of the war upon the livestock of the country has been most disastrous', wrote F. B. Smith, the Director of Agriculture in the Transvaal. 'The native stock has been nearly exterminated, and the country has been impregnated with disease.'[10] In these circumstances competition to control the scarce livestock resources in the countryside was naturally keen.

Many returning Boers took the law into their own hands and organised sorties against black communities to seize cattle which they claimed belonged to them. To overcome the difficulties presented by the distribution of valuable cattle resources the Transvaal administration resolved to permit African and Boer farmers rights of inspection over each other's herds. An order was issued obliging blacks in possession of Boer cattle to restore them to their owners, but the system broke down when most whites refused to hand over cattle to black claimants, and the order was eventually withdrawn.[11] Sir Godfrey Lagden believed the most practical solution was for magistrates to encourage blacks to surrender Boer cattle, compensate them for the animals received, and hand these over to the Repatriation Department.[12] However, little progress was made because blacks refused to surrender cattle for cash, which because of the scarcity of livestock on the market could not be used immediately to purchase animals of comparable quality to replace them. Many disputes concerning the ownership of cattle were left to be sorted out in the courts, where white claimants were usually able to win their cases.[13]

It was the issue of labour, more so than any other factor, that lay at the heart of difficulties in the countryside in the aftermath of war. Farmers returning to their land after the peace were in urgent need of plentiful labour for the construction of new buildings and the preparation of land for the new season's crops. A customary means of attempting to mobilise workers by returning farmer-landlords was to demand from labour-tenants services that had been unfulfilled because of their wartime absence. As a result of the changed economic and political circumstances in the countryside, however, immediate problems often followed, for in the post-war period farm tenants in a number of districts were in a much stronger bargaining position than during the final years of the republican regime.

While stories of blacks being 'full of money' after the war were frequently exaggerated, and while those blacks released from the concentration camps often found themselves in desperate straits, there can be little doubt that in the annexed colonies, especially in those areas not devastated by scorched earth or military operations, many blacks had prospered during the war – from earning good wages in army employment, from being able to extend their area of crop cultivation, and from receiving inflated prices for the produce they sold. Many were more independent financially than for a number of years. Furthermore, during the period of British administration after the war, more opportunities were presented for expressing their increased independence.

With the collapse of the Boer state, the local burgher administration was supplanted by a smaller professional bureaucracy. Veldkornets and landdrosts, who usually had themselves been local farmers, had in some areas practised labour coercion on a regular basis. But after the war the new colonial officials, however sympathetic they might be to the difficulties of Boer farmers, generally felt unable to set aside the law or turn a blind eye on those who exceeded their legal rights in recruiting and maintaining their labour force. Africans were thereby allowed a greater measure of economic leverage than hitherto, and many blacks took advantage of the prevailing circumstances to move off private farms, where they had resided as labour-tenants, and settle on land owned by absentee proprietors or land held by the crown, where they could establish themselves as rent-tenants. On crown land the liability to work was much less onerous than for labour-tenants, and the rent of £1 per annum much lower than rents paid to farmers. There were benefits too from the much less rigorous collection of taxes and rents in the immediate post-war years, and also from the British administration's abandonment of the system of taxing rent-tenants more heavily than labour-tenants, Lagden and his staff being especially mindful of the important role played by black peasants in supplying cereals for the Transvaal market. Further economic leverage was afforded peasants when in 1905 the Transvaal Supreme Court declared in a test case that Africans were able to register land in their own name, thereby enabling blacks to purchase land on their own account, instead of having to use a white intermediary, usually a missionary, as before. Africans thereafter used every available opportunity to purchase land for their own settlement and use.[14]

A pattern of resistance to returning landlords emerged. Having in some instances tried to prevent the reoccupation by Boer families of their farms, tenants then refused to provide labour on the same terms as before the war, instead insisting in some cases on paying rents only in cash or in kind (as was a prevalent claim in Vryheid and Utrecht, for example), and in other cases negotiating more favourable terms of tenure under the threat of simply moving away to find rent tenancies elsewhere, a phenomenon more common in the northern and western districts of the Transvaal. The British administration seemed confronted with difficulties wherever it turned. 'The great question in this district is still the old question of landlord and tenant', reported Scholefield from Waterberg. 'Many Boers are still being repatriated and the native, who resides on his farm, and who generally had beneficial occupation during the war, now refuses to fulfil his part of the contract by supplying the stipulated amount of labour.'[15] In the southeast many Zulu informed officials they never intended to work for Boers again. 'From the farms which I have visited, I hear almost without exception the same story', reported Colonel Roch. 'The kaffirs will not work.'[16]

In some areas of the Transvaal, but more especially in the maize-producing regions of the Orange River Colony, sharecropping arrangements after the war proliferated, with farmers, unable to attract labour-tenants, welcoming returning families to the region on the basis of supplying land and seeds in return for sharing the produce of the soil. Many Basotho, leaving Basutoland with their families and livestock and often in possession of ploughs, were welcomed as sharecroppers by labour-starved Boer landlords with only limited capital assets across the Caledon river.[17]

The resilience of the peasant sector during the reconstruction period, and the accompanying difficulties faced by farmer-landlords in obtaining labour and competing effectively with peasant cultivators, were amply testified to by witness after witness before the Transvaal Labour Commission (1903) and the South African Native Affairs Commission (1903–5), whose report proposed the elimination of all tenancy arrangements and their replacement by relations of wage labour, with labour tenancies as a suitable transition stage between the two where necessary. In the aftermath of war poor whites left the land in thousands.

The war, however, did not usher in a new era of stable prosperity for black peasant farmers in the former republics. Rather, processes of social change were accelerated by the war which in the long term would undermine their economic independence. White farmers had legal rights to land and access to agricultural credit and therefore to more advanced technology. With such government assistance and encouragement, more white holdings and operations began to be commercialised, and when self-government was restored to the Transvaal in 1907 it was Het Volk that took over the reins of power, the party dominated by representatives of the wealthiest Afrikaner commercial farming interests. Colin Bundy has summarised the consequences for black peasant cultivators.

The re-assertion by Afrikaans farmers in the Transvaal of political power was marked, almost immediately, by a series of moves against the independence of the share-cropper and the rent-paying squatter-peasant. The 1908 Natives Tax Act imposed a levy of £2 on 'squatters', while labour tenants were wooed with a tax of only £1. In the northern districts, rent squatters were removed from some farms by direct governmental action in 1909 and 1910 . . . In 1911 and 1912, the revived anti-squatter legislation of 1895 as well as the 1908 Act were pressed in central and northern districts, and by their very nature they attacked those squatter-peasants who had most to lose.[18]

The Natives Land Act followed in 1913, three years after the inauguration of the Union. By this legislation land purchase by Africans in 'white' areas was prohibited, and less than 13 per cent of South Africa's land area demarcated as 'Native Reserves'. A principal function of the Act was the reduction of rent-tenants and sharecroppers to the status of labour-tenants, and a separate part of the legislation specifically outlawed sharecropping in the Orange Free State. Though the processes of social change took time to run their course, the transformation of peasant into wage labourer had been set further along its path.

UNREST IN THE GOLD-MINING INDUSTRY

Although there had existed among many black industrial workers an expectation that the establishment of British rule in the Transvaal would mark the end of the harsh wartime regime on the Rand and signal the introduction of a less closely regulated and more remunerative labour system there, conditions of work for blacks in the industrial region worsened rather than improved after the British occupation. The monthly wages of black mine-workers were reduced by the Chamber of Mines in December 1900 from their pre-war level, about 50s, to 30–35s; workers were conscripted into British military employment; law and order in the industrial area was rigorously enforced; and martial law restrictions were placed on the movement of blacks, so that many workers (especially from Mozambique) found it impossible to return home and were compelled to remain in the industrial region long after their original contracts had expired.

The mining industry and the new British administration combined to reduce inter-company competition for labour on the Rand and to develop a much more sophisticated system of direction and control over black industrial workers. During the 1890s many mining companies had systematically recruited workers from each other by employing labour 'touts' to procure the labour of newly arrived workers to the industrial area and to encourage desertions from men in the Rand locations and even from the compounds of neighbouring mines. This practice had assisted workers to exercise some selection in their ultimate choice of employer. Following the British annexation of the Transvaal, however, workers were confronted by a more uniform and inflexible wage system; by the establishment of a monopoly recruiting agency, the Witwatersrand Native Labour Association (WNLA), which was created with the expressed intention of 'rendering impossible in the future the indiscriminate touting and traffic in Natives which in the past existed among the mining companies';[19] and by an administration determined on regulating black labour to a greater degree within the industrial area. The Milner regime extended the pass department and tightened up the administration of the pass laws, developed improved legal procedures under masters and servants legislation for dealing with breaches of contract, introduced a scheme to register the fingerprints of all mine employees to help identify those who deserted one employer for another, and established regulations to prohibit mining companies recruiting workers in labour districts.[20] The possibility of workers exchanging one employer for another to find the most congenial living and working conditions was therefore considerably reduced, though desertions were by no means eradicated.

It was the intention of both the mining industry and the Milner regime to take steps to improve health facilities and living conditions for black miners in the interests of labour efficiency, but few steps were taken immediately to effect improvements other than intensive efforts to control liquor (in December 1901 the mineowners claimed that only 1 per cent of their workforce was absent owing to liquor consumption in one day, compared to an average 10–15 per cent in pre-war times).[21] While there may have been many fewer workers incapacitated from alcohol following the resumption of gold-mining operations, general health conditions deteriorated markedly. The number of deaths among workers in the industry rose steeply from 92 deaths in May 1902 to 247 in November, and in July 1902 a death rate of 112.54 per 1000 workers was reached.[22] Men too long in arduous work for the mines and the military during the difficult war years were numbered among the fatalities, but so were many newer recruits. Workers were often in a poor physical condition when they arrived to begin work, having travelled long distances on foot or in cramped railway trucks with no sanitary facilities. Trains transporting workers were classed as 'goods' rather than 'passenger' vehicles and were in consequence subject to long delays en route. The problem immediately after the war was exacerbated by the congestion of the railway system, the shortage of rolling stock which caused terrible overcrowding in available trucks, and further delays in the transportation of workers from Braamfontein station to the men's places of employment.[23] One in eight mining recruits was found physically unfit to begin work immediately.[24]

The response of black workers to this state of affairs was twofold: Africans in large numbers refused to work in the gold-mining industry; and in the mining region a series of protests took place among workers.

The gold-mining companies on the Rand were only able to recruit a labour force of black workers in 1903 which was two-thirds the size of that which they had employed in 1899 (64,454 workers compared to 96,704 before the beginning of the war). The argument was frequently advanced by those with responsibility for recruiting labour for the gold mines that the scale and conditions of military employment had disrupted the whole system of labour in South Africa. Speaking at the annual meeting of the Chamber of Mines in 1903, Sir Percy FitzPatrick stated that the shortfall of labour in the industry could be accounted for by 'the position of affluence and comfort which the native at present enjoys owing to the excessive rates paid by the military and the bountiful harvests of the last two years',[25] a view that may have been popular among employers at the time, but which can scarcely be maintained as the whole explanation for the labour scarcity of the post-war years.

In fact there appears to have taken place after the war, in general terms, a redistribution of black workers rather than an overall decline in the number of men entering the labour market. In 1903 the number of Africans from Natal seeking work in the Transvaal was greater than in any pre-war year.[26] Between 60,000 and 70,000 workers migrated from Basutoland in 1902–3 compared to under 40,000 in 1898–9.[27] Labour migration from the Transkei increased from 61,033 in 1898, to 66,695 in 1902, and to 76,556 in 1903.[28] Although precise statistics are unavailable, the number of workers travelling to South Africa from Mozambique may not have significantly declined; rather, more workers seem to have migrated independently and clandestinely to avoid WNLA recruitment for employment on the gold mines.[29] The only regions from which fewer Africans appear to have migrated to work immediately after the war are the western and northern districts of the Transvaal, where relative immunity from direct military action, and the absence of Boers on commando, enabled a larger cross-section of the black population than elsewhere in the territory to live relatively independently during the war and prosper from the sale of agricultural produce. After the war there were also more opportunities in the former republics for Africans to avoid the necessity of wage labour, as we have seen.

There can be little doubt that one of the most important reasons why Africans declined to work on the gold fields was the wage reduction enforced by the Chamber of Mines. The new rate of 30–35s a month compared unfavourably with the wages earned by almost every other category of labour in South Africa except farm workers and domestic servants. During the immediate post-war economic boom it was relatively easy for Africans to find better-paid and more congenial employment in repatriation work, in public works projects to improve road and railway communications, in the construction industry, and at the seaports. Whereas in 1897 the Chamber of Mines had been able to enforce wage reductions with some resistance on the part of workers but very little effect on the overall supply of labour, in 1901–3 the demand for workers in South Africa was greater than the supply. Magistrates frequently drew attention to the reluctance of workers to migrate to the gold mines when higher wages were available elsewhere. African newspapers poured scorn on the first attempts of the mining companies to alleviate their labour shortage without introducing a substantial rise in black wages. 'If in addition to supplying them with blankets, overcoats and warm clothing, they should give higher wages to those working underground . . .

they will soon find they have all the labour they require', *Ilanga lase Natal* suggested in an editorial in mid-1903.[30]

Another important reason for the labour scarcity in the gold-mining industry appears to have been the greater control exercised by employers and the state over black workers. One of the main factors keeping men from the Transkei away from the Rand was said to be the intensification of police activity and the placing of vindictive 'Zulu' gangers over Xhosa workers.[31] According to the Native Commissioner in Pietersburg, black workers declined to travel to the gold mines after the war because they could not choose on which mine they were to work.[32] *Ipepa lo Hlanga* especially criticised the consensus among the white community that black workers should have as few rights as possible in the labour market.

> The natives as people are looked upon by many as camels or any other beast of burden, and not as reasoning animals . . . We admit that a native as an unskilled labourer is to do all the rough work, but it does not follow that he has no right to choose his own master, and to sell his labour at the best possible market . . . everyone looks to the native as a cheap labourer not because they have his improvement at heart; but because they want to improve themselves.[33]

Reports of wartime hardship among black workers on the Rand, and the number of deaths in the compounds, also discouraged workers from travelling to the gold fields. In December 1903 *Imvo* published interviews with the Tswana chiefs Lentshwe and Sekhoma on the issue of labour conditions in the gold-mining industry. Both men alluded to the intensive campaign by the Randlords to bring indentured Chinese workers to South Africa to solve the labour crisis.

> *Lentshwe*: I am not in a position to help the Rand mines, as I am Chief of the Bakhatla, and not Emperor of China. They want Chinamen and not my people, who, they say, are too expensive. If Mokibesa (De Beers) wants labourers, I may give him some, as he appears to be satisfied with my men, but it is not within my power to satisfy the wish of a Company which wants cheap Chinamen. Earlier this year I sent a batch of labourers to the Rand as was understood at £3 per month 'all found', for three months on surface work. On arrival there, they were forced into a contract of six months against their wishes, at 45s. The death rate there was something appalling. Dead bodies were hurled into an open Scotch Cart, and thrown into a large trench . . . Altogether such horrors are reported from Johannesburg that I thought it advisable never to hire my people to the Rand Mines except by their own desire.
> *Sekhoma*: If anyone tells you there are not enough labourers in this country, it is a falsehood. They want our people to leave their families, go to Johannesburg, stay away for six months, suffer to enrich the mine owners and bring nothing back, what's the good for going to work then? If one is to come back empty handed after six months or eight months service like prisoner. There is something to their advantage in the employment of Chinamen, the mine owners mean to do away with the natives.[34]

On the reef itself workers protested against the prevailing conditions. In spite of the intensity of the new system of labour regulations, individual desertions continued on a large scale. Desertions and gaolings for breach of contract accounted for an annual average of 7.2 per cent of the total wastage of the unskilled black workforce on the mines between 1902 and 1909. 'Loafing', a term used by management to describe a labourer's failure to perform a minimum amount of work, was another type of informal resistance practised by workers, and was regarded by managers sufficiently seriously to warrant an agreement with government in 1905 permitting mine managers to deduct pay from a worker for failure to complete a 'fair day's work' and to add such days to the man's contracted term of service.[35]

The first endeavours of WNLA to recruit workers for the resumption of gold-mining operations met with some overt resistance on the part of workers. In 1901, 192 Venda workers refused on arrival at the gold fields to begin work, and only after a dispute lasting ten days were they eventually persuaded to do so. Twenty-nine Barolong workers also refused to commence work, expressing dissatisfaction with the rates of pay they found to exist on the mines, and the Association eventually had to return the men to Mafeking.[36] On 1 January 1902 a riot occurred at the Johannesburg location when six Zulu policemen and two white constables were attacked by two hundred, mostly Xhosa, mineworkers. The assembly of angry workers was dispersed only after shots had been fired into the crowd, killing two men and wounding a number of others. Later, forty-three of those who took part were sentenced to terms of imprisonment of up to twelve months. At the root of the unrest lay the increased intensity of police supervision of workers, especially by unpopular 'Zulu' constables.[37]

Discontent on the reef erupted once again at the beginning of April 1902 when 116 of the 183 black workers employed at the Consolidated Main Reef Mine went out on strike. In spite of the intervention by the Inspector of Labour, S. M. Pritchard, the workers refused to return to work, and were arrested en masse. The origin of the unrest was the mineworkers' low pay; their dissatisfaction came to a head when other black workers on the mine employed by an outside contractor were found to be receiving wages higher than their own.[38]

Mass walk-outs by workers became almost a feature of life on the Rand during the middle of 1902. In May, 164 workers deserted from the Ginsberg Mine and camped in protest outside Boksburg. A further hundred black workers left the East Rand Mines rather than stay to complete their contracts. Both groups of protesters were permitted to return home. When, however, 448 Pedi at the Geldenhuis Mine struck work and demanded to be allowed to leave their jobs, a large detachment of the Germiston Mounted Police was called in to arrest the strikers, who were given the choice of either paying a £2 fine or serving sentences of up to two months. Most men decided to go to gaol.[39] Shortly after midnight on 28 June, 1100 workers at the Langlaagte Deep Mine deserted the compound armed with knobkerries, bottles and stones. A detachment of the Johannesburg Mounted Police pursued the protesters and eventually they were persuaded to return to the mine, where they stoned the office of the compound manager, Joseph Woichowsky, before going back to their quarters. Because of the restrictions on the movement of blacks in the

Transvaal during the war many of the workers at the mine had been unable to return home directly their contracts had expired, and they had been cajoled into signing on for another period there. In these circumstances the actions of the compound manager had become unbearable; Woichowsky had rejected almost all applications by men for temporary passes to leave the compound, and had presided over acts of gross cruelty to workers.[40]

Within a month of the Langlaagte protest further unrest was evident at the Durban Roodepoort Mine, where on 21 July the black workforce of 700 men held a meeting before the morning shift and refused to go underground unless they were given an increase in the 30s a month for which they had been contracted. Within two hours, however, the strikers had been induced to return to work under the threat that if the stoppage continued the men would be punished in the same way as the Geldenhuis workers.[41]

The protests took place in circumstances of restrictions on the free movement of black workers in the Transvaal; institutional and legislative measures to control more rigidly the black labour force; more intensive police supervision on the reef; a rapidly rising death rate among black workers; wage reductions; and a decline in the purchasing power of workers' wages. Above all, the protests occurred in an environment of unfulfilled expectations on the part of black workers that following the British annexation of the Transvaal a more humane, flexible and remunerative labour system would be introduced.[42]

The individual protests almost all failed in their immediate objectives because of the swift and harsh action of the police, both black and white. Some improvements took place afterwards in the conditions of life in the compounds, but this did not begin to occur significantly until almost a year later, and improvements basically stemmed from the mining companies' desire for greater labour efficiency rather than from direct pressures for change from the mineworkers themselves. However, collectively the protests of workers on the Rand and the refusal of many Africans to migrate to work on the gold fields did force the Chamber of Mines to re-introduce the 1897 wage schedule at the beginning of 1903, which restored the levels of wages earned by workers at the outbreak of war. The Chamber also permitted companies, in the interests of productivity, to reward with higher wages and bonuses their most skilled and industrious workers, and those men who signed on again after their original contract had expired. A continued upward movement in black wage levels in the gold-mining industry was nevertheless prevented by the introduction to the Rand of indentured Chinese workers in 1904. The bargaining power in the labour market exercised by black workers in the aftermath of war was thereby undermined, and from 1907 onwards both the real and money value of black wages in the mining industry progressively fell.[43]

POLITICAL HOPES DASHED

The gradual but assured evolution of a society in South Africa ordered on non-racial principles, in which the influence of educated and talented black people would be progressively advanced by their own industry and determination, was a guiding vision among members of the black elite. It was a vision of the future in which the Cape Colony's non-racial franchise represented a fountainhead, and one from which most members of the elite drew personal confidence and inspiration. It helped them to make sense of their own lives and their struggles for advancement and recognition in the wider colonial society. For this reason the impact on black political thinking of clause eight of the peace agreement, which effectively precluded the introduction of a non-racial franchise in the annexed states, was profound. The optimism of 1899, and indeed of earlier years, was dealt a punishing blow. It soon became clear, too, that the clause was no aberration in imperial policy, for after the war the racially discriminatory legislation in the annexed colonies inherited from the republics was largely maintained intact; municipalities in the Transvaal authorised the formal segregation of blacks in locations; the Municipalities Ordinance of 1903 embodied an all-white franchise; and Ordinance 17 of 1904 introduced for the first time a statutory industrial colour bar.

Black political activity grew in scale after the war as political associations were formed in response to the trend of events: the African Political Organisation, a predominantly Coloured association, was initiated in Cape Town in 1903, later changing its name to the African People's Organisation; a Native Vigilance Association, based in the Transkei, and a South African Native Congress, based in the Western Cape, were formed; an Orange River Colony Native Vigilance Association was established in 1902, later changing its name to the Orange River Colony Native Congress in 1906; and in the Transvaal various political associations were formed, including a Native United Political Association. These various organisations had as one of their primary purposes the lobbying of the British government and its representatives in South Africa with a view to annulling clause eight of the peace agreement and reversing the discriminatory legislation entrenched by the Milner regime in the Transvaal and Orange River Colony.

The English columns of African newspapers brimmed over with condemnations of imperial policy in the immediate post-war years. On the first day of *Imvo*'s reappearance in October 1902 Jabavu condemned clause eight of the peace agreement, and wrote that because the British, the Boers and the African population were all entitled to live in the country, 'each should be accorded by the others the common rights of citizenship'.[44] Petitions to the British government were the means commonly employed by black groups and most of the African political organisations of the period to bring their point of view to bear on official decision-making. In 1902 a petition signed by 1400 Africans from the Orange River Colony, setting out four demands, was despatched to Joseph Chamberlain.

> 1. We pray that we may be permitted to enjoy political rights with all other British subjects in the Orange River Colony.
> 2. We pray that the existing laws whereby we are prevented from acquiring rights to land be repealed.
> 3. We pray that we may be granted the same facilities for education as may be

extended to the white population of this colony.

4. We further pray that the Native population of this colony may be given special representatives in any elected Assembly of Representatives of People when such may be hereafter allowed to this colony.[45]

The petition neatly encapsulates some of the fundamental concerns of members of the black elite after the war – political rights, land and education – concerns that were repeated in other petitions of the post-war years, though the final clause pressing in effect for a separate electoral roll for black people was not a typical request of the period. Much more representative in this respect was a petition drawn up later in the same year by leading members of the Seleka-Barolong community at Thaba Nchu, which requested that the African people of the Orange River Colony 'be placed on the same level with the Native subjects of the Crown in the Colony of the Cape of Good Hope'.[46] The largest petition of the immediate post-war years was submitted in 1905 by the United Political Association in the Transvaal and was signed by 46 chiefs and 25,730 other Africans. It simply requested, in the light of the British government's intention of pressing ahead as soon as possible with the restoration of self-government for the Transvaal, that African interests 'should be safeguarded in the granting of the constitution to the New Colonies'.[47]

More than any other single issue it was clause eight of the peace agreement that was the focus of political discussion and protest. As early as December 1900 *Ipepa lo Hlanga* in Natal had noted the inconsistency of British political principles when applied to whites and blacks: 'what is the matter at issue between the Boers and the English – one thing only – the English want a voice in the government of the Transvaal – the very thing they refuse to give us here'.[48] In a petition sent to Edward VII in 1906 the Orange River Colony Native Congress pursued a similar theme.

Your petitioners earnestly deprecate the clause in the Vereeniging Peace Terms which compromised the claim of the Natives to what they feel is a legitimate franchise. Indeed, it seemed to them deplorable that before bloodshed ceased the avowed cause of Justice, Freedom, and Equal Rights, for which the war had been undertaken, should have been so easily abandoned.[49]

As reconstruction progressed so African political leaders became increasingly despondent and critical of imperial policy. There were even those who wished 'to call back the days of the republic' for, they argued, their people had received better treatment and higher wages 'when the Boers dominated'. The Kgatla chief, Segale, reported that in the Transvaal there existed profound disillusionment among black people.

Having lately gone to the Transvaal, I heard the complaints of Natives who live in all parts of the Transvaal . . . They say that they are not satisfied with the present administration, they say that they hoped that the British Government had come to release them from the bonds of oppression . . . And I truly believe that if there is war again the people of the Transvaal will assist the Boers. I assure you they have become disgusted . . . The Natives of the Transvaal say 'we expected deliverence whereas we have gone deeper into bonds'.[50]

In an anonymous contribution to *South African Outlook*, published in 1906, 'An African Resident' came to much the same conclusion.

> One strong incentive reason that impelled the Natives of the New Colonies to put themselves at the disposal of His Majesty's troops in the late war was that the British Government, led by their known and proverbial sense of justice and equity, would, in the act of general settlement, have the position of the black races upon the land fully considered, as at the conclusion of the war the whole land would revert to the British Nation, when it would be a timely moment, they thought, for the English to show an act of sympathy towards those who have been despoiled of their land and liberties. Alas! This was not the case. The black races in these Colonies feel today that their last state is worse than their first.[51]

Disappointment and disillusionment was expressed, too, after the war by leaders of the Asian and Coloured communities. Restrictive legislation which prevented Asians from owning land in the Transvaal and Orange River Colony was maintained by the British administration. In 1906 an ordinance was drafted to make compulsory the registration of fingerprints by Asians in the Transvaal. Vigorous protest by the Asian community, led by Gandhi, persuaded Lord Elgin, the Colonial Secretary, to order the abandonment of the proposed legislation. After the granting of responsible government in 1907, however, the measure was reintroduced and approved unanimously by the new legislature, and further measures discriminating against Asians soon followed. Gandhi's anger was aimed equally against the Transvaal and British governments: 'Our lot today is infinitely worse than under the Boer regime', he informed Lord Elgin in 1906.[52]

One of the sternest critics of post-war British policy was Dr Abdullah Abdurahman, the Cape Malay member of the Cape Town City Council, and after 1905 President of the African People's Organisation. Abdurahman was a devoted anglophile and admirer of the British constitution, but he refused to sign a farewell address to Milner from the City Council, and later condemned Milner for leaving the country with the rights of Coloureds at a lower ebb than when he had arrived. In his first address as President of the African People's Organisation – speaking before a largely Coloured audience, many of whom had signed a petition in 1901 declaring their 'firm and unalterable' loyalty to the British government – Abdurahman vigorously criticised the conduct of imperial policy in South Africa, and claimed that 84 per cent of Britain's 400 million colonial peoples were governed 'in a more or less despotical manner'.[53]

In 1906 the African People's Organisation sent Abdurahman and P. J. Daniels to England to press the government to introduce a non-racial franchise in the Transvaal and Orange River Colony before responsible government was granted. The men argued that clause eight of the peace agreement had referred only to 'natives', and therefore at the very least it was possible to extend the franchise to Coloureds and Asians. In the same year Jabavu and thirteen other prominent Africans from the eastern Cape forwarded to the House of Commons a petition requesting that the franchise in the north be extended to eligible black people as a whole.

In 1908 South Africa's white political leadership assembled at a National Convention to consider the terms upon which greater cooperation between the four settler colonies might be achieved. Out of their deliberations emerged the blueprint for union, later enshrined in the South Africa Bill that was approved by the British parliament. In March 1909, at Bloemfontein, a South African Native Convention was held and attended by sixty delegates elected from earlier regional conventions in each of the four colonies. Of the prominent elite politicians of the era only Jabavu was absent. The delegates condemned the draft constitution as 'illiberal and short-sighted in its conception of the people of South Africa'. In particular delegates criticised the terms which set out that every member of the South African parliament was to be of 'European descent'; that the existing franchise laws in each province of the Union were to be maintained, thereby preserving the all-white suffrage in the former republics; and that a two-thirds majority of both Houses of the South African parliament could approve a Bill introduced to disfranchise black voters in the Cape. Afterwards the African People's Organisation and the South African Native Convention sent a joint multi-racial delegation to London, which included W. P. Schreiner, J. T. Jabavu, Dr Abdurahman and the Rev. Walter Rubusana, to hold meetings with members of the British government and to present a petition to parliament calling for the removal of the discriminatory articles of the South Africa Bill. Their efforts were to no avail.[54]

Between 1902 and 1910 African political activity increased in scale, and groups of black politicians from the four South African colonies came together to advance their common interests, foreshadowing the establishment of the South African Native National Congress in 1912. The post-war years were a period when disillusionment with the role played by the imperial government in South African affairs became widespread, though the confidence of members of the black elite in the good intentions of the British government was not yet completely shattered; it was still believed that petitions addressed to the British government and visits by delegations to London could awaken Britain to her responsibilities towards the welfare of South Africa's black population. With the achievement of Union, however, a new era had begun in which to formulate fresh programmes of political action.

Conclusion

The South African war was one of the most costly and bitterly contested military encounters between whites on African soil. The issues over which it was fought, the way in which events unfolded between 1899 and 1902, and the nature of the state that was created in its aftermath, these affected all the people of the subcontinent – mining magnate, commercial farmer, poor white tenant, black schoolteacher, clerk, peasant and worker alike. By looking afresh at the war as a social as well as a military and political phenomenon, and in particular by examining the ways in which it affected the lives and livelihoods of black people, the preceding chapters have sought to shed new light on some of the more familiar episodes and historical concerns of the period, and to pave the way for a more complete understanding of the war's social history.

In 1899 neither side chose to take for granted the subordination of all the black communities within and along its borders. The colonial incorporation of the major African states of the region was a relatively recent occurrence, and while the processes of social change engendered by the mineral revolution were clearly in evidence, the structures of a society transformed by mining capital were less rigid and secure than they were to become in the twentieth century. In Natal less than one in five white males of military age were called up for active service. Colonial forces were posted to the eastern Cape to be on hand to deal with black resistance as well as Afrikaner rebellion and invasion. At the start of the war only between 56 and 65 per cent of the Boers' fighting strength was placed in the field, and burghers were garrisoned in a number of areas of the republics where the security of white farms seemed endangered from within.

The weakness of the pre-war colonial regime in the Transvaal was particularly marked, and within a year of hostilities beginning the Boer state had collapsed, from internal black resistance as well as from military invasion. Boer families and officials were driven from a large area of the western Transvaal, and when Smuts entered the region in mid-1900 he found almost all the farms deserted by whites. Kgatla regiments effectively controlled the Rustenburg–Marico area for the final two years of the war. Following the withdrawal of burghers from Pedi territory in June 1900 the remaining Boer officials were driven from the district, and during the guerrilla war no commando dared to move into the region between the Olifants and Steelpoort rivers controlled by the Sekhukhune party. In the neighbourhood of Ohrigstad farm tenants led a ruthless campaign against local landlords. Throughout areas of the northern and western Transvaal Boer land was seized and occupied by black people, new homesteads built and fresh gardens established. In the southeast many of the Zulu whose lands had been alienated to Boer settlers during the 1880s conducted a determined campaign of harassment against the local republican forces. Following the destruction of Qulusini on General Botha's orders in reprisal for the Zulu's activities, fifty-six members of the Vryheid commando were killed in a fierce attack by the Qulusi on the burghers' encampment at Holkrans.

The incident at Holkrans, more than any other episode late in the war, has led to the hypothesis, advanced by Donald Denoon, that the war ended 'because factors in the black–white dimension intruded upon the white–white dimension'.[1] The implications of the Qulusi attack on the Vryheid commando were important indeed, especially since the assault occurred only a matter of days before the meeting of Boer representatives at Vereeniging to discuss proposals for peace. The third reason for making peace cited in the Vereeniging resolution stated that: 'the Kaffir tribes, within and without the frontiers of the territories of the two Republics, are mostly armed and are taking part in the war against us, and through the committing of murders and all sorts of cruelties have caused an unbearable condition of affairs in many districts of both Republics'.[2] A number of Boer delegates drew attention to the threat of the complete loss of their livelihoods.

From a military point of view many Boers argued in the discussions that the evacuation of the southeastern districts of the Transvaal, which Zulu hostility appeared to make necessary, would endanger the whole guerrilla war strategy. The struggle could only be maintained by dispersing the superior numbers of the British army through operating over as large an area as possible. If the Boers were to have left the southeastern Transvaal they would have been obliged to concentrate to a dangerous extent in the vicinity of British blockhouses and columns. Following the British decision in December 1901 not to assemble any more Boer families in refugee camps, the guerrillas had been obliged to assume responsibility for the protection of their dependents in the countryside. If the commandos left the southeastern Transvaal they would have been forced to take those families living there with them (which would seriously have impaired their mobility), or else leave them behind unprotected. The Boers did not have unlimited access to fresh supplies, and increasingly during the guerrilla war they were compelled to plunder provisions from African homesteads. If commandos moved into the northern Transvaal in force as a result of evacuating other districts, then serious further difficulties in the Boers' relations with black communities would have followed. Louis Botha told the assembled representatives at Vereeniging:

In only one portion of the country, namely in Zoutpansberg, is there still food, but how do we obtain our provisions there? It [sic] must be taken, and thereby we create more enemies. Our safety in Zoutpansberg lay in this: that hitherto the kaffirs were divided, but if the enemy were to pour into that district the kaffirs will join against us.[3]

There can be little doubt therefore that black resistance to the republican forces and collaboration with the British army of occupation in the annexed states was a crucial factor in accounting for the Boers' decision to surrender. But equally it would be too simplistic to argue that in some way the events at Holkrans, or black resistance and irregular participation in the war in general, directly precipitated the signing of peace. Botha and Smuts, among others, argued at Vereeniging that Boer aspirations were incapable of being achieved by military methods, and discussions focused on a number of other important considerations such as the Boers' shortage of military supplies, the extension of the blockhouse system, Kitchener's mobilisation of Afrikaner National Scouts and Volunteers, and the failure of the rebellion in the Cape.[4]

Elsewhere in southern Africa the props of colonial society were loosened by the circumstances of war because of Britain's need to mobilise support and resources for the war effort from such areas as Basutoland, Bechuanaland and Zululand. There was naturally some concern about the implications of this among both British and colonial officials. By backing the British campaign and supporting Zulu resistance against the Boer farming community in the southeastern Transvaal, Dinuzulu was able during the war to shake free of some of the rigid, and in a time of crisis unworkable, conditions laid down for his return from exile. There can be no question that war conditions gave rulers such as Khama, Lentshwe and Lerotholi more room for manoeuvre in their relations with the colonial authorities. For the duration of the struggle the balance of power shifted perceptibly in their favour, and they were able to enhance their positions within the framework of the colonial system. It is important to note, however, that among rulers such as Khama and Lerotholi, whose wealth and influence had grown in collaboration with the colonial authorities and who had benefited from the stability and market opportunities engendered by colonial rule, there was little serious doubt about their support for Britain's war effort: they had potentially too much to lose from a British defeat.

The British enjoyed considerable political and military support from black people during the war. The reasons for this are not difficult to discover. On the part of the black elite it was widely believed on the basis of Britain's past record and war propaganda that a British victory would presage a new and more enlightened era in the management of African affairs. It was expected that the Cape's non-racial franchise would be extended to the northern states once these were administered by Britain, and more opportunities provided for the commercial, educational and political advancement of black people. In the Cape the enforcement of republican native law in the occupied districts, and the systematic campaign by guerrillas and rebels against black peasant and artisan interests, served as a poignant reminder of the dangers inherent in a Boer victory.

For a variety of reasons the British received direct and indirect support from other quarters. The Dlamini hoped that a British victory would enable them to secure their dominance in Swazi society more successfully under renegotiated terms of colonial incorporation. The Sekhukhune party among the Pedi, having ousted the Boers from the Pedi heartland, entered into military cooperation with the British army in the hope that much of their former influence in Pedi affairs could be restored, their lands substantially extended and a new colonial relationship forged. Elsewhere in the Transvaal black communities collaborated with the army of occupation in the hope of regaining alienated farms on a permanent basis and as a means of defending their land and its produce against raids by the Boer guerrilla forces. Among the thousands of black workers who directly supported Britain by entering into military employment, the issues over which the war was being fought, and the opportunities that might follow a British victory, were for many less important considerations than economic necessity following the disruption to the migrant labour system at the outbreak of war, the poor harvests in a number of areas in 1899–1900, and later the devastation wrought by Kitchener's scorched earth campaign.

The props upon which colonial society rested were, therefore, loosened during the war, and in the Transvaal they collapsed under the strain of internal resistance and external conquest. The signing of peace, however, ushered in an era when the foundations of the settler states were urgently repaired and strengthened. The immediate post-war period was one of unfulfilled expectations for many black people. The terms of the peace agreement effectively made it impossible for a non-racial franchise to be introduced in the annexed colonies. The discriminatory legislation of the republics was largely maintained in force by the British and in some instances reinforced and extended. State control over workers was intensified and wages in the mining industry reduced. For every £4 officially assessed as war compensation to Africans in the Transvaal, only £1 was in fact paid out. Boer farmers, meanwhile, received much more generous compensation, they were given legal rights to their lands and military assistance to reoccupy their farms, and provided with access to agricultural credit and therefore to more advanced technology. The Kgatla hoped that in return for their military assistance against the Boers they might be granted, by right of conquest, a reserve in the western Transvaal between the Crocodile and Elands rivers, but the request was turned down. The Pedi were granted no more land following the conclusion of peace. Zululand was opened up to white settlement in the years after the war, and a system of land partition implemented in Swaziland. Opportunities that might have presented themselves during the war were in most instances swiftly terminated once the peace agreement was signed.

The overriding objective of British reconstruction after the war was to return the gold-mining industry to full production and to create the conditions necessary to improve the industry's productivity. Britain set out to create a modernised state compatible with the needs of mining capital, and it is this that was to be the most enduring legacy of the period. The impact on social change of the war itself was nonetheless of some importance. It enabled a younger generation of men to achieve political leadership of the Boer community, men who were themselves mostly progressive commercial farmers, and who were much more amenable to capitalist interests than their predecessors. The scorched earth campaign, the agricultural difficulties of the immediate post-war years and the growing commercialisation of white farming accelerated the already serious social divisions within Boer society, driving thousands of poor whites into the industrial region to seek work.

The devastation of large areas of the Orange Free State and the southern, central and eastern districts of the Transvaal also drove many black peasants into wage employment. But in those areas of the annexed states unaffected by scorched earth, and especially in those districts that remained relatively immune from military operations, black peasants were able to prosper in the larger locations mostly untroubled by direct state interference, and in a number of localities blacks were able to occupy white farms and extend their area of cultivation. Because of the increased demand for food and the dislocation of white agriculture during the war, inflated prices were available for grain and other produce. During the reconstruction period in the former republics the economic leverage afforded some black agriculturalists during the war did not immediately disappear, and during the first decade of the century competition between black and white farmers was a matter of some economic and political importance.

Elsewhere in the subcontinent during the war those peasants with the resources to produce a surplus of grain and other produce for sale were also able to benefit from the remunerative market for food. Those who gained most were likely already to belong to the most affluent section of the rural black population. It was also the most prosperous peasant farmers who were able to benefit from hiring waggons and draught animals to the military at inflated prices, and who filled many of the highest paid skilled and semi-skilled occupations available to blacks in British military employment.

Conversely, it was those poorer blacks already dependent on wage labour before the war who generally benefited least from the upheavals. The dislocation of the migrant labour system at the start of military operations threw many workers out of employment, driving them back to the rural areas. Pressure on food resources increased as a consequence, and in some of the most overpopulated and poorest districts of Natal, Zululand and the Ciskei and Transkei, where the first months of war were acccompanied by especially meagre harvest yields, famine conditions rapidly spread. Employment with the British army was the obvious escape route from impoverishment. Although the wages available from a number of military departments were relatively good – and indeed there was a modest upward movement in the levels of wages earned by black workers outside the gold-mining sector during the war and immediately afterwards – the prices of food, cattle and other goods also increased. In some areas of food scarcity mealies sold for as much as 40s for a bag of 200 lbs, compared to the usual price of under 10s. The price of cattle rose appreciably: from £7–£15 to £10–£18 in Basutoland, to as high as from £10 to £25–£30 in the Bechuanaland Protectorate (a level not reached again until the 1960s). It is questionable therefore whether there was any significant increase in the real wages of most workers.

For two men in particular memories of the war and its significance for black people were to remain especially strong for the rest of their lives. Both Sol Plaatje and Silas Molema were Mafeking veterans, men who had witnessed the hardships of life and death for the Barolong people during the seven-month siege, and both referred back to the events of the war in their later writings. Of the implications of the 1913 Land Act for the black defenders of Mafeking, Plaatje wrote, 'what must be the feelings of these people . . . now that it is decreed that their sons and daughters can no longer have any claim to the country for which they bled'.[5] Writing in 1920, Molema also concluded that the support given to the British by black people during the war had been in vain: 'It is a fact . . . the position of the Bantu after the South African War was worse than before it . . . their condition has grown worse and worse every year, their rights, never many, nor mighty, have been curtailed systematically from then to now; and the future is dark and dreary.'[6]

Notes

The following abbreviations have been used in the notes.

AC	Assistant Commissioner
AG	Attorney-General, Cape Colony
BNA	Botswana National Archives, Gaborone
CA	Cape Archives, Cape Town
CBBNA	Cape Blue Book on Native Affairs
CMK	Chief Magistrate of East Griqualand
CMT	Chief Magistrate of the Transkei
CO	Colonial Office, London
Col.Col.	Colenso Collection
conf.	confidential
CSO	Colonial Secretary's Office, Bloemfontein
DC	District Commissioner
DD	Defence Department, Cape Colony
DMI	Director of Military Intelligence, London
encl.	enclosure
GS	Government Secretary, Orange Free State
JAH	*Journal of African History*
JSAS	*Journal of Southern African Studies*
LMS	London Missionary Society
LNA	Lesotho National Archives, Maseru
LtG	Lieutenant-Governor, Transvaal
Mag.	Magistrate
MG	Military Governor, Bloemfontein
MGP	Military Governor, Pretoria
Mills Report	*Report by Colonel G. A. Mills, C.B., on the Causes which Led to the Ill-Feeling between the Boers and the Zulu, Culminating in the Attack on the Boers by the Zulu Chief Sikobobo at Holkrantz, 6th May 1902,* Colony of Natal, 1902
MM	Mafeking Municipality Notice
NA	Natal Archives, Pietermaritzburg
NAD	Native Affairs Department, Cape Colony
NBBNA	Natal Blue Book on Native Affairs
NC	Native Commissioner
OFS	Orange Free State
OHSA	M. Wilson and L. M. Thompson, eds., *The Oxford History of South Africa,* 2 vols., Oxford University Press, 1969, 1971

PWD	Public Works Department, Natal
RM	Resident Magistrate
SANAC	South African Native Affairs Commission, 1903–5
SLD	Secretary to the Law Department, Cape Colony
SN	Superintendent of Natives, South African Republic
SNA	Secretary for Native Affairs
SRC	Superintendent of Refugees, Orange River Colony
TA	Transvaal Archives, Pretoria
tel.	telegram
Times History	L. C. M. S. Amery, *The Times History of the War in South Africa, 1899–1902*, 7 vols., Sampson, Low & Marston, London, 1900–9
USPG	United Society for the Propagation of the Gospel, London
WO	War Office, London
ZA	Zululand Archive, Pietermaritzburg

1. Myth of a white man's war

1 R. Kruger, *Good-Bye Dolly Gray*, Cassell, London, pp. 421–2.

2 *OHSA*, vol. 2, p. 326.

3 CO 179/210/8629, statement by Lieutenant Lambton, 12 Feb. 1900.

4 WO 32/8048, Kemp to Kitchener, 15 July 1901.

5 This section is mostly based on S. Marks and A. Atmore, eds., *Economy and Society in Pre-Industrial South Africa*, Longman, London, 1980, especially pp. 1–43 and the chapters by Stanley Trapido and Roger Wagner; S. Marks and R. Rathbone, eds., *Industrialisation and Social Change in South Africa*, Longman, London, 1982, especially pp. 1–43; and Stanley Trapido, 'Landlord and Tenant in a Colonial Economy: The Transvaal 1880–1910', *JSAS*, 5, 1 (1978), pp. 26–58.

6 See Donald Moodie, ed., *The Record*, reprint, Balkema, Amsterdam and Cape Town, 1960, part 3, pp. 26–30; J. S. Marais, *The Cape Coloured People 1652–1937*, Longman Green, London, 1939, p. 12; T. R. H. Davenport, *South Africa: A Modern History*, Macmillan, London, 1977, p. 23. I have used the term 'Coloureds' in the text to refer to people of mixed descent, though the term 'Bastards' was generally used in the eighteenth century.

7 Marais, *The Cape Coloured People*, pp. 131, 134.

8 See G. Tylden, 'The Development of the Commando System in South Africa 1715–1922', *Africana Notes and News*, 13, 8 (1961), pp. 303–13.

9 Shula Marks, 'Khoisan Resistance to the Dutch in the Seventeenth and Eighteenth Centuries', *JAH*, 13, 1 (1972), p. 76; M. Whiting Spilhaus, *South Africa in the Making 1652–1806*, Juta, Cape Town, 1966, p. 129.

10 D. C. F. Moodie, *The History of Battles and Adventures*, reprint, Cass, London, 1968, vol. 1, p. 339; Marais, *The Cape Coloured People*, p. 133; R. Elphick and H. Giliomee, eds., *The Shaping of South African Society 1652–1820*, Longman Penguin Southern Africa, Cape Town, 1979, pp. 222, 352.

11 Spilhaus, p. 383.

12 G. M. Theal, ed., *Documents Relating to the Kaffir War of 1835*, South African Government, 1912, p. 329.

13 G. E. Cory, *The Rise of South Africa*, Winderley, Cape Town, 1930, vol. 5, pp. 357–8. The background to the Kat River rebellion is to be found in Tony Kirk, 'The Cape Economy and the Expropriation of the Kat River Settlement, 1846–53', in Marks and Atmore, eds., pp. 226–46.

14 R. Moyer, 'The Mfengu, Self-Defence and the Cape Frontier Wars', in C. C. Saunders and R. M. Derricourt, eds., *Beyond the Cape Frontier*, Longman Penguin Southern Africa, Cape Town, 1974, p. 106.

15 *OHSA*, vol. 1, p. 411; vol. 2, pp. 269, 282.

16 Marks, 'Khoisan Resistance' p. 76; Moodie, *History of Battles*, vol. 1, pp. 175, 182, 185; Marais, *The Cape Coloured People*, pp. 132, 133; G. M. Theal, *History of the Boers in South Africa*, reprint, Struik, Cape Town, 1973, p. 255; James Darling, 'Boomplaats, an Eye-Witness Account', South African Historical Society Records, 1913–16, University of the Witwatersrand Library, MS. A241.

17 J. S. Marais, *Maynier and the First Boer Republic*, Maskew Miller, Cape Town, 1944, pp. 102, 107; W. M. Macmillan, *Bantu, Boer and Briton*, Faber and Gwyer, London, 1928, p. 33; Martin Legassick, 'The Frontier Tradition in South African Historiography', in Marks and Atmore, eds., p. 66; Leonard Thompson, *Survival in Two Worlds: Moshoeshoe of Lesotho 1786–1870*, Oxford University Press, 1975, pp. 236–7.

18 Marais, *The Cape Coloured People*, p. 134; G. Tylden, 'The Cape Mounted Riflemen 1827–1870', *Journal of the Society for Army Historical Research*, 17 (1938). pp. 227–31; B. Williams, *Record of the Cape Mounted Riflemen*, Causton, London, 1909.

19 See W. R. Nasson, 'Race and Civilisation in the Anglo-Boer War of 1899–1902', unpublished MA dissertation, University of York, 1977; Christine Bolt, *Victorian Attitudes to Race*, Routledge and Kegan Paul, London, 1971; V. G. Kiernan, *The Lords of Human Kind*, Penguin, Harmondsworth, 1972.

20 Settler views in South Africa were rather different from those in the metropolis, where the use of indigenous troops was regarded as a vital ingredient of imperial defence, in India and tropical Africa for example. See C. E. Callwell, *Small Wars*, 2nd edn, HMSO, London, 1899, and Sir Garnet Wolseley, 'The Negro as Soldier', *The Fortnightly Review*, 44 (1889).

21 CO 179/206/26305, desp. 28 Sept. 1899, minutes by Sir Hartmann Just, Sir Frederick Graham and Joseph Chamberlain.

22 *Parliamentary Debates*, 4th series, Commons, lxxix, col. 57, 15 Feb. 1900.

23 *Ibid.*, Commons, xcviii, col. 1155, 2 Aug. 1901.

24 *Ibid.*, Commons, lxxix, col. 57, 15 Feb 1900. A number of Indian bearers and other ancillary workers accompanied British troops from India to South Africa, a total of 7071 men, who worked as skilled labourers in the transport and remount departments, as water-carriers, stretcher-bearers and washermen. See *Minutes of Evidence before the Royal Commission on the War in South Africa*, Cd.1791, 1904, p. 496.

25 *Parliamentary Debates*, 4th series, Commons, xcviii, cols. 1123–4, 2 Aug. 1901. For the later development of this theme see B. P. Willan, 'The South African Native Labour Contingent 1916–1918', *JAH*, 19, 1 (1978), pp. 61–86; Robert C. Reinders, 'Racialism on the Left, E. D. Morel and the "Black Horror on the Rhine"', *International Review of Social History*, 13 (1968), pp. 1–28; Keith L. Nelson, 'The Black Horror on the Rhine: Race as a Factor in Post-World War I Diplomacy', *Journal of Modern History*, 42, 4 (1970), pp. 606–27.

26 See pp. 115–16.

27 CO 48/551/2411, encl. 6 in Milner to Chamberlain, 3 Jan, 1901, Spriggs to Milner, 31 Dec. 1900.

28 CO 179/210/4948, transmitted by the Governor, Hely-Hutchinson, to Chamberlain (tel.) 14 Feb. 1900.

29 S. B. Spies, *Methods of Barbarism? Roberts and Kitchener and Civilians in the Boer Republics, January 1900–May 1902*, Human and Rousseau, Cape Town, 1977, p. 19; OFS Archives, GS 2113, R6286-2/1899 contains a list of seventy members of the commando raised from the Bethlehem district, of which at least twenty are signified as Coloureds. Some members of the coloured De Buys family from Mara in the Zoutpansberg evidently accompanied the Boer forces, see TA, LtG 121, 110/5, report of NC Zoutpansberg, 30 Jan, 1903.

30 J. B. Scott, *The Hague Peace Conferences of 1899 and 1907*, vol. 2, John Hopkins University Press, Baltimore, 1909, pp. 111–42 (for the text of the convention). For further details about the general implications of the convention for the war in South Africa see S. B. Spies, 'The Hague Convention of 1899 and the Boer Republics', *Historia*, 15, 1 (1970), and *Methods of Barbarism?*, pp. 10–15 and *passim*.

31 W. K. Hancock and J. van der Poel, eds., *Selections from the Smuts Papers*. vol. 1, Cambridge University Press, 1966, p. 484, Smuts to W. T. Stead, 4 Jan, 1902.

32 Trapido, 'Landlord and Tenant', pp. 42–4; P. Delius, 'Abel Erasmus: Power and Profit in the Eastern Transvaal', unpublished research paper, Institute of Commonwealth Studies, University of Oxford, 1981, *passim*.

33 Breytenbach quoted by Spies, *Methods of Barbarism?*, p. 17; P. Warwick, 'African Societies and the South African War 1899–1902', unpublished DPhil thesis, University of York, 1978, p. 20.

34 Schreiner Papers, South African Public Library, Cape Town, MSS. SA Sect.B, 'Situation in South Africa – miscellaneous correspondence October–November 1899', Steyn to Schreiner (tel.), 20 Nov. 1899.

35 CO 417/287/9529, sub. in encl. in Milner to Chamberlain, 7 Mar. 1900, Steyn and Kruger to Roberts, 19 Feb. 1900, and Roberts to Milner, 23 Feb. 1900; CO 179/216/4904, encl. 1, Roberts to Steyn and Kruger, 7 Mar. 1900.

36 CO 179/207/33825, desp. 6 Nov. 1899, minute by Lucas; CO 179/207/31437, desp. 12 Nov. 1899, minute by Lucas. Charles Lucas was knighted in 1907.

37 WO 32/7958, De Wet to Kitchener, 18 Mar. 1901; WO 32/8027, encl. in Kitchener to Brodrick (conf.), 30 Aug. 1901, memorandum by General Sir Bindon Blood giving an account of his interview with Viljoen at Lydenburg on 25 and 27 Aug. 1901; General B. Viljoen, *My Reminiscences of the Anglo-Boer War*, Hood, Douglas and Howard, London, 1903, pp. 523–4, 540–1; *Parliamentary Debates*, 4th series, Commons, xcviii, cols. 1124–5, 28 Aug. 1901.

38 See p. 44.

39 *Times History*, vol. 2, p. 297; vol. 3, pp. 113–14.

40 See p. 121.

41 S. M. Brown, *With the Royal Canadians*, Publishers' Syndicate, Toronto, 1900, p. 248; (Lady) E. C. Briggs, *The Staff Work of the Anglo-Boer War 1899–1901*, Grant Richards, London, 1901, p. 75; R. C. Billington, *A Mule Driver at the Front*, Chapman and Hall, London, 1901, p. 3; P. Bonner, 'African Participation in the Anglo-Boer War of 1899–1902', unpublished MA dissertation, University of London, 1967, p. 3; W. R. Nasson, '"These Infernal Mahogany Brats": Black Transport Workers and the British Army in the Cape Colony during the South African War', unpublished research paper presented to the conference on research in progress, Centre for Southern African Studies, University of York, March 1980.

42 R. C. A. Samuelson, *Long, Long Ago*, Knox, Durban, 1929, pp. 142, 149, 170–1, 176; *Times History*, vol. 5, p. 613.

43 CA, CMK 6/21, AG circular memorandum no. 37, 17 May 1901.

44 Sir F. P. Fletcher Vane, *War and One Year After*, South African Newspaper Co., Cape Town, 1903, p. 30; B. Farwell, *The Great Boer War*, Harper and Row, New York, 1976, p. 357; T. Pakenham, *The Boer War*, Weidenfeld and Nicolson, London, 1979, p. 540.

45 TA, MGP 25, 3470/00, J. S. Marwick to secretary to General Maxwell, the Military Governor, Pretoria, 15 Sept. 1900; E. Hobhouse, *The Brunt of the War and Where it Fell*, Methuen, London, 1902, p. 219, petition of the women of the Klerksdorp Women's Laager, 5 Jan. 1901; see also pp. 100–1.

46 Spies, *Methods of Barbarism?*, pp. 155–6.

47 WO 32/7951/5363, Staff Diary 8th Infantry Division, 10 Dec. 1900.

48 See Warwick, 'African Societies', pp. 27–8.

49 Kitchener Papers, Public Records Office, PRO 30/57/20, Roberts to Kitchener, 31 Jan. 1901; 30/57/22, Brodrick to Kitchener, 8 Feb. 1901, and Kitchener to Brodrick, 16 Feb. 1901.

50 CO 48/553/29712, encl. 2 in Hely-Hutchinson to Chamberlain, 5 Aug. 1901, Kitchener to Hely-Hutchinson, 31 July 1901; *Further Correspondence Relating to Affairs in South Africa*, Cd.903, 1902, p. 137, Boer proclamation by P. H. Kritzinger, Nov. 1901.

51 *Times History*, vol. 5, p. 250.

52 *Parliamentary Debates*, 4th series, Commons, xcviii, col. 1123, 2 Aug. 1901, and cv, col. 658, 20 Mar. 1902.

53 *Ibid.*, xcix, col. 34, 8 Aug. 1901; civ, col. 811, 7 Mar. 1902.

54 Kitchener Papers, PRO 30/57/22, Kitchener to Brodrick, 9 Mar. 1902.

55 J. F. C. Fuller, *The Last of the Gentlemen's Wars, a Subaltern's Journal of the War in South Africa, 1899–1902*, Faber and Faber, London, 1937, pp. 113–16; Farwell, p. 351.

56 Kitchener Papers, PRO 30/57/22, Brodrick to Kitchener, 22 Mar. 1902.

57 G. H. L. Le May, *British Supremacy in South Africa 1899–1907*, Oxford University Press, 1965, p. 101.

58 Kitchener Papers, PRO 30/57/22, Kitchener to Brodrick, 13 Apr. 1902.

59 *Parliamentary Debates*, 4th series, Commons, cv, col. 647, 20 Mar. 1902.

60 *Mills Report*, pp. 16, 19, evidence of Mpela, a Zulu from Vryheid, and C. S. Jordaan, member of British intelligence department.

61 *The War in South Africa, October 1899 to February 1900, Prepared in the Historical Section of the Great General Staff, Berlin*, trans. W. H. H. Waters and H. du Cane, 2 vols., Murray, London, 1904–6, vol. 1, p. 137.

62 *Mills Report*, pp. 6, 8, evidence of Coenraad Meyer, Assistant Veldkornet, Ward 3, Utrecht, and Jacobus Vermaak, farmer from Morgenson.

63 Hancock and Van der Poel, eds., *Smuts Papers*, vol. 1, p. 485.

64 Statement by Brodrick in *Parliamentary Debates*, 4th series, Commons, xciv, col. 1455, 20 May 1901.

65 CO 417/335/41844, encl. in Milner to Chamberlain, 12 Oct. 1901.

66 Roberts Papers, Public Records Office, WO 105/14, French to Roberts, 26 Oct. 1899.

67 CO 179/219/27864, encl. in McCallum to Chamberlain, 15 July 1901, Lawson to McCallum, 10 July 1901.

68 CO 179/210/8629, encl. 4, Buller to Hely-Hutchinson (tel.), 13 Feb. 1900; see also Winston Churchill, *London to Ladysmith via Pretoria*, Longman, London, 1900, p. 357.

2. Mafikeng and beyond

1 Pakenham, pp. 398–9.

2 *Times History*, vol. 4, p. 199.

3 S. T. Plaatje, *Native Life in South Africa*, King, London, 1916, p. 239; *Cape Times*, 6 Oct. 1899; CA, NAD 445, Bell to SNA (tel.), ? Oct. 1899.

4 F. D. Baillie, *Mafeking, a Diary of the Siege*, Constable, London, 1900, p. 146; C. Harding, *Frontier Patrols*, Bell, London, 1937, p. 135; J. L. Comaroff, ed., *The Boer War Diary of Sol T. Plaatje, an African at Mafeking*, Macmillan, London, 1973, 3 Jan. 1900, p. 64 (henceforth Plaatje, *Diary*).

5 Baillie, p. 108; B. Gardner, *Mafeking, A Victorian Legend*, Cassell, London, 1966, pp. 44–5; Comaroff in Plaatje, *Diary*, p. xxxvii; CA, NAD 445, Bell to SNA (tel.), ? Oct. 1899.

6 Mafeking Municipality Notice (MM) 34, 30 Oct. 1899.

7 Baillie, pp. 56–7, 166, 167, 172–4, 263; MM 39, 3 Nov. 1899; Pakenham, pp. 410–14; Edward Ross, *Diary of the Siege of Mafeking, October 1899 to May 1900*, edited by B. P. Willan, Van Riebeeck Society, Cape Town, 1980, 22 Dec. 1899. p. 75.

8 Baillie, p. 212; Gardner, p. 37 n. 2; Plaatje, *Native Life*, p. 242; CBBNA, G.52–1901, p. 32; MM 108, 23 Jan. 1900; MM 143, 28 Feb. 1900; MM 150(b), 7 Mar. 1900; CO 417/287/11859, sub. in encl. 2 in Milner to Chamberlain (conf.), 28 Mar. 1900, Baden-Powell to Chief Staff Officer (tel.), 9 Feb. 1900; Roberts Papers, WO 105/15, T/14/1, Baden-Powell to Plumer (tel.), 6 Mar. 1900; Ross, 23 Jan. 1900, p. 110. Ross gives the number of Rapulana armed as 3000 and Baden-Powell as 2000, but these figures are almost certainly grossly inflated.

9 J. E. Neilly, *Besieged with B-P*, Pearson, London, 1900, p. 198; Plaatje, *Diary*, 8 Dec. 1899, pp. 33–5.

10 Baden-Powell to Snyman, 23 Jan. 1900, letter reproduced in B. P. Willan, 'The Siege of Mafeking' in P. Warwick, ed., *The South African War*, Longman, London, 1980, p. 151.

11 MM 143, 28 Feb. 1900.

12 Ross, p. 95.

13 C. G. H. Bell, 'Diary during the Siege of Mafeking', 16 Oct. 1899 (unpublished MS., Cory Library, Rhodes University, Grahamstown – copy kindly shown me by Dr Brian Willan); MM 76, 9 Dec. 1899; *Mafeking Mail (Special Siege Slip)*, 8 Feb. 1900; Neilly, p. 252; Willan, p. 152; Ross, 11 Jan. 1900, p. 95, 13 Apr. 1900, p. 212.

14 The details of Baden-Powell's 'loaves and fishes' exercise are set out in Pakenham, pp. 406–9.

15 *Ibid.*, p. 402.

16 J. A. Hamilton, *The Siege of Mafeking*, Methuen, London, 1900, p. 196; CO 417/285/4659, encl. 2 in Milner to Chamberlain (conf.), 24 Jan. 1900, Nicholson to Milner, 16 Jan. 1900; Roberts Papers, WO 105/15, T/14/1, Baden-Powell to Nicholson (tel.), 8 Jan. 1900; Willan, p. 150; Ross, 2 Jan. 1900, p. 85.

17 Willan, p. 163.

18 Plaatje, *Diary*, 21 Mar. 1900, p. 121.

19 'Mafeking Besieged, Seven Months of a Lifetime – the Diary of Miss Ina Cowan, 9 Oct. 1899–17 May 1900', p. 30 (unpublished typescript kindly shown me by Mrs C. Minchin of Mafeking).

20 Bell, 'Diary', 22 Mar. 1900; Willan, p. 155; Ross, 14 Feb. 1900, p. 147.

21 Willan, p. 155.

22 Neilly, pp. 227–31.

23 CBBNA, G.52–1901, p. 32; report by Mafeking Municipal Council on Baden-Powell's evidence to the Royal Commission on the War in South Africa, 8 Dec. 1903, reproduced in Ross, p. 241.

24 MM 115, 30 Jan. 1900; MM 126, 11 Feb. 1900; MM 183, 12 Apr. 1900; Plaatje, *Diary*, 27 Feb. 1900, pp. 102 3; *De Volksstem*, 13 Feb. 1900, Pakenham, p. 410; Willan, pp. 151, 155.

25 Z. K. Matthews, 'A Short History of the Tshidi-Barolong', *Fort Hare Papers*, 1, 1 (1945), p. 24; Baillie, pp. 284–5.

26 Plaatje, *Native Life*, pp. 249, 251.

27 A. Sillery, *Founding a Protectorate, a History of Bechuanaland 1885–95*, Mouton, The Hague, 1965, pp. 62–3; I. Schapera, *A Short History of the BaKgatla-bagaKgafela*, Communications from the School of African Studies, University of Cape Town, New Series, No. 3, 1942, p. 13; L. W. Truschel, 'Nation-Building and the Kgatla: The Role of the Anglo-Boer War', *Botswana Notes and Records*, 4 (1972), p. 185; BNA, HC 108, 'A petition from the Bakgatla raad to the English government, Cape Town', November 1894 (which provides a history of the Kgatla and their version of the land dispute with the Koena).

28 CO 417/258/32008, sub. in encl. 6 in Milner to Chamberlain, 1 Nov. 1899, Arthur Lawley to British Consul, Beira, 22 Oct. 1899; CO 417/269/34320, encl. 2 in Milner to Chamberlain (conf.), 22 Nov. 1899, Nicholson to Milner, 30 Oct. 1899.

29 CO 417/258/33853, encl. 2 in Milner to Chamberlain, 15 Nov. 1899, Nicholson to Milner, 23 Oct. 1899; CO 417/268/33043, encl. 4 in Milner to Chamberlain, 8 Nov. 1899, Lawley to Milner, 31 Oct. 1899; CO 417/283/3024, Milner to Chamberlain, 10 Jan. 1900; CO 417/283/13205, encl. in Milner to Chamberlain, 4 Apr. 1900, Nicholson to Milner, 23 Feb. 1900; Boer Official Telegram, 22 Oct. 1899; G. H. J. Teichler, 'Some Historical Notes on Derdepoort-Sikwane', *Botswana Notes and Records*, 5 (1973), pp. 126, 131.

30 Milner Papers, Bodleian Library, University of Oxford, 17, 622, Lawley to Milner (conf.), 11 Nov. 1899; CO 417/309/1011, encl. 2, Lawley to Milner, 13 Nov. 1899.

31 CO 417/269/34320, encls. 7 and 9 in Milner to Chamberlain (conf.), 22 Nov. 1899, Clarke to Milner (tel.), 13 Nov. 1899, and Milner to Clarke (tel.), 20 Nov. 1899; J. Ellenberger, 'The Bechuanaland Protectorate and the Boer War 1899–1902', *Rhodesiana*, 11 (Dec. 1964), p. 5; Schapera, p. 19; Teichler, p. 127; CO 417/291/21851, sub. in encl. 1 in Milner to Chamberlain

(conf.), 20 June 1900, Surmon to Clarke, 31 Mar. 1900, and statement by Jules Ellenberger, 14 May 1900.

32 BNA, RC 5/4/962, Ashburnham to Ellenberger, 19 July 1901 and evidence of Ramono and Mongale, 3 Aug. 1901; Truschel, 'Nation-Building', p. 191.

33 CO 417/269/33599, Milner to Chamberlain (tel.), 3 Dec. 1899, and minutes of Chamberlain and other Colonial Office officials; CO 417/287/11788, encl. in Milner to Chamberlain, 28 Mar. 1900, undated extract from *Kreutz Zeitung*; BNA, RC 4/14, statement by Ramono, 29 May 1900; CO 417/292/24285, encl. various affidavits collected by Ellenberger.

34 Boer Official Telegrams, 25 Nov. 1899, 28 Nov. 1899.

35 W. van Everdingen, *De Oorlog in Zuid-Afrika*, vol. 1, Delft, 1911, p. 87.

36 Boer Official Telegram, 1 Dec. 1899; article in the journal, *Keur*, cited by Teichler, p. 129. For further details of the assault from the Boer's point of view see Kmnd. H. J. Botha, 'Die moord op Derdepoort, 25 November 1899: Nie-blankes in oorlogsdiens', *Militaria*, 1 (1969), pp. 1–97.

37 CO 417/283/3848, encl. 1 in Milner to Chamberlain (conf.), 17 Jan. 1900, Nicholson to Milner, 25 Dec. 1899; Boer Official Telegram, 26 Dec. 1899; Teichler, p. 129; Schapera, p. 20; Van Everdingen, pp. 142–3. The *Standard and Diggers' News*, 29 Dec. 1899, states that the Boer commando was only 200 strong, and that five Boers were killed and three wounded.

38 Neil Parsons, 'The Economic History of Khama's Country in Botswana, 1885–1930', in R. Palmer and N. Parsons, eds., *The Roots of Rural Poverty in Central and Southern Africa*, Heinemann, London, 1977, pp. 119–24.

39 Sillery, pp. 63–6, 202–11; L. W. Truschel, 'Accommodation under Imperial Rule: The Tswana of the Bechuanaland Protectorate 1895–1910', PhD thesis, Northwestern University, 1970, chapters 2 and 3; BNA, S 1/13, Goold-Adams to Milner, 20 Dec. 1898; BNA HC 130/2, Khama to Milner, n.d., and Khama to J. A. Ashburnham, 14 Dec. 1898, and HC 190/1, J. S. Moffat to Loch, 20 Feb. 1894, and HC 108, statement by Ratshosa, 23 Apr. 1894.

40 CO 417/258/33863, encl. 2 in Milner to Chamberlain, 15 Nov. 1899, Nicholson to Milner, 23 Oct. 1899.

41 BNA, RC 4/14/169, Grobler to Khama, 20 Oct. 1899, and Khama to Grobler, 23 Oct. 1899.

42 CO 417/258/32008, sub. in encl. 6 in Milner to Chamberlain, 1 Nov. 1899, Lawley to British Consul, Beira, 22 Oct. 1899; CO 417/309/1011, encl. 2, Lawley to Milner, 13 Nov. 1899.

43 BNA, RC 4/14/109, Ashburnham to Goold-Adams, 5 June 1900; CO 417/309/1011, encl. 3, Nicholson to Milner, 13 Nov. 1899. It was reckoned that a cyclist scout could cover 150 miles in four days. Colonel Plumer also employed thirty 'reliable' Ndebele scouts. CO 417/258/33863, encl. 1 in Milner to Chamberlain (conf.), 15 Nov. 1899, Nicholson to Milner, 16 Oct. 1899; CO 417/283/14881, encl. in Milner to Chamberlain, 22 Apr. 1900, Ashburnham to Milner, 21 Feb. 1900.

44 CO 417/290/20056, encl. 1 in Milner to Chamberlain, 5 June 1900, Nicholson to Milner, 7 May 1900; BNA, RC 4/14/169, Ashburnham to Goold-Adams, 5 June 1900; CO 417/283/22749, sub. in encl. 2 in Milner to Chamberlain (conf.), 26 June 1900, Lt Beale Brown to DMI, David Henderson, 31 May 1900; BNA, RC 4/14/112, Grobler to Ashburnham, 20 Feb. 1901; CO 417/320/20757, encl. in Milner to Chamberlain, 24 May 1901, Surmon to Milner, 15 May 1901; CO 417/320/22393, encl. 1 in Milner to Chamberlain, 7 June 1901, Surmon to Milner (tel.), 1 June 1901.

45 Hancock and Van der Poel, eds., *Smuts Papers*, vol. 1, 'Memoires of the Boer War', p. 597.

46 Teichler, pp. 129–30; Boer Official Telegram, 16 Mar. 1900.

47 CO 417/282/22749, encl. Surmon to Plumer, 12 May 1900; CO 417/290/20056, sub. in encl. 1 in Milner to Chamberlain, 5 June 1900, Lentshwe to Surmon (tel.), 4 May 1900; CO 417/290/21003, encl. in Milner to Chamberlain, 13 June 1900, Clarke to Surmon (tel.), 13 May 1900; Hancock and Van der Poel, eds., *Smuts Papers*, vol. 1, pp. 598, 626–7; TA, SNA 4, 429/01, W. McDonald to Capt. de Bertodano, 29 Nov. 1901; TA, SNA 13, 1569/02, NC Rustenburg, C. Griffith, to SNA, 20 Aug. 1902.

48 CO 417/283/25614, encl. 2 in Milner to Chamberlain (conf.), 16 July 1900, Baden-Powell to Roberts (tel.), 28 June 1900.

49 CO 417/283/23669, encl. 3 in Milner to Chamberlain (conf.), 4 July 1900, Milner to Roberts (tel.), 28 June 1900; CO 417/283/25614, minute by Lord Selborne.

50 TA, LtG 122, 110/7, Edmeston to Griffith, 27 Apr. 1903.

51 BNA, RC 4/14, Lord Methuen to ADC Mafeking (tel.), 30 Oct. 1900, Capt. C. M. Ryan to Surmon, 29 Nov. 1900, Capt. C. E. Morgan to Ryan, 27 Nov. 1900; TA, LtG 122, 110/7, Edmeston to Griffith, 27 Apr. 1903; CO 417/321/1773, encls. 1 and 2 in Milner to Chamberlain, 20 Dec. 1901, Ralph Williams, Resident Commissioner, to Milner, 3. Oct. 1901; BNA, RC 6/3/129, Williams to Milner, 7 Nov. 1901, 20 Dec. 1901, Williams to Milner (tel.), 17 Dec. 1901, and Milner to Williams (tel.), 18 Dec. 1901; TA, LtG 122, 110/17, Kgatla petition to Sir Arthur Lawley, 1903.

52 BNA, HC 130/2, Goold-Adams to Ashburnham, 10 Nov. 1898, 15 Sept. 1899; CO 417/283/14881, encl. in Milner to Chamberlain, 22 Apr. 1900, Ashburnham to Milner, 21 Feb. 1900; BNA, HC 82, Goold-Adams to Milner, 26 July 1900.

53 CO 417/321/45360, encl. 3 in Milner to Chamberlain, 29 Nov. 1901, Milner to Williams, 29 Nov. 1901; CO 417/343/5418, encl. 1 in Milner to Chamberlain, 10 Jan. 1902, Williams to Milner, 28 Dec. 1901; Truschel, 'Accommodation under Imperial Rule', pp. 102–15; Parsons, in Palmer and Parsons, eds., p. 129.

54 LMS, South Africa, Box 59, Rev. H. Williams to Rev. Wardlaw Thompson, 2 May 1901; Box 58, Rev. D. Carnegie to Thompson, 10 Feb. 1900, Willoughby to Thompson, 4 Oct. 1900; Box 60, Willoughby to Thompson, 26 Apr. 1902; W. C. Willoughby Papers, Selly Oak Colleges Library, Birmingham, file 804, Willoughby to Thompson, 5 June 1901; Parsons, in Palmer and Parsons, eds., pp. 125–8.

55 BNA, RC 6/3/129, Williams to Milner, 7 Nov. 1901, and report of visit to Mochudi, 25 Oct. 1901.

56 TA, SNA 13, 1569/02, Griffith's weekly report, 23 Aug. 1902; TA, SNA 17, 2482/02, AG's Office, Circular No. 15, 1902; BNA, S259/13/4259, Williams to Milner (tel.), 2 June 1902; Truschel, 'Nation-Building', p. 190.

57 Schapera, p. 20.

58 CO 417/344/28505, encl. 1 in Milner to Chamberlain, 21 June 1902, Williams to Milner, 2 June 1902; TA, LtG 122, 110/17, Littake, Segale, Ramono and Kgari Pilane to Lawley, 9 Feb, 1903.

59 TA, SNA 15, 2160/02, Milner to Lagden, 1 Nov. 1902; BNA, RC 8/8/496, Griffith to Lagden, 6 Feb. 1903.

60 TA, SNA 15, 2160/02, W. J. S. Driver to Griffith, n.d.

61 BNA, S 1/9, J. C. Macgregor to High Commissioner, 1 Mar. 1916.

62 Truschel, 'Nation-Building', p. 191.

63 TA, SNA 15, 2160/02, Driver to Griffith, n.d.

64 Matthews, p. 24; Plaatje, *Native Life*, p. 252; TA, SNA 12, 1477/02, William Mkuzangwe to Colonel Vyvyan, CSO Vryburg, 4 July 1902; *Minutes of Evidence before the Royal Commission on the War in South Africa*, Cd. 1790, 1904, vol. 1, p. 427; *Mafeking Mail*, 23 Dec. 1903; Pakenham, p. 418; Willan, pp. 159–60; Ross, appendix p. 241.

3. An encircling struggle

1 Quoted by G. Tylden, *The Rise of the Basuto*, Juta, Cape Town, 1950, p. 145. See also Sandra Burman, *Chiefdom Politics and· Alien Law: Basutoland under Cape Rule 1871–1884*, Macmillan, London, 1981.

2 Tylden, *The Rise of the Basuto*, p. 200.

3 *Basutoland Annual Report for 1899–1900*, Cd. 431, 1901, p. 5.

4 Colin Murray, *Families Divided: The Impact of Migrant Labour in Lesotho*, Cambridge University Press, 1981, p. 12.

5 *Ibid.*, pp. 12–13.

6 *Report 1894–5*, C.7944, 1896, pp.5–6; see also *Report 1895–6*, C.8279, 1897, p.6.

7 Judy Kimble, 'Labour Migration in Basutoland, *c*.1870–1885', in Marks and Rathbone, eds., pp.130–60.

8 *Report 1893–4*, C.7629, 1895, p.5.

9 *Report 1897–8*, C.9046, 1899, p.4; Sandra Burman, 'Masopha, *c*.1820–99', in Christopher Saunders, ed., *Black Leaders in Southern African History*, Heinemann, London, 1979, pp.100–13.

10 CO 417/270/15502, encls. in Milner to Chamberlain, 31 May 1899, esp. Notes of *pitso* held at Griffith's Village, 8 May. 1899.

11 *Report 1899–1900*, pp.25, 30; Tylden, *The Rise of the Basuto*, p.195.

12 See C. Van Onselen, 'Reactions to Rinderpest in Southern Africa 1896–7', *JAH*, 13, 3 (1972), pp.473–88.

13 LNA, S8/2/2/6, Letter Book to Chiefs, Nov. 1897–Feb. 1902, Lagden to Lerotholi, 19 Sept. 1899.

14 *Report 1899–1900*, p.4; G. Y. Lagden, *The Basutos*, Hutchinson, London, 1909, vol. 2, p.602.

15 CO 417/270/19926, Milner to Chamberlain, 10 July 1899.

16 CO 417/270/30588, encl. 1 in Milner to Chamberlain, 18 Oct. 1899, Lagden to Milner, 4 Oct. 1899.

17 CO 417/270/23436, encl. in Milner to Chamberlain, 18 Oct. 1899, Lagden to Fiddes, 10 Aug. 1899; LNA, S7/1/1/13, AC Berea to GS (Herbert Sloley), 6 Dec. 1899, and encl. statement by Bose of Mamatha; USPG, Reports, Africa 1899A, 4 (33284), Rev. Spencer Wrigall, Masite, to Rev. H. W. Tucker, 31 Dec. 1899; LNA, S7/1/2/17, AC Leribe to Sloley, 28 Sept. 1899.

18 *Report 1898–9*, Cd. 3, 1900, p.5; LNA, S7/3/16, Lerotholi to Lagden, 24 Sept. 1899.

19 Lagden, vol. 2, p.603.

20 CO 417/270/31511, Milner to Chamberlain, 25 Oct. 1899, and encl. 4, Lagden to Milner, 15 Oct. 1899; encl. 7, Milner to Lagden, 16 Oct. 1899; encl. 12, Lagden to Milner, 18 Oct. 1899.

21 LNA, S7/3/15, Lagden to Lerotholi, 12 Oct. 1899; *Report 1899–1900*, pp.6, 11.

22 LNA, S8/2/2/6, Lagden to Lerotholi, 2 Feb. 1900; *Times History*, vol. 2, p.189; vol. 4, p.320.

23 CO 417/297/14085, encl. 2 in Milner to Chamberlain 18 Apr. 1900, Milner to Lagden (tel.), 6 Apr. 1900; C. R. de Wet, *Three Years War*, Constable, London, 1902, p.104; Lagden Papers, Rhodes House Library, Oxford, MSS. Afr.s. 213, Box 5/1 MSS. diary, 7 Apr. 1900, 14 Apr. 1900; CO 417/297/14910, encl. 4 in Milner to Chamberlain 25 Apr. 1900, Lagden to Milner (tel.), 12 Apr. 1900; *Report 1899–1900*, p.45; *Times History*, vol. 4, p.63. The *History* suggests that the proximity of the Basotho inspired the besieged force since 'they felt it would never do for the "niggers" to see them beaten by the Boers' (p.61).

24 CO 417/293/31108, encl. tels. in Milner to Chamberlain, 5 Sept. 1900; 1, Lagden to Milner, 29 Aug. 1900; 12, Lagden to Milner, 3 Sept. 1900; 13, Milner to Lagden, 3 Sept. 1900; 17, Lagden to Milner, 3 Sept. 1900.

25 J. B. Seely (Lord Mottistone), *Fear and Be Slain*, Hodder and Stoughton, London, 1931, p.105; *Report 1901–2*, Cd.1388, 1903, p.18; Pakenham, 439; Lagden Papers, MSS. Afr.s.213, Box 5/1, Rundle to Lagden (tel.), 22 Sept. 1900; CO 417/328/7007, encl. 1 in Milner to Chamberlain, 6 Feb. 1901, Sloley to Milner (tel.), 28 Jan. 1901; CO 417/328/15236, encls. 1 and 2 in Milner to Chamberlain, 5 Apr. 1901, Sloley to Milner (tel.), 27 Mar. 1901, Milner to Sloley (tel.), 27 Mar. 1901; CO 417/328/27907, encl. 1 in Milner to Chamberlain, 19 July 1901, Sloley to Milner, 10 June 1901.

26 *Times History*, vol. 2, p.124; Lagden Papers, MSS. Afr.s.172, bound diary, 20 Oct. 1899; P. Hadley, ed., *Doctor to Basuto, Boer and Briton, 1877–1906, Memoires of Dr Henry Taylor*, Philip, Cape Town, 1972, p.167. For the first part of the war Dr Taylor practised at Ficksburg.

27 LNA, S7/1/4/10, Lagden to AC Maseru, 31 Oct. 1899; CO 417/270/33043, encl. in Milner to Chamberlain, 8 Nov. 1899, Lagden to Milner (tel.) 30 Oct 1899.

28 LNA, S7/1/2/17, AC Leribe to Sloley, 23 Oct. 1899. The proclamation is also reproduced in Lagden, vol. 2, pp.600–1.

29 Extract from *The Friend* reproduced in *Report 1899–1900*, pp.14–16; CO 417/267/28295,

encl. 3 in Milner to Chamberlain, 26 Sept. 1899, Lagden to Milner (tel.), 22 Sept. 1899; CO 417/270/31511, encl. 9 in Milner to Chamberlain, 25 Oct. 1899, Lagden to Milner (tel.), 16 Oct. 1899; LNA, S8/2/2/6, Lagden to Lerotholi, 10 Oct. 1899, and S7/3/16, Lerotholi to Lagden, 15 Jan. 1900; CO 417/270/30588, encl. 2 in Milner to Chamberlain, 18 Oct. 1899, Lagden to Milner (tel.), 16 Oct. 1899; *Report 1899–1900*, pp. 9, 52, 53.

30 CO 417/270/34332, encl. 6 in Milner to Chamberlain, 22 Nov. 1899, Lagden to Milner (tel.), 19 Nov. 1899.

31 *Further Correspondence Relating to Affairs in South Africa*, Cd. 261, 1900, p. 4, encl. in Milner to Chamberlain, 10 Jan. 1900, Lagden to Milner, 22 Dec. 1899, and sub. encl. H. Potgieter to chief Letsie, 12 Dec. 1899.

32 CO 417/291/23612, encl. 1 in Milner to Chamberlain, 4 July 1900, Lagden to Milner (tel.), 29 June 1900; CO 417/297/24298, encl. in Milner to Chamberlain, 11 July 1900, Orange Free State War Commission to Lerotholi, 19 June 1900.

33 CO 417/270/1010, encl. 19 in Milner to Chamberlain, 20 Dec. 1899, Lagden to Milner (tel.), 17 Dec. 1899.

34 CO 417/270/31511, Milner to Chamberlain, 25 Oct. 1899; CO 417/270/33043, encl. 5 in Milner to Chamberlain, 8 Nov, 1899, Lagden to Milner (tel.), 1 Nov. 1899.

35 CO 417/267/28295, encl. 3 in Milner to Chamberlain, 26 Sept. 1899, Lagden to Milner (tel.), 22 Sept. 1899.

36 Lagden Papers, MSS. Afr.s. 173, MSS. diary, 5 May 1900; CO 417/328/37991, Milner to Chamberlain, 28 Oct. 1900; LNA, S7/1/4/11, Regina v. Sesha, Tlatsinyane and Maboka, 5 Mar. 1902; LNA, S7/6/13, Commander Ladybrand to Sloley (tel.), n.d.; J. D. Kestell, *Through Shot and Flame*, Methuen, London, 1903, p. 150; De Wet, p. 231.

37 Lagden Papers, MSS. Afr.s. 172, bound diary, 3 Oct. 1899.

38 LNA, S7/3/15, Lerotholi to Lagden, 18 Oct. 1899.

39 Lagden Papers, MSS. Afr.s. 172, bound diary, 24 Oct. 1899.

40 *Report 1899–1900*, p. 51; LNA, S7/1/7/15, Lagden to Barrett, 17 Oct. 1899; LNA, S8/2/2/6, Lagden to Lerotholi, 11 Oct. 1899, 18 Oct. 1899, 3 Nov. 1899.

41 CO 417/270/31511, encl. 1 in Milner to Chamberlain, 25 Oct. 1899, Lagden to Milner (tel.), 14 Oct. 1899; *Report 1899–1900*, p. 51; D. B. Hook, *With Sword and Statute*, Greaves, London, 1906, pp. 369–72; CO 417/270/32071, encl. in Milner to Chamberlain, 1 Nov. 1899, Milner's diary of events, 29 Oct. 1899; CO 417/270/33043, encls. 4 and 6 in Milner to Chamberlain, 8 Nov. 1899, Lagden to Milner (tel.), 1 Nov. 1899, and Milner to Lagden (tel.), 8 Nov. 1899; W. E. Stanford Papers, Jagger Library, University of Cape Town, diary D. 24, 1899, 30 Oct. 1899.

42 USPG, Reports, Africa 1899A, 5 (26904), Rev. John Widdicombe, Thlotse Heights, to Rev. H. W. Tucker, 30 Sept. 1899; *Report 1899–1900*, pp. 9, 14–15; LNA, S11/6, Pitso Book (9 May 1899–16 Aug. 1915), p. 23.

43 LNA, S7/1/2/18, AC Leribe to Sloley (tel.), 25 Nov. 1899; LNA, S7/1/2/17, AC Leribe to Sloley, 29 Nov. 1899; LNA S8/2/2/6, Lagden to Lerotholi, 6 Feb. 1900, 13 May 1900; Lagden, p. 607.

44 LNA, S7/3/15, Lerotholi to Lagden, 21 Oct. 1899.

45 LNA, S7/3/15, Lerotholi to Lagden, 30 Sept. 1899.

46 Lagden Papers, MSS, Afr.s. 172, bound diary, 19 Nov. 1899.

47 LNA, S7/1/1/1, AC Berea to Lagden, 28 Nov. 1899.

48 CO 417/270/35840, Milner to Chamberlain, 26 Dec. 1899; LNA, S7/1/1/14, AC Berea to Lagden (tel.), 19 Dec. 1899, and Lerotholi to Lagden 21 Nov. 1899.

49 CO 417/270/112, encl. 2 in Milner to Chamberlain, 13 Dec. 1899, Lagden to Milner, 3 Dec. 1899.

50 *Report 1899–1900*, pp. 5, 10.

51 CA, NAD 445 (tel. 1169), Elliot to Sec. to NAD, Cape Town, 5 Dec. 1899; CO 417/270/112, encl. in Milner to Chamberlain, 13 Dec. 1899, Milner to Lagden (tel.), 7 Dec. 1899.

52 LNA, S7/3/15, Lerotholi to Lagden, 15 Dec. 1899.

53 LNA, S7/3/15, Lagden to Lerotholi, 17 Jan. 1900; S7/1/5/10, AC Mohale's Hoek to Lagden (tel.), 3 Feb. 1900; S7/3/15, Lagden to Lerotholi, 17 Jan. 1900; Lagden Papers, MSS. Afr.s. 173, bound diary, 30 Jan. 1900, 23 Jan. 1900.

54 Stanford Papers, F(x)21, Barrett to Stanford, 11 Feb. 1900; LNA, S8/2/2/6, Lagden to Lerotholi, 19 Jan. 1900; LNA, S7/3/16, Lerotholi to Lagden, 17 Jan. 1900.

55 Lagden Papers, MSS. Afr.s. 173, bound diary, 13 Mar. 1900.

56 LNA, S7/3/16, Lerotholi to Lagden, 18 Feb. 1900; *Further Correspondence Relating to Affairs in South Africa*, Cd. 261, 1900, p. 52.

57 LNA, S7/1/1/15, Schedule of European and Native Refugees, 30 Apr. 1902; *Report 1901–2*, p. 30.

58 *Report 1899–1900*, p. 20; *Report 1900–1*, Cd. 788, 1902, p. 12; LNA, S7/6/14, Assistant Government Secretary to O. C. Steam Transport, Bloemfontein, 28 Aug. 1901.

59 *Report 1899–1900*, p. 34; *Report 1901–2*, Cd. 1388, 1903, p. 6; LNA, S7/1/2/21, AC Leribe to Sloley, 14 Jan. 1902; LNA, S7/1/5/12, Enquiry at Mohale's Hoek, 19 Mar. 1901.

60 CO 417/328/27907, encl. 1 in Milner to Chamberlain, 19 July 1901, Sloley to Milner, 10 June 1901.

61 LNA, S7/1/5/12, AC Mohale's Hoek to Sloley, 6 July 1901; LNA, S11/6, proceedings of *pitso* at Mohale's Hoek, 17 June 1902.

62 *Report 1900–1*, p. 11.

63 OFS Archives, MG1, Intelligence Officer III Division to MG, 24 June 1900; Lagden Papers, MSS. Afr.s. 173, MSS. diary, 18 May 1900; OFS Archives, MG2, Capt. A. J. Trollope to General Ridley, 2 Nov. 1901; Tylden, *The Rise of the Basuto*, pp. 205–6.

64 *Report 1899–1900*, p. 38; *Report 1900–1*, p. 6.

65 *Report 1899–1900*, p. 22; *Report 1902–3*, Cd. 1768, 1904, p. 15.

66 R. W. Thornton, *The Origin and History of the Basuto Pony*, Morija Printing Works, Morija, 1936, pp. 16, 19; CO 417/328/13206, Milner to Chamberlain, 22 Mar. 1901; LNA, S7/1/6/9, AC Qacha's Nek to Sloley (tels.), 1 Mar. 1901, and 4 Apr. 1901; CO 417/328/21407, encl. in Milner to Chamberlain, 1 June 1902, report of an outbreak of disease amongst cattle in Orange River Colony and Basutoland, by T. Flintoff, Veterinary Staff Officer, Maseru; *Report 1900–1*, p. 27; *Report 1901–2*, p. 3.

67 *Report 1899–1900*, pp. 12, 18; *Report 1900–1*, p. 11.

68 Royal Commonwealth Society Library, London, South African Diary of Amy M. Wilson, 1901–2, 29 Mar. 1902; Palmer and Parsons, eds., p. 22.

69 LNA, S7/1/6/9, AC Qacha's Nek to Sloley (tel.), 21 Feb. 1901; CO 417/293/31108, encl. 5 in Milner to Chamberlain, 5 Sept. 1900, Lagden to Milner (tel.), 30 Aug. 1900; *Report 1902–3*, p. 7; LNA, S7/1/4/14, Maama to Sloley, 5 June 1902.

70 LNA, S8/2/2/6, Lagden to Lerotholi, 4 Feb. 1900; *Report 1901–2*, p. 35; LNA, S11/6, Pitso Book, pp. 98–113; CO 417/355/31855, encl. in Milner to Chamberlain, 11 July 1902, Sloley to Milner, 29 June 1902.

71 *Report 1899–1900*, pp. 52, 59; *Report 1900–1*, p. 33; LNA, S7/3/17, Lerotholi to Sloley, 1 Dec. 1901; LNA, S7/3/18, Lerotholi to Sloley, 16 May 1902.

72 LNA, S11/6, Pitso Book, pp. 73–97; CO 417/355/22781, encl. 1 in Milner to Chamberlain, 17 May 1902, Sloley to Milner, 17 May 1902, and sub. encl. report of the trial of Mocheka and Semenekane; CA, NAD 544, folio 754, Mag. Herschel to Sec. to NAD (tel.), 26 July 1902, Sloley to Mag. Herschel, (tel.), 11 June 1902, Milner to Hely-Hutchinson, Governor of Cape Colony, 23 Apr. 1904.

73 LNA, S7/3/16, Lerotholi to Lagden, 13 Feb. 1900, 15 Feb. 1900; CO 417/355/5702, Milner to Chamberlain, 19 Jan. 1902, and encl. medical report on Lerotholi, which concluded 'his life must be considered very uncertain'.

74 LNA, S7/1/1/4, AC Berea to Lagden (tel.), 19 Nov. 1900, Lerotholi to Lagden, 21 Nov. 1900; *Report 1899–1900*, pp. 6, 10, 59; *Report 1900–1*, p. 20; LNA, S7/1/2/18, report by Api, Selta, Abiathara, Neftale and Mothepu, 26 June 1900.

4. The Zulu's war

1 NA, SNA 1/4/6, C118/1899, circular memorandum, 9 Sept. 1899.
2 CO 179/206/26305, Hely-Hutchinson to Chamberlain, 28 Sept. 1899.
3 NA, SNA 1/4/7, C1678/1899, Mag. Estcourt to F. R. Moor, 18 Sept. 1899.
4 NA, SNA 1/4/7, 49/1899, Mag. Dundee to Moor, 13 Sept. 1899.
5 NA, SNA 1/4/7, 550/1899, Mag. Lions River to Moor, 6 Nov. 1899; SNA 1/4/6, C97/1899, Inspector Natal Native Trust to Moor, 12 Oct. 1899, and C138/1899, report of Native Intelligence Officer, 12 Oct. 1899.
6 NA, ZA 32, CR49/1899, Hime to Saunders, 9 Sept. 1899.
7 NA, ZA 32, CR49/1899, Saunders to Hime, n.d.; SNA 1/4/7, CR73/1899, RM Mahlabathini to Saunders, 19 Sept. 1899, and encl. minutes of meeting with chiefs.
8 NA, ZA 32, CR49/1899, Saunders to Hime, n.d.
9 NA, SNA 1/4/7, CR43/1899, RM Nquthu to Saunders, 6 Sept. 1899; NA, SNA 1/4/7, CR368/1899, RM Ndwandwe to Saunders, 4 Sept. 1899.
10 *Mills Report.* p. 70.
11 NA, SNA 1/4/6, C248/1899, Mag. Alfred to Moor, 23 Sept. 1899; NA, SNA 1/4/7, C1678/1899, Mag. Umvoti to Moor, 14 Oct. 1899; NA, SNA 1/4/7, CR60/1899, RM Hlabisa to Saunders, 10 Sept. 1899; NA, SNA 1/4/6, C74/1899, Mag. Dundee to Moor, 27 Sept. 1899; NA, SNA 1/4/6, C458/1899, H. Steadman to Mag. Lions River, n.d.; CO 179/207/33005, encl. in Hely-Hutchinson to Chamberlain, 31 Oct. 1899, minutes of a public meeting at Kranskop, 18 Oct. 1899.
12 NA, SNA 1/4/6, C155/1899, circular minute no. 59, 21 Sept. 1899.
13 NA, SNA 1/8/25A, Moor to Mags. Weenen, Umsinga, Mapumulo, 2 Oct. 1899.
14 J. J. Guy, *The Destruction of the Zulu Kingdom*, Longman, London, 1979, p. 243 and *passim*, and 'The Destruction and Reconstruction of Zulu Society', in Marks and Rathbone, eds., pp. 167–94.
15 NA, SNA 1/4/7, CR60/1899, RM Hlabisa to Saunders, 10 Sept. 1899.
16 NA, SNA 1/4/7, CR96/1899, RM Nquthu to Saunders, 27 Sept. 1899; NA, SNA 1/4/7, C53/1899, RM Emthonjaneni to Saunders, 14 Sept. 1899.
17 NA, SNA 1/4/7, C550/1899, Mag. Lower Tugela to Moor, n.d.
18 NA, SNA 1/4/7, CR195/1899, Acting RM Ubombo to Saunders, 9 Nov. 1899.
19 CO 179/206/2666, report by Hely-Hutchinson to Chamberlain, 2 Oct. 1899; CO 179/207/33013, encl. 2 in Hely-Hutchinson to Chamberlain, 31 Oct. 1899, Gibson to Saunders, 23 Oct. 1899.
20 CO 179/207/33013, encl. 1, Saunders to Hime, 27 Oct. 1899.
21 CO 179/207/33013, minute by Graham.
22 CO 179/207/33011, encl. in Hely-Hutchinson to Chamberlain, 3 Nov. 1899, Rev. Dr J. Dalzell to Hime, 28 Oct. 1899.
23 CO 179/207/33828, encl. 1 in Hely-Hutchinson to Chamberlain, 9 Nov. 1899, Rev. Dalzell to Hime, 3 Nov. 1899.
24 CO 179/213/24322, encl. in Hely-Hutchinson to Chamberlain (conf.), 10 July 1900, Criminal Investigation Officer to Hime, 3 July 1900.
25 CO 179/210/10436, encl. in Hely-Hutchinson to Chamberlain, 10 Mar. 1900, Z. M. Masuku to Moor, 26 Feb. 1900; NA, SNA 1/4/8, C181/1900, diary of chief Dumisa of events during the Boer occupation of Dundee division, 12 Mar. 1900; NA, SNA 1/4/8, C59/1900, Mag. Weenen to Moor, 31 Jan. 1900.
26 NA, SNA 1/8/10A, Moor to Hime, 19 Jan. 1900.
27 NA, SNA 1/4/8, C226/1900, Dumisa to Mag. Weenen, 1 Apr. 1900; NA, SNA 1/4/8, C200/1900, Dumisa to Mag. Weenen, 21 Mar. 1900.
28 NA, SNA 1/4/8, C178/1900, Dumisa to Moor, 27 May 1900 and SNA 1/8/10A, C42/1900, Samuelson to Dumisa, 9 June 1900.

29 CO 179/209/6271, encl. 2 in Hely-Hutchinson to Chamberlain (secret), 1 Feb. 1900, statement by Untiloyi kaMpaka, 19 Dec. 1899.

30 NA, SNA 1/4/8, C38/1900, statement of Sayimana kaSikonkwana, 22 Jan. 1900; NA, SNA 1/4/8, C58/1900, chief Kula to Moor, 1 Feb. 1900; NA, SNA 1/4/8, C227/1900, Z. M. Masuku to Mag. Weenen, 25 Mar. 1900.

31 CO 179/207/29776, Hely-Hutchinson to Chamberlain, 29 Oct. 1899; CO 179/207/30424, Hely-Hutchinson to Chamberlain, 4 Nov. 1899; CO 179/207/34368, encl. in Hely-Hutchinson to Chamberlain, 18 Nov. 1899, Colenbrander to Saunders, 18 Nov. 1899; Alistair M. Miller Papers, Killie Campbell Africana Library, Durban, MS MIL 1.08.70, Reminiscences of Van Wissell, Zululand trader.

32 CO 179/208/35887, encl. in Hely-Hutchinson to Chamberlain (conf.), 1 Dec. 1899, Governor's diary of events, 30 Nov. 1899; CO 179/208/1854, encl. in Hely-Hutchinson to Chamberlain (conf.), 22 Dec. 1899, Governor's diary of events, 15 Dec. 1899; CO 179/208/1828, encl. in Hely-Hutchinson to Chamberlain, 23 Dec. 1899, Saunders to Hime (tel.), 22 Dec. 1899.

33 CO 179/208/2477, encl. in Hely-Hutchinson to Chamberlain (conf.), 30 Dec. 1899, Saunders to Hime (tel.), 26 Dec. 1899.

34 NA, ZA 33, CR47/1900, Saunders to Hime (secret tel.), 13 Jan 1900; CO 179/209/6275, encl. 4 in Hely-Hutchinson to Chamberlain (conf.), Saunders to Hime (tel.), 2 Feb. 1900.

35 CO 179/210/4387, Hely-Hutchinson to Chamberlain, 8 Feb. 1900.

36 CO 179/210/4816, encl. in Hely-Hutchinson to Chamberlain, 13 Feb. 1900.

37 CO 179/210/4816, minute by Chamberlain.

38 CO 179/210/4947, Hely-Hutchinson to Chamberlain, 13 Feb. 1900.

39 CO 179/210/4937, minute by Sir Frederick Graham.

40 NA, ZA 33, CR202/1900, Buller to Hely-Hutchinson, 21 Mar. 1900; Hime to Hely-Hutchinson, 21 Mar. 1900, Saunders to Hime, 28 Mar. 1900.

41 CO 179/210/8621, encl. 4 in Hely-Hutchinson to Chamberlain (conf.), 4 Mar. 1900, depositions regarding the taking of Nkandla magistracy, evidence of Manqezu, brother of chief Sitshitshili; encl. 3, statements made to J. L. Knight at Eshowe by messengers from the chiefs in the occupied districts, 19 Feb. 1900, evidence corroborated by chief Moses Afrikander and chief Mpumela.

42 CO 179/210/8621, encl. 6, weekly report by RM Emthonjaneni to Saunders, 21 Feb. 1900.

43 CO 179/210/8621, encl. 4 evidence of Ntika kaBede; USPG, Reports, Africa 1900B, 63 (11290), diary of the Rev. Charles Johnson during the Boer occupation of Nquthu.

44 CO 179/210/8621, encl. 4, evidence of Manqezu. This evidence is corroborated by the statement of a Zulu constable to the Chief Commissioner, see encl. 8, Saunders to Hime, 21 Feb. 1900.

45 CO 179/210/8621, encl. 4, evidence of Nongamulana.

46 CO 179/211/23583, encl. 10, Hignett to Saunders, 31 May 1900.

47 Guy, *Destruction of the Zulu*, p. 239, and 'The Destruction and Reconstruction of Zulu Society', *passim*.

48 CO 179/216/11833, Rev. C. Johnson to RM Nquthu, 1 Mar. 1900; also see Johnson's diary of the Boer occupation.

49 NA, SNA 1/4/7, CR233/99, RM Nkandla to Saunders, 28 Nov. 1899; NA, SNA 1/4/7, CR272/99, RM Emthonjaneni to Saunders, 14 Dec. 1899; Col.Col., NA, Pietermaritzburg, 73, Harriet Colenso to Sec. of the Mansion House Fund, 5 Dec. 1899.

50 CO 179/216/4527, H. R. Fox Bourne to Chamberlain, 12 Feb. 1900; Col.Col. 37, Fox Bourne to Harriet Colenso, 26 Jan. 1900; *The Times*, 26 Jan. 1900, 10 Feb. 1900; CO 179/216/4527, minutes by Chamberlain and other officials, and Fox Bourne to Chamberlain, 12 Feb. 1900.

51 NA, SNA 1/4/7, CR275/99, RM Nkandla to Saunders, 19 Dec. 1899.

52 NA. SNA 1/1/289, RM Ndwandwe to Saunders, 8 Jan. 1900.

53 CO 179/211/8621, encl. 4, evidence of Nongamulana.

54 CO 179/212/20946, encl. in Hely-Hutchinson to Chamberlain (conf.), diary of events, 6 June 1900.

55 CO 179/212/20949, encls. 1 and 2 in Hely-Hutchinson to Chamberlain (conf.), 9 June 1900, Hely-Hutchinson to Milner, 7 June 1900, and to Buller (tel.), 25 May 1900.

56 Col.Col, 101, Dinuzulu to General Buller, 31 May 1900; Col.Col 100, Colonel H. E. Sandbach to Dinuzulu, 30 July 1900.

57 NA, SNA 1/6/25, R989/1901, Kitchener to Hely-Hutchinson, 31 May 1901, forwarding general regulation of 3 Feb. 1901.

58 CO 179/218/12308, Hely-Hutchinson to Chamberlain, 7 Mar. 1901, forwarding a memorandum from the Natal government; for further details of the background see Warwick, 'African Societies', p. 189.

59 CO 179/218/12308, schedule B, 3 and 29, Hildyard to Hime, (tels.), 30 Mar. 1901, 3 Apr. 1901.

60 NA, SNA 1/6/25, C121/1901, Saunders to Hime, 2 Apr. 1901; Col.Col. 101, Dinuzulu to Bottomley, 4 Apr. 1901 and Dinuzulu to Officer Commanding Nongoma, 4 Apr. 1901; Col.Col. 100, Bottomley to Dinuzulu, 12 Apr. 1901; *Mills Report*, pp. 6, 7; NA, SNA 1/6/25, R546/1901, RM Ndwandwe to Saunders, 8 May 1901; CO 179/218/19687, encl. 8 in McCallum to Chamberlain (conf.), 11 May 1901, Saunders to Hime (tel.), 9 May 1901; NA, SNA 1/6/25, R989/1901, Saunders to Hime (tel.), 4 Apr. 1901; J. Stuart, *A History of the Zulu Rebellion 1906*, Macmillan, London, 1913, p. 485; S. Marks, *Reluctant Rebellion*, Oxford University Press, 1970, pp. 112–13.

61 Col.Col, 100, RM Ndwandwe to Dinuzulu, 6 Apr. 1901.

62 CO 179/218/12308, schedule B, 35, Saunders to Hime, 3 Apr. 1901; 39, Saunders to Hime, 3 Apr. 1901; 42, Saunders to Hime, 4 Apr. 1901; 49, Saunders to Hime, 10 Apr. 1901.

63 CO 179/218/12308, schedule B, 47, Kitchener to Governor's Office Natal, 7 Apr. 1901; NA, SNA 1/6/25, R989/1901, Kitchener to McCallum, 1 June 1901; also see CO 179/218/19701, minute by Chamberlain.

64 *Mills Report*, pp. 6, 7.

65 NA, SNA 1/6/25, R989/1901, Minister of Agriculture to Saunders (tel.), 18 Apr. 1901; NA, SNA 1/6/25, C121/1901, Hime to McCallum, 27 June 1901.

66 Col.Col. 101, Dinuzulu to Bottomley, 17 Oct. 1901.

67 Col.Col. 100, RM Ndwandwe to Dinuzulu, 30 Oct. 1901.

68 Col.Col. 100, RM Ndwandwe to Dinuzulu, 8 Mar. 1902 and 1 Apr. 1902, A. J. Shepstone to Dinuzulu, 11 May 1902; Col.Col. 101, Dinuzulu to (?), 20 Mar. 1902; *Mills Report*, pp. 19,69.

69 CO 179/212/22719, encl. in Hely-Hutchinson to Chamberlain, 19 June 1900, Gibson to Saunders, 11 June 1900.

70 CO 179/229/3538, sub. in encl. 1 in McCallum to Chamberlain, 6 Jan. 1904, Botha to Acting High Commissioner (Sir Arthur Lawley), 10 Nov. 1903; *Natal Mercury*, 21 Dec. 1935.

71 *Mills Report*, passim. See also J. F. Shelton, 'The Holkrans Massacre, 6 May 1902', unpublished BA Honours dissertation, University of Natal, 1969. Mr Shelton kindly showed me a copy of the dissertation. Government Notice No. 62, 1903, report by Colonel G. A. Mills, p. 90.

72 CO 179/229/3538, Botha to Lawley, 10 Nov. 1903.

73 Government Notice No. 62, 1903, p. 89.

74 *Mills Report*, p. 3.

75 CO 179/229/3538, encl. 2, McCallum to Hime, 22 Dec. 1903.

76 See, for instance, Col.Col, 101, Dinuzulu to Officer Commanding Vryheid, 11 Apr. 1901.

77 Col.Col. 101, Dinuzulu to RM Ndwandwe, 13 Dec. 1900.

78 Col.Col. 100, RM Ndwandwe to Dinuzulu, 8 Oct. 1901.

79 Marks, *Reluctant Rebellion*, p. 98.

80 *Ibid.*, especially chapters 6, 10 and 11. There appears to be little direct relationship between events during the war and the Zulu rebellion. It seems coincidental that the most important area of conflict in Zululand later, the Nquthu and Nkandla districts, was that invaded by the

Boers during the war; the Ladysmith, Dundee and Newcastle divisions of Natal, occupied by the Boers and the scene of the most intense military activity in the colony, later remained immune from conflict. Many of the Zulu who fought against the insurgents during the disturbances had earlier cooperated fully with the government during the war, Sibindi and Sitshitshili for example, but so too had some of the prominent leaders of the rebellion, such as Bambatha and Mehlokazulu. Bambatha in fact contributed £3 to the War Relief Fund. See Marks, *Reluctant Rebellion*, p. 157 and CO 179/212/1999, encl. in Hely-Hutchinson to Chamberlain, 28 May 1900, Native Contributions to the War Relief Fund.

5. Allies and neutrals

1 For the background to Pedi history see Peter Delius, 'Migrant Labour and the Pedi, 1840–80' in Marks and Atmore, eds., pp. 293–312, and 'Abel Erasmus: Power and Profit in the Eastern Transvaal', *passim*; D. R. Hunt, 'An Account of the Bapedi', *Bantu Studies*, 5, 4 (1931), pp. 303–10; K. W. Smith, 'The Fall of the Bapedi of the North-Eastern Transvaal', *JAH*, 10, 2 (1969), pp. 237–52; *OHSA*, vol. 2, pp. 282–3.

2 TA, SNA 3, 182/01, 'The Last Rising in Sekukuni's Land' by J. A. Winter, 8 Sept. 1900; Hunt, p. 311; Delius, 'Abel Erasmus', p. 41.

3 TA, SNA 13, 1753/02, Sekhukhune to Winter, 19 June 1900.

4 TA, SNA 1,475/01, 'The Story of the Native-war which occured [sic] in the Low Country from July to November 1900', by Rev. H. A. Junod, 19 June 1901; CO 291/36/6457, H. Pattern to Sir Montagu Ommaney, 19 Feb. 1901.

5 TA, SNA 13, 1753/02, Sekhukhune to Winter, n.d.

6 TA, SNA 3, 182/01, 'The Last Rising in Sekukuni's Land', p. 11.

7 *Ibid.*, p. 12; Hunt, pp. 312–13.

8 Hunt, p. 313.

9 *Times History*, vol. 5, pp. 328n, 614; Viljoen, pp. 407–15; Peter R. Kruger, 'M'pisana's Fort', *Historia* (Sept. 1973), pp. 200–1; CO 417/360/10247, encl. 9 in DMI. to Under Sec. St. Colonies, 12 Mar. 1902, diary of Sgt Major Mauchle, 12 Sept. 1901.

10 SNA 3, 210/01, Baird to Henderson, n.d.; CO 417/360/10274, encl. 14, Reitz to Botha, 5 Sept. 1901.

11 TA, SNA 3, 210/01, Baird to Henderson, n.d.

12 CO 417/333/45389, encl. in DMI to Under Sec. St. Colonies, 2 May 1901, Henderson to DMI, 5 Apr. 1901, reporting interview with Erasmus.

13 TA, SNA 13, 1569/02, General F. W. Kitchener to Sekhukhune, 10 Apr. 1901.

14 CO 417/360/10274, encl. 9, diary of Sgt Major Mauchle, 23 July 1901.

15 R. W. Schikkerling, *Commando Courageous (a Boer's Diary)*, Keartland, Johannesburg, 1964, pp. 326–7.

16 TA, SNA, 194/01, Haigh to Henderson, 22 Sept. 1901.

17 TA, SNA 15, 1891/01, Haigh to Henderson, 7 Sept. 1901; TA, SNA 3, 187/01, Sekhukhune to G. Roy, Intelligence Officer, Lydenburg, 31 Oct. 1901.

18 TA, SNA 3, 194/01, Haigh to Henderson, 22 Sept. 1901; TA, SNA 13, 1569/02, Hogge to Lagden, 18 Aug. 1902.

19 TA, SNA 3, 187/01, Haigh to Henderson, 16 Oct. 1901; TA, SNA 3, 78/01, Maxwell to Henderson, 17 Oct. 1901.

20 TA, SNA 15, 2103/01, Baird to Henderson, 12 Nov. 1901; TA, SNA 3, 187/01, Haigh to Henderson, 16 Oct. 1901.

21 TA, SNA 15, 1891/01, Haigh to Henderson, 7 Sept. 1901.

22 TA, SNA 13, 1569/02, weekly report by E. H. Hogge, Lydenburg, 23 Aug. 1902.

23 TA, SNA 3, Haigh to Henderson, 4 Oct. 1901.

24 TA, SNA 13, 1569/02, Hogge to Lagden, 18 Aug. 1902.

25 TA, SNA 13, 1569/02, 'Notes of a meeting held at Schoonoord in Sekukuni's location', 9 Aug.

1902, and 'Conference held at Schoonoord on 6th September, 1902'.

26 TA, SNA 13, 1569/02, Hogge to Lagden, 31 July 1902, 18 Aug. 1902.

27 Hunt, pp. 314–15.

28 CO 417/267/28345, encl. 1 in Milner to Chamberlain (secret), 27 Sept. 1899, Milner to Smuts (secret), 25 May 1899.

29 CO 417/267/28345, encl. 8 Smuts to Milner (tel.), 14 Sept. 1899.

30 *Further Correspondence Relating to Affairs in South Africa*, Cd. 43, 1900, p. 197, report of meeting between Smuts and Labotsibeni, 13 Oct. 1899.

31 *Ibid.*, p. 118, precis of letter from Joubert to Bhunu, 9 Oct. 1899 (author's emphasis).

32 *Standard and Diggers' News*, 18 Nov. 1899.

33 CO 417/289/14911, sub. in encl. 5 in Milner to Chamberlain (conf.), 25 Apr. 1900, interview with Labotsibeni and Swazi Council, 30 Mar. 1900; CO 417/295/27475, encl. 9 in Milner to Chamberlain (conf.), 31 Oct. 1899, Smuts to Milner (tel.), 19 Oct. 1899; see also Warwick, 'African Societies', pp. 221–3. The description of Labotsibeni is that of Sir Robert Coryndon.

34 CO 417/290/18243, encl. 2 in Milner to Chamberlain (conf.), 21 May 1900, Forbes to Smuts, 18 Apr. 1900.

35 For full details of the attack and other events in Swaziland during the war see Warwick, 'African Societies', pp. 224–7, and J. S. M. Matsebula, *A History of Swaziland*, Longman, Cape Town, 1972, pp. 86–90.

36 CO 291/29/43104, encl. 4 in Milner to Chamberlain (conf.), 15 Nov. 1901, Smuts to Milner, 18 Apr. 1901.

37 CO 291/27/4357, encl. 3, Kitchener to Milner (tel.), 10 Jan. 1901, and sub. in encl. 1, Major Congreve to Smuts, 1 Jan. 1901.

38 CO 417/335/43539, Henderson to Selborne, 7 Dec. 1901, forwarding captured correspondence between Botha and Tobias Smuts; encl. 1, Botha to T. Smuts, 16 July 1901; encl. 2, T. Smuts to Botha, 29 July 1901; encl. 5, Botha to T. Smuts, 31 Aug. 1901; encl. 9, diary of Sgt Major Mauehle, 31 July 1901. Miller Papers, 1.08 29 MS a h. Tobias Smuts went beyond his orders by burning Bremersdorp and was relieved of his command by Botha.

39 CO 291/29/35841, sub. in encl. 2 in Milner to Chamberlain (conf.), 20 Sept. 1901, Smuts to General T. E. Stephenson, 29 Apr. 1901.

40 CO 291/35841, encl. 2, memorandum by General Stephenson, 15 Apr. 1901.

41 CO 291/56/14308, Swaziland Report for 1902.

42 For two detailed studies of land apportionment in Swaziland and the opposition of the Dlamini see F. J. Mashasha, 'The Swazi and Land Partition (1902–1910)', *The Societies of Southern Africa in the 19th and 20th centuries*, Institute of Commonwealth Studies, University of London, vol. 4, 1974, pp. 87–107; and Martin Fransman, 'The Colonial State and the Land Question in Swaziland, 1903–1907', *ibid.*, vol. 9, 1979, pp. 27–38.

6. The war in the Cape

1 See S. Trapido, 'African Divisional Politics in the Cape Colony 1884–1910', *JAH*, 9, 1 (1968), pp. 79–80. For the role of the black elite in Cape society see Trapido, '"The Friends of the Natives": Merchants, Peasants and the Political and Ideological Structure of Liberalism in the Cape 1854–1910', in Marks and Atmore, eds., pp. 247–74.

2 J. S. Marais, *The Fall of Kruger's Republic*, Oxford University Press, 1961, pp. 180–1, 235–7.

3 *Parliamentary Debates*, 4th series, Commons, lxxvii, col. 271, 19 Oct. 1899; Lords, lxxviii, col. 257, 1 Feb. 1900; *Further Correspondence Relating to Affairs in South Africa*, Cd. 547, 1901, p. 34.

4 CO 417/266/27246, encl. 1 in Milner to Chamberlain, 20 Sept. 1899, resolutions passed at a meeting of Coloured men, 6 Sept. 1899; CO 48/543/31479, encl. 2 in Milner to Chamberlain, 24 Oct. 1899, Alfred Mangena and Toise B. Skenjana to Milner, 3 Oct. 1899.

5 CO 48/551/3277, encl. in Milner to Chamberlain, 9 Jan. 1900, petition, 5 Jan. 1900.

6 NA, SNA 1/4/8, 3308/1900, resolutions passed at a meeting of Native British subjects from Natal, 8 June 1900; *Natal Mercury*, 8 June 1900, 9 June 1900.
7 *Imvo Zabantsundu*, 16 Oct. 1899.
8 See *Imvo Zabantsundu*, 13 Nov. 1899, 24 Oct. 1899.
9 D. D. T. Jabavu, *The Life of John Tengo Jabavu*, Lovedale Institution Press, Lovedale, 1922, p. 49; L. D. Ngcongco, 'Jabavu and the Anglo-Boer War', *Kleio*, 2 (1970), pp. 6–18, and 'Imvo Zabantsundu and Cape "Native" Policy 1884–1902', unpublished MA thesis, University of South Africa, 1974; Anti-Slavery Papers, Rhodes House Library, Oxford, MSS. Brit. Emp. s. 18, C/83/96, Jabavu to Travers Buxton, 27 Aug. 1909.
10 CO 48/543/35055, encl. 23 in Milner to Chamberlain (secret), 29 Nov. 1899, RM Queenstown to Sec. to Law Dept Cape Town (tel.), 24 Nov. 1899; CBBNA, G.50–1900, p. 28; Warwick, 'African Societies', pp. 132–3.
11 Schreiner Papers, Sect. B, Private Secretary's Letter Book 1898–9, Schreiner to Milner, 24 Nov. 1899.
12 CO 417/269/33058, encl. in Milner to Chamberlain (conf.), 9 Nov. 1899, Milner's diary of events, 6 Nov. 1899.
13 CA, NAD 445, Scott to SNA (tel. 1215), 27 Nov. 1899, and Elliot to SNA (tel. 1333), 17 Dec. 1899.
14 CA, CMK 1/236, RM Mount Ayliff to Scott (tel. 1205), 30 Nov. 1899; CMT 3/51, 2/99, Stanford to Elliot (conf.), 21 Nov. 1899; CMT 3/7, 2/711E, Sam Majeke to RM Qumbu, 13 Oct. 1899.
15 *Imvo Zabantsundu*, 15 Jan. 1900.
16 Stanford papers, D.25a, 8 Dec. 1899; *Times History*, vol. 3, pp. 96–7; Williams, *Record of the Cape Mounted Riflemen*, pp. 59–61.
17 CA, CMT 3/225, RM Engcobo to Elliot (tel. 955), 8 Dec. 1899; CBBNA, G.50–1900, p. 28.
18 CA, DD 7/175, Thembuland Levies – Intelligence Corps; CBBNA, G.50–1900, p. 29.
19 CBBNA, G.52–1901, p. 35.
20 Stanford Papers, F(x)19, J. B. Moffat to Stanford, 23 Dec. 1899; CA, NAD 253, S. C. van Niekirk to SNA, 20 Dec. 1899; Schreiner Papers, Sect. B, correspondence bearing on the situation in South Africa, Dec. 1899–Jan. 1900, J. F. du Toit to Schreiner, 14 Dec. 1899, Rev. W. P. de Villiers to Schreiner, 17 Jan. 1900, D. W. Schoeman to Schreiner, 26 Dec. 1899.
21 For an excellent discussion of the significance of the disfranchisement issue see W. R. Nasson, '"These Natives Think This War to Be Their Own"': Reflections on Blacks in the Cape Colony and the South African War 1899–1902', research paper presented at the Institute of Commonwealth Studies (SSA/79/7), University of London, May 1980, pp. 6–7.
22 CO 48/543/3430, G. E. Dugmore to SNA (tels.), 8 Nov. 1899, 10 Nov. 1899; CO 417/288/13209, diary of the High Commissioner's visit to the northeast Cape, 4 Apr. 1900; CA, NAD 445, St Quintin, West Barkly to SNA (tel. 414), 17 Apr. 1900.
23 CO 48/543/35055, encl. 24 in Milner to Chamberlain (secret), 29 Nov. 1899, RM Upington to Sec. to Law Dept (tel.), 25 Nov. 1899; encl. 26, Sec. to Law Dept to RM Upington (tel.), 25 Nov. 1899; encl. 52, RM Upington to Sec. to Law Dept (tel.), 28 Nov, 1899; CO 48/545/10422, encls. 6 and 24 in Milner to Chamberlain (secret), 14 Mar. 1900, RM Calvinia to Sec. to Law Dept, 6 Mar. 1900, 7 Mar. 1900; CO 48/546/13216, encl. 1 in Milner to Chamberlain (secret), 11 Apr. 1900, statement by F. Jooste, prisoner-of-war, 3 Apr. 1900.
24 CO 48/555/42296, encl. 1 in Hely-Hutchinson to Chamberlain (conf.), Lt McIntyre to CSO Cape Town, 26 Oct. 1901; CO 48/552/17247, schedule 2 in encl. 1 in Hely-Hutchinson to Chamberlain (conf.), RM Gordonia to Sec. to Law Dept, 19 Apr. 1901; *Times History*, vol. 5, pp. 550–1, 612, 613; G. Tylden, *The Armed Forces of South Africa*, City of Johannesburg Africana Museum, 1954, pp. 44, 49, 92, 118; D. Reitz, *Commando, A Boer Journal of the Boer War*, Faber and Faber, London, 1931, pp. 201–5; Hook, *With Sword and Statute*, p. 402.
25 CO 48/553/29712, encl. 2 in Hely-Hutchinson to Chamberlain, 5 Aug. 1901, Kitchener to Hely-Hutchinson, 31 July 1901; *Further Correspondence Relating to Affairs in South Africa*,

Cd. 903, 1902, p. 137, Boer proclamation by P. H. Kritzinger, Nov. 1901.

26 Marais, *The Cape Coloured People*, p. 96.

27 Reitz, pp. 298–9. A full analysis of the Leliefontein attack is given by Nasson in '"These Natives Think This War to Be Their Own"', pp. 1–4.

28 CO 48/551/9079, memorandum by G. V. Fiddes, Imperial Secretary, 18 Feb. 1901; *Cape Times*, 20 Feb. 1901; *Telegram from Sir Alfred Milner to the Secretary of State for War, Relating to the Reported Outrage on Esau at Calvinia*, Cd. 464, 1901. Nasson, '"These Natives Think This War to Be Their Own"', provides further details. The most comprehensive collections of documents relating to the executions and ill-treatment of blacks by guerrillas and rebels can be found in WO 32/8085–8, Kitchener to Under-Secretary of State for War, 22 Nov. 1901–21 Mar. 1902; and in CA, AG 2071, 'Anglo-Boer War correspondence relating to the shooting and outrages on Natives, 1899–1902'.

29 CBBNA, G.50–1900, pp. 19, 37, 41; CA, CMT 3/8, 2/199E, SNA to Elliot, 18 May 1900.

30 CBBNA, G.50–1900, P. 52; CA, CMT 3/60, 9/758/00, Brownlee to Elliot, 31 Oct. 1900.

31 CBBNA, G.52–1901, p. 45; *Izwi Labantu*, 21 Jan. 1902.

32 Stanford Papers, D.29, 31 Dec. 1900, 13 Jan. 1901; D.30, 18 July 1901, 3 Sept. 1901; 'Facts and Dates for Report of OC East Griqualand', 6 Sept. 1901, 23 Sept. 1901.

33 Stanford Papers, F(x)14, Capt. W. F. Raw to Stanford, 21 Nov. 1899; *Cape Times*, 22 Oct. 1901.

34 J. W. Macquarrie, ed., *The Reminiscences of Sir Walter Stanford*, 2 vols., Van Riebeeck Society, Cape Town, 1958 and 1962, vol. 2, p. 223; CA, NAD 445, J. Bezuidenhout to T. L. Graham, 27 Oct. 1902.

7. Black workers

1 Colin Bundy, 'The Emergence and Decline of a South African Peasantry', *African Affairs*, 71 (1972), pp. 369–88, and the enlarged study, *The Rise and Fall of the South African Peasantry*, Heinemann, London, 1979.

2 *Report of the Transvaal Labour Commission*, Cd. 1896, 1904, p. 15. It is impossible to rely on more precise figures since before the war no uniform system of compiling labour statistics existed. Some mines returned men actually at work; others the total number of men in the compounds; yet other mines included workers employed on site by surface contractors.

3 Chamber of Mines, *Annual Report for 1898*, p. 453.

4 J. P. Fitzpatrick (Sir), *The Transvaal from Within*, Heinemann, London, 1899, p. 105; Chamber of Mines, *Annual Report for 1897*, p. 107; Peter Richardson and Jean Jacques Van-Helten, 'The Gold Mining Industry in the Transvaal 1886–99', in Warwick, ed., *The South African War*, pp. 31–2; Parsons and Palmer, 'The Roots of Rural Poverty; Historical Background', in Palmer and Parsons, eds., p. 4.

5 See, for example, CBBNA, G.50–1900, pp. 31, 39; G.52–1901, p. 9.

6 Chamber of Mines, *Annual Report for 1898*, p. 78.

7 *Ibid.*, pp. 312, 314, 317.

8 Alan Jeeves, 'The Control of Migratory Labour on the South African Gold Mines in the Era of Kruger and Milner', *Journal of Southern African Studies*, 2, 1 (1975), p. 11. Also see Peter Warwick, 'Black Industrial Protest on the Witwatersrand, 1901–1902', in Eddie Webster ed., *Essays in Southern African Labour History*, Ravan, Johannesburg, 1978, pp. 20–31.

9 *Standard and Diggers' News*, 10 Oct. 1899, 30 Oct. 1899, 3 Nov. 1899, 20 Nov. 1899; *Bechuanaland News*, 14 Oct. 1899, report from Johannesburg, 13 Oct. 1899; J. H. Breytenbach, *Die Geskiedenis van die Tweede Vryheidsoorlog in Suid-Africa 1899–1902*, 4 vols., Die Staats-drukker, Pretoria, 1969–78, vol. 1, p. 130; Charles van Onselen, 'The World the Mineowners Made', *Review*, 3, 2 (1979), p. 295.

10 A small number of mines continued working after the start of the war, their output being taken over by the state.

11 'Regulaties van de Regeerings Commissie Ruste en Orde, Witwatersrand', in *Standard and Diggers' News*, 19 Oct. 1899, 21 Mar. 1900; CO 48/552/15654, encl. in Milner to Chamberlain (conf.), 15 Apr. 1900, J. Sundt to Capt. P. Robinson, 29 Dec. 1899; *Standard and Diggers' News*, 30 Oct. 1899, 3 Jan. 1900.

12 *Further Correspondence Relating to Affairs in South Africa*, Cd. 43, 1900, pp. 167–70; J. S. Marwick Papers, Killie Campbell Africana Library, Durban, MAR 2.08.5, 'March with Zulus from Johannesburg to Natal'; C. H. Stott, *The Boer Invasion of Natal*, Partridge, London, 1900, pp. 30–1; *Ipepa lo Hlanga*, 20 Nov. 1902; Pakenham, pp. 120–1. For Marwick's role in Johannesburg see Guy, 'The Destruction and Reconstruction of Zulu Society', in Marks and Rathbone, eds., p. 187.

13 NA, SNA 1/4/7, C1678/99, Mag. Umvoti Division to F. R. Moor (conf.), 14 Oct. 1899; NA, SNA CR231/99, Mag. Lower Umfolozi to Saunders, 25 Nov. 1899; CO 179/207/35070, Hely-Hutchinson to Chamberlain, 24 Nov. 1899.

14 *Standard and Diggers' News*, 16 Oct. 1899, 17 Oct. 1899.

15 NA, SNA 1/4/6, C92/99 Mag. Umsinga Division to Moor, 5 Oct. 1899, and encl. deposition by Mrabula; Stanford Papers, F(x)11, George Dugmore to Stanford, 19 Oct. 1899; CO 179/208/35796, encl. statement by Sebastian Msimang, 29 Nov. 1899; CBBNA, G.50–1900, p. 59; G. W. Steevens, *From Capetown to Ladysmith*, Blackwood, London, 1900, p. 34.

16 USPG, Reports, Africa 1899A, 47 (4377), Rev. E. M. Dixon to Rev. H. W. Tucker, Dec. 1899.

17 CBBNA, G.50–1900, p. 27.

18 W. A. J. O'Meara, *Kekewich of Kimberley*, Medici Society, London, 1926, pp. 55–6.

19 'The Siege of Kimberley', special illustrated number of *The Diamond Fields Advertiser* (1900), pp. 52–3, 132; Roberts Papers, WO 105/14, Col. Kekewich to Roberts (tels.), 20 Jan. 1900, 10 Feb. 1900; E. D. Ashe, *Besieged by the Boers, A Diary of Life and Events in Kimberley*, Hutchinson, London, 1900, pp. 117–19; Brian Gardner, *The Lion's Cage*, Barker, London, 1969, pp. 152–3; USPG, Reports, Africa 1900A, 5(11979), Rev. G. Mitchell to Rev. H. W. Tucker, March 1900; Farwell, p. 205; *Reports etc.*, Cd.902, encl. 5 in Hely-Hutchinson to Chamberlain, 27 Nov. 1901, memorandum on infant mortality in the Cape Colony, 25 Nov. 1901, pp. 27–8.

20 CBBNA, G.50–1900, p. 69; Ashe, p. 9; O'Meara, p. 56.

21 CO 417/270/34332, encl. 5 in Milner to Chamberlain (conf.), 22 Nov. 1899, Lagden to Milner (tel.), 19 Sept. 1899; CO 417/270/35089, encl. 2 in Milner to Chamberlain (conf.), 29 Nov. 1899, Lagden to Milner tel., 21 Nov. 1899. Before the siege Ladysmith was inundated by African and Asian workers from the Natal coalfield. Conditions there were equally bad if not worse than in Kimberley. So frustrated became workers that at the end of January 1900 a strike of conscript labourers occurred that was only overcome by the use of force, see Harry H. Balfour, *Diary kept during the Siege of Ladysmith*, 1901, Killie Campbell Africana Library, PAM 968.042.

22 See p. 123, and CBBNA, G.50–1900, p. 41.

23 Breytenbach, vol. 1, pp. 36–7, 132; vol. 3, 362–6; TA, Leyds-Argief, 781 (i), 'Gebruik van zoogenaamde wilde volkstammen, rapport van Luit. Thomson en Kapt. Ram', n.d., pp. 66–73; Spies, *Methods of Barbarism?*, p. 22.

24 *Standard and Diggers' News*, 25 Nov. 1899.

25 *Ibid.*, 20 Oct. 1899.

26 *Ibid.*, 11 Jan. 1900. Resistance by some workers in fact led to the partial relaxing of the order only a week after its introduction.

27 See the experiences of Africans described in CO 179/207/35885, sub. in encl. in Hely-Hutchinson to Chamberlain (conf.), 29 Nov. 1899, statement by Jim, a prisoner-of-war; CO 179/211/11865, encls. 1 and 2 in Hely-Hutchinson to Chamberlain, 29 Mar. 1900, statements by Tom and Simon.

28 See numerous letters in TA, SN 71–4, and OFS Archives, GS 2108, R6128/99, GS to Station Master, Viljoen's Drift (tel.), 9 Oct. 1899.

29 CA, AG 814, 65/1900, encl. in Civil Commissioner, Albert, to SLD, 14 May 1900, statement by Jack Sohai; CO 48/547/29006, encl. 13 in Milner to Chamberlain, 14 Aug. 1900, RM Hay to SLD, 2 July 1900; 'Seven Months under Boer Rule', by the Rev. Gerard Chilton Bailey of Dundee, bound typescript, shown to me by the late Canon C. T. Wood, Cape Town, p. 108.

30 *Times History*, vol. 2, p. 87.

31 CO 179/207/35885, encl. in Hely-Hutchinson to Chamberlain (conf.), 29 Nov. 1899, minute by Criminal Investigation Officer, 18 Nov. 1899; CO 179/211/11865, encl. statements by Tom and Simon, 26 Mar. 1900; Billington, p. 22.

32 WO 32/8136, Ladysmith Staff Diary, 1 Dec. 1899.

33 TA, MGP 1, 05B/00, S. J. Brander and J. T. Mikane to Roberts, 8 June 1900.

34 See the case of a clerk, Meyer, who 'commandeered some hundreds of cattle from the natives . . . and delivered less than a hundred to the authorities', *Standard and Diggers' News*, 8 Feb. 1900.

35 For the Boers' wartime control of the mining industry and mine labour see *ibid.*, 26 Dec. 1899, 19 Feb. 1900.

36 *Ibid.*, 25 Oct. 1899, 3 Jan. 1900, 15 Jan. 1900, 6 Mar. 1900, 21 Mar. 1900.

37 *Times History*, vol. 6, p. 595; H. J. Batts, *Pretoria from Within during the War, 1899–1900*, Shaw, London, 1901, p. 192.

38 Churchill, *London to Ladysmith*, p. 126.

39 The *isibalo* system in Natal obliged chiefs to call out 15 per cent of the adult males among their people for work on public works programmes, usually local road-building. The labour was, to all intents and purposes, forced, and the wages uncompetitive, see Marks, *Reluctant Rebellion*, pp. 43–5, S. T. van der Horst, *Native Labour in South Africa*, Cass, London, 1971, p. 141.

40 NA, PWD 4623/99, J. Donelly, District Engineer, to J. F. E. Barnes, 10 Nov. 1899; NA, PWD 4599/99, Barnes to Minister of Lands and Works, 8 Nov. 1899, Barnes to Minister of Lands and Works, 27 Oct. 1899; NA, PWD 604/00, Secretary for Native Affairs Circular no. 26 of 1899; NA, PWD 4633/99, Mag. Mapumulo to Moor, 10 Nov. 1899; NA, PWD 4746/99, Mag Mapumulo to Minister of Lands and Works, 27 Oct. 1899.

41 Marwick Papers, MAR 2.08.2, Barnes to Marwick, 14 Dec. 1899; NA, PWD 3571/00, 'Pioneer Batallion: Conditions of Enrolment', 1 Dec. 1899; NA, PWD 2827/02, 'Native Labour Corps', memorandum by Barnes, 4 June 1902.

42 NA, PWD 4964/99, Barnes to Principal Medical Officer, 13 Dec. 1899; NA, PWD 5117/99, Barnes to Minister of Lands and Works, 13 Jan. 1900; Mabel Palmer, *The History of the Indians in Natal*, Oxford University Press, Cape Town, 1957, pp. 63–4.

43 Capt. A. B. Ritchie, *The Record of the 4th Battalion (PWO) West Yorkshire Regiment during the Boer War 1899–1902*, John Sampson, York, 1903, p. 23.

44 Royal Engineers' Institute, *Detailed History of the Railways in the South African War, 1899–1902*, Chatham, 1904, pp. 257–62.

45 TA, MGP, 2A/00, Italian consul to Maxwell, 7 June 1900; Royal Engineers' Institute, *Detailed History*, p. 260.

46 *Times History*, vol. 6, p. 595.

47 Spies, *Methods of Barbarism?*, pp. 68, 154.

48 *Times History*, vol. 6, p. 596.

49 Spies, *Methods of Barbarism?*, pp. 68, 82.

50 TA, MGP 1, 08/00, Capt. A. R. Hoskins to Officer Commanding Supplies, 9 June 1900; TA MGP 63, 605/01, Marwick to Director of Supplies, 8 Feb. 1901; TA, SNA 1, 592/01, 'Report on the routine work of the Superintendent of Natives office, Pretoria, and of the offices attached thereto', 24 Aug. 1901; Spies, *Methods of Barbarism?*, p. 154.

51 Milner Papers, 47, Milner to Kitchener, 18 Feb. 1901.

52 TA, SNA 2, 882/01, T.M.C. Nourse, in charge Native Affairs, to Mine Managers' Association, 1 Mar. 1901; Spies, *Methods of Barbarism?*, pp. 174, 247.

53 Of course there were factors other than the shortage of African labour that determined the

slow progress of the resumption of gold mining. In particular, Kitchener was reluctant to agree to large numbers of *uitlanders* returning to Johannesburg because their transport there, and in particular the food they would need when they arrived, would place an additional burden on the railway system. He also insisted that travelling permits could only be granted in return for an undertaking that *uitlanders* would join the Rand Rifles, see Spies, *Methods of Barbarism?*, pp. 173–4, 246–7.

54 For a valuable study of transport workers in the Cape see W. R. Nasson, 'Black Transport Workers and the British Army in the Cape Colony during the South African War', *Collected Papers*, vol. 6, Centre for Southern African Studies, University of York, 1981.

55 J. Ralph, *Towards Pretoria*, Pearson, London, 1900, pp. 99–100; Archive of the Methodist Church Overseas Division, Transvaal incoming correspondence 1899–1903, Methodist Missionary Society Library, London (cxxxxiii), Rev. George Lowe to Rev. Hartley, 25 Aug. 1900.

56 CBBNA, G.25–1902, pp. 21–2, 31, 33; NBBNA, 1901, pp. C2, C4, C11; 1902, p. 42; Nasson, 'Black Transport Workers'.

57 Warwick, 'African Societies', pp. 256–7; Bundy, *The Rise and Fall*, pp. 122, 155.

58 Warwick, 'African Societies', pp. 140, 258–9; Nasson, 'Black Transport Workers'. Notions of 'loyalty' and 'patriotism' played an important role too in the recruitment of black people to the South African Native Labour Contingent during the First World War, see B. P. Willan, 'The South African Native Labour Contingent, 1916–1918', p. 67.

59 Lloyd George, speaking in the Commons on the 'iniquity' of employing so many Africans in the war, drew attention to the allure of acquiring loot, 'a much greater inducement to human nature than regular pay', *Parliamentary Debates*, 4th series, Commons, cv, col. 652, 20 Mar. 1902.

60 *Izwi Labantu*, 9 July 1901; CBBNA, G.52–1901, p. 7; G.25–1902, p. 49.

61 CBBNA, G.52–1901, pp. 2, 16, 17, 21.

62 W. R. Nasson, 'Tommy Atkins in South Africa', in Warwick, ed., *The South African War*, pp. 131–2.

63 For conditions in the shanty village at De Aar see CA, NAD 102, 1496/01D, Acting Ass. RM De Aar to Sec. to NAD, 12 Dec. 1901 and various enclosures; see also Nasson, 'Black Transport Workers'.

64 For efforts to root out deserters from the industrial region see TA, SNA 2, Commissioner of Mines 3/01, Capt. A. E. Hodgins to Acting Commissioner of Mines, 16 Nov. 1900.

65 LNA, S7/3/16, Lerotholi to Lagden, 25 Apr. 1900; LNA, S3/2/5/2, Lerotholi to Lagden, 10 May 1900, 18 May 1900, and Lagden to Girouard (tel.), 5 May 1900; Royal Engineers' Institute, *Detailed History*, p. 257.

66 LNA, S7/3/18, Lerotholi to Sloley, 28 Feb. 1902; LNA, S7/6/14, confidential army circular.

67 CO 179/222/7666, encl. in McCallum to Chamberlain, 26 Jan. 1902, Proceedings of the Native Labour Conference, Newcastle, 23 Jan. 1902, evidence of Major Hamnett.

68 CA, CMT 3/9, 2/606G, SNA to Elliot, 17 May 1901 and encl. David S. Mokuena to RM Mount Fletcher, 23 Mar. 1901.

69 CA, NAD 500, folio 103, 'Complaints by Native Labourers of their ill-treatment by the Military Authorities, 1901–02', and other enclosures.

70 CO 417/309/1011, encl. in Milner to Chamberlain (conf.), 20 Dec. 1899, Nicholson to Milner, 13 Nov. 1899; CO 417/309/7000, encl. 2 in Milner to Chamberlain, 6 Feb. 1901, F. Perry to Sec. to Transvaal Chamber of Mines, 31 Jan. 1901. CBBNA, G.52–1901, p. 38. C. van Onselen, *Chibaro*, Pluto Press, London, 1976, p. 87.

71 Warwick, 'African Societies', pp. 262–3.

72 CBBNA, G.25–1902, p. 3; *Izwi Labantu*, 9 July 1901; Van der Horst, pp. 162–3.

73 *Izwi Labantu*, 6 Aug. 1901.

74 CA, CMT 3/445, Elliot to magistrates (tel. 467), 7 May 1900; NA, SNA 1/4/12, C106/1903, various enclosures.

75 See various documents in CA, NA 580, folder 1340.
76 CO 179/222/7666, Proceedings of the Native Labour Conference, 23 Jan. 1902; CO 224/11/16833, encl. in Milner to Chamberlain (conf.), 18 Apr. 1903, petition from civil servants of ORC as to the inadequacy of salaries; CA, CMT 3/9, 2/1287H, SNA to Elliot, 22 Dec. 1901; SANAC, vol. 5, Sir John Colley, p. 18; *Cape Times*, 6 Sept. 1901; *Imvo Zabantsundu*, 15 July 1901.
77 *Cape Times*, 6 Sept. 1901.
78 NBBNA, 1902, pp. 11, 38.
79 CA, NA 503, folder 132, Ass. Sec. to General Manager of Railways, 4 Apr. 1902.
80 *Ipepa lo Hlanga*, 17 July 1902; SANAC, vol. 3, R. C. A. Alexander, Superintendent of Durban Police.
81 Stanford Papers, D.27a, 27 Sept. 1900, 3 Oct. 1900; Macquarrie, ed., *The Reminiscences of Sir Walter Stanford*, vol. 2, pp. 213–15; *South Africa*, 50, 15 June 1901; Chamberlain Papers, Birmingham University Library, JC 11/17/6, Hely-Hutchinson to Chamberlain, 27 Mar. 1901; Milner Papers, 47, Sir F. Walker to Kitchener (tel.), 8 Mar. 1901 and Kitchener to Walker (tel.), 8 Mar. 1901.
82 *Eastern Province Herald*, 11 June 1901, 12 June 1901, 13 June 1901; *Izwi Labantu*, 2 July 1901; *Imvo Zabantsundu*, 15 July 1901; *Ipepa lo Hlanga*, 14 June 1901.
83 For further details see Maynard W. Swanson, 'The Sanitation Syndrome: Bubonic Plague and Urban Native Policy in the Cape Colony 1900–9', *JAH*, 18, 3 (1977), pp. 387–410; C. C. Saunders, 'Segregation in Cape Town: The Creation of Ndabeni', *Centre for African Studies Collected Papers*, University of Cape Town, 1 (1978), pp. 43–63.

8. Refugees

1 S. B. Spies, 'Women in the War', in Warwick, ed., *The South African War*, p. 170.
2 P. Magnus, *Kitchener: Portrait of an Imperialist*, Penguin, Harmondsworth, 1968, p. 219.
3 N. Devitt, *The Concentration Camps in South Africa during the Anglo-Boer War of 1899–1902*, Shuter and Shooter, Pietermaritzburg, 1941, p. 21.
4 E. Hobhouse, *Report of a Visit to the Camps of Women and Children in the Cape and Orange River Colonies*, Friars Printing Association, London, 1901, p. 8.
5 H. R. Fox Bourne to Chamberlain, 24 Mar. 1902, reprinted in Hobhouse, *The Brunt of the War*, pp. 350–2.
6 Library of the Religious Society of Friends, London, Box P, Friends' South African Relief Fund, *Report of A Deputation to South Africa*, December 1902, p. 18. This statement is inaccurate in at least two respects. First, the rates of remuneration available to *refugees from the camps* who enlisted for work with the army were certainly no higher than those that had been current before the outbreak of war. Secondly, De Lotbinière, the Superintendent of the Native Refugee Department, vetoed a proposal that schools for Africans should be established in the camps because he believed 'the introduction of a new element in the shape of a Schoolmaster or Clergyman . . . would only tend to unsettle the natives' present system of control, and weaken the hands of my Superintendents', TA, SNA 8, 1037/02, De Lotbinière to Lagden, 17 May 1902.
7 'Questions Affecting the Natives and Coloured People Resident in British South Africa', reprinted in T. Karis and G. M. Carter, eds., *From Protest to Challenge, a Documentary History of African Politics in South Africa*, vol. 1, *Protest and Hope, 1882–1934*, Hoover Institution Press, Stanford, 1972, pp. 18–29.
8 *Bechuanaland News*, 15 Dec. 1900.
9 TA, MGP 57, 8270/00, Capt. J. Vaughan to Provost Marshall, 3 July 1900, and Col. C. V. Hume to Maxwell, 3 July 1900, and Maxwell's reply, 6 July 1900; TA, MGP 54, 7891/00, DC Heidelberg to Maxwell (tel.), 21 Dec. 1900.
10 TA, MGP 54, 7891/00, DC Heidelberg to Maxwell (tel.), 21 Dec. 1900.

11 CA, CMK 6/21, Adjutant-General Circular Memorandum No. 29, 21 Dec. 1900.

12 TA, MGP 63, 679/01, Lt E. A. Wood to Commissioner of Police, Pretoria, 14 Jan. 1901.

13 TA, MGP 109, 9370A/01, DC Heidelberg to Maxwell (tel.), 26 July 1901. For the importance of the army 'living off the land' see CA CMK 6/21, Chief of Staff Circular Memorandum No. 5, 11 Apr. 1900.

14 TA, SNA 2, 33/01, Officer Commanding Eerst Fabrieken to Marwick, 9 Oct. 1901, and minutes by Major Weston Peters, 11 Oct. 1901, and Marwick, 25 Oct. 1901; SNA 3, 147/01, Lagden to DMI, South Africa (tel.), 22 Oct. 1901.

15 *Reports etc. on the Working of the Refugee Camps*, Cd. 819, 1902, pp. 158, 217, 227, 300, 215; Cd. 902, p. 56; Hobhouse, *Report*, p. 4.

16 *Reports etc. on the Working of the Refugee Camps*, Cd. 819, pp. 74, 154; TA, MGP 73, 2062/01, DC Heidelberg to Maxwell (tel.), 17 Feb. 1901; Hobhouse, *Report*, p. 13; CO 224/3/27027, encl. in Kitchener to Chamberlain, 12 July 1901, report of refugee camps and returns for week ending 9 June 1901; Transvaal Administration Reports, *Final Report of the Work Performed by the Native Refugee Department of the Transvaal from June 1901 to December 1902*, p. 2.

17 TA, MGP 78, 2713/01, George Turner, Medical Officer Heidelberg (tel.), to Maxwell, 13 Mar. 1901; Spies, *Methods of Barbarism?*, p. 201.

18 Transvaal Administration Reports, *Final Report*, p. 1.

19 *Ibid*. In the Orange River Colony camps before they were taken over by the Department, rations had been issued without charge but £1 per month taken from the wages of those in employment. This was reported to have caused unrest among workers, and was clearly also a disincentive to work.

20 OFS Archives, CSO 86, 358/02, De Lotbinière to Major H. J. Goold-Adams, Deputy Administrator, ORC, 18 Jan. 1902; see the statistics for the Transvaal presented on p. 150, together with the less complete ones from the ORC contained in OFS Archives, CSO 81, 29/02, CSO 90, 586/02, CSO 96, 895/02, and CSO 108, 1493/02, Reports on Native Refugee Camps for November, January, February and April respectively.

21 The death rate among blacks in the camps was by no means as exceptional as it may seem. Infant mortality rates at this time were remarkably high, even among whites. In the principal thirty-two towns of the Cape Colony the proportion of deaths under one year per thousand births registered was in 1896 195.51 for whites and 362.47 for blacks, and in 1900 214.40 for whites and 409.20 for blacks. See Cd. 902, pp. 27–8. The British government naturally drew attention to these statistics in answering its critics over the concentration camp policy.

22 OFS Archives, SRC 8, 'Native Refugee Camps, 1901–02'.

23 Transvaal Administration Reports, *Final Report*, p. 3.

24 OFS Archives, CSO 85, 326/02, Capt. F. Wilson Fox, Superintendent Native Refugee Department ORC, to De Lotbinière, 3 Feb. 1902.

25 Mortality rates in the white camps were of course in some cases much higher than 344 per thousand per annum. The rate in the Middelburg camp reached 622 per thousand per annum in July 1901 (Spies, *Methods of Barbarism?*, p. 221). It is significant, however, that the response this elicited from the authorities made possible a reduction in the rate to 199 per thousand per annum in the following month. Such rapid reductions in death rates brought about by an immediate administrative response were rare indeed in the case of the African camps.

26 Spies, *Methods of Barbarism?*, p. 228; CO 224/5/42229, Kitchener to Chamberlain, 9 Nov. 1901, and encl. general recommendations of Concentration Camps Commission and remarks by Chief Superintendent, Refugee Camps ORC. The Commission recommended compulsory labour for all adult white males, but this was never put into practice. G. B. Beak *The Aftermath of War, an Account of the Repatriation of Boers and Natives in the Orange River Colony 1902–1904*, Arnold, London, 1906, p. 26. Transvaal Administration Reports, *Final Report*, p. 5. Warwick, 'African Societies and the South African War', pp. 282–4.

27 Transvaal Administration Reports, *Final Report*, p. 4; OFS Archives, CSO 86, 358/02, De Lotbinière to Goold-Adams, 18 Jan. 1902, pp. 6, 13.

28 CA, CMK 6/21, Adjutant-General Circular Memoranda Nos. 44 (1 July 1901) and 50 (12 Aug. 1901); Beak, p. 26; Transvaal Administration Reports, *Final Report*, p. 4; OFS Archives CSO 86, 358/02, De Lotbinière to Goold-Adams, 18 Jan. 1902, pp. 14–15.

29 OFS Archives, CSO 93, 704/02, F. Wilson Fox to H. F. Wilson, Colonial Secretary ORC, 10 Mar. 1902, and encl. Defence of Native Refugee Camps: Instructions for Camp Superintendents.

30 TA, MGP 86, 3885/01 Major H. P. Sykes, DC Potchefstroom to Maxwell, 13 Apr. 1901 and Lt D. Grant to Sykes, 9 Apr. 1901.

31 OFS Archives, CSO 82, 71/02, Fox to Wilson, 6 Jan. 1902, and encl. report on attack on Taaibosch camp by W. T. Mills, 4 Jan. 1902, and Mills to Lt J. M. Court, Officer Commanding Armed Natives, 4 Jan. 1902; CSO 93, 704/02, Fox to Wilson, 10 Mar. 1902, and encl. Court to Fox, 7 Mar. 1902.

32 OFS Archives, CSO 93, 704/02, circular letter by Lt Court, 11 Mar. 1902; WO 108/16/580, De Lotbinière to Military Secretary to General Kitchener, 4 June 1902.

33 OFS Archives, CSO 82, 71/02, Fox to Wilson, 6 Jan. 1902; CSO 85, 326/02, Fox to De Lotbinière, 3 Feb. 1902.

34 Beak, p. 29.

35 USPG, Reports, Africa 1901, 47 (11435), Rev. E. Farmer to Rev. H. W. Tucker, 22 Feb. 1901.

36 Archive of the Methodist Church Overseas Division Transvaal, incoming correspondence 1901–1903, Rev. Hugh Morgan to Rev. Hartley, 3 Sept. 1901.

37 USPG, Reports, Africa 1901, 1 (27347), Rev. W. H. R. Brown to Rev. W. H. Tucker, 3 Sept. 1901.

38 OFS Archives, CSO 75, 4353/01, RM Harrismith to Wilson, 26 Nov. 1901 and 27 Nov. 1901.

39 OFS Archives, CSO 74, 4283/01, encl. in RM Kroonstad to Wilson, 31 Dec. 1901, Marome and Oliphant to Goold-Adams, 23 Nov. 1901.

40 OFS Archives, CSO 85, 326/02, Fox to De Lotbinière, 3 Feb. 1902.

41 OFS Archives, CSO 86, 358/02, De Lotbinière to Goold Adams, 18 Jan. 1902, p 14; TA, SNA 6, 519/02, De Lotbinière to Lagden, 3 Mar. 1902; CO 417/349/9619, encl. in Milner to Chamberlain, 14 Feb. 1902, Summary of Refugees, Transvaal, 26 Dec. 1901.

42 OFS Archives, CSO 86, 358/02, De Lotbinière to Goold-Adams, 18 Jan. 1902, pp. 15–18; CSO 132, 2679/02, RM Thaba Nchu to Wilson, 23 July 1902.

43 OFS Archives, CSO 86, 390/02, encl. in Fox to Wilson, 10 Feb. 1902, Superintendent Native Refugees Thaba Nchu to Fox, 8 Feb. 1902.

44 LNA, S7/6/13, Goold-Adams to Sloley (tel.), 5 Mar. 1901, and Sloley to Goold-Adams (tel.), 5 Mar. 1901; LNA, S7/1/1/15, Schedule of Native and European Refugees, 30 Apr. 1902.

45 SANAC, *Minutes of Evidence*, vol. 3, Qu. 25523 Petrus Mazarine, African farmer.

46 CO 291/42/41289, encl. in McCallum to Chamberlain, 15 Sept. 1902, De Lotbinière to John Buchan, Milner's Private Secretary, 5 Sept. 1902.

47 Transvaal Administration Reports, *Final Report*, p. 7.

48 *Ibid.*, pp. 2, 7, 8; Beak, pp. 162, 163.

49 NA, SNA 22, 142/03, Samuelson to De Lotbinière, 9 Jan. 1903, and encl. Leslie to Samuelson, Dec. 1902; SNA 1/1/296, Leslie to Moor, 9 July 1902; SANAC, *Minutes of Evidence*, vol. 3, Qus. 25523–5, Petrus Mazarine, African farmer.

50 Beak, p. 162.

51 Transvaal Administration Reports, *Final Report*, p. 7.

52 Beak, p. 162; Transvaal Administration Reports, *Final Report*, p. 7.

53 TA, SNA 3, 171/01, NC Zoutpansberg to Lagden, 26 Oct. 1901.

54 TA, LtG 121, 110/5, monthly report by N. C. Rustenburg, 5 Feb. 1903.

55 Quoted by D. J. N. Denoon, 'Participation in the "Boer War": People's War, People's Non-War or Non-People's War?', in B. A. Ogot, ed., *War and Society in Africa*, Cass, London, 1972, pp. 115–16.

56 TA, SNA 15, 2075/02, De Lotbinière to Lagden, 22 Oct. 1902.

57 Transvaal Administration Reports, *Report of the Native Affairs Department for 1902*, pp. A18, A22.
58 TA, SNA 15, 2075/02, De Lotbinière to Lagden, 22 Oct. 1902.
59 TA, LtG 124, 110/42(5), report of Sub-Native Commissioner, Wakkerstroom.
60 For details see D. J. N. Denoon, *A Grand Illusion*, Longman, London, 1973, p. 63.
61 *Progress of Administration in the Transvaal and Orange River Colony*, Cd. 1551, 1903, p. 32; Transvaal Administration Reports, *Final Report*, p. 7; Beak, pp. 164–5.
62 Denoon, 'Participation in the Boer War', p. 116.
63 TA, SNA 16, 2369/02, monthly report of Capt. Vignoles, South African Constabulary, Amsterdam, 13 Oct. 1902.
64 TA, SNA 17, 2500/02, De Lotbinière to Lagden, 7 Nov. 1902.
65 Beak, p. 184.
66 TA, SNA 16, 2217/02, encl. in Assistant RM Wakkerstroom to Lagden, 4 Oct. 1902, Rev. C. Poulson to Assistant RM, 1 Oct. 1902, and reply by Lagden, 11 Oct. 1902.
67 TA, SNA 17, 2640/02, G. H. Hogge to Lagden, 20 Dec. 1902.
68 Transvaal Administration Reports, *Final Report*, p. 12.

9. Aftermath

1 *Ipepa lo Hlanga*, 14 Dec. 1900.
2 *Izwi Labantu*, 3 Sept. 1901.
3 Transvaal Administration Reports, *Report of the Native Affairs Department for 1903*, p. B18.
4 Transvaal Administration Reports, *Report of the Native Affairs Department for 1902*, p. A17.
5 CO 179/224/39318, encl. 1(g), Roch to CSO Natal, 23 Aug. 1902.
6 TA, SNA 13, 1569/02, NC Rustenburg to SNA, 6 Aug. 1902; Basil Williams Papers, Rhodes House Library, Oxford, MSS. Afr.s 131, vol. 2, conversation with General Beyers, 29 June 1902; S. B. Steele, *Forty Years in Canada (and South Africa)*, Dodd Mead, New York, 1915, p. 375.
7 Transvaal Labour Commission, *Minutes of Proceedings and Evidence*, Cd. 1891, 1904, evidence of Louis Botha.
8 TA, SNA 16, 2243/02, memorandum by W. Windham, 25 Oct. 1902; Transvaal Administration Reports, *Report of the Native Affairs Department for 1902*, appendix 9, 'Schedule of Arms Surrendered by Native Commissioners', pp. A18 and A27; TA, SNA 13, 1569/02, NC Rustenburg to SNA, 17 Sept. 1902.
9 TA, SNA 13, 1569/02, NC Pretoria to SNA, 8 Sept. 1902; CO 291/44/48451, encl. 12 in Milner to Chamberlain, 3 Nov. 1902, NC Lydenburg to SNA, 6 Oct. 1902.
10 *Further Correspondence Relating to Affairs in South Africa*, Cd. 1463, 1904, p. 20.
11 TA, SNA 17, 2482/02, AG's Circular No. 15; Transvaal Administration Reports, *Report of the Native Affairs Department for 1902*, p. A14.
12 TA, SNA 13, 1644/02, memorandum by Lagden, 3 Sept. 1902.
13 There were some exceptions, see Transvaal Administration Reports, *Report of the Native Affairs Department for 1902*, p. A15.
14 Bundy, *The Rise and Fall*, pp. 208–10; Denoon, *A Grand Illusion*, pp. 127–8; Stanley Trapido, 'Landlord and Tenant' pp. 46–55.
15 TA, SNA 13, 1569/02, NC Waterberg to SNA, 26 Sept. 1902.
16 CO 179/224/39318, encl. 1(f), Roch to CSO Natal, 16 Aug. 1902.
17 Bundy, *The Rise and Fall*, pp. 213–14; T. Keegan, 'Peasants, Capitalists and Farm Labour: Class Formation in the Orange River Colony, 1902–1910', *The Societies of Southern Africa in the 19th and 20th Centuries*, 9 (1979), p. 18, and 'The Sharecropping Economy', in Marks and Rathbone, eds., pp. 195–211.
18 Bundy, *The Rise and Fall*, p. 212.
19 Chamber of Mines, *Annual Reports for 1900 and 1901*, p. 111.

20 See Alan Jeeves, 'The Control of Migratory Labour' pp. 12f.

21 C. van Onselen, 'Randlords and Rotgut, 1886–1903', *History Workshop Journal*, 2 (1976), p. 81.

22 TA, SNA 17, 2515/02, return of deaths on the Witwatersrand mines, May to September 1902; *Return of Statistics of Mortality, Sickness and Destitution amongst the Natives employed in the Rand Mines during the period October 1902 to March 1903* (345), 1903; SANAC, 4, Qus. 42913, 42917, evidence of Dr L. Irvine, Mine Medical Officer.

23 TA, SNA 16, 2256/02, T. M. C. Nourse, Joint General Manager WNLA, to Chairman WNLA, 22 Oct. 1902, and T. W. Butt, Compound Manager, Nigel Gold-Mining Company, to Inspector of Labour, Springs, 1 Oct. 1902; TA, SNA 2195/02, Secretary, Chamber of Mines, to SNA, 11 Oct, 1902.

24 SANAC, 4, evidence of T. J. M. Macfarlane, General Manager, WNLA, p. 735.

25 *Rand Daily Mail*, 27 Feb. 1903.

26 Marks, *Reluctant Rebellion*, p. 135.

27 *Basutoland Annual Report for 1899–1900*, p. 22; *1902–3*, p. 15.

28 *Report of the Transvaal Labour Commission*, Cd. 1894, 1904, p. 22; Bundy, *The Rise and Fall*, p. 121.

29 See p. 142.

30 *Ilange lase Natal*, 29 May 1903.

31 SANAC, 5, evidence of J. H. Scott, p. 79.

32 TA, LtG 121, 110/5, report of NC, Pietersburg, n.d.

33 *Ipepa to Hlanga*, 14 June 1901.

34 *Imvo* interviews reproduced in *Ipepa lo Hlanga*, 11 Dec. 1903.

35 Peter Richardson and Jean Jacques Van-Helten, 'Labour in the South African Gold Mining Industry 1886–1914', in Marks and Rathbone, eds., pp. 91–2.

36 TA, SNA 5, 172/02, report of the Witwatersrand Native Labour Association for 1901.

37 CO 291/56/1 '8, encl. in Milner to Chamberlain, 30 Mar. 1903, Johannesburg Town Police Report for 1902, p. 13.

38 TA, SNA 8, 861/02, General Manager Consolidated Main Reef Mine to General Manager WNLA, 2 Apr. 1902, and TA, SNA 7, 783/02, 4 Apr. 1902.

39 CO 291/40/32789, encl. 1 in Milner to Chamberlain, 19 July, 1902, Mag. Native Court, Johannesburg to SNA, 14 July 1902; TA, SNA 11, 1342/02, Pritchard to SNA, 15 July 1902.

40 TA, SNA 11, 1308/02, report by Trooper G. W. Brickhill, Johannesburg Mounted Police, 28 June 1902, Pritchard to SNA, 2 July 1902.

41 TA, SNA 12, 1480/02, Pritchard to SNA, 22 July 1902, and encl. evidence of H. R. Skinner, Manager; J. C. Gray, compound manager; and Madoda, a worker from Mozambique.

42 For further details of these industrial protests see Peter Warwick 'Black Industrial Protest on the Witwatersrand, 1901–1902', in Webster, ed., pp. 20–31.

43 The definitive work on the Chinese labour experience, its background and effects, is Peter Richardson, *Chinese Mine Labour in the Transvaal*, Macmillan, London, 1982.

44 *Imvo*, 8 Oct. 1902.

45 CO 224/7/16319, sub. in encl. 1 in Milner to Chamberlain, 4 Apr. 1902.

46 CO 224/8/39322, encl. in Milner to Chamberlain, 30 Aug. 1902.

47 Denoon, *A Grand Illusion*, p. 108.

48 Quoted in *Imvo*, 14 Dec. 1900.

49 Petition reprinted in Karis and Carter, vol. 1, pp. 48–9.

50 BNA, RC 10/7, extract from *Koranta ea Becoana*, 6 Aug. 1903.

51 Francis Wilson and Dominique Perrot, eds., *Outlook on a Century 1870–1970*, Spro-cas, Lovedale, 1973, p. 271.

52 For further details of the Asian question in South Africa at this time see H. J. and R. E. Simons, *Class and Colour in South Africa 1850–1950*, Penguin, Harmondsworth, 1969,

pp. 69–71; R. A. Huttenback, *Ghandi in South Africa, British Imperialism and the Indian Question, 1860–1914*, Cornell University Press, 1971.

53 R. van der Ross, *The Founding of the African Peoples Organisation and the Role of Dr Abdurahman*, Munger Africana Library Notes 28, Pasadena, 1975, pp. 20f.

54 For further details of African political activity preceding Union and the response of the Liberal government in Britain see Karis and Carter, vol. 1, pp. 10–12, 52–7; P. Walshe, 'The Origins of African Political Consciousness in South Africa', *Journal of Modern African Studies*, 7, 4 (1969), pp. 583–610; R. Hyam, 'African Interests and the South Africa Act 1908–1910', *The Historical Journal*, 13, 1 (1970), pp. 85–105; N. Mansergh, *South Africa 1906–1961, The Price of Magnanimity*, Allen and Unwin, London, 1962, chapter 3.

Conclusion

1 Denoon, 'Participation in the "Boer War"', p. 120.

2 J. D. Kestell and D. E. van der Velden, *The Peace Negotiations*, Clay, London, 1912, contains the full text.

3 *Ibid.*, p. 85.

4 *Ibid.*, *passim*, and De Wet, pp. 401–506. An interesting account of the Boer discussions is provided by T. D. Moodie, *The Rise of Afrikanerdom*, University of California Press, Berkeley, 1975, pp. 33–6.

5 Plaatje, *Native Life*, p. 252. Some eighty years after the end of the war Mafeking has become part of the 'independent' homeland of Bophuthatswana.

6 S. M. Molema, *The Bantu Past and Present*, Green, Edinburgh, 1920, p. 292.

Select Bibliography

I UNPUBLISHED SOURCES

A Official

1 Britain

Public Records Office, London
CO 417 Africa South despatches and correspondence 1899–1902
CO 48 Cape Colony despatches and correspondence 1899–1902
CO 179 Natal despatches and correspondence 1899–1903
CO 224 Orange River Colony despatches and correspondence 1901–3
CO 291 Transvaal despatches and correspondence 1901–3
WO 32 South African War despatches and correspondence 1899–1902

2 South Africa

Cape Archives, Cape Town
NAD Native Affairs Department, correspondence files 1899–1902
CMT Archive of the Chief Magistrate of the Transkei 1899–1902
CMK Archive of the Chief Magistrate Griqualand East 1899–1902
AG Attorney-General's Department, Anglo-Boer War files
DD Defence Department, Native Levies and Intelligence 1899–1902 (7/175)

Natal Archives, Pietermaritzburg
SNA 1/1 Secretary for Native Affairs, minute papers 1899–1902
SNA 1/4 Secretary for Native Affairs, confidential and semi-official correspondence 1899–1902
SNA 1/6/25 Papers relating to the actions of Colonel Bottomley 1901–2
SNA 1/8/25A Secretary for Native Affairs, confidential letterbook 1855–1911
ZA 32–33 Zululand Archive, Resident Commissioner and Chief Magistrate's confidential correspondence 1899–1902
PWD Public Works Department, minute papers and correspondence 1899–1902

Orange Free State Archives, Bloemfontein
GS Government Secretary, letters received and minute papers, September–December 1899
MG Military Governor, letters received and minute papers 1900–1
CO Colonial Secretary, correspondence 1901–2

212

SRC Archive of the Superintendent of Refugees 1901–2

Transvaal Archives, Pretoria
SN Archive of the Superintendent of Natives 1899–1900
MGP Archive of the Military Governor, Pretoria 1900–1
SNA Archive of the Secretary for Native Affairs 1901–3
LtG Archive of the Lieutenant-Governor 1903–5

Leyds Argief 781(i), 'Gebruik van zoogenamde wilde volksstammen, rapport van Kapt. Ram en Luit. Thomson' (Dutch military attaches)

3 Lesotho

Lesotho National Archives, Maseru
S3/2 Correspondence relating to the Anglo-Boer War 1899–1902
S7 In-letters of the Office of the Resident Commissioner, Maseru 1899–1902
S8 Out-letters of the Office of the Resident Commissioner, Maseru 1897–1902
S11 Pitso Books

4 Botswana

Botswana National Archives, Gaborone
The following correspondence files were consulted.
HC 82; 108; 116/3; 130/2; 163/2; 177/6; 186; 190/1
RC 4/14; 4/20; 5/4; 5/11; 6/2; 6/3; 6/12; 6/13; 8/8; 10/2; 10/7; 10/13; 12/13
S 1/9; 1/13; 29/4; 259/13

B Non-official

1 Britain

Public Records Office
Roberts Papers (WO 105)
Kitchener Papers (PRO 30/57)

Bodleian Library, University of Oxford
Milner Papers

Rhodes House Library, Oxford
Anti-Slavery Papers (MSS. Brit.Emp.s. 18)
Lagden Papers (MSS. Afr.s. 172–5, 210, 213)
Basil Williams Papers (MSS. Afr.s. 130, 131)

Birmingham University Library
Chamberlain Papers

Selly Oak Colleges Library, Birmingham
W. C. Willoughby Papers

Library of the Religious Society of Friends, London
Letters of W. H. F. Alexander, comprising a journal of the visit to South Africa by Alexander and
   L. Richardson on behalf of the Friends' South African Relief Fund

213

Select bibliography

Royal Commonwealth Society Library, London
South African Diary of Amy M. Wilson 1901–2

Library of the School of Oriental and African Studies, London
The Archives of the Council for World Mission (incorporating the London Missionary Society)
South Africa, incoming letters 1899–1902
South Africa, reports 1899–1902
W. C. Willoughby Papers

Methodist Missionary Society Library, London
Archive of the Methodist Church Overseas Division, Transvaal incoming correspondence 1899–1903
Papers relating to the South African Conference 1883–1901, 1890–1905

Archive of the United Society for the Propagation of the Gospel, London
Reports, Africa (E MSS.) 1899–1902
Letters received from South Africa (C MSS.) 1899–1902

2 South Africa

South African Public Library
W. P. Schreiner Papers (MSS. SA Sect.B)

Jagger Library, University of Cape Town
W. E. Stanford Papers
W. P. Schreiner Papers

Killie Campbell Africana Library, Durban
J. S. Marwick Papers
Alistair M. Miller Papers

Natal Archives, Pietermaritzburg
Colenso collection (boxes 37, 73, 100, 101, the latter two boxes comprising the papers of Dinuzulu)

Mrs C. Minchin, Mafeking
'Mafeking Besieged, Seven Months of a Lifetime – the Diary of Miss Ina Cowan, 9 Oct. 1899–17 May 1900', unpublished typescript

The late Canon C. T. Wood, Cape Town
'Seven Months under Boer Rule', by the Rev. Gerard Chilton Bailey of Dundee, bound typescript

II PUBLISHED CONTEMPORARY SOURCES

A Official

1 Britain

Parliamentary Debates 1899–1902

Parliamentary Papers
1887–8 to 1903–4, C.5249, C.5897, C.6221, C.6563, C.6857–12, C.6857–39, C.7629, C.7944, C.8279, C.8650, C.9046, Cd.3. Cd.431, Cd.788, Cd.1388, Cd.1768, Cd.2238, *Basutoland Annual Reports*
1899, C.9206, *Further Correspondence Relative to the Affairs of Swaziland*
1900–4, Cd.43, Cd.261, Cd.420, Cd.547, Cd.903, Cd.1163, Cd.1463, *Further Correspondence Relating to Affairs in South Africa* 1901, Cd.457, *South Africa Despatches, Vol. 1*
1901, Cd.464, *Telegram from Sir Alfred Milner to the Secretary of State for War, Relating to the Reported Outrage on Esau at Calvinia*
1901–2, Cd.608, Cd.694, Cd.789, Cd.793, *Returns of Numbers of Persons in the Concentration Camps*
1901–2, Cd.819, Cd.853, Cd.902, Cd.934, Cd.936, *Reports etc. on the Working of the Refugee Camps in the Transvaal, Orange River Colony, Cape Colony and Natal*
1902, Cd.893, *Report on the Concentration Camps by the Committee of Ladies Appointed by the Secretary of State for War*
1902, Cd.939, Cd.942, Cd.1161, *Statistics of the Refugee Camps in South Africa*
1903, Cd.1551, Cd.1553, *Papers Relating to the Progress of Administration in the Transvaal and Orange River Colony*
1903, 345, *Return of Statistics of Mortality, Sickness and Desertion amongst the Natives Employed in the Rand Mines during the Period October 1902 and March 1903*
1904, Cd.1789, Cd.1790, Cd.1791, Cd.1792, *Report, together with Minutes of Evidence (2 vols.) and Appendices, of the Commissioners Appointed to Enquire into the Military Preparations and Other Matters Connected with the War in South Africa*
1904, Cd.1894, Cd.1896, Cd.1897, *Report, Minutes of Proceedings and Evidence of the Transvaal Labour Commission*
1905, Cd.2399, *Report of the South African Native Affairs Commission*

2 South Africa

1899–1903, G.50, G.52, G.25, G.29, Cape Colony, *Blue Books on Native Affairs*
1899–1903, Colony of Natal, Department of Native Affairs, *Magistrates' Annual Reports/Blue Books on Native Affairs*
1902, Colony of Natal, *Report by Colonel G. A. Mills on the Causes which Led to the Ill-Feeling between the Boers and the Zulu Culminating in the Attack on the Boers by the Zulu Chief Sikobobo at Holkrantz 6 May 1902*
1902, Transvaal Administration Reports, *Final Report of the Work Performed by the Native Refugee Department of the Transvaal from June 1901 to December 1902*
1902, 1903, Transvaal Administration Reports, *Annual Reports of the Native Affairs Department*
1905, *South African Native Affairs Commission, Minutes of Evidence* (5 vols.)
Mafeking Municipality Notices, October 1899–May 1900

B Newspapers and periodicals

1 Britain

Aborigines' Friend
The Times

2 South Africa

Cape Times
Eastern Province Herald

Select bibliography

Mafeking Mail (Special Siege Slip)
Natal Mercury
Standard and Diggers' News
Vryheid Herald
Ilanga lase Natal
Imvo Zabantsundu
Ipepa lo Hlanga
Izwi Labantu

The above items were consulted at Colindale Newspaper Library, London; Rhodes House Library, Oxford; and the Natal Archives, Pietermaritzburg. The South African Public Library, Cape Town, kindly provided microfilms of *Imvo* and *Izwi*. Only the English columns of the African newspapers were read, though articles in Zulu from *Ipepa* and *Ilanga* can sometimes be found in translation among the files of the Natal Secretary for Native Affairs. Some articles from *Koranta ea Becoana* were consulted in the Botswana National Archives, Gaborone, where they were found in various administrative files.

C Contemporary books, pamphlets and unofficial reports

Aborigines' Protection Society, *Transactions of the Aborigines' Protection Society*, published by the Society, Westminster, 1899–1902
Ashe E. D., *Besieged by the Boers, a Diary of Life and Events in Kimberley*, Hutchinson, London, 1900
Baden-Powell R. S. S., *The Downfall of Prempeh*, Methuen, London, 1896
Baillie F. D., *Mafeking, a Diary of the Siege*, Constable, London, 1900
Batts H. J., *Pretoria from Within during the War, 1899–1900*, Shaw, London, 1901
Beak G. B., *The Aftermath of War, an Account of the Repatriation of Boers and Natives in the Orange River Colony 1902–1904*, Arnold, London, 1906
Billington R. C., *A Mule Driver at the Front*, Chapman and Hall, London, 1901
Briggs E. C. (Lady), *The Staff Work of the Anglo-Boer War 1899–1901*, Grant Richards, London, 1901
Brown S. M., *With the Royal Canadians*, Publishers' Syndicate, Toronto, 1900
Butler E. J. (Lady), *Native Races and the War*, Gay and Bird, London, 1900
Callwell C. E., *Small Wars, Their Principles and Practice*, 2nd edn, HMSO, London, 1899
Chamber of Mines (Transvaal), *Annual Reports*, 1896–1903
Churchill W. S., *London to Ladysmith via Pretoria*, Longman, London, 1900
Conan Doyle A. (Sir), *The Great Boer War*, Smith and Elder, London, 1903
FitzPatrick J. P. (Sir), *The Transvaal from Within*, Heinemann, London, 1899
Friends' South African Relief Fund, *Report of a Deputation to South Africa*, December 1902
Fuller J. F. C., *The Last of the Gentlemen's Wars*, Faber and Faber, London, 1937
Gandhi M. K., *Satyagraha in South Africa*, Ganesan, Madras, 1928
Gibson J. Y., *The Story of the Zulus*, Longman, London, 1911
Hamilton J. A., *The Siege of Mafeking*, Methuen, London, 1900
Hobhouse E., *The Brunt of the War and Where it Fell*, Methuen, London, 1902
Hobson J. A., *The War in South Africa*, Nisbet, London, 1900
Hook D. B., *With Sword and Statute*, Greaves, London, 1906
Indicus (pseud.), *Labour and Other Questions in South Africa*, Fisher Unwin, London, 1903
Kestell J. D., *Through Shot and Flame*, Methuen, London, 1903
  and Van der Velden D.E., *The Peace Negotiations*, Clay, London, 1912
Lagden G. Y. (Sir), *The Basutos*, 2 vols., Hutchinson, London, 1909
Maxeke M., 'The Black Man's Side in the Transvaal War', *Independent*, 51 (7 December 1899)
Molema S. M., *The Bantu Past and Present*, Green, Edinburgh, 1920

Neilly J. E., *Besieged with B-P*, Pearson, London, 1900

Plaatje S. T., *Native Life in South Africa*, King, London, 1916

Reitz D., *Commando, a Boer Journal of the Boer War*, Faber and Faber, London, 1931

Royal Engineers' Institute, *Detailed History of the Railways in the South African War 1899–1902*, Chatham, 1904

Samuelson R. C. A., *Long, Long Ago*, Knox, Durban, 1929

Seely J. B. (Lord Mottistone), *Fear and Be Slain*, Hodder and Stoughton, London, 1931

Stuart J., *A History of the Zulu Rebellion 1906*, Macmillan, London, 1913

Thierry C. de, 'The South African Native and the War', *English Illustrated Magazine* (December 1899), pp. 266–72

Thomas O., *Agricultural and Pastoral Prospects of South Africa*, Constable, London, 1904

Viljoen B., *My Reminiscences of the Anglo-Boer War*, Hood, Douglas and Howard, London, 1903

Waters W. H. H. and Du Cane H. (translators), *The War in South Africa, October 1899 to February 1900, Prepared in the Historical Section of the Great General Staff, Berlin*, 2 vols., Murray, London, 1904–6

Wet C. R. de, *Three Years War*, Constable, London, 1902

Wolseley G. (Sir), 'The Negro as Soldier', *The Fortnightly Review*, new series, 44 (1888), pp. 689–703

D Documentary material subsequently published

Comaroff J. L., ed., *The Boer War Diary of Sol T. Plaatje, an African at Mafeking*, Macmillan, London, 1973

Ellenberger J., 'The Bechuanaland Protectorate and the Boer War 1899–1902', *Rhodesiana*, 11 (December 1964)

Hadley P., ed., *Doctor to Basuto, Boer and Briton 1877–1906, Memoires of Dr Henry Taylor*, Philip, Cape Town, 1972

Hancock W. K. and Van der Poel J., eds., *Selections from the Smuts Papers*, vol. 1, Cambridge University Press, 1966

Headlam C., ed., *The Milner Papers, South Africa 1897–1905*

Karis T. and Carter G. M., eds., *From Protest to Challenge, a Documentary History of African Politics in South Africa*, vol. 1, Hoover Institution Press, Stanford, 1972

Macquarrie J. W., ed., *The Reminiscences of Sir Walter Stanford*, 2 vols., Van Riebeeck Society, Cape Town, 1958 and 1962.

Schikkerling R. W. *Commando Courageous (A Boer's Diary)*, Keartland, Johannesburg, 1964

Willan B. P., ed., *Diary of the Siege of Mafeking, October 1899 to May 1900, by Edward Ross*, Van Riebeeck Society, Cape Town, 1980

Wilson F. and Perrot D., eds., *Outlook on a Century, South Africa 1870–1970*, Spro-cas, Lovedale, 1973

III SECONDARY SOURCES

A Books

Amery L. C. M. S., ed., *The Times History of the War in South Africa 1899–1902*, 7 vols., Sampson, Low & Marston, London, 1900–9

Breytenbach J. H., *Die Geskiedenis van die Tweede Vryheidsoorlog in Suid-Afrika 1899–1902*, 4 vols., Die Staatsdrukker, Pretoria, 1969–78

Brookes E. H. and Webb C., *A History of Natal*, University of Natal Press, 1965

Bundy C., *The Rise and Fall of the South African Peasantry*, Heinemann, London, 1979

Davenport T. R. H., *The Afrikaner Bond (1880–1911)*, Oxford University Press, Cape Town, 1966

Select bibliography

South Africa: A Modern History, Macmillan, London, 1977

Denoon D. J. N., *Southern Africa since 1800*, Longman, London, 1972

A Grand Illusion, Longman, London, 1973

Devitt N., *The Concentration Camps in South Africa during the Anglo-Boer War of 1899–1902*, Shuter and Shooter, Pietermaritzburg, 1941

Elphick R. and Giliomee H., eds., *The Shaping of South African Society 1652–1820*, Longman Penguin Southern Africa, Cape Town, 1979

Farwell B., *The Great Boer War*, Harper and Row, New York, 1976

Gardner B., *Mafeking, A Victorian Legend*, Cassell, London, 1966

Grinnell-Milne D., *Baden-Powell at Mafeking*, Bodley Head, London, 1957

Guy J. J., *The Destruction of the Zulu Kingdom*, Longman, London, 1979

Hancock W. K., *Smuts*, vol. 1, *The Sanguine Years*, Cambridge University Press, 1962

Huttenback R. A., *Gandhi in South Africa, British Imperialism and the Indian Question, 1860–1914*, Cornell University Press, 1971

Jabavu D. D. T., *The Life of John Tengo Jabavu*, Lovedale Institution Press, 1922

Kiewiet C. W. de, *A History of South Africa, Social and Economic*, Oxford University Press, 1941

Kruger R., *Good-Bye Dolly Gray*, Cassell, London, 1959

Lehmann J.H., *The First Boer War*, Cape, London, 1972

Le May G. H. L., *British Supremacy in South Africa 1899–1907*, Oxford University Press, 1965

Magnus, P., *Kitchener: Portrait of an Imperialist*, Penguin, Harmondsworth, 1968

Marais J. S., *The Cape Coloured People 1652–1937*, Longman Green, London, 1939

The Fall of Kruger's Republic, Oxford University Press, 1961

Marks S., *Reluctant Rebellion*, Oxford University Press, 1970

and Atmore A., eds., *Economy and Society in Pre-Industrial South Africa*, Longman, London, 1980

and Rathbone R., eds., *Industrialisation and Social Change in South Africa*, Longman, London, 1982

Martin A. C., *The Concentration Camps 1900–2*, Timmins, Cape Town, 1957

Matsebula J. S. M., *A History of Swaziland*, Longman, Cape Town, 1972

Maurice F. (Sir) and Grant M. H., *History of the War in South Africa 1899–1902*, Hurst and Blackett, London, 1906–10

Moodie T. D., *The Rise of Afrikanerdom*, University of California Press, Berkeley, 1975

Muller C. J. F., ed., *500 Years, a History of South Africa*, Academica, Pretoria, 1969

Pakenham T., *The Boer War*, Weidenfeld and Nicolson, London, 1979

Palmer R. and Parsons N., eds., *The Roots of Rural Poverty in Central and Southern Africa*, Heinemann, London, 1977

Price R., *An Imperial War and the British Working Class*, Routledge and Kegan Paul, London, 1972

Pyrah G. B., *Imperial Policy and South Africa 1902–10*, Oxford University Press, 1955

Reynolds E. E., *Baden-Powell*, Oxford University Press, 1942

Roux E., *Time Longer than Rope*, Gollancz, London, 1948

Sacks B., *South Africa, an Imperial Dilemma; Non-Europeans and the British Nation 1902–14*, University of New Mexico Press, 1967

Schapera I., *A Short History of the BaKgatla-bagaKgafela*, Communications from the School of African Studies, University of Cape Town, New Series, No. 3, 1942

Scott J. B., *The Hague Peace Conferences of 1899 and 1907*, vol. 2, John Hopkins University Press, Baltimore, 1909

Sillery A., *Founding a Protectorate, a History of Bechuanaland 1885–95*, Mouton, The Hague, 1965

Simons H. J. and R. E., *Class and Colour in South Africa 1850–1950*, Penguin, Harmondsworth, 1969

Spies S. B., *Methods of Barbarism? Roberts and Kitchener and Civilians in the Boer Republics,*

January 1900–May 1902, Human and Rousseau, Cape Town, 1977

Thompson L. M., *The Unification of South Africa 1902–10*, Oxford University Press, 1960

Thornton R. W., *The Origin and History of the Basuto Pony*, Morija Printing Works, 1936

Tylden G., *The Rise of the Basuto*, Juta, Cape Town, 1950

    The Armed Forces of South Africa, City of Johannesburg Africana Museum, 1954

Van der Horst S.T., *Native Labour in South Africa*, 2nd edn, Cass, London, 1971

Van der Ross R., *The Founding of the African Peoples Organisation and the Role of Dr Abdurahman*, Munger Africana Library Notes 28, Pasadena, 1975

Walshe, P., *The Rise of African Nationalism in South Africa*, Hurst, London, 1970

Warwick P., ed., *The South African War*, Longman, London, 1980

Webster E., ed., *Essays in Southern African Labour History*, Ravan, Johannesburg, 1978

Williams B., *Record of the Cape Mounted Riflemen*, Causton, London, 1909

Wilson M. and Thompson L. M., eds., *The Oxford History of South Africa*, 2 vols., Oxford University Press, 1969, 1971

B Articles

Blainey G., 'Lost Causes of the Jameson Raid', *Economic History Review*, second series, 18, 2 (1965), pp. 350–66

Botha H. J., 'Die moord op Derdepoort, 25 November 1899: Nie-blankes in oorlogsdiens', *Militaria*, 1 (1969), pp. 1–97

Denoon D. J. N., 'The Transvaal Labour Crisis 1901–6', *Journal of African History*, 7, 3 (1967), pp. 481–94

    'Participation in the "Boer War": People's War, People's Non-War or Non-People's War?', in B. A. Ogot, ed., *War and Society in Africa*, Cass, London, 1972, pp. 109–23

Hunt D. R., 'An Account of the Bapedi', *Bantu Studies*, 5, 4 (1931), pp. 275–326

Hyam R., 'African Interests and the South Africa Act 1908–10', *The Historical Journal*, 13, 1 (1970), pp. 85–105

Jeeves A., 'The Control of Migratory Labour on the South African Gold Mines in the Era of Kruger and Milner', *Journal of Southern African Studies*, 2, 1 (1975), pp. 3–29

Keegan T., 'Peasants, Capitalists and Farm Labour: Class Formation in the Orange River Colony 1902–10', *The Societies of Southern Africa in the 19th and 20th Centuries*, 9 (1979), pp. 18–26

Killingray D., 'The Idea of a British Imperial Army', *Journal of African History*, 20, 3 (1979), pp. 421–36

Marks S., 'Scrambling for South Africa', *Journal of African History*, 23, 1 (1982), pp. 97–113 and Trapido S., 'Lord Milner and the South African State', *History Workshop Journal*, 8 (1979), pp. 50–80

Moyer R., 'The Mfengu, Self-Defence and the Cape Frontier Wars', in C. C. Saunders and R. M. Derricourt, eds., *Beyond the Cape Frontier*, Longman Penguin Southern Africa, Cape Town, 1974, pp. 101–26

Ngcongco L. D., 'Jabavu and the Anglo-Boer War', *Kleio*, 2 (1970), pp. 6–18

Pilane A. K., 'A Note on Episodes from the Boer War', *Botswana Notes and Records*, 5 (1973), p. 131

Richardson P., 'Coolies and Randlords, The North Randfontein Chinese Miners' "Strike" of 1905', *Journal of Southern African Studies*, 2, 2 (1975), pp. 151–77

Saunders C. C., 'Segregation in Cape Town: The Creation of Ndabeni', *Centre for African Studies Collected Papers*, University of Cape Town, 1 (1978), pp. 43–63

Savage D. C. and Forbes-Munro J., 'Carriers Corps Recruitment in the British East African Protectorate 1914–18', *Journal of African History*, 7, 2 (1966), pp. 313–42

Swanson M., 'The Sanitation Syndrome: Bubonic Plague and Urban Native Policy in the Cape Colony 1900–9', *Journal of African History*, 18, 3 (1977), pp. 387–410

Select bibliography

Teichler G. H. J., 'Some Historical Notes on Derdepoort-Sikwane', *Botswana Notes and Records*, 5 (1973), pp. 125–30

Trapido S., 'African Divisional Politics in the Cape Colony 1884–1910', *Journal of African History*, 9, 1 (1968), pp. 79–98

'Landlord and Tenant in a Colonial Economy: The Transvaal 1880–1910', *Journal of Southern African Studies*, 5, 1 (1978), pp. 26–58

Truschel L. W., 'Nation-Building and the Kgatla: The Role of the Anglo-Boer War', *Botswana Notes and Records*, 4 (1972), pp. 185–93

Tylden G., 'The Cape Mounted Riflemen 1827–1870', *Journal of the Society for Army Historical Research*, 17 (1938), pp. 227–31

'The Development of the Commando System in South Africa 1715–1922', *Africana Notes and News*, 13, 8 (1961), pp. 303–13

Van-Helten J. J., 'German Capital, the Netherlands Railway Company and the Political Economy of the Transvaal 1886–1900', *Journal of African History*, 19, 3 (1978), pp. 369–90

'British Capital, the British State and Economic Investment in South Africa 1886–1914', *The Societies of Southern Africa in the 19th and 20th Centuries*, 9 (1979), pp. 1–17

Van Onselen C., 'Reactions to Rinderpest in Southern Africa 1896–7', *Journal of African History*, 13, 3 (1972), pp. 473–88

'Randlords and Rotgut 1886–1903', *History Workshop Journal*, 2 (1976), pp. 33–89

Warwick P., 'African Labour during the South African War 1899–1902', *The Societies of Southern Africa in the 19th and 20th Centuries*, 7 (1977), pp. 104–16

'The African Refugee Problem in the Transvaal and Orange River Colony 1900–2', *Centre for Southern African Studies, University of York, Collected Papers*, 2 (1977), pp. 61–81

Will D. and Dent T., 'The Boer War as seen from Gaborone', *Botswana Notes and Records*, 4 (1972), pp. 195–209

Willan B. P., 'The South African Native Labour Contingent 1916–1918', *Journal of African History*, 19, 1 (1978), pp. 61–86

C Unpublished theses and research papers

Bonner P., 'African Participation in the Anglo-Boer War of 1899–1902', MA dissertation, University of London, 1967

Delius P., 'Abel Erasmus: Power and Profit in the Eastern Transvaal', research paper, Institute of Commonwealth Studies, University of Oxford, 1981

Nasson W. R., 'Race and Civilisation in the Anglo-Boer War of 1899–1902', MA dissertation, University of York, 1977

'"These Infernal Mahogany Brats": Black Transport Workers and the British Army in the Cape Colony during the South African War', research paper presented at the University of York, March 1980

'"These Natives Think This War to Be Their Own": Reflections on Blacks in the Cape Colony and the South African War 1899–1902', research paper presented at the Institute of Commonwealth Studies, University of London, May 1980

Ngcongco L. D., 'Imvo Zabantsundu and Cape "Native" Policy 1884–1902', MA thesis, University of South Africa, 1974

Shelton J. F., 'The Holkrans Massacre, 6 May 1902', BA Hons. dissertation, University of Natal, 1969

Siwundhla H. T., 'The Participation of Non-Europeans in the Anglo-Boer War 1899–1902', PhD thesis, Claremont Graduate School, 1977

Spies S. B., 'Roberts, Kitchener and Civilians in the Boer Republics, January 1900–May 1902', PhD thesis, University of the Witwatersrand, 1973

Warwick P., 'African Societies and the South African War 1899–1902', DPhil thesis, University of York, 1978

Index

Abdurahman, Dr Abdullah, 177, 178
Aborigines' Protection Society, 86, 146
Addison, Colonel R.H., 83
African People's Organisation, 175, 177
Afrikaner Bond, 115, 117–18
agterryers, 11, 25, 26, 130
Alfred, 77
Aliwal North, 59, 63, 67
Asaf, 98
Ashburnham, J.H., 44
Asian community, 4, 133, 177, 178

Baden-Powell, Colonel R.S.S.: Mafeking, 28–9, 30, 31, 33, 34, 35, 36, 37, 38, 50; given command of South African Constabulary, 46; and Kgatla campaign against the Boers, 46
Badrile, 33
Baillie, Major F.D., 33
Balfour, A.J., 15, 16
Bande, 81–2
Bapedi Lutheran Church, 97, 98
Barkly East, 69, 116, 119, 123
Barnard, J.H., 40
Barolong: Rapulana-, 33–4, 38, 50, 189 n.8; Seleka-, 176; Tshidi-, 13, 21, 31–8, 50, 51, 173, 184
Basotho, 8, 26, 52–74, 129–30, 140, 158, 168
Basutoland, 8, 15, 52–74, 141, 157–8, 171
Basutoland Mounted Police, 59–60
Basutoland National Council, 74
Beak, G.B., 155, 160
Bechuanaland Protectorate, 9, 20–1, 28–51, 141
Beit, Alfred, 2
Bell, Charles, 31
Beyers, General C., 20, 44
Bezuidenhout, Frederick, 13
Bhunu, 104, 105, 106
black elite: perception of the war, 110–14;

franchise question, 110, 112, 181–2, 184; views on black involvement in the war, 116; concern about wartime developments, 163–4; views on Peace of Vereeniging, 164, 175, 176, 177; post-war political activity, 174–8
blockhouses, 4, 24
Bloemfontein, 3, 68, 157
Boer army: casualties, 1; attitude towards arming blacks, 17–19, 25–6; *see also* labour; workers
Boomplaats, battle of (1848), 13
Border Scouts (Upington), 121
Botha, Chris, 105
Botha, General Louis, 3, 90; Holkrans incident, 91, 92, 93, 180; and Swazi, 107, 200 n.38; run off his farm by tenants, 165; and Peace of Vereeniging, 180–1
Bottomley, Colonel H., 87, 88–90
Bremersdorp (Manzini), 105, 108
British army: casualties, 1, 23; and arming blacks, 22–5, 27; *see also* labour; workers
British government, 1, 2, 5, 7; attitude towards arming blacks, 15–17, 22–5; propaganda concerning black liberties, 111; post-war policies, 164, 175, 177, 178, 182–3; *see also* Chamberlain, Joseph; Colonial Office; Salisbury, Lord; War Office
British South Africa Company Police, 30, 39–40
Brodrick, St John, 23, 24–5
bubonic plague, 144
Buller, General Sir Redvers, 6, 26, 75, 83, 84, 87, 115, 133
Burger, Schalk, 20, 106
Burgher Forces and Levies Act (Cape Colony, 1878), 14
Bushmansland Borderers, 121
Buthelezi people, 88, 89

221

DH

968.
048
089
96
WAR

Lightning Source UK Ltd.
Milton Keynes UK
UKOW041428190513

210910UK00001B/64/A